THE NATURE AND DYNAMICS OF
ORGANIZATIONAL CAPABILITIES

The Nature and Dynamics of Organizational Capabilities

edited by
Giovanni Dosi,
Richard R. Nelson, and
Sidney G. Winter

OXFORD

UNIVERSITY PRESS

OXFORD
UNIVERSITY PRESS

Great Clarendon Street, Oxford OX2 6DP

Oxford University Press is a department of the University of Oxford.
It furthers the University's objective of excellence in research, scholarship,
and education by publishing worldwide in

Oxford New York

Athens Auckland Bangkok Bogotá Buenos Aires Calcutta
Cape Town Chennai Dar es Salaam Delhi Florence Hong Kong Istanbul
Karachi Kuala Lumpur Madrid Melbourne Mexico City Mumbai
Nairobi Paris São Paulo Singapore Taipei Tokyo Toronto Warsaw
and associated companies in Berlin Ibadan

Published in the United States
by Oxford University Press Inc., New York

First published 2000

British Library Cataloguing in Publication Data
Data available

Library of Congress Cataloging in Publication Data
Data available

ISBN 0-19-829680-0

1 3 5 7 9 10 8 6 4 2

Typeset in Garamond by
Kolam Information Services Pvt. Ltd, Pondicherry, India
Printed in Great Britain
T.J. International Ltd
Padstow, Cornwall

Preface

This book has painstakingly but excitingly emerged from an international research project which originally grew at the International Institute of Applied System Analysis (IIASA), Laxemburg, Austria within the *Technological and Economic Dynamics* (TED) Project and was completed drawing on the precious support of the '*Dynacom*' Project financed by the European Union (under the TSER/DG XII Programme).

It has been made possible by the enthusiastic effort of a wide invisible college of scholars who accepted to forgo any reasonable cost-benefit analysis in terms of time investment vs. financial rewards in order to contribute to an enterprise which at the start most would have regarded as a far-cry into the properties of self-organization. At least in the judgement of the editors of this book, it turned out to be indeed a major success, possibly a future reference in the field.

It is hopeless to try to acknowledge all friends and colleagues who contributed with their comments and criticism throughout the process. Within the large community of collaborators who made this book possible, we would like just to mention the patient and loyal help of Yasmine Taher, our secretary at IIASA, who motherly followed the vicissitudes of chapter contributors and editors of the book.

Contents

List of Figures

List of Tables

List of Contributors

MELISSA APPLEYARD, Assistant Professor of Business Administration, Darden Graduate School of Business Administration, University of Virginia, Charlottesville, USA.

LINDA ARGOTE, Kirr Professor of Organizational Behaviour, Graduate, School of Industrial Administration, Carnegie Mellon University, Pittsburgh, USA.

IAIN COCKBURN, Professor of Management, Boston University, Cambridge, USA.

BENJAMIN CORIAT, Professor of Economics, University of Paris XIII, France.

ERIC DARR, Senior Manager, Knowledge and Learning Studies, Ernst & Young, LLP, USA.

GIOVANNI DOSI, Professor of Economics, Santa Anna School of Advanced Study, Pisa, Italy.

M. THÉRÈSE FLAHERTY, Wharton School, University of Pennsylvania, Philadelphia, USA.

RICHARD FLORIDA, Senator H. John Heinz III Professor of Regional Economic Development, Carnegie Mellon University, Pittsburgh, USA.

TAKAHIRO FUJIMOTO, Faculty of Economics, University of Tokyo, Tokyo, Japan.

NILE HATCH, Assistant Professor, College of Commerce and Business Administration, University of Illinois at Urbana, Champaign, USA.

REBECCA HENDERSON, Eastman Kodak Professor of Management, Sloan School of Management, Massachusetts Institute of Technology, Cambridge, USA.

MARTIN KENNEY, Professor in the Department of Human and Community Development, University of California at Davis, and Senior Research Assistant in the Berkeley Roundtable on International Economy, University of California at Berkeley, USA.

DANIEL LEVINTHAL, Julian Aresty Professor of Management Economics, Wharton School (Levinthal), University of Pennsylvania, Philadelphia, USA.

DAVID C. MOWERY, Professor, Haas School of Business, University of California at Berkeley, USA.

ALLESSANDRO NARDUZZO, Department of Management and Computer Science, University of Trento, Italy.

RICHARD R. NELSON, School of International and Public Affairs, Columbia University, New York, USA.

PARI PATEL, Senior Research Fellow, Science Policy Research Unit, University of Sussex, Falmer, Brighton, UK.

KEITH PAVITT, Professor, Science Policy Research Unit, University of Sussex, Falmer, Brighton, UK.

GARY PISANO, Harry E. Figgie, Jr. Professor of Business Administration, Harvard University, Boston, USA.

ELENA ROCCO, Visiting Scholar at the Collaboratory for Research on Electronic Work (CREW), School of Information, University of Michigan, USA.

AMY SHUEN, Visiting Professor, Haas School of Business, University of California at Berkeley, USA.

GABRIEL SZULANSKI, Assistant Professor of Management, Wharton School, University of Pennsylvania, Philadelphia, USA.

DAVID TEECE, Mitsubishi Bank Professor, Haas School of Business, University of California at Berkeley, USA.

MASSIMO WARGLIEN, Associate Professor of Industrial Management, Department of Business Economics and Management, Universita'Ca'Foscari de Venezia, Italy.

SIDNEY G. WINTER, Deloitte and Touche Professor of Management, Wharton School of Business, University of Pennsylvania, Philadelphia, USA.

Introduction: The Nature and Dynamics of Organizational Capabilities

GIOVANNI DOSI, RICHARD R. NELSON, AND SIDNEY G. WINTER

It is familiar enough that business firms and other organizations 'know how to do things'—things like building automobiles or computers, or flying us from one continent to another. On second thoughts, what does this mean? Is there not a sense in which only a human mind can possess knowledge? If so, can this proposition somehow be squared with the idea that organizations know how to do things? And if organizational knowledge is a real phenomenon, what are the principles that govern how it is acquired, maintained, extended, and sometimes lost?

Our focus here is on the particular forms of organizational knowledge that account for the organization's ability to perform and extend its characteristic 'output' actions—particularly, the creation of a tangible product or the provision of a service, and the development of new products and services. The range of activities we have in mind is broad, embracing for example automobile manufacturing, brain surgery, identifying and developing new pharmaceuticals, putting on an effective art exhibition, and shipping a package across a continent. Pending a more thorough discussion of terminology, we identify the term 'organizational capabilities' with the know-how that enables organizations to perform these sorts of activities.

The authors represented in this volume share the belief that organizational knowledge is real and a phenomenon of central importance to the understanding of the modern world. Their studies explore the role played by organizations in linking the general fund of knowledge in a society to its practical affairs. Understanding how organizations develop, maintain, and advance their capabilities is, in their view and ours, fundamental to understanding how society works and how it changes. This belief obviously contributes importantly to the intellectual interest that the subject holds for the participants in this undertaking.

As we shall explain in more detail below, research on capabilities is an area invigorated from the 'supply side' by the convergence of different lines of scholarly inquiry, and from the 'demand side' by a range of potential areas of practical and theoretical application. The studies collected here illustrate that range, if they do not fully cover it, and we expect that this volume will be of interest to a number of different audiences.

Accordingly, in this introduction we seek to introduce the subject in a manner accessible to a diverse audience. We first explain what the capabilities discussion is about. It relates, we argue, to distinct phenomena that have not been adequately addressed by the various disciplines and sub-fields that lie adjacent to this subject matter. We hope to evoke the sense that, notwithstanding their familiarity as part of the backdrop of everyday life, organizational capabilities are complex and even somewhat mysterious social phenomena. A further goal in this introduction is to sketch the complex intellectual background of current research on capabilities, and to identify some of the areas where improved understanding of capabilities would be particularly useful.

We do not, however, attempt a full survey of the book and the principal issues raised by the various contributions; this task is addressed in a 'distributed' way by the introductions to the individual sections. The sections are presented in order of increasing scope. We begin with studies that examine the development of particular capabilities at the microlevel within organizations, then proceed to studies at the level of the firm or productive establishment, then to industry-level patterns. The final section contains a perspective on the development of the capabilities view in strategic management and a theoretical paper that illuminates the causes of some of the basic patterns observed in the empirical studies.

1. The Concept of Organizational Capability

To be *capable* of some thing is to have a generally reliable capacity to bring that thing about as a result of intended action. Capabilities fill the gap between intention and outcome, and they fill it in such a way that the outcome bears a definite resemblance to what was intended.

In the behaviour of organizations, however, the most relevant intentions are often remote from the particular action and outcome. They may lie deep in the background of the specific actions that occur, which often come about in a variety of ways not involving intentions—including habitual responses of human beings and the automatic, physically determined responses of machines. The local telephone company intended to provide phone service in the sense that its executives, past and present, construed many of their own decisions in those terms—but the realization of a particular call is automatic. Its feasibility reflects an accumulation of equipment, individual skills, and organizational arrangements generated by a series of specific decisions that implemented and re-implemented the general intention to provide phone service—including a variety of arrangements that link the services of the provider of local service to other organizations in the global telecommunications system.

This example illustrates the typical situation: it is in the building of organizational capabilities that the role of intentionality is most reliably displayed; specific exercise may be intentional (as when an engineering firm builds a factory or bridge to fulfil its contract to do so), but it may be also be quite automatic (as in the phone-call example).

Although the phone call is a simple and familiar action from the caller's point of view, it is made feasible by the operation of an extraordinarily complex system. The system in turn is the product of a long and complex process of technological and organizational change, with associated investments in facilities and training—a process in which intentions to develop a (better) telephone system played a role that was important but intermittent and fragmented. The contemporary global telecommunications system was not produced through the execution of a coherent and comprehensive plan. In this case, and many others, the structure of capabilities at the highest level reflects the outcome of a self-organizing, bottom-up process rather than realization of any comprehensive intention.

The distinction we make here—between the capability itself and the numerous instances of its exercise—parallels similar distinctions expressed in varying terminology about a variety of contexts. In particular, it parallels the distinction at the individual level between a skill and the exercise of the skill. In organizations, there is a distinction between the execution of high-frequency, repetitive daily business by low-level employees and the decisions of executives about the development and deployment of capabilities (serving the french fries versus opening another hamburger stand). There is a corresponding distinction at the individual level between the relatively tacit, subconscious, automatic, and high-frequency character of exercise and the more intentional, deliberate, and intermittent processes involved in skill development and deployment (learning to drive or choosing the destination versus the exercise of skill in keeping the car on the road). The parallels extend to learning processes; different processes are involved in the sort of learning that improves exercise than in original development of skills and capabilities. This parallelism presents an opportunity to use the individual realm as a metaphor to explicate the organizational, and vice versa. The opportunity has been exploited more than once. One significant fact that has become clear only in recent years is that, for individuals, the exercise of skills involves brain processes quite different from those displayed in fully conscious thought and the command of facts.[1]

It has been said that the mark of high skill in an individual is the ability to make some activity look easy when it is actually very difficult, and much the same point applies to organizational capabilities. The more polished the performance, the less attention gets directed to the innumerable hazards of failure that have been overcome, and the more the performance itself assumes a taken-for-granted character. Also, performances that are commonplace in the sense of being reproduced at high frequency come to seem less mysterious and easier than accomplishments that occur only occasionally—although it should be obvious on reflection that frequency *per se* is no indicator of ease or difficulty, once the threshold question of feasibility is settled. The more organizations succeed in making customer encounters simple and uneventful, the more the complex reality of capabilities tends to disappear behind the veil of familiarity.

2. A Note on Terminology

The term 'capabilities' floats in the literature like an iceberg in a foggy Arctic sea, one iceberg among many, not easily recognized as different from several icebergs near by.

---

[1] For the use of organization as a metaphor for the individual, see e.g. Alfred Marshall (Marshall 1920: 21). Marshall's discussion in a footnote anticipates reasonably well recent discoveries relating to brain function and physiology: 'It seems that the exercise of nerve force under the immediate direction of the thinking power residing in the cerebrum has gradually built up a set of connections, involving probably distinct physical change, between the nerves and nerve centres concerned; and these new connections may be thought of as a sort of capital of nerve force. There is probably something like an organized bureaucracy of the local nerve centres; the medulla, the spinal axis and the larger ganglia generally acting the part of provincial authorities, and being able after a time to regulate the district and village authorities without troubling the supreme government.' More of the bureaucracy lives in the brain than Marshall thought. See e.g. Squire, 1987 *Memory and Brain*, esp. ch. 11.

In this section, we attempt to survey this terminological flotilla and point out distinctive features of some of the floating objects. We make suggestions about terminology that reflect our own understanding and preferences, but we are not under the illusion that terminological anarchy is easily suppressed.

In surveying this somewhat confusing scene, it is useful to keep in mind a distinction between the use of a given term as a label on a black box and the use of that same term as a label on a more transparent box—which can be seen to have other boxes inside it, themselves somewhat transparent. Both types of usage are quite legitimate, and sometimes an author will slip smoothly from one to the other as attention shifts from one issue to another. The chapters that follow are generally concerned with the 'transparent box' version of capability, and even with unpacking the transparent box to examine more closely the boxes inside. This is less true of some of the works that introduced the terms discussed below.

Following the discussion above, it should be clear that we think of 'capability' as a fairly large-scale unit of analysis, one that has a recognizable purpose expressed in terms of the significant outcomes it is supposed to enable, and that is significantly shaped by conscious decision both in its development and deployment. These features distinguish 'capability' from 'organizational routines' as that term is used in organization theory and evolutionary economics—subject to the qualification that *some* organizational routines might equally well be called capabilities. In general, however, the notion of a routine involves no commitment regarding size—large routines are typically structured sets of medium-sized routines, and so on. It involves no presumption regarding evident purpose; one of the interesting things about routines is that they are often found in contexts where nobody can explain what they are for except in the vague terms of 'the way things are done around here'. And there is no presumption of deliberation or conscious choice; a flight crew probably does not choose its response to unexpected turbulence any more than a batter chooses to hit the dirt when the pitch appears to be coming toward his head.

On the other hand, the notion of a routine certainly does not *exclude* the possibility of conscious decisions about exercise. Hence, some routines may appropriately be called capabilities, if they satisfy the other criteria.

Capabilities involve organized activity and the exercise of capability is typically repetitious in substantial part. Routines are units or 'chunks' of organized activity with a repetitive character. Hence, it is basically well said that 'routines are the building blocks of capabilities'—although routines are not the *only* building blocks of capabilities. A marketing capability might require a customer database, for example, which is neither a routine itself nor does it resemble a routine in the way that the working of complex equipment sometimes does. The database is, instead, a contextual requisite of some of the organizational routines supporting the capability.

Individual skills, in turn, are among the building blocks of organizational routines. What we commonly think of as individual skills are quasi-modular components of routines; their names are useful in expressing, for example, the idea that the role played by one skilled machine operator might well be played by another. But 'knowing the job' involves knowing things that are relational—involving other participants—and organization-specific (Nelson and Winter 1982: 100–3). That is why the skilled operator still needs to learn the job when joining an unfamiliar organization to operate a familiar machine—and why someone who is a perfectly adequate machine operator might nevertheless fail to learn the job. Some of the non-modular knowledge required is skill-like, regardless of what it is called—but these are skills that can be learned only through experience in the specific organization.

In our view, clarity would be served by reserving the term 'skills' to the individual level and 'routines' to the organizational level. 'Routines are the skills of an organization' is a metaphorical truth not a literal truth.[2] In the existing literature, however, our proposed usage convention is violated in both directions. For example, Waterman *et al.* (1980) used 'skills' for what we would prefer to call routines or capabilities, whereas Nelson and Winter (1982: 100) slipped into using 'routines' at the individual level when they should have said 'skills' or perhaps 'constituent skills'. Transgressions of this kind will no doubt continue, but, we hope, not by us.

Consistent with this proposal, a useful meaning for the 'skills of the organization' would simply be the collectivity of skills possessed by individuals in the organization, regardless of whether the skills are modular, organization-specific, or not organization-related at all. Then it could be said that organizational routines have the major function of coordinating the skills of the organization, i.e. of turning that collectivity of skills to useful effect.

Turning to another area of the concept flotilla, we find a cluster centred on 'competence'. In organization theory, the idea that an organization tends to be good at some particular thing (if anything) has long been referenced by the term 'distinctive competence'. This term was introduced by Selznick (1957) in his classic work *Leadership in Administration*. In Selznick's original discussion, however, the idea of distinctive competence seems to be at least as close a relative of the organization's mission statement, or perhaps its 'strategic intent' (Hamel and Prahalad 1989) as of its capabilities. Selznick's concern is with the infusion of means with shared ends, 'the transformation of an engineered, technical arrangement of building blocks into a social organism'. He suggests, as other management theorists have subsequently, that a highly effective organization emerges when a leader helps the organization to transcend a merely technical understanding of its own functioning.[3] An indicator of the distance from the capabilities concept is Selznick's reference to *standardized* building blocks; apparently it is the value-laden 'transformation' and not the building blocks that account for the 'distinctive' part. While Selznick (and others) may well be right to emphasize the importance of values, especially among the best organizations, capabilities theorists think the technical building blocks are often quite distinctive in their own right.

An influential article by Prahalad and Hamel (1990) popularized the term 'core competence'. Only a brief encounter with the article is required to note four points:

---

[2] The statement is in Nelson and Winter (1982: 124), and it is there introduced as a metaphor.
[3] Peters and Waterman (1982) were emphatic and interesting on this point, see esp. ch. 4.

(i) that large corporations have multiple core competencies (five or six at a maximum, they suggest, not twenty or thirty—but not one, either); (ii) that competencies are fundamental to the *dynamics* of the firm's competitive strength, lending strategic coherence to a string of new and improved products appearing over an extended period; (iii) that the competencies referred to are all areas of 'hard' technology (if Procter & Gamble is properly thought to have core competence in marketing and distribution, or Wal-Mart in logistics, the authors don't mention it); (iv) that while the relationship of competencies to large-scale structural features of the organization is a featured issue, the organizational aspects of the competencies themselves do not capture the authors' attention. Some of the subsequent discussion of core competence seems to lose track of one or more of these points. The fact that the authors titled their article 'The Core Competence of the Corporation' (note singular) may have contributed to a partial eclipse of point (i).[4]

The last two points noted above are much at odds with the concept of organizational capabilities, which need not relate to technology and certainly have significant internal organization. If, however, we ourselves exercise the prerogative of simply ignoring a couple of points, we can move closer to the capabilities concept by focusing on the first two. We then arrive at the idea that a successful large corporation derives competitive strength from its excellence in a small number of capabilities clusters where it can sustain a leadership position over time. This comes very close to the concept of 'dynamic capabilities' advanced by Teece *et al.* (1997: 516): 'We define dynamic capabilities as the firm's ability to integrate, build, and reconfigure internal and external competences to address rapidly changing environments.' (See also Teece *et al.* in this volume) In areas of 'hard' technology, the dynamic capabilities of a firm depend heavily on its R&D resources; in other areas that label may not be applied but analogous investments are made.

There is general agreement, however, that dynamic capabilities cannot be built simply by spending on R&D or making analogous investments. On the contrary—and to an increasing extent as the competitive pace quickens—coordination between R&D and other functions, and often with suppliers or alliance partners, is of the essence. Such coordination is needed, among other things, for effective identification and linking of technological options and market opportunities, and for identifying the strengths and weaknesses of existing resources relative to the requirements of a new product or process.

Thus the concepts of 'core competence' and 'dynamic capabilities' point in the same direction, being broadly concerned with the firm's ability to carry off the balancing act between continuity and change in its capabilities, and to do so in a competitively effective fashion. The discussion of dynamic capabilities has, however,

---

[4] The use of the singular in 'core competence' encourages a conflation with 'core business'. In practice, 'core business' seems to have primarily a historical connotation: your core business is the one you were in before you started (or resumed) diversifying. Recommendations that a corporation retreat to its core business do, however, seem to rest on the presumption that some resources offering potential competitive advantage do remain there, current poor performance notwithstanding. And there is a presumption that if you can't be good at your core business, you probably can't be good at anything else.

been both broader in scope and more explicit in its treatment of the details of capabilities than the core competence discussion.

Another important idea in this general area is referred to as 'combinative capabilities' by Kogut and Zander (1992). Here again the emphasis is on the firm's ability to handle change by transforming old capabilities into new ones. Two points about the nature of this transformation are emphasized: (i) that firms produce new capabilities by *recombining* existing capabilities and other knowledge, (ii) that the ability of the firm to do this is affected by the organizing principles guiding its operations—principles that include matters of formal structure but, more importantly, internal social relations shaped in part by differences in the knowledge bases of individuals and groups within the firm. Pursuing these ideas the authors develop a view of the firm and the make-or-buy decision quite different from that put forward in transaction cost economics.

There are also examples in the literature where the word 'competence' is not used as an abbreviation for 'core competence' nor as a rough synonym for what we would call a 'capability' or a 'dynamic capability'. Usage in these cases appears to be most closely akin to usage of the same terms in reference to individuals, and has if anything a connotation of breadth rather than specificity—something closer to judgement than to skill. Eliasson (1990), for example, discusses the role of the 'top competent team' in the firm—the *de facto* top management team—which involves making strategic judgements that are not readily amenable to analysis. Such decisions are informed instead by the experience-based tacit knowledge of individuals and by the dialectical interaction within the team. This sort of competence relates not to a specific subject matter or task, but to an entire realm of highly consequential decisions that are difficult to get right, where small percentage improvements over judgements of average quality can be very valuable.

The character of decision-making in this realm, and in contexts in which both competence (or vision) and capabilities play an important role, has been explored by Fransman (1994*a*, 1994*b*). The question of the value that top management competence brings to the firm, and its relation to managerial compensation, has also been studied by Castanias and Helfat (1991), although both the orientation and language is different.

This discussion of terminology would certainly be incomplete without reference to what was (at least to our knowledge) the original use of the term 'capabilities', in a sense closely akin, if not identical, to our own. George B. Richardson, in his article 'The Organization of Industry', (Richardson 1972: 888) made the fundamental point that 'organizations will tend to specialize in activities for which their capabilities offer some comparative advantage', and that the pursuit of activities that are similar in the sense of drawing upon the same capabilities may lead a firm 'into a variety of markets and a variety of product lines' (ibid.).[5] Richardson's analysis includes a capabilities-based account of the boundaries of the firm that is both clear and plausible—though

---

[5] This point was further expounded by Teece (1980) in his article on the multiproduct firm, and subsequently reintroduced by Prahalad and Hamel (1990), with 'core competences' rather than 'capabilities' in the starring role.

he does not anticipate every question that today's transaction cost theorists might ask. Finally, Richardson did not see large-scale organizational choices as a spectrum between markets and hierarchies, but saw cooperation as a third alternative. Co-operation includes relational contracting, but also more formal arrangements such as equity participation.

3. The Role of the Organization

Scouting around for wood for the campfire is an example of a productive activity that can be described with no reference to organizations. It is something human beings do today—in parks, on ranches, in wilderness areas, and other settings. Viewed narrowly as an activity, it is not all that different from what humans have done for millennia, from times long before there were formal organizations in their sociocultural environment. Thus, not every activity we engage in today involves a close encounter with an organization. But a great many of them do.

Everyday experience in the modern world involves us in a series of encounters with products and services that permit us to accomplish remarkable things with remarkable consistency and in a remarkably short time—although the remarkable often goes unremarked for the reason previously suggested. The realms of commun-ication, computation, and transportation are particularly rich in examples of remark-able capabilities of very recent origin. It takes only a modicum of historical perspective to recognize that the everyday environment contains many products and services that did not exist five years ago, many more that did not exist twenty-five years ago, and that truly drastic changes have reshaped life in the past century and a half. If we inquire as to where these novelties come from, the straightforward answer is that they come to us from business firms—from the telephone companies, the computer companies, and the airlines, for example.

Obviously this everyday appearance is to some extent deceiving; we must avoid replicating the error of the US congressman who questioned the need for (publicly funded) weather satellites on the ground that the Weather Channel is available on cable TV. The question is, just how deceiving is the appearance? What is the appro-priate perspective on the role of organizations in supplying products and services, old as well as new? Our basic proposal here is that everyday appearances are not all that deceiving, especially if we take into account that there are organizational perform-ances that support the organizational performances that deliver the products and services to us. This is not to deny, however, that there are other credible contenders for attention in the grand story of how society creates and uses productive knowledge.

To get a sense of the role of organizations in one of these remarkable contem-porary performances, it is helpful to begin by standing close to the action (as many of our authors have). From a vantage point close in, it is possible to see many contributing details of the overall performance that might otherwise be over-looked—even, in some cases, by the managers in charge. Having identified various requisites of the performance as it exists today, we can ask questions about the provision of those requisites and about the historical development of each of them—

with particular attention to the development of the specific knowledge base. What know-how does it take for this to happen, and where did it come from? Each element identified as a requisite of the contemporary performance has its own distinct trail of technological and organizational history, however much that trail may interweave with those of other elements or with broader historical themes. To explore a major fraction of these interweaving trails in any depth would be an enormous project, which would take volume upon volume to report—and there is an important lesson in that observation. It is, however, possible to sketch in the rudiments of an example of such an undertaking.

Consider an airline flight. From the time the passenger arrives at the check-in counter or gate, he or she is pretty much the captive of the airline's organizational routines. The counter routines cover the baggage-checking and providing a boarding pass and directions to the gate. At the gate, the passenger is processed through the boarding routine—first-class passengers and families with small children 'pre-board', please. The ticket is collected and in some cases electronically processed immediately. Behind the scenes there may be a routine matching the passengers who have boarded to the baggage that has been put aboard. The airline has arranged the presence at the gate of the airplane, the flight crew, the baggage handlers, and the food to be put aboard—although the latter may well be a delivery from another company, as may the fuel that is also being put aboard.[6] Of course, the availability of the gate itself has also been arranged by the airline, probably by contract with the airport authority. Behind the scenes again there is a set of routines comprising a broad capability for monitoring and maintaining the aircraft, and another capability for handling the scheduling of crews. As the airplane departs, the crew begins an interaction with a highly complex air traffic control system that will continue intermittently for the duration of the flight.

And so on; any frequent flyer can fill in further details that are somewhere between commonplace and absolutely generic across flight experiences. The airline has accomplished a massive feat of coordination and orchestration to bring all of this together and make it work, as it typically does, quite smoothly. Of course, sometimes the airplane isn't there; sometimes it is there but it doesn't work. Sometimes the flight crew shows up late. Sometimes it seems that gate personnel telling lies about the departure time is also an organizational routine, evoked in the subset of cases where something has gone wrong. Sometimes you may later wish the food hadn't shown up after all. Such 'eventfulness' is an indicator of malfunctioning routines (Szulanski 1996); it serves as a reminder that there actually are routines and that they usually succeed in making flights uneventful.

Of course, the airplane is a prominent artefact in this story. The airline didn't build its airplanes, it bought them, perhaps from Boeing or Airbus. Those companies and their ancestors created capabilities, over an extended period, for designing and building aircraft. They too accomplished massive feats of coordination and orches-

[6] This example of the fact that capabilities sometimes involve intimate operational connections among distinct firms points to the broader observation that significant capabilities sometimes reside in networks of firms rather than in individual firms. See e.g. Saxenian (1994); Powell *et al.* (1996); Orsenigo *et al.* (1999).

tration of design engineers, production-line workers, parts suppliers, metal producers, and so on. But the aircraft companies didn't make the engines, they purchased
them from companies with long traditions in engine manufacture. Although it
wouldn't seem so central to the story of the flight, a similar tale could be told about
the food service or the baggage-handling equipment. Down a multitude of pathways,
the story of a single airline flight leads back into the capabilities of a multitude of
organizations, each contributing their capabilities in a long story of technological and
organizational evolution.

Back along the trail were two brothers who had a bicycle shop, some equipment,
and high ambition. Many history books will tell you quite a lot about those brothers,
but they say very little about how a multitude of organizations respond to your desire
today to get across a continent or an ocean, or how some of those same organizations
and many others now extinct contributed to spanning the enormous gap between a
few hundred feet of low, slow, uncomfortable, and hazardous flight and thousands of
miles of high, fast, comfortable, and remarkably safe flight. Research on organizational capabilities seeks, among other things, to right this balance.

4. Capabilities and Decisions

In economics and other disciplines that employ the theoretical tools of decision
theory, key assumptions about skills and capabilities often remain implicit. Consider,
for example, the simple and basic tool called the pay-off matrix: an array with choice
alternatives on one side, 'states of the world' (or opponent's choices) on the other,
and the outcome utility values in the cells. Typically, the choices are actions or entail
actions. While in some cases the choices listed are everyday actions that are familiar
and perhaps available to the typical reader of the analysis ('carry umbrella'), in other
cases they emphatically are not ('conduct seismic tests', 'shut down nuclear reactor').
In these latter cases, the availability of the actions is apparently presumed to inhere in
the identity of the decision maker, and this presumption goes unremarked. Arguably,
the development of the menu of future choices would be a candidate for the first
exercise introducing the topic of sequential decision analysis. In fact, the question of
where the menu comes from is generally ignored.

Further, choices available to the decision maker are, in decision theory, feasible by
definition—any uncertainty attached to the consequences of *trying* to take a specific
action (the sort of choice that is in fact readily available) is subsumed in the
uncertainty attached to states of the world. This is in principle an inconsequential
formal convention, but in practice significant questions of feasibility tend to get
swept under the rug in the process of abstracting an analysable problem from a real
situation. The rich sequences of unfolding events that often follow a failed attempt—
sequences that may involve wholly unanticipated outcomes and learning, among
other things—could be represented in a sufficiently elaborate decision-theoretic
formalism, but generally are not.

These habits of decision-theoretic thought contribute to the obscurity in which
capabilities issues have long resided in economic analysis. The entries in the menu of

choices are specified and promptly taken for granted, one situation at a time—even when the choices involve complex action. Little is seen of the costly and protracted learning processes that place alternatives on the menu. The consequences for future menus of the choices made today—for example, the likely strengthening of the capabilities that are exercised and the likely withering of those that are not—are generally abstracted away. These practices may well represent sound, if largely tacit, judgement about the domain where decision theory is useful. They nevertheless leave a major gap in the understanding of behaviour—a gap best filled, perhaps, by the use of other tools.

Just as the market system accomplishes remarkable feats of coordination without the aid of a central plan, organizational learning produces the coordinated performances of organizational capabilities without the aid of a recipe—alternatively, without the aid of a comprehensive plan, optimized or not. According to the mainstream tradition in economics, economic actors do not have to understand the price system for it to work. Similarly, an organization produces coordinated activity without anyone knowing how it works—although participants may be well aware of managerial intentions to achieve coordination. As learning proceeds, innumerable procedural details are settled by individual participants, with or without conscious awareness or consideration. There are far more of these details than any amount of observation will uncover or any imaginable set of manuals will ever record. Tentative choices that are actually incompatible or substantially subversive of the overall performance get rooted out in the course of learning—not in response to the imperative 'follow the recipe' but in response to 'try something different!' Choices compatible with the overall performance are allowed to stabilize and become habitual, without either the choices or the habits necessarily being recognized as such along the way. Finally, in the well-established capability, the activity in progress is its own best (and only) operating manual.

5. Capabilities Research: Areas of Inquiry and Application

The discussion above locates the organizational capabilities discussion and suggests why many of us consider it to be a fascinating area of research, and one that is in large part novel—because of the several factors that have long tended to shroud it in obscurity. Here we extend the case by pointing to areas where improved understanding of capabilities has important applications. These are also areas that have participated in the building of existing understanding of capabilities, and involve ongoing research that continues to contribute to the broad effort to improve that understanding.

5.1. *Evolutionary economics and firm capabilities*

A fundamental proposition in evolutionary economics is that firms have ways of doing things that show strong elements of continuity. A related and equally fundamental proposition is that firms have *distinctive* ways of doing things: firms are generally heterogeneous even in the ways they accomplish functionally similar tasks, to say nothing of the large-scale differences that separate the chemical firm, the automobile manufacturer, the mass retailer, and the hospital. Taken together, these propositions set the stage for the dynamic interplay of the evolutionary triumvirate of variation, selection, and retention. Variety in the form of heterogeneous firm behaviour patterns gives the market selection process something to work on; because the patterns persist, the market's selection and promotion of successful ones has significant systemic consequences over time.

Research on capabilities advances the evolutionary economics agenda in three significant ways. First, it provides concrete examples and specific empirical evidence that illustrates and supports the view of firm behaviour taken in evolutionary theory. The analysis of firm capabilities illustrates one very fruitful way of conceptualizing the elements of continuity and idiosyncrasy that are central to the evolutionary view of firm behaviour. To the best of our knowledge, no student of firm capabilities has ever proposed that firm capabilities often change radically in short periods of time, except perhaps by the outright acquisition of another firm that already possesses different capabilities. Rather, the emphasis is on the accumulation of capabilities and the fact that the options for further development at each point of time are sharply constrained by the heritage of the past.[7]

The second contribution involves the relationship between capabilities and organizational routines. Routines play a central role in the formulation of evolutionary theory offered by Nelson and Winter. In their introductory discussion, they noted that much business behaviour is not routine within the ordinary meaning of that term, but then remarked '[The point] . . . is that most of what is *regular and predictable* about business behaviour is plausibly subsumed under the heading "routine", especially if we understand that term to include the relatively constant dispositions and strategic heuristics that shape the approach of a firm to the non-routine problems it faces' (1982: 15). The story of the development of capabilities in a firm is very much a story of the shaping role of 'relatively constant dispositions and strategic heuristics' that provide an element of continuity that extends even over time spans long enough for radical change to accumulate in the firm's specific performances. Thus, the capabilities discussion relates specifically to a realm of behaviour infused with intentionality, conscious deliberation, planning, and expertise—as contrasted with the quasi-automatic character of performance of low-level operating routines. And it shows how these elements of intelligence and intendedly rational calculation not only coexist with, but give expression to, the historically grounded uniqueness of the individual firm.

The third contribution is closely akin to the second. Precisely because the development of capabilities also includes elements of intentionality and deliberation, the capabilities discussion provides a bridge between the predominantly descriptive concerns of evolutionary theory and the prescriptive analysis of firm strategy. Accurate description requires acknowledgement of the role of intentionality; likewise, sound advice must be founded on an accurate characterization of the system

---

[7] These patterns of accumulation are well illustrated by Miyazaki (1995) and Patel and Pavitt (1998).

the decision makers are guiding. Thus the two areas of inquiry are mutually supportive, notwithstanding the substantial difference between their focal concerns.

Evolutionary economics has long been identified with an emphasis on the role of institutions in economic life, and this long-standing connection has recently been revitalized (Hodgson 1988, 1993). The narrower but still extensive set of institutions that shape a nation's science and technology resources and, generally, innovative abilities is another area of institutional and policy concern that has a long-standing connection to evolutionary economics.[8] It is hard to review the history of the aircraft industry, or of computers, or biotech, or many other industries, without getting the distinct impression that something more is going on than the exploitation of the 'given' production functions of firms. Evolutionary economists view firms as building their capabilities in an institutional and policy context, and the exploration of the connections to those contexts remains very much on the research agenda (Metcalfe 1994).

5.2. Firm capabilities and strategic management

As many observers have noted, the past decade or so has seen a marked swing in the attention focus of scholars and practitioners interested in business strategy. Among the aspects of strategic doctrine that now capture attention, issues surrounding the quality of firm capabilities now loom very large. A number of factors have contributed to this development. On the academic side, there is an element of the familiar phenomenon of the swinging pendulum of attention: the concern with capabilities followed a period in which strategy research had been re-energized by economic concepts drawn from industrial organization economics and focused primarily on the firm's relation to its competitive environment. As often happens, one of the truths discovered in this research programme was that its orienting ideas were not as fruitful in illuminating the key issues as had been hoped. The quest for the sources of competitive advantage turned back toward the internal workings of the firm, and in particular to the development of Edith Penrose's idea (1959) that the profitability and growth of a firm should be understood in terms of its possession and development of unique and idiosyncratic resources. Scholars who identify themselves with the 'resource-based view' examine the question of what sorts of resources confer lasting competitive advantages, how these advantages can be extended or 'leveraged', and what considerations prevent the elimination of the gap between the cost of the resources and the market value of the output produced. Many discussions in this vein seem to imply that firm resources are 'idiosyncratic' in only a weak sense; they are relatively discrete and separable from the context of the firm and are the sorts of things that would naturally carry a market price. On this interpretation, the resource rubric does not subsume capabilities. Some authors, notably Dierickx and Cool (1989), offer a sharply contrasting view, suggesting that competitively significant resources are gradually accumulated and shaped within the firm, and are generally non-tradeable. Unique, difficult-to-imitate capabilities acquired in a protracted

---

[8] On the germane field of 'national systems of innovation' see Lundvall (1992) and Nelson (1993).

process of organizational learning are prominent example of the sorts of resources they see as sources of competitive advantage.

Another recent theme in the strategy literature is the idea that the most distinctive role of the business firm in the economic system is the way it brings knowledge to bear on productive effort. This and related ideas have been discussed under the heading of the 'knowledge-based theory of the firm' (Grant 1996, Kogut and Zander 1992, and Dosi and Marengo 1994).[9] As with the notion of resources, this discussion converges with the capabilities discussion in proportion as the knowledge is conceived as know-how embedded in the organization's activities, as opposed to passive, library-like stocks in the heads of participants.

There is, however, much more to the rising concern with capabilities than simply the swinging pendulum of scholarly interest. One important background fact (in the USA) is the stock market's scepticism toward unrelated diversification, which has been manifested quite consistently for at least fifteen years (even if one could always argue that this phenomenon itself is a scholar-induced fad!). Episodes like Sears Roebuck's 1992 retreat from its strategy of diversification into financial services, and the broadly similar evolution at American Express in 1993 and after, illustrated the power of the market to 'jerk the chain' of wandering CEOs and force a retreat to the 'core business'.[10] That being the case, it is unsurprising that managers and consultants became inclined to focus more on the relatively concrete and specific issues affecting the individual firm's competitiveness in particular markets. Another impulse in the same direction was provided by the rising concern with American manufacturing vis-à-vis Japanese competition in the early and mid-1980s.

So far has this trend progressed that Professor Michael Porter of Harvard, a long-time leader in the strategy field who is active in both the academic and consulting segments, has recently felt compelled to enter an objection in the form of an article titled 'What Is Strategy?' beginning with Section I: 'Operational Effectiveness Is Not Strategy' (Porter 1996). It remains to be seen whether this assessment will do much to diminish the prevailing interest in capabilities-based competition.

Although the discussion of capabilities issues has been quite extensive in both the business press and the academic strategy literature, the fund of solid empirical research that is specifically on the strategic aspects of the subject has accumulated rather slowly.[11] As a result, much of the discussion has remained at a relatively high level of abstraction. Several of the studies in this volume should be of considerable value in promoting understanding of capabilities at a sufficiently detailed level so that the relationships to managerial action become visible.

Of course, as noted above in our discussion of the 'competence' terminology, the capabilities perspective reveals a world where enormous challenges face strategic

[9] For an earlier discussion with similar emphasis but cast in terms of reforming the theory of production, see Winter 1982.

[10] For a more detailed discussion of the relationship between capabilities and diversification patterns, see Teece *et al.* (1994).

[11] For broader discussion of the recent emphasis on capabilities in the strategic management literature, see Rumelt *et al.* (1991), Teece *et al.* (1997), and Stalk *et al.* (1992). The discussion in Robert Grant's excellent textbook illustrates the appearance of these ideas in the business school curriculum (Grant 1995: ch. 5).

decision makers who must try to accommodate to an uncertain future. In general, scholars of capabilities and evolutionary economics are less sanguine about the response to these challenges than a mainstream economist would be, and they are perhaps less readily reassured by the guidance of management theorists than a strategic management scholar would be. There has been interest in getting the strategic decision process into realistic focus and attempting to determine what approaches might actually generate superior decision in an uncertain world. This concern has been addressed in contributions by Loasby (1983), Kay (1992, 1997), and Fransman (1994*a*, 1994*b*).

5.3. *Technology and organization*

Capabilities studies with a strategic management orientation are separated by a not-very-bright line from a large literature that examines the way organizations deal, or fail to deal, with technological challenges. And, more generally, they link with an equally large literature which has studied the patterns of change in the knowledge bases underlying innovative activities and the related dynamics of 'technological paradigms' (cf., among others, Dosi 1984 and Freeman 1982). A broad theme that unites these areas of inquiry is the response of an industry to the appearance of a technology that provides a new way of performing functions of central importance to the industry's activities. Such episodes can be identified on a very large scale—such as the replacement of mechanical and electro-mechanical devices by electronic devices in a wide range of types of equipment—and on a quite small scale—such as the successive generations of displacement of larger disk drives by smaller disk drives in computers (Chistensen and Rosenbloom 1995; Christensen and Bower 1996; Christensen 1997). A common pattern in such episodes is that the leading firms in an industry often seem to react slowly to the challenge, with the result that leadership passes to some of the pioneers of the new technology. Sometimes a previously leading firm even fails to survive, or has a very close call. This pattern is, of course, illustrative of Schumpeter's discussion of capitalism's 'perennial gale of creative destruction', which he saw as the essential contextual feature for 'every piece of business strategy' (1950: 83–4).

One problem is to understand why this happens. Another problem is to understand why it *doesn't* happen—the pattern described is not universal, and the intuitive expectation that a 'bigger' technological change ought to make it more likely is not always confirmed. Among a number of explanations that are complementary and hence difficult to untangle, considerations related to the nature of the adjustment of firm capabilities needed to cope with the challenge have received considerable attention. Two mainstays of this literature are Henderson and Clark (1990) and Tushman and Anderson (1986), two papers that describe different conceptual litmus tests for when new technologies are likely to cause incumbents to stumble, and illustrate the conceptual schemes with careful empirical studies. These four authors, in subsequent individual work and in various collaborations, have substantially advanced understanding of capabilities in other directions as well—as have a number of other scholars.

In acquiring and adapting their capabilities over a period of time, organizations are doing something that can reasonably be called organizational learning. Here again there is a large literature embracing a wide range of specific intellectual ambitions, methodologies, and techniques. There are books that seek to speak directly to managers, a notable and influential example being Senge (1990). Facilitating certain types of organizational learning is a major objective of quality management, and thus the large literature of quality management provides another port of entry into the subject of organizational learning and hence to organizational capabilities. Classics in this area include Deming (1982), and Juran (1989); for a recent assessment of the quality movement see Cole (1999). More recently, consultants and corporate executives have evinced great interest in 'Knowledge Management', a rubric that seems to span a substantial number of distinguishable concerns—but some of these concerns clearly relate to the effort to improve capabilities through learning.[12] In particular, the quest of improved performance through 'benchmarking' and the identification and transfer of 'best practices' is an activity that is widely and systematically pursued. Careful studies of the microprocesses of organizational learning have been conducted both in the field as in Hutchins (1991), Adler (1993), and von Hippel and Tyre (1995), and in the laboratory, Cohen and Bacdayan (1994) and Egidi (1995).

In general, a major challenge which the whole perspective of research is painstakingly beginning to address is the identification of robust statistical proxies for capabilities themselves, allowing also further exploration of the links between capabilities and revealed organizational performances. So, statistical studies have explored the building of dynamic capabilities through sustained financial commitments to R&D programmes (Helfat 1994, 1997), and a few statistical surveys, especially in Europe, have begun to search for organization-related proxies. However it is fair to say that most of the work is still to be done.

Within any organization, capabilities, in principle aimed to 'solve problems' in the broadest sense – ranging from carrying a passenger across the Atlantic to more purposeful activities of search for new drugs or new machines – come anyhow together with specific mechanism of governance of potentially conflicting interests and incentives. Indeed, the links (and, over time, the co-evolution) between organizational capabilities and governance structures is another major field of inquiry ahead (for some hypotheses, cf. Coriat and Dosi 1998; see also Langlois and Foss 1999 and the remarks in Marengo *et al.* 1999).

Organizational learning has also begun to be illuminated by various styles of formal modelling. Nearer the richness of the historical evidence, 'history-friendly' models attempt to formalize the evolution of technological capabilities of heterogeneous firms nested in the competitive dynamics of particular industries (on computers, see Malerba *et al.* 1999). At the other, more abstract, end a few works—drawing also from 'artificial sciences' (e.g. artificial intelligence etc.), complexity theory, and cognitive psychology—try to formally represent the properties of

---

[12] On this, a valuable reference is the special issue on 'Knowledge and the Firm' (R. E. Cole, ed.) of the *California Management Review* (v. 40, Spring 1998)

organizational capabilities as emergent from some combinatorial dynamics among multiple underlying 'bits of elementary knowledge' (Marengo 1992; Birchenhall *et al.* 1997; Marengo *et al.* 1999).

5.4. *Firm capabilities in business history*

In this area, empiricism led the way. One of the more important spurs leading to the new interest in organizational capability was the pioneering series of business histories written by Alfred Chandler.[13] Prior to Chandler, most business history simply involved a recounting of the history of a firm, in a manner akin to the 'leaders and battles' approach to the history of nations. Chandler's focus was, originally, on the new forms of business organization that were needed in order to exploit the potential for 'economies of scale and scope' opened by the development of the railroads and the telegraph system in the middle of the nineteenth century. For Chandler, the way a firm was organized and governed was an essential constraint on, and key facilitator of, what it could do. In later work, Chandler came to stress what he called the 'three-pronged investments' in large-scale manufacturing facilities, marketing, and distribution systems, and modern management methods. Companies that were among the first to commit to such investments often dominated their industries for decades thereafter. Much of the work on strategy referred to above drew heavily on Chandler. And Chandler's work set in train a whole new tradition of historical work on business capabilities and how they have evolved.[14]

5.5. *Organizational capabilities and economic growth*

Over the past several years a number of scholars studying the processes of economic development in rapidly growing countries have come to focus on organizational learning and organizational capabilities. For example, detailed studies of the processes through which Korean firms learn to master progressively more complex technologies have been done by Westphal *et al.* (1985), Pack and Westphal (1986), Amsden (1989), and Pack (1994). Hobday's recent work (Hobday 1995) is concerned with the processes by which East Asian firms acquired competence in electronics.

A related body of literature grew up somewhat earlier, concerned with exploring the reasons behind the competitive ascendancy of Japanese firms in electronics, automobiles, and other industries during the 1970s and 1980s. The book *Made in America* (Dertouzos *et al.* 1989) attracted much attention with its discussion of the prowess of Japanese firms and, later, *Made in France* (Taddei and Coriat 1993) addressed the general theme of the institutional and organizational roots of competitive performances. More recently, as competitive advantage has shifted back to

[13] Especially *Scale and Scope: The Dynamics of Industrial Capitalism* (1990), but also *Strategy and Structure: Chapters in the History of American Industrial Enterprise* (1962), and *The Visible Hand: The Managerial Revolution in American Business* (1977).

[14] And it also set in train a lot of fruitful controversies: for example, on the importance of organizational scale as a factor conducive to persistent learning and competitive advantages (for refinements of, and debate upon, that view, see Chandler *et al.* 1998); or, on the role of organizational factors nearer to the shop floor—as opposed to sheer managerial strategies—as determinants of corporate competitiveness (Lazonick 1990).

American firms, there has been a spate of analyses stating that the organizational flexibility and dynamism of American firms vis-à-vis Japanese and European ones is what is giving the American firms the advantage. Although neither of these sets of accounts provides a comprehensive picture of the forces at work in the respective historical phases, both are concerned with considerations that did play an important role. The chapters on automobiles in this volume describe, for example, some of the responses to the very real competitive challenge posed by the Japanese firms.

By a number of different routes, analysis focused on organizational capabilities is influencing the literature on economic development and international competitiveness. Improved understanding of the dynamics of capabilities at the level of the individual organization provides the foundation for an improved and qualitatively different understanding of the mechanisms of aggregate economic growth. While there has long been wide agreement on the centrality of innovation and technical progress in the growth process, the concepts and tools employed in the quest for analytical understanding have typically sought causal insight at the aggregate level, where the phenomena themselves—often characterized as the 'stylized facts' about national economic growth—reside.

Innovation, however, is intrinsically a matter of specifics and details in its origins and impacts—in inspiration, incentives, products, processes, firms, markets—and innovations do not aggregate in any simple way. Nevertheless, the tendency in mainstream growth theory, old and new, has been to try to have it both ways—to acknowledge innovation's centrality to growth but to resist the implication that better understanding of growth must be grounded in better understanding of the microlevel processes that produce economic change.[15]

An emphasis on firms as fundamental repositories of economic knowledge leads to quite a different view of many issues in growth theory than is suggested by standard approaches in neoclassical growth theory, old and new. Perspectives that regard technology as a highly codified public resource fail to apprehend the role of a variety of factors shaping the effectiveness with which the actual role is performed (Pack 1994). Similarly, the emphasis on capital accumulation tends to focus on saving rates and on capital allocation processes at the sectoral level, rather than on capital allocation among firms and within firms. The capabilities-based view, on the other hand, sees aggregate economic progress largely as the consequence of a multiplicity of actions at the firm level. Among the external forces that affect the quality of these performances are a number of aspects of the environment that might be subject to policy influence—particularly the competitive characteristics of input and output markets, the determinants of firm access to financial capital, and the legal framework surrounding 'intellectual property'.

As noted above, capabilities research is burgeoning today in the areas we have surveyed. Compelling evidence for that claim is provided in the chapters that follow.

---

[15] Research agendas on growth well in tune with the centrality of microeconomic capabilities and learning are discussed in Nelson 1998 and Dosi *et al.* 1993. When such an agenda is put to practice, it yields indeed quite different interpretative results from standard growth theories: see, on the 'Asian Miracle', Nelson and Pack 1999.

References

Adler, P. (1993). 'The learning bureaucracy: New United Motor Manufacturing, Inc.', *Research on Organization Behavior*, 15: 111–94.

Amsden, A. (1989). *Asia's Next: South Korea and Late Industrialization*. New York: Oxford University Press.

Birchenhall, C., N. Kastrinos, and S. Metcalfe (1997). 'Genetic algorithms in evolutionary modeling', *Journal of Evolutionary Economics*, 7: 375–93.

Castanias, R., and C. Helfat (1991). 'Managerial resources and rents', *Journal of Management*, 17: 155–71.

Chandler, A. (1962). *Strategy and Structure: Chapters in the History of American Industrial Entrerprise*. Cambridge, Mass.: Harvard University Press.

—— (1977). *The Visible Hand: The Managerial Revolution in America Business*. Cambridge, Mass.: Harvard University Press.

—— (1990). *Scale and Scope: The Dynamics of Industrial Capitalism*. Cambridge, Mass.: Harvard University Press.

—— F. Amatori, and T. Hikino (eds.) (1998). *Big Business and the Wealth of the Nations*. Cambridge/New York: Cambridge University Press.

—— P. Hagström, and Ö. Sölvell (eds.) (1998). *The Dynamic Firm: The Role of Technology, Strategy, Organization, and Regions*. Oxford/New York: Oxford University Press.

Christensen, C. M. (1997). *The Innovator's Dilemma: When New Technologies Cause Great Firms to Fail*. Boston: Harvard Business School Press.

—— and R. Rosenbloom (1995), 'Explaining the attacker's advantage: technological paradigms, organizational dynamics, and the value network', *Research Policy*, 23: 233–57.

—— and J. L. Bower (1996). 'Customer Power, Strategic investment and the failure of leading firm', *Strategic Management Journal*, 17: 197–218.

Cohen, M., and P. Bacdayan (1994). 'Organizational routines are stored as procedural memory', *Organization Science*, 5: 554–68.

Cole, R. E. (1999). *Managing Quality Fads: How American Business Learned to Play the Quality Game*. New York: Oxford University Press.

Deming, W. E. (1982). *Out of the Crisis*, Cambridge, Mass.: MIT Center for Advanced Engineering Study.

Dertouzos, M. L., R. K. Lester, and R. M. Solow (1989). *Made in America: Regaining the Productive Edge*. Cambridge, Mass.: MIT Press.

Dierickx, I., and Cool, K. (1989). 'Asset stock accumulation and sustainability of competitive advantage', *Management Science*, 35: 1504–11.

Dosi, G. (1984). 'Technological paradigms and technological trajectories: A suggested interpretation of the determinants and directions of technical change', *Research Policy*, 11: 147–162.

—— and L. Marengo (1994). 'Some elements of an evolutionary theory of organizational competences', in R. W. England, *Evolutionary Concepts in Contemporary Economics*, Ann Arbor: University of Michigan Press.

—— C. Freeman, and S. Fabiani (1994). 'The process of economic development: introducing some stylized facts and theories on technologies, firms and institutions', *Industrial and Corporate Change*, 3: 1–32.

—— and F. Malerba (eds.) (1996). *Organizations and Strategy in the Evolution of the Enterprise*. London: Macmillan.

Egidi, M. (1995). 'Routines, hierarchies of problems, procedural behavior: some evidence from experiments', in K. J. Arrow, *The Rational Foundations of Economic Behavior*. London: Macmillan.

Eliasson, G. (1990). 'The firm as a competent team', *Journal of Economic Behavior and Organization*, 13: 275–98.

Fransman, M. (1994*a*). 'AT&T, BT and NTT: A comparison of vision, strategy and competence', *Telecommunications Policy*, 18: 137–53.

—— (1994*b*). 'Information, knowledge, vision and theories of the firm', *Industrial and Corporate Change*, 3: 713–58.

Freeman, C. (1982). *The Economics of Industrial Innovation*. London: Pinter, 2nd edn.

Grant, R. M. (1995). *Contemporary Strategy Analysis: Concepts, Techniques, Applications*, 2nd. edn. Cambridge, Mass.: Blackwell.

—— (1996). 'Toward a knowledge-based theory of the firm', *Strategic Management Journal*, 17 (Winter Special Issue): 109–22.

Hamel, G., and C. K. Prahalad (1989). 'Strategic intent', *Harvard Business Review*, 66 (May–June): 63–76.

Helfat, C. (1994). 'Evolutionary trajectories in petroleum firm R&D', *Management Science*, 40: 1720–47.

—— (1997). 'Know-how and asset complementarity and dynamic capability accumulation: The case of R&D', *Strategic Management Journal*, 18: 339–60.

Henderson, R., and K. Clark (1990). 'Architectural innovation: the reconfiguration of existing product technologies and the failure of established firms', *Administrative Science Quarterly*, 35: 9–30.

Hobday, M. (1995). *Innovation in East Asia: The Challenge to Japan*. London: Edward Elgar.

Hodgson, G. M. (1988). *Economics and Institutions: A Manifesto for a Modern Institutional Economics*. Philadelphia: University of Pennsylvania Press.

—— (1993). *Economics and Evolution*. Ann Arbor: University of Michigan Press.

Hutchins, E. (1991). 'Organizing work by adaptation', *Organization Science*, 2: 14–39.

Juran, J. M. (1989). *Juran on Leadership for Quality: An Executive Handbook*. New York: Free Press.

Kay, N. (1992). 'Markets, false hierarchies and the evolution of the modern corporation', *Journal of Economic Behavior and Organization*, 17: 315–33.

—— (1997). *Patterns in Corporate Evolution*. Oxford: Oxford University Press.

Kogut, B., and Zander, U. (1992). 'Knowledge of the firm, combinative capabilities, and the replication of technology', *Organization Science*, 3: 383–97.

Loasby, B. J. (1983). 'Knowledge, learning and the enterprise', in J. Wiseman, *Beyond Positive Economics?*, London: Macmillan.

Langlois, R. N., and N. J. Foss (1999). 'Capabilities and governance: the rebirth of production in the theory of economic organization', *Kylos*, 52: 201–18.

Lazonick, W. (1990). *Competitive Advantage on the Shopfloor*. Cambridge, Mass.: Harvard University Press.

Lundvall, B. A. (ed.) (1992). *National Systems of Innovation*. London: Pinter.

Malerba, F., R. Nelson, L. Orsenigo, and S. Winter (1999). 'History-friendly models of industry evolution: the computer industry', *Industrial and Corporate Change*, 8: 3–40.

Marengo, L. (1992). 'Coordination and Organizational Learning in the Firm', *Journal of Evolutionary Economics*, 2: 313–26.

—— G. Dosi, P. Legrenzi, and C. Pasquali (1999). 'The structure of problem-solving knowledge and the structure of organizations', Pisa, St. Anna School of Advanced Studies, Working Paper.

Marshall, A. (1920). *Principles of Economics*, 8th edn. New York: Macmillan.

Metcalfe, J. S. (1994). 'Evolutionary economics and technology policy', *Economic Journal*, 104: 931–44.

Miyazaki, K. (1995). *Building Competences in the Firm: Lessons from Japanese and European Optoelectronics*. New York: St. Martin's Press.

Nelson, R. (ed.) (1993). *National Innovation Systems*. Oxford/New York: Oxford University Press.

——(1998). 'The agenda for growth theory: a different point of view', *Cambridge Journal of Economics*, 22: 497–520.

——and S. G. Winter (1982). *An Evolutionary Theory of Economic Change*. Cambridge, Mass.: Harvard University Press.

——and H. Pack (1999). 'The Asian miracle and modern growth theory', *The Economic Journal*, 109: 416–36.

Orsenigo, L., F. Pammolli, and M. Riccaboni (1999). 'Variety and irreversibility in scientific and technological systems: the pharmaceutical industry after the molecular biology revolution', in U. Pagano (ed.), *Evolution and Economics*, London: Routledge (forthcoming).

Pack, H. (1994). 'Endogenous growth theory: intellectual appeal and empirical shortcomings', *Journal of Economic Perspectives*, 8: 55–72.

—— and L. E. Westphal (1986). 'Industrial strategy and technological change: theory vs. reality', *Journal of Development Economics*, 22: 87–128.

Patel, P., and K. Pavitt (1998). 'The wide (and increasing) spread of technological competences in the world's largest firms: a challenge to conventional wisdom', in Chandler, Hagström, and Sölvell (1998).

Penrose, E. (1959). *The Theory of the Growth of the Firm*. New York: Wiley.

Peters, T. J., and R. H. Waterman (1982). *In Search of Excellence: Lessons from America's Best-Run Companies*. New York: Warner Books.

Porter, M. E. (1996). 'What is strategy?', *Harvard Business Review*, 74: 61–78.

Powell, W., K. Koput, and L. Smith-Doerr (1996). 'Inter-organizational collaboration and the locus of learning: networks of learning in biotechnology', *Administrative Science Quarterly*, 41: 116–45.

Prahalad, C. K., and G. Hamel (1990). 'The core competence of the corporation', *Harvard Business Review* (May): 79–91.

Richardson, G. B. (1972). 'The organisation of industry', *Economic Journal*, 82: 883–96.

Rumelt, R., D. Schendel, and D. Teece (1991). 'Strategic management and economics', *Strategic Management Journal*, 12: 5–29.

Saxenian, A. (1994). *Regional Advantage: Culture and Competition in Silicon Valley and Route 128*. Cambridge: Harvard University Press.

Schumpeter, J. (1950). *Capitalism, Socialism and Democracy*, 3rd edn. New York: Harper & Row.

Selznick, P. (1957). *Leadership in Administration: A Sociological Interpretation*. Evanston, Ill.: Row, Peterson & Co.

Senge, P. M. (1990). *The Fifth Discipline: The Art and Practice of the Learning Organization*. New York: Doubleday.

Squire, L. R. (1987). *Memory and Brain*. New York: Oxford University Press.

Stalk, G., P. Evans, and L. E. Shulman (1992). 'Competing on capabilities: the new rules of corporate strategy', *Harvard Business Review*, 70(2): 57–69.

Szulanski, G. (1996). 'Exploring internal stickiness: impediments to the transfer of best practice within the firm', *Strategic Management Journal*, 17 (Winter Special Issue): 27–43.

Taddei, D., and B. Coriat (1993). *Made in France*. Paris: Hachette/Livre de Poche.

Teece, D. J. (1980). 'Economies of scope and the scope of the enterprise', *Journal of Economic Behavior and Organization*, 1: 223–33.

——R. Rumelt, G. Dosi, and S. Winter (1994). 'Understanding corporate coherence: theory and evidence', *Journal of Economic Behavior and Organization*, 23: 1–30.

——G. Pisano and A. Shuen (1997). 'Dynamic capabilities and strategic management', *Strategic Management Journal*, 18: 509–33.

Tushman, M., and P. Anderson (1986). 'Technological discontinuities and organization environments', *Administrative Science Quarterly*, 31: 439–65.

Von Hippel, E., and M. J. Tyre (1995). 'How learning by doing is done: problem identification in novel process equipment', *Research Policy*, 24: 1–12.

Waterman, R. H., T. J. Peters, and J. R. Phillips (1980). 'Structure is not organization', *Business Horizons*, June: 14–86.

Westphal, L. E., L. Kim, and C. Dahlman (1985). 'Reflections on Korea's acquisition of technological capability', in N. Rosenberg, *International Technology Transfer*. New York: Praeger.

Winter, S. (1982). 'An essay on the theory of production', in S. Hymans (ed.), *Economics and the world around it*. Ann Arbor: University of Michigan Press.

——(1987). 'Knowledge and competences as strategic assets', in D. Teece (ed.), *The Competitive Challange*. Cambridge, Mass.: Ballinger.

PART I

Introduction to Part I

ORGANIZATIONAL CAPABILITIES: THE MICRO EVIDENCE

The four papers in Part I put a microscope on the particularities of organizational capabilities and learning. The paper by Narduzzo, Rocco, and Warglien, is concerned with two sets of capabilities developed and implemented by a cellular phone network company. One of these capabilities is for the installation of new stations. The other is for maintenance and problem-solving. The authors use the study of these complex examples of capabilities as an opportunity to explore the usefulness, limits, and meaning of the treatment of capabilities as bundles of routines. They conclude that, in their case at least, effective capabilities certainly do involve the mastery and use of certain routines, but also the ability to do particular and often idiosyncratic things that are appropriate to a particular context.

The company studied in this paper has different operations in different regions. The authors also explore the question of the extent to which capabilities, and practices, are company-wide, as contrasted with developing regional- or group-specific idiosyncratic elements. They conclude that the latter are important.

The chapter by Argote and Darr is concerned with the apparently humble capabilities in making a good pizza in an economical way. One of their central questions is the extent to which learned capabilities are built into particular people, and the mechanisms and extent to which capabilities can be regarded as organizational, in the sense that individuals can leave and be replaced without erosion of the capability. They also are concerned with the extent to which new learned capabilities are transmitted and contained within an organization, in this case a set of franchise operations, as contrasted with all comers. A hallmark of the chapter is detailed examination of the way new knowledge is made organizational, and spread throughout the franchise.

The chapter by Szulanski also is concerned with the mechanisms through which routines are made common across a group of related organizations, in this case the member banks of a bank group. The group of banks associated with Banc One has been expanded through acquisition. Banks choose to become members of the group because of the significant financial success that group members continue to have, and because of a strong belief that that success is due in good part to certain bundles of routines that are used in Banc One operations. At the same time, the philosophy of Banc One admits that individual units should have a certain freedom to accommodate to the particularities of their individual circumstances. The study describes in elaborate detail the processes through which a new acquisition of Banc One is taught and learns the basic routines that define the Banc One system.

The chapter by Flaherty is concerned with learning and effective control in semiconductor manufacturing. In contrast with the technologies considered by other papers in Part I, semiconductor manufacturing is extraordinarily complex. There are many different processes involved, and each process, and the interactions across the various processes, easily can get 'out of control'. There is a major problem in assuring quality of the output.

A central problem, therefore, in semiconductor manufacture is to be able quickly to spot production aspects that seem to be getting 'out of control', to diagnose these problems, and to solve them. An essential aspect of these processes is that the relevant 'knowledge' generally is distributed among a number of different people. Another factor is that certain kinds of experimentation to diagnose and solve a problem can themselves be highly expensive in terms of lost production. Flaherty's study puts a microscope on these issues, and illustrates nicely the complexities that often are involved in organizational capabilities.

1

Talking about Routines in the Field: The Emergence of Organizational Capabilities in a New Cellular Phone Network Company

ALESSANDRO NARDUZZO, ELENA ROCCO, AND MASSIMO WARGLIEN

1. Introduction: Unbundling Routines

To many students of organizational life, part of the attractiveness of the routine concept lies in its capacity to tie together familiar features of how organizations do and know how to do things. Rather than being defined once-for-all, the concept of organizational routine is progressively circumscribed by the set of properties one learns to associate with it. A familiar list of such properties would include adjectives like tacit, automatic, repetitive, distributed, situated, rule-based, political. Attempts to provide an unambiguous definition of routines have proved to be only mildly successful, and Sid Winter has legitimately claimed that the polysemy of the concept is part of its strength (Winter 1986; Cohen *et al*. 1996). In fact, the concept of routines is caught in a fancy recursion, since it reproduces at a higher level part of the features it describes. It is somehow tacit, since there is more in the concept than one can say (and people learn it mostly through examples); it is distributed in the community of its users and, in some cases, it is a truce among the different and sometimes conflicting claims students make on the definition of organizational capabilities (see again Cohen *et al*. 1996).

Thus, the concept of routine looks like a bundle of features, among which users can emphasize those that better fit the specific aims and context of their analysis. However, what in most cases is a point of strength, turns out to be more problematic when one deals with case studies in the field. Being samples of one, case studies tend to emphasize the descriptive and interpretive accuracy of concepts, rather than their ability to capture recurring features across multiple experiences. Thus, when dealing with the field, some reverse engineering is needed and unbundling concepts becomes the dominant strategy.

This is what this chapter is mostly about. It is a case study in the emergence of organizational capabilities in a newborn cellular phone company. The case study looks at how competencies are accumulated in the key activities of network

We wish to thank Omnitel and those who allowed us to make our observations in the field. We are grateful to Chiara Medioli and the BTS technicians working in Emilia Romagna and Sicily for their support, their kindness, and their tolerance.

installation and maintenance in the first year of operations. During such year, we have been tracking the capabilities building process through multiple data-gathering activities, including interviews, systematic screening of internal documents, and a six months' presence in the field with two network technicians' teams by one of us. Inevitably, compressing in a few pages the huge amount of (often unstructured) information such observations have generated implies some subjective selection and the usual trade-offs among accuracy, generality, and simplicity (Weick 1979). In doing so, we have been guided by a twofold concern. On the one hand, we have tried to understand whether the concept of routine provides a suitable framework for describing and interpreting the emergence of organizational capabilities, and how the concept should be articulated to account for our observations; on the other hand, we have tried to learn from the field some lessons on the nature of organizational routines. Thus, our chapter can be better framed as a 'conversation with the field' about routines, a round trip between concepts and data.

After a short presentation of the field setting (Section 2), we focus on four key processes related to capabilities building. Section 3 reconstructs some key features of organizational imprinting, or the original accumulation of a stock of capabilities in the early months of organizational life. Section 4 deals with how technicians learn to fix troubles, looking into the way individual skills and collective capabilities interweave. Section 5 describes the emergence of network installation routines, calling on processes of emergent division of labour and the recombination of elementary routines in more complex patterns of action. Section 6 looks at the evolution of coordination within technicians' teams, reconstructing the emergence of hierarchical roles. Finally, we summarize what we have learned from the field.

2. A Case Study: Network Technicians in a New Cellular Phone Company

Omnitel Pronto Italia (henceforth OPI) provides a service of wireless communication through cellular phones in Italy. By the time of this study, OPI was a just-born company which has been in the market since the end of 1995. The organization is decentralized and physically distributed in the country. There are four zones covering four different geographical areas coordinated by the headquarters located in one of the four zones.

The first year activity has been extremely intensive and in a few months OPI has created a nationwide GSM[1] network. Over 600 transceiver stations have been installed in less than six months (see Figure 1.1).

OPI has performed a rapid growth to meet the legal requirements that define the minimal network dimension. Such a quick growth has generated heavy pressures on competence accumulation, especially with regards to competencies which are less known and understood. Among them, network technical competencies have high strategic relevance, meeting current definitions of organizational capabilities

---

[1] GSM (Global System of Mobile Communication) is the European standard technology for digital cellular communication.

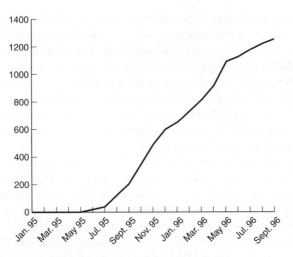

Fig. 1.1 Number of BTS stations installed

(Teece 1984; Barney 1991; Amit and Schoemaker 1993). Such competencies mainly refer to installation and maintenance activities. The capacity to rapidly install new stations is needed for both legal and marketing reasons. On the one hand, it facilitates meeting the national legal threshold for becoming authorized providers of cellular communication services; on the other hand, the geographic area of network coverage is a key parameter of service quality to customers' eyes. A second key technical competence is network maintenance: a high service reliability is considered by OPI a source of competitive advantage.

Installation and maintenance are complex tasks accomplished by a large number of organizational units and subunits. Different units plan which parts of the country have to be covered, how many transceiver stations (called BTS[2] stations) they need, where the stations should be placed, and which configuration has to be chosen. Once the locations are identified they rent the space and build the sites. When the room is ready the GSM transceivers are installed and connected to the network. These last steps are followed by the so-called BTS specialists; they are the technicians in charge of the maintenance of the network. In a few months OPI has recruited over one hundred skilled repairmen as BTS technicians. Most of them had previous experience with telecommunication technology (e.g. wireless communication, radio links), but none was familiar with the digital cellular GSM adopted by OPI.

BTS technicians are grouped in teams which are responsible for network activities over well-defined areas. The main activities on BTS stations are: installation, trouble-fixing, and periodical maintenance. They have to handle a variety of problems and situations concerning the telecommunication system, electric (e.g. batteries) and electronic (e.g. smoke detectors) devices, and the air-conditioning system. Taking

---

[2] BTS stands for Base Transceiver Station and is the radio unit of the GSM infrastrucure that exchanges signals with cellular phones.

care of BTS stations and the GSM network over a geographical area requires monitoring of communication traffic, making periodical checks and cleaning the sites, upgrading hardware and software configurations, and documenting the activity. BTS technicians also have close relationships with a variety of different external suppliers.

BTS technicians are organized in quasi-independent teams. These teams are spatially distributed and they are the most decentralized units of the company. Technicians' daily work follows a weekly schedule. The team's scheduling often changes during the week because of unexpected events such as alarms in the BTS stations which require immediate solutions.

During the first months BTS technicians belonging to the same team used to work together; later on, as the network size increased, they started spreading around and working alone. Increasing physical isolation made face-to-face interaction a more rare event and the BTS technicians began to use their cellular phones as the main communication device to keep in touch and coordinate with others.

BTS technicians spend most of their time in the field, and some of them go to the office only once or twice a week. When they are in the field they (a) participate in the installation phase to build new BTS stations, (b) fix troubles when BTS alarms turn on. In fact, the BTS technicians may receive phone calls from other colleagues who monitor the whole network and (c) carry out the maintenance activity.

3. Organizational Imprinting: The 'Primitive Accumulation' of Capabilities

The initial phase of OPI's activity has been thus characterized by at least two key constraints. First, there has been an urgency to reach a territorial network coverage sufficient to meet the deadline imposed by the National Telecommunication Department. That deadline marks the conclusion of the set-up phase and the opening of the full-fledged working phase. The second constraint has been the need to provide customers a regular and reliable service since the first day of the working phase. This implies that OPI had to reach a critical threshold of competence within a short time span, running the new technology, concentrating learning, testing, and trouble-shooting in a few months. This process of 'primitive accumulation' of capabilities had to occur in the absence of direct feedback from fully operating conditions, in what was commonly referred to as a 'simulated' working environment. Thus, most learning had to resort to substitutes of experience (Weick 1991) rather than to direct experience.

Besides knowledge and technology supplied by providers, the initial pool of resources needed to create OPI own-operating capabilities was brought in, recruiting skilled people coming from pre-existing organizations. Of course, it was impossible to buy such capabilities already packaged; therefore, OPI had to accumulate knowledge by hiring people from a host of 'neighbour' organizations in the telecommunication industry (i.e. Telecom, Ericcson, Italtel, Bell Atlantic). All those people were bringing in different individual skills and practices from different systems of organizational routines and mapping them onto the new context. As a consequence, organizational learning initially occurs mainly through the 'import' and replication of others' experience (vicarious learning) rather than directly.

In the new, rapidly growing firm, field practice is to a large extent a space to fill, only partially structured by organizational policies, where people can recognize familiar cues and transfer their own past experience. For example, the use of maps is widespread in radio frequency activities. BTS technicians with previous jobs in radio frequency draw maps for supporting their trouble diagnostic activity, while others use text based information. Similarly, people with former experience in the domain of power stations tend to introduce new procedures for maintenance inspired by their previous job. Thus, the initial stock of competencies looks like an organizational patchwork, an assembly of heterogeneous elements borrowed from the environment.

Of course, some coherence needs to be conferred to such collection of practices. The key role in shaping more ordered patterns of action has been played by the zone technical supervisors, who have been hired among the first and have been in charge of recruiting the technicians' teams and shaping their local organization. However, since supervisors of different zones come from different organizations, each zone has developed an idiosyncratic work style. For example, a zone (that we will label 'zone A') tends to reproduce the technocratic style of the organization its supervisor comes from. This means that trouble-fixing is conceived as a highly standardizable activity, and most efforts are devoted to creating a detailed set of standard operating procedures to deal with each possible trouble. The process of generating such procedures is inherited from the source organization of the supervisor, and often single procedures use SOPs from such organizations as templates. Technicians are trained as executors of such procedures, and coordination is bureaucratic and rule-based. Conversely, in another zone ('zone B') the supervisor brings from his original organization a conception of trouble-fixing as a complex task which requires reflection and diagnostic reasoning. In zone B, the accent is on shared information rather than standard procedures, and efforts are devoted to creating databases and technical notes that can support such an information-sharing process. The structure of databases and technical notes is directly imported from the supervisor's previous experience. Coordination is informal and based on mutual adjustment.

Such local heterogeneity of practices is not surprising in a new, decentralized organization. What matters here is that those imported practices and the system of routines they generate tend to persist in spite of pressures for organization-wide homogeneity from the headquarters, and create an 'organizational imprinting effect' that gives each zone a peculiar style and organizational flavour. Still now people easily identify the source of such flavour (e.g. it is common to refer to a given zone as being 'Telecom style')

There are multiple reasons for such local persistence of early routines. A first reason is simply sunk costs. Once a given routine has generated investments in diagnostic software, formal procedures, databases, training and so forth, it creates economic and psychological inertia. Sometimes sunk costs are strategically exploited by zones, e.g. committing skills and investing in costly software systems that support a given set of procedures makes it less likely that headquarters will change such procedures.

A second reason is complementarities. Single routines do not stand alone, but usually are complementary to others. For example, the way a trouble is fixed has relationships with how troubles are communicated, how jobs are scheduled, how databases are built and updated, and how past troubles are documented. Once a more or less coherent system of routines is installed, it cannot be changed piecemeal without damaging the global performance—it is trapped in a local optimum, to use a mathematical metaphor (Levinthal and Warglien 1997). Consequently, complementarities protect single routines from change pressures and defer change to major restructurings that often never come, because they are too costly, risky, and disruptive.

There are also insulation factors that preserve localism and inhibit the convergence in practice among zones. One obvious insulation factor is space. Spatial proximity is a fundamental facilitator of processes of imitation and mutual learning; it favours communication, trust, and generates opportunities for joint work. Individuals who work on stations significantly distant from others, rarely meet team members, have to rely mostly on their own direct experience, and develop idiosyncratic, often poor skills—for example, they develop too simplistic diagnostic models of troubles (see Section 4).

However, distance among individuals does not depend only on geographical space, but also on organizational structure that affects communication opportunities and creates a sense of belonging to the same social unit. For example, interactions between Naples and Palermo, that are in the same zone, are more frequent than interactions between Naples and Rome, that belong to different zones, although the geographical distance among the latter is less than the one between the former. Indeed, both geographical and organizational distance seem to matter in our case. Interactions and exchange of experiences are more frequent within zones but to a lesser extent also across zones that are closer in space.

Time also matters. As different zones have started the set-up of the network in different moments, time delays play against the diffusion of local competencies. Since zones have not started at the same time, people do not simultaneously face the same problems and inter-zone meetings are often considered as a waste of time. This fact is also strategically used as an excuse to apply local solutions to common problems and intentionally avoid exchange of solutions among zones. For instance, during inter-zone meetings zone managers talk about problems they face, but they do not share and discuss solutions. As a result, there are indeed rare examples of imitation of solutions earlier developed in other zones.

However, distance in space, organizational structure, and time act as insulation mechanisms also because there are powerful incentives to keep low levels of inter-zone learning and diffusion. Some competition among geographical units is commonplace in any decentralized organization. However, in our case headquarters have pushed competition among zones to improve zones' performance, especially with regards to effectiveness in setting up the network. The side effect is that the diffusion of best practices is inhibited—each zone has an incentive to perform better than the other ones.

This kind of strategic behaviour is not only visible in the relations among zones, but also in the relations between each zone and the headquarters. Headquarters have an interest to drive a process of convergence of work practices and documentation, in order to foster diffusion of best practices and keep monitoring and control of zone activities. On the converse, zones tend to preserve autonomy, maintaining local coherence. In the context of new organization building, this often implies the search for 'first mover advantages' in the establishment of work practices. In other words, zones tend to anticipate headquarters in establishing procedures and documentation, tailoring such elements to their emergent routines. For example, headquarters have been developing a system that had to keep together the nationwide monitoring of network troubles, the dispatching of trouble-fixing tasks to technicians, and the recording of trouble histories. However, only the network monitoring activity and the dispatching to teams (not to team members) has been immediately available. In the meanwhile, some zones have developed their own parallel dispatching and trouble-history-recording systems. This implies that different zones now have different systems, making standardization increasingly difficult and leaving the key control functions in local hands (for example, reliably assessing the average trouble-fixing time is now possible only at the local level). Of course, the development of local systems is motivated by operating needs and the urgency to have key information without waiting for the full development of the central system. The point is that those local systems are developed without searching for an *ex ante* agreement with headquarters and other zones on procedural and technological standards, thus creating the premises for *ex post* incompatibility with low reversibility.

3.1. *Wrapping up*

Observing a newborn organization with rapid growth rates provides a unique opportunity to analyse the nature of organizational imprinting (Stinchcombe 1965; Ginsberg and Baum 1994).

We have stressed that vicarious learning plays a fundamental role in performing the 'primitive accumulation' of OPI's organizational capabilities. Having no time to resort to direct experience, the firm has found its competencies in the environment. The process of assimilation of such (heterogeneous) competencies has stressed local coherence versus firm-level integration and has generated within zones patterns of action that, once established, have proved stable and resilient to efforts of firm-wide standardization.

The local stabilization of initial capabilities is the key feature of the imprinting process. Our case study suggests that the process has a dual nature (Coriat and Dosi 1994). On the one hand, there are 'functional' reasons supporting the stability in each zone of the initial core of organizational practices: urgency, sunk costs, complementarities among routines, the costs of communication and coordination. On the other hand, all these elements are strategically manipulable by organizational actors, and in fact there is evidence that actors do exploit such strategic opportunities to maintain control of key resources and processes.

In a newborn organization there are wide empty territories to occupy, and first movers have a good chance to win the gold race. The incentive system of a decentralized organization reinforces strategies of anticipation and sinking costs. Under such pressures, the system of local routines quickly crystallizes and prevents further change.

4. Fixing Troubles

4.1. Fixing simple troubles

Troubles range from very simple to very complex ones. Simple trouble-fixing is usually an individual task that reflects individual skills (although, as we shall see, these are embedded in the community links of the individual) and whose correct execution is mostly taken for granted. Thus, such simple troubles are a good starting point for describing capabilities that seem elementary both in terms of technical and social complexity.

One of the most common and simple troubles results in the inability of a single station to transmit a signal. The trouble is very easy to detect as it interrupts the whole station activity and it is also revealed by the automated control systems of the network. Thus, when a technician reaches the station whose transmission breakdown has been signalled, he has already been told the type and possible causes of the trouble. In particular, if transmission breaks down totally, he must expect that something pertaining to the transmission system of the station (including a transmitter and a receiver) has been damaged.

In theory, since the transmission system is all integrated in a single board, the trouble could be easily fixed by changing the transmission board. This simplistic view is also the one encoded in the technical handbook provided by the technology supplier and adopted as the training platform for technicians. Thus, the formal standard procedure in case of such trouble is just 'if a transmission error is signalled then change the board'. However, even in this elementary case, the formal 'official' knowledge is often misleading, and the experience of technicians has developed an alternative fixing routine. Failures of the standard procedure have created the ground for the emergence of the new routine. In fact, most technicians have soon learned that in many cases changing the transmission board would not eliminate the transmission breakdown. The reason is that there are interactions with other components of the technology that may result in a 'transmission error' signal without directly concerning the transmission board itself. Instead of the official standard procedure, technicians have developed a more elaborate procedure which is grounded on a more complex diagnostic model of the trouble. The most surprising feature of the technicians' actual 'expert' behaviour in front of a transmission trouble is that their first intervention is rarely the transmission board substitution. Instead, they usually start resetting components of the station that affect indirectly the transmission process. The official standard procedure becomes only the last-resort procedure when such preliminary tests have failed. This behaviour is rooted in the model of trouble technicians have developed through collective experience. The model implies the belief that the transmission board technology is quite robust so it rarely fails, while other components are more fallible and have to be tested before. Thus, the implicit representation technicians use is not the simplistic one of the handbook but implies a more complex causal structure (Figure 1.2).

A few remarks need to be made at this stage of our discussion. Such 'enriched' representation is not derived from an explicit representation of the station inner working, but instead is induced from diagnostic experience: it is a diagnostic model of the test to be performed rather than a causal model of the technology. People learn this representation by calling more expert technicians, when a diagnostic impasse is experienced, and asking 'what should I do then?' rather than asking which components are connected to the transmission board. We shall return to this remark more in depth later, but we can suggest that technicians tend to develop a model of their activity rather than a model of the technology they work on.

Individual technicians differ in terms of the diagnostic model they adopt. Differences are affected by the number of years of experience and membership to a particular subset of the whole technicians' 'community of practice' (Lave and Wenger 1991; Seely Brown and Duguid 1991). For example, more experienced technicians differ from novice ones in terms of the number of possible causal links they test and degree of complexity they can handle: the model of the trouble is usually richer in expert subjects. Also, expert technicians in different geographic areas may adopt different sets of causal links in their actual diagnostic activities. This seems to be closely related to the way expertise is accumulated and diffused. The enrichment of the diagnostic model is not only the outcome of individual experience with the technology, but to a large extent it is the result of communication among colleagues (Orr 1987). Communication sometimes arises as an *ad hoc* call in case of difficulties in

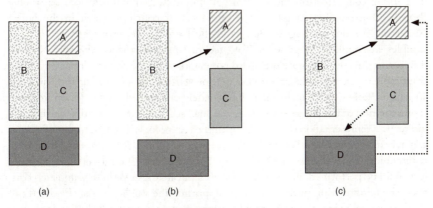

Fig. 1.2 Fixing a trouble

An alarm is signalled by the control system on board A. According to the control system (a) the trouble is localized in the board A. The BTS technicians' manuals sometimes suggest some alternative causes (b) for the problems, as for instance the board B. None the less, on the basis of their field experience BTS technicians have learned that there are some more complex relationships among the boards and that the alarm on board A may be caused by some problems on board C.

trouble-fixing, or as a 'war story' told on the occasion of face-to-face encounters in the office, during lunch, or other meeting events (Orr 1990). Also, communication has tight boundaries defined by physical constraints (i.e. face-to-face meeting constrained by geographic distance) and social constraints (i.e. belonging to the same organizational unit). Thus, expertise is not only a matter of cumulated personal experience, but also a matter of membership of a community of practice within which experience is shared (a typically social dimension of expertise, thus, is the amount of people one personally knows and can call in case of need). For example, we have observed the case of an isolated technician, working in a physically remote area with low levels of integration within the community of colleagues, displaying more simplistic diagnostic activities despite having a long personal experience. This in turn has isolated him from colleagues, making him perceived as an 'outgroup', further deepening his social distance from the work community and thus further impoverishing his personal skills.

4.2. Testing alternative causes of a trouble

Troubles can be more complex than that, however. Not all troubles have a repetitive and predictable nature. They often require a more subtle diagnostic task, involving the identification of the trouble and the construction of *ad hoc* sequences of tests identifying the appropriate repair operations. In those cases, the concept of routine as a mere behavioural pattern would be of little use to portray the technicians' activity. Nevertheless, the structure of diagnostic and repair activities shares important features with the one depicted in the example above. Another example will provide some illustration of this point.

One night, the automatized network control system was signalling that the fourth of the eight time slots managing multiple simultaneous calls in a station was affected by a 70 per cent error (this means that communication in that time slot was totally flawed). One possible source of the error was of course a defect in the board containing the time slot itself. But, as in the former case, errors can result from troubles in coupled components. Two technicians had reached the site. No one thought to directly substitute the board containing the time slot (again, just as in the trouble-fixing example described above), nor started debating about the hardware structure. Rather, both technicians immediately contended about the appropriate representation of the diagnostic task. As we shall see, such representation carries only indirectly a representation of subsystems of the technology. The first object of debate was whether it was possible or not to perform a loop test, i.e. a simulation of a communication loop controlled by a portable computer. Once ascertained that the test could be performed, the first step was to replicate the error in the simulated context. The confirmation of the error was supporting the validity of the simulated call loop in reproducing the real trouble. Once this was established, the loop test structure was suggesting three possible sources of the error: (a) a default in the time slot; (b) a default in the receiver sending inputs to the time slot; or (c) a default in both. This was because the loop test was passing messages through those two elements.

The implicit sequence of tests suggested by this representation was thus to eliminate possible alternative causes of error, selecting among the three possible sources (from a logical point of view, thus, the diagnostic test was similar to what psychologists of thinking call a selection task—Wason and Johnson-Laird 1972).

The first test actually performed was to let the simulated call pass through another time slot connected to the same receiver. Since this alternative time slot was working well, it was logically clear that the receiver was not defective, and thus the only possible cause of error was a default in time slot four. However, the technicians didn't stop their test sequence, but performed all the sequence of tests suggested by the loop test structure, repeating a loop test by coupling the fourth time slot to another receiver. Thus, technicians ignored the selective value of the first evidence and performed all the sequence despite the uselessness of the last tests. This provides an interesting paradox. Technicians appear to follow a seemingly 'automated' sequence of actions, but this happens in a context that they are experiencing for the first time and with a sequence that they are generating for the first time.

In order to interpret this paradox, it may be useful to look at the drawings one technician made to explain what he had just done to one of us (see Figure 1.3). The drawing was *not* representing the actual functional structure of the hardware (Figure 1.4), with its connections among components, but instead was representing the logical structure of the loop test, connecting together components of the station hardware, not through their actual physical links, but in their functional position within the test scheme (that brings out a representation which is inconsistent with the physical structure of the hardware). Thus, they built a model of their activity, not

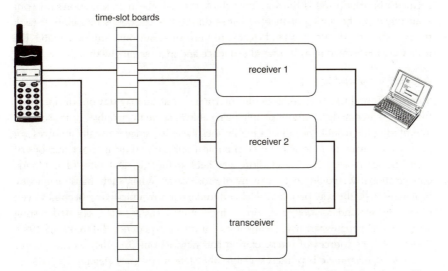

Fig. 1.3 Representation of the hardware drawn by a BTS technician to explain the time-slot trouble
The representation of the hardware as drawn by a BTS technician is based on the structure of the test applied to reproduce the alarm. This model is not consistent with the physical structure of the hardware, as shown in Fig. 1.4. Here the technician draws the same component twice (as input and output unit) and leaves the fact that the eight time slots are physically settled into two different boards.

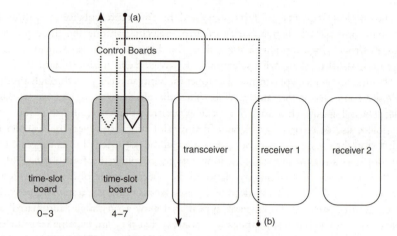

Fig. 1.4 Scheme of the hardware structure involved in the time-slot trouble
Communication flows (a) and (b) are regulated by a system of control boards that exchange signals with the
transceiver and the receivers through the time-slot boards.

of the station structure. What seems to be routinized, thus, is not the sequence of actions itself (the series of tests) but how technicians derive a sequence of actions from the representation of the task they build. Within this representation, they ignore the evidence made available by experience until the sequence is entirely performed (as in the 'batch' routine mode defined by Stinchcombe 1990). In other words, what seems to be routinized is the way they think through the representation and consequently act. The timing of their activities during this episode is revealing. It took them a while to identify the kind of test to perform—but once this was made, the tests were performed in a very rapid sequence and in a seemingly 'thoughtless' way.

4.3. Interpreting troubles

Sometimes troubles are even harder to interpret. A station may stay out of operation for more than one day, without people being able to solve the trouble. In those cases interpreting the trouble becomes a highly social activity, since it usually involves the presence of many technicians and communications with an even larger number of them. In such cases, long discussions are held at the site, at lunch, or in phone conversations. We could observe many of those cases. When such 'hard' diagnostic problems arise, the way people model and understand trouble-fixing becomes even more relevant and an object of open discussion. Usually, after repeated testing activities fail, people start using 'substitutes of direct experience' (March *et al.* 1991; Weick 1991) as sources of interpretation and new actions. In other words, people stop testing diagnostic hypotheses against the station and starts testing hypotheses against mental entities. Typically, this process takes two forms.

Testing hypotheses against models.   The typical situation is one in which a test is proposed, and other technicians deny its validity on the ground of their model of the technology. This is the only case in which we have seen an explicit model of the technology emerging beyond the model of the test activity. Sometimes discussions can be so general that they concern not only the GSM technology, but broader notions of communication technology. This is not surprising given the higher level of abstraction and explicitness of such discussions: a sort of 'academic' style emerges in these cases, leading to an explicit comparison of representations of how a station works. Since models of different scope and width are confronted, these are also opportunities in which individual representations are enriched and diffused in explicit form.

Testing hypotheses against case histories. In most cases, however, the discussion is less academic and resorts to analogous cases as sources of comparison and validation/discrediting for proposed interpretations. The usual format of these discussions is that a technician describes his difficulties in dealing with the trouble and his new hypotheses, and another technician starts a tale concerning situations he has faced that might provide useful analogies. Those tales are highly interactive, since they often imply questions and answers and the intervention of other persons. These tales closely resemble the 'war stories' described by Orr (1987, 1990). Interpretations are provided in the context of narratives of action, and they are tightly coupled to descriptions of the activity involved. They rarely present an abstract picture of the problem, but instead follow a plot dictated by the actual sequence of actions tried in those similar contexts. It is noteworthy that when such tale-tellers are asked to join the station and try a sequence of tests, they reproduce the same sequence of actions they have been narrating. Sometimes this involves the repetition of tests that they know have already been tried without success by former technicians. We find here again the emergence of 'useless' tests that are nevertheless performed. The close tie to the narrative form of case-telling suggests that useless tests are repeated because they are part of the story—in other words, they act as 'evoking steps' (March and Simon 1993) necessary to the technician to reconstruct in action the pattern experienced in past cases.

4.4. *Wrapping up*

Trouble-fixing is not just an automatic execution of a behavioural repertoire, but implies reasoning through a model of the trouble—there is some flexibility in actions that is hardly amenable to a strict behavioural view of routines

The model of the trouble, however, is embedded in a model of the trouble-fixing task that ties together representations of the technology, diagnostic activities, and repair actions.

Once such a model is active, technicians execute all the actions it suggests in a batch mode, substantially ignoring the feedback from experience until the sequence is completed.

Although trouble-fixing skills may look as individual ones, elements of the individual representation are acquired not only through direct experience, but also through social activities of communication and debate within the boundaries of a 'community of practice'. The content of such communication rarely takes the form of abstract, explicit representations of the technology, while most often such representations are embedded in tales of the activity.

Thus, there is a mixed evidence of routinization in a strict (behavioural) sense. In order to describe trouble-fixing activities, one needs to account for both automatic action and reasoning, and feedback from experience seems to be relevant at some levels (defining the trouble) and irrelevant at some other level (performing sequences of actions). We suggest that introducing an explicit distinction between representations and behaviour may be helpful. People seem to reason through representations (although these are highly context-dependent, task-oriented ones) and act automatically on the basis of such representations. Furthermore, the diffusion of representations is not less relevant than the replication of behaviours—but representations are mostly diffused in ways that depend on the social and practical context.

5. Building a Network Station

As we have seen, trouble-fixing routines are social in nature, but their execution is mostly an individual task; however, technicians are also engaged in activities implying joint coordinated execution and a more complex division of labour. The network station installation and set-up is the most prominent example of such more complex patterns of action. Basically, the station installation and set-up consists of three phases (see Figure 1.5):

- 'Room-Ready' phase in which the physical location (walls, pylons, public utilities connections) is predisposed for hosting the electronic hardware of the station;
- 'Commissioning phase' during which the hardware is installed, configured, and tested;
- 'Integration phase', during which the station is further configured and connected to the GSM network.

Each of these phases belongs formally to different units, both OPI internal units and/or providers ones. There are very detailed standard procedures, agreed between OPI and its main technology provider, prescribing accurately how phases should be sequenced in time and how they should be executed (a technician compared the almost pedantic nature of such instructions to the one of his first motorcycle manual, specifying even that 'one should put the parking-bar down when he parks). In particular, such procedures prescribe a strictly sequential arrangement of the phases and of single activities, and a rigid division of labour between OPI units and the providers' ones.

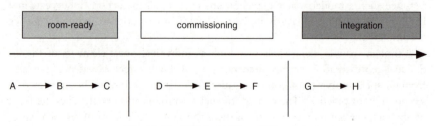

Fig. 1.5 The SOP for building a BTS station

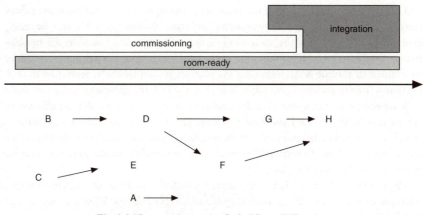

Fig. 1.6 The emerging routine for building a BTS station

Despite their very detailed structure, such standard procedures are in fact system-atically violated in the field. Phases are overlapping, single activities are often executed in parallel, and the division of labour is rearranged as a function of the timing of the activities. Moreover, OPI technicians participate in all phases (they shouldn't) and often substitute providers' technicians. Thus, the standard procedure is in fact 'spontaneously re-engineered' by participants, generating an entirely differ-ent sequence of activities and division of labour (see Figure 1.6).

The relevant point here is that such a reorganization violates the procedure in a peculiar way. In fact the official procedure is not 'thrown away', but instead is used only for its descriptive value, while its prescriptive aspects are eluded. Para-doxically, it is just because the procedure is so detailed that activities can be restructured: participants tend to use the procedure as a check list of activities, whose official sequence can be ignored as far as their precise description allows to treat them as 'modules' to reassemble in practice (Pentland and Reuter 1994). In other words, the procedure allows a clear punctuation of the flow of activities, providing unam-biguous labels for them, and thus provides a system of manipulable elements (Holyoak and Spellman 1993). Since the installation work has to be performed under a relevant time pressure (OPI had to quickly achieve a broad coverage of the national territory), activities that can be anticipated are consequently performed in parallel, reducing the cycle time. Some participants to the restructured routine that had previously worked on the same task with a different organization reported that in their former occupation, since activities were less clearly defined in highly detailed procedures, it was harder to subvert the customary sequence of actions—which implied a much longer cycle time. Thus, the formal procedure is not merely executed nor ignored, but instead it is used as a 'structuring resource' (Suchman 1987) for manipulating the list of activities and restructuring their position in time.

Notice that the new arrangement of activities in time is not a rigid one: it is easily adapted to the specific contexts of each installation (e.g. to delays in some activity)

and can be renegotiated among the actors (for example, when a different providers' team is encountered, new arrangements on who should do what can be easily generated). We find here the same kind of flexibility that was found in the trouble-fixing examples: once a representation of the problem is constructed, activities can be performed in routine ways following the plan suggested by the representation. The usefulness of the standard procedure is in that it allows the technicians to easily build such representation in a shared and unambiguous way, so that a coherent division of labour can be established and single actions can be performed. In a way, what is strictly routinized is the execution of the single 'activity modules', or chunks (Cohen and Bacdayan 1994). In turn, such a modularity is possible thanks to the descriptive power of the formal procedure.

The power of the modularity of routines is well shown by a subsequent example, which emphasizes the recombination possibilities (Nelson and Winter 1982; Zander and Kogut 1995) modularization provides.

After their first installation, some stations had to be empowered by the addition of further boards for the reception and transmission of phone calls ('oversizing'). This was a somehow new activity, since it implied the restructuring of pre-existing installations. The main novelty was constituted by something like an 'open heart' surgery over a working station. Furthermore, this activity had to be performed under a severe time constraint.

The structuring of the new activity was not procedurally specified by headquarters, but instead was delegated to team leaders. We could observe the emergence of the new 'oversizing' routine in two different geographic areas.

The new routine took shape through initial pilot oversizing experiments in a few stations where a group of technicians participated—after those early experiences, each technician could perform it individually. The main problem was that oversizing had to be performed by technicians without any direct feedback on the success of the operation. They were executing a kind of package of tasks whose effect could only be verified by the subsequent activation by a different organizational unit (the radio frequency technicians), often with some days of delay. This mix of novelty, time constraints, and lack of feedback was creating a strong sense of anxiety in technicians. Facing this uncertainty about the outcomes and in the absence of an official procedure, technicians heavily resorted to past experience as a source of structuring for the new activity. The activity was not redesigned from scratch, but instead was organized though a new recombination of single 'building blocks' of the installation routine. This way, technicians' attention was focused on the few entirely new operations and on the connection among different building blocks, leaving un-changed the execution of the building blocks themselves, that were performed in an automatic way and were somehow taken for granted. The sequence of building blocks was heavily driven by the characteristics of the hardware. Thus, the correct-ness of operations was only assured to network technicians by the correct execution of a sequence of familiar tasks. Being unable to evaluate the outcomes, they had to rely on the process (March 1994).

5.1. *Wrapping up*

The emergence of the new installation routine shows how establishing a new routine may imply redefining the division of labour among actors and the distribution of knowledge among them.

The story shows the paradoxical power of formal rules and procedures in facilitating the coordination of such a process. By supplying labels that punctuate the flow of activities and provide a shared representation of the task, the standard procedures act as descriptive resources that allow violation of their own prescriptive implications. BTS technicians are able to manipulate the formal representation to achieve a different sequence of actions, stressing once more the need to distinguish representations from expressions.

The punctuation of activities enhances the modularity of the routine, facilitating the architectural restructuring of the same set of building blocks or their selective recombination in a new routine (oversizing). Within single modules, actors are able to act in a semi-automatic way even in front of novel situations.

Furthermore, the familiarity of the single building blocks recombined in an unfamiliar task allows the use of process feedback (the correct execution of each module) as a substitute for outcome feedback, guiding behaviour in front of substantive uncertainty about the success of a sequence of actions.

6. Coordination and Hierarchy: The Emergence of Team Leadership

Coordination processes are at the core of organizational routines. The multi-actor nature of routines implies that individual behaviours have to be matched in order to ensure a smooth flow of actions. In complex action settings, coordination not only is part of virtually any routine, but becomes a specific process, connecting and interfacing single routines through communication, scheduling, task assignment, and other related activities. In other words, coordination processes become crucial elements of the architecture of systems of interdependent routines.

A remarkable feature of the evolution of coordination practices in the technicians' organization is the emergence of an unplanned coordination structure ending up in the institutionalization of a formal hierarchy. At the beginning of our field observations, the technicians structure was a quite flat one: there were three to four teams per geographic area (the 'zones'), within which roles were homogeneous, under the global responsibility of a zone manager. The team was explicitly designed as a group of peers, where any member of the team had to be on the same footing and cover equivalent functional roles, developing equal skills. At the end of our observations, after about one year, teams had developed a hierarchical structure, with the emergence (and subsequent formalization) of team leaders that had assumed coordination tasks as their almost exclusive activity. The process through which this hierarchical structure emerged is worth telling.

In the early months of activity, technicians' field activity was still performed by small groups (usually pairs), and a significant amount of technicians' time (almost 50 per cent) was jointly spent in the office, where a rich amount of many-to-many communication flows was taking place through conversations, meetings, and all sorts of informal communication practices within each team. Scheduling and task assignment were performed through collective decision-making in meetings at the beginning of the week or on *ad hoc* occasions. In fact, most coordination was not perceived as a *per se* process, but was instead immersed in the flow of ongoing activity. This practice was coherent with the original organizational design that was explicitly emphasizing the homogeneity of individual competencies and roles within each team.

However, since the beginning it was clear that there were emerging pressures that might disrupt the planned homogeneity of team roles. Those pressures were originated by four main processes:

(1) The number of technicians per zone was rapidly increasing.

(2) The number of stations was increasing more rapidly than the number of technicians (from eight to twenty per technician in a few months), causing a shift from joint activity to individual activity on single stations.

(3) Stations were installed increasingly far from local offices, increasing the time spent out of the office itself.

(4) The amount of documentation to be produced by technicians was rapidly growing.

As a result, there was an increasing coordination need for scheduling activities during the week, assigning tasks, signalling unexpected troubles, filling reports on executed tasks. The dramatic decrease of time spent together in the office (from about half the working time to a few hours a week) was forcing the creation of communication nodes that might efficiently substitute for direct, many-to-many communication (Simon 1981). Moreover, it was increasingly difficult for zone managers to communicate with all team members. The shift from a full networked to a star topology of communication was thus almost unavoidable. However, there are some less obvious features of this process.

In contrast with the official 'team of peers' philosophy, those central communication nodes were quickly and steadily occupied by a single person. Such a person was emerging from the team on the basis of quite occasional differentiation elements. In some teams, it was the one with more seniority. In other teams, it was the one who was controlling critical resources for bureaucratic work, like a computer. In other cases, it was the one having acquired more status symbols, like the use of the company car. The key point is that no one of those distinctive elements was officially recognized as relevant—each technician had to be like the others—nor was it based on major competencies related to the technicians' core task. But as such distinctive elements were making a team member easier to recognize from others, it was creating a spontaneous 'reference' for hierarchy that was quickly acquiring centrality in the communication flow. In other words, although zone managers were denying any difference among technicians, they were quickly recognizing elements of differentiation and using them for creating gate-keeping positions. Initially, labels of 'team leader' were utilized, but under the premiss that team leadership would not imply any differentiation in task or resource allocation—team leaders had to be *primi inter pares*. However, soon first among peers became first among unequals.

Once this initial (and, as we have seen, based on quite accidental criteria) differentiation was established, it was creating a sort of monopoly over communication resources. To provide just an anecdote, at the beginning the team leader in one zone was just the most able in using the laptop where some critical software was residing. Subsequently, being the best one in using it he was keeping it with himself most of the time. Finally, a password was creating a *de facto* monopoly in its use and was inhibiting others from filling the competence gap.

As coordination tasks were increasingly loading team leaders' activity, team leaders were starting to spend more time in the office than others, thus reducing their direct involvement in field operations. Once more, this was contradicting in facts the official policy on teams. When, talking to managers, we were remarking that there was an increasing pressure towards the specialization of team leaders, they were strongly denying the desirability of such specialization. Nevertheless, they were reinforcing it in practice, for example increasing the reporting tasks of team leaders over team activities. In fact, the responsibility for communication was becoming implicitly a responsibility for activity, and the team leader was increasingly asked to be responsible for the outcomes of the team activity. This implicit shift from communication gate-keeping to accountability for the team performance was the key passage in establishing hierarchical roles.

A related process is that as specialized coordination activities are created, they tend to bootstrap themselves: for example, a team leader has less time to visit the field because he needs to spend time in creating software that will help him in dealing with the existing software, or in creating procedures that he will have to manage. Coordination recursively generates coordination needs. The process is very similar to the one observed in studies of managerial work (Mintzberg 1973; Hannaway 1989).

The process through which the gap between practice and formal prescriptions has been filled is an example of 'crawling institutionalization' of practice. The emerging hierarchical structure of team coordination has not been recognized through a single, deliberate decision, but instead has been frozen into a series of formal devices and acts.

For example, the emerging hierarchy has been progressively embedded in administrative software. There has been an increasing number of applications in which team leaders have writing access, while technicians only have reading access.

More generally, procedures started making explicit differences between team leaders and the others. For example, procedures regulating night availability of technicians had been revised to explicitly exclude team leaders from night shifts.

Finally, the process of institutionalization of team leadership has reached its achievement when team leaders have been formally relieved of field operations (e.g. maintenance or trouble-fixing). This exemption makes the final symbolic detachment of coordination activities from the field, separating the physical and social territory of the team from the one of its leader.

6.1 *Wrapping up*

Thus, this picture of the evolution of hierarchy in coordination processes keeps some classical flavour, but adds some new ingredients. On the one hand, it clearly reflects pressure of the growing task complexity on communication structures that creates opportunities for their increasing centralization (Simon 1981). On the other one hand, the way such opportunities are seized and the dynamics of the process of centralization suggest a few additional features.

• Hierarchical roles seem to evolve out of quite occasional initial differentiation elements. In particular, those elements of differentiation provide initial cues (tags: cf. Holland 1995) helping the management to select gate-keeping persons in the communication process.

• The amplification of such initial differences into stable hierarchical roles is not only favoured by the pressure of task complexity, but is also sustained by self-reinforcing processes, driven by the acquisition of critical resources (Coriat and Dosi 1994) by team leaders and by some recursive, bootstrapping features of the coordination work.

• The most relevant outcome of such process is the progressive enucleation of coordination activities from ongoing activities. Once these coordination activities are singled out, they cease to be coupled to single persons and become stable elements of the architecture of the system. Thus the emergence of hierarchy restructures the system of routines, changing the way they are interfaced and aggregated in higher-level patterns of activity.

• Finally, 'organizational artefacts' such as software, procedures, and job descriptions are the vehicles through which emerging hierarchical roles are formalized and some irreversibility is introduced in the process.

7. Concluding Remarks

Inferences one can draw from a case study are highly local and, in many senses, subjective. What we have learned is most of the time how the concept of routine should be articulated in order to allow us to tell our story. A different story might require a different 'unbundling' of routines, and different observers might tell differently the same story. The main implications of our case study can be usefully summarized by starting from the definition of routines in their narrow sense, and suggesting in which directions we had to enrich it to describe what we have observed. Sid Winter has recently defined routines in the narrow sense as:

complex, highly automatic (and at least in that sense 'unconscious') behaviors that 'function as a unit' and typically involve high levels of information processing that is largely repetitive over separate invocation of the routine. (Cohen *et al.* 1996: 663)

If one looks at the way key capabilities (such as installation or trouble-fixing) are learned and stored by network technicians, routines in their narrow sense are only a part of the picture, and probably not the most relevant. To be sure, there are many examples of automatized, tacit behaviours in our story. But all of them are embedded in more complex patterns of action in which interpretation, reasoning, more or less explicit manipulation of mental representations, deliberation, and design take a relevant part. Routines in the narrow sense are important, but they don't suffice in any case to sustain a reasonable performance in activities of strategic relevance to the firm.

More broadly, a 'behavioural' view of routines seems of little use to tell our story. We rarely found highly repetitive behaviour. In general, a certain degree of flexibility seems to be a relevant component of skilled action, both at the individual and the collective level. The single technician dealing with a trouble-fixing task or a team dealing with a new station installation rarely repeat the same behaviour, and are usually able to adapt to different situations with different behaviour. In turn, those different behaviours are not apparently drawn from a given behavioural repertoire, but come out of an interpretive activity that implies some manipulation of a representation of the task at hand.

The most economic way to account for the interplay between such interpretive activity and actual behaviour is to make a distinction between representations and expressions (Cohen *et al.* 1996). We suggest that our technicians store representations of the task under the form of mental models, i.e. a reduced-scale model of the external reality and of available actions (Craik 1943; Johnson-Laird 1983; Holland *et al.* 1986), and construct a model of the problem at hand by retrieving such representations and combining them into new ones. Once this representation is achieved, it suggests appropriate behaviours (expressions) that usually exhibit properties of modularity, tacitness, and high automaticity. Thus, 'routines in the narrow sense' are often found at the lower level of action patterns, as 'behavioural modules' that are activated and assembled following the definition of the problem that has been reached. Automated sequences of tests in trouble-fixing or elementary action modules in installation are examples of routines in the narrow sense that are recurrent in our observations. Our point is that they cannot be understood without resorting to a broader architecture of skills within which mental models play a key role.

The term 'mental model' may be misleading if it suggests that representations are only stored in people's minds (Norman 1991). In fact, we have shown that many representations are stored in people's minds *and* in artefacts such as procedures, software, or physical features of the environment that are resources structuring mental models of individuals and teams (Hutchins 1991): see the example of how detailed procedures help to spontaneously re-engineer the installation process. It is a relevant matter of fact that design can shape the emergence of routines through such artefacts.

Looking at representations not only helps to account for behavioural flexibility, but makes it easier to understand how capabilities are stored and diffused within the organization. Although there is evidence of processes of direct imitation of behaviour, most diffusion processes are vehiculated by the explicitation of models of the task, as we have seen for trouble-fixing activities. Needless to say, representations are diffused in context-dependent forms (Holyoak and Spellman 1993), rather than in abstract ways. Technicians suggest to each other new causal connections among components or interpretations of the technology in the context of sequences of tests or in narrative forms, and the availability of evoking inputs in task-related descriptions of the trouble are critical in eliciting colleagues' representations. Nevertheless, there is little doubt about the fact that 'replicators' in the process of diffusion are often (incomplete) representations rather than expressions (behaviours). External representations embedded in artefacts play a similar role in storing and replicating productive knowledge, as we have seen above.

The nature of diffusion/replication processes is especially relevant in defining how individual and collective competencies are interrelated, and hence in bridging the gap between individuals and collective entities such as groups, organizational units, or firms at large. Nelson and Winter (1983) heavily draw on the analogy between individual skills and routines. Our observations support such analogy, but suggest that more attention should be devoted to the complicated interrelationships between the individual and the collective level. The case study highlights three elements of special relevance.

(a) On the one side, processes of diffusion help to frame individual skills in the context of collective activities. Although many of the competencies we have observed are ultimately individual (they are not 'distributed' among actors), like in trouble-fixing activities, they are developed and maintained within a community of actors whose boundaries, structure, and communication patterns deeply affect what individuals know. In this peculiar sense, individual skills are organizational phenomena.

(b) Moreover, the diffusion of competencies within groups of actors relies on a shared language that enables making representations communicable (Hutchins and Hazelhurst 1990). Such shared language is an organizational construct, and it interfaces individual skills and genuinely collective capabilities, which are distributed among participants.

(c) Artefacts provide structuring resources (Suchman 1987) that are shared by actors. We have seen how the hardware and software used for diagnostic activity provide both a common representation of the task and suggest sequences of actions (Hutchins 1995).

Finally, organizational capabilities are not mere collections of routines (however defined, narrowly or broadly). As far as there are complementarities among routines, some form of architectural coherence among them is needed to achieve efficiency and coordination. For example, the initial patchwork of competencies generates locally coherent 'work styles' at the zone level. We have also seen how the coordination architecture of a system of routines evolves into a hierarchical structure, extracting coordination processes out of single routines and transforming coordination into a *per se* activity attributed to a specialistic, hierarchical role. We have also seen how in both examples the architecture of systems of routines is shaped by the pressure of 'functional' needs (exploiting complementarities among them) but also by strategic moves of actors motivated by local interest (Coriat and Dosi 1994). We suggest that further exploring issues of complementarities among routines and architectural coherence would considerably enlarge our understanding of organizational capabilities.

References

Amit, R., and P. J. H. Schoemaker (1993). 'Strategic Assets and Organizational Rent', *Strategic Management Journal*, 14: 33–46.

Barney, J. (1991), 'Firm Resources and Sustained Competitive Advantage, *Journal of Management*, 1: 99–120.

Baum, J. A. C., and J. V. Singh (eds.) (1994). *Evolutionary Dynamics of Organizations*. New York: Oxford University Press.

Cohen, M. D. (1991). 'Individual learning and organizational routines: emerging connections', *Organization Science*, 1: 135–9.

—— and P. Bacdayan (1994). 'Organizational routines are stored as procedural memory: Evidence from a laboratory study', *Organization Science*, 5: 545–68.

—— R. Burkhart, G. Dosi, M. Egidi, L. Marengo, and M. Warglien (1996). 'Routines and other recurring action patterns of organizations: contemporary research issues', *Industrial and Corporate Change*, 5(3): 653–98.

Coriat, B., and G. Dosi (1994). *Learning How to Govern and Learning How to Solve Problems. On the Co-evolution of Competences, Conflicts and Organizational Routines*, IIASA Working Paper, Laxenburg, Austria.

Craik, K. (1943). *The Nature of Explanation*. Cambridge: Cambridge University Press.

Egidi, M., and A. Narduzzo (1997). 'The emergence of path-dependent routines in cooperative contexts', *International Journal of Industrial Organization*.

Gersick, C., and J. R. Hackman (1990). 'Habitual routines and task-performing groups', *Organizational Behavior and Human Decision Processes*, 47: 65–97.

Ginsberg, A., and J. A. C. Baum (1994). 'Evolutionary processes and patterns of core business change', in J. A. C. Baum and J. V. Singh (eds.), *Evolutionary Dynamics of Organizations*. New York: Oxford University Press.

Hannaway, J. (1989). *Managers Managing: The Working of an Administrative System*. Oxford: Oxford University Press.

Holland, J. H. (1995). *Hidden Order: How Adaptation Builds Complexity*. Reading, Mass.: Addison-Wesley.

—— K. J. Holyoak, R. E. Nisbett, and P. R. Thagard (1986). *Induction*. Cambridge, Mass.: MIT Press.

Holyoak, K. J., and B. A. Spellman (1993). 'Thinking' in *Annual Review of Psychology*, 44: 265–315.

Hutchins, E. (1991). 'The social organization of distributed cognition', in L. B. Resnick, J. M. Levine, and S. P. Teasley (eds.), *Perspectives on Socially Shared Cognition*, American Psychological Association, 283–307.

—— (1995). *Cognition in the Wild*. Cambridge, Mass.: MIT Press.

—— and B. Hazelhurst (1990). 'Learning in the cultural process', in C. G. Langton, C. Taylor, J. D. Farmer, and S. Rusmussen (eds.), *Artificial Life II*: Proceedings of the Workshop on Artifical Life held February 1990 in Santa Fe, New Mexico. Reading, Mass.: Addison Wesley.

Johnson-Laird, P. N. (1983). *Mental Models*. Cambridge, Mass: Harvard University Press.

Kogut, B., and U. Zander (1992). 'Knowledge of the firm, combinative capabilities, and the replication of technology', *Organization Science*, 3: 383–97.

Lave, J., and E. Wenger (1991). *Situated Learning*. Cambridge: Cambridge University Press.

Levinthal, D., and M. Warglien (1999). 'Landscape design: designing for local actions in complex worlds', *Organization Science*, 10(3).

March, J. G. (1994). *A Primer on Decision Making: How Decisions Happen*. New York: Free Press.

——and H. A. Simon (1993). *Organizations*, 2nd edn. (1st edn. 1958) Cambridge: Blackwell.

——L. S. Sproull, and M. Tamuz (1991). 'Learning from samples of one or fewer', *Organization Science*, 2(1): 14–39.

Mintzberg, H. (1973). *The Nature of Managerial Work*. New York: Harper & Row.

Nelson, R. R., and S. G. Winter (1982). *An Evolutionary Theory of Economic Change*. Cambridge, Mass.: Harvard University Press.

Norman, D. A. (1991). 'Cognitive artifacts', in J. M. Carroll (ed.), *Designing interaction: Psychology at the Human-Computer Interface*, Cambridge: Cambridge University Press, 17–38.

Orr, J. (1987). 'Narratives at work: story telling as cooperative diagnostics activity', *Field Service Culture* (June): 47–60.

——(1990). 'Sharing knowledge, celebrating identity: war stories and community memory in a service culture', in D. S. Middleton, and D. Edwards (eds.), *Collective Remembering: Memory in Society*. Sage Publication.

Pentland, B. T., and H. H. Rueter (1994). 'Organizational routines as grammars of action', *Administrative Science Quarterly*, 39: 484–510.

Seely Brown, J., and P. Duguid (1991). 'Organizational learning and communities-of-practice: toward a unified view of working, learning, and innovation', *Organization Science*, 1: 40–57.

Simon, H. A. (1981). *The Sciences of Artificial*. Cambridge, Mass.: MIT Press.

Stinchcombe, A. C. (1965). 'Social structure and organization', in J. G. March (ed.), *Handbook of Organizations*. Chicago: Rand McNally.

——(1990). *Information and Organizations*. Berkeley and Los Angeles: University of California Press.

Suchman, L. (1987). *Plans and Situated Action*. Cambridge: Cambridge University Press.

Teece, D. (1984). 'Economic analysis and strategic management', *California Management Review*, 26(3): 87–110.

——(ed.) (1987). *The Competitive Challenge: Strategy and Organization for Industrial Innovation and Renewal*. New York: Harper & Row, Ballinger Division.

Wason, P. C., and P. N. Johnson-Laird (1972). *Psychology of Reasoning. Structure and Contest*. Cambridge, Mass.: Harvard University Press.

Weick, K. E. (1979). *The Social Psychology of Organizing*, 2nd edn. Wokingham: Addison-Wesley.

——(1991). 'The nontraditional quality of organizational learning', *Organization Science*, 2(1): 41–73.

Wernerfelt, B. (1984). 'A resource-based theory of the firm', *Strategic Management Journal*, 5: 171–80.

Winter, S. G. (1986). 'The research program of the behavioral theory of the firm', in B. Gilad, and S. Kaish (eds.), *Handbook of Behavioral Economics*, 151–88.

——(1987). 'Knowledge and competence a strategic assets', in Teece (1987).

Zander, U., and B. Kogut (1995). 'Knowledge and the speed of the transfer and imitation of organization capabilities: An empirical test', *Organization-Science*, 6(1): 76–92.

2

Repositories of Knowledge in Franchise Organizations: Individual, Structural, and Technological

LINDA ARGOTE AND ERIC DARR

Abstract

Where is knowledge embedded in organizations? The chapter describes results on the persistence and transfer of knowledge in fast food franchises. Results on the productivity of the franchises are summarized; results on the timeliness of their service are presented. Qualitative evidence about where knowledge was embedded in the franchises is presented. The qualitative evidence suggests that knowledge gained from experience at the franchises was embedded in individual workers and in the organizations' routines, structures, and technologies. The fast food franchises were able to realize significant productivity gains in the face of extraordinarily high turnover because a significant component of the knowledge was embedded in the organization's structure and technology rather than in individual employees. Further, embedding knowledge in structure and technology appeared to facilitate the transfer of knowledge across organizations.

Significant productivity gains typically occur as organizations gain experience in production. This phenomenon, referred to as a 'learning curve' or learning by doing, has been documented in many industries (see Yelle 1979; and Dutton and Thomas 1984, for reviews).

Figure 2.1 shows an example of an organizational learning curve. The figure is based on data obtained from one pizza store. The cumulative number of pizzas produced is plotted on the horizontal axis; the cost of producing each pizza is plotted on the vertical axis. The figure indicates that the unit cost of pizza production decreased at a decreasing rate as experience was gained in production.

The classic form of the learning curve is a power function:

$$y_i = ax_i^{-b} \tag{1}$$

where y is the unit cost of the xth unit of output, a is the unit cost of the first unit, x is the cumulative number of units produced, b is a parameter measuring the rate unit costs change as cumulative output increases, and i is a time subscript. In this formulation, cumulative output is viewed as a measure of organizational 'knowledge'.

Prepared for the *Nature and Dynamics of Organizational Capabilities*, edited by G. Dosi, R. Nelson, and S. Winter. This research was supported by a grant from the Carnegie Bosch Institute for Applied Studies in International Management at Carnegie Mellon University.

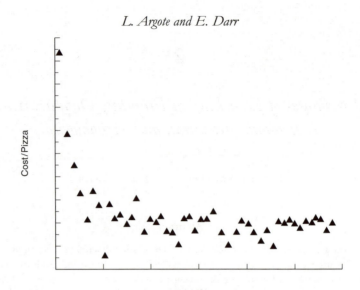

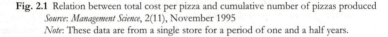

Cumulative pizzas produced

Fig. 2.1 Relation between total cost per pizza and cumulative number of pizzas produced
Source: *Management Science*, 2(11), November 1995
Note: These data are from a single store for a period of one and a half years.

If unit costs change as a function of this knowledge, other things equal, organizational learning is said to occur.

Interest in organizational learning and productivity has increased markedly in the 1980s and 1990s. Several themes are evident in this new wave of research (Argote 1999). Recent research on organizational learning has extended organizational performance measures to include other outcomes such as quality (e.g. Argote 1993). Research has also focused on understanding the variation observed in organizational learning rates. Researchers are interested in the fundamental question of why some organizations are more productive than others (e.g. see Lieberman 1984; Hayes and Clark 1986; Argote and Epple 1990; Adler and Clark 1991). Researchers are also examining organizational 'forgetting' or depreciation and the effect of interruptions on organizational performance (e.g. Argote *et al.* 1990; Cohen and Bacdayan 1994). There has also been considerable interest in the transfer of knowledge across organizations or units of organizations (Joskow and Rose 1985; Adler 1990; Argote *et al.* 1990; Cohen and Levinthal 1990; Zimmerman 1992; Henderson and Cockburn 1994; Irwin and Klenow 1994; Miner and Haunschild 1995; Zander and Kogut 1995; Epple *et al.* 1996; Szulanski 1996; Baum and Ingram 1998). These researchers examine whether one organization (or unit of an organization) benefits from knowledge acquired in another.

This chapter addresses the question of where the knowledge acquired through learning by doing is embedded in organizations. It begins with a discussion of various repositories or 'retention bins' of knowledge in organizations. Empirical evidence on the extent to which knowledge acquired through learning by doing is embedded in different repositories is discussed. Qualitative evidence from a study of learning in fast food franchises is presented to illustrate where knowledge is embedded in organizations. Quantitative results on productivity from the study are summarized. New results on service timeliness are then presented. The implications of where knowledge is embedded for its persistence and transfer are developed.

1. Repositories of Knowledge in Organizations

Where is the knowledge about productivity gains acquired through learning by doing embedded in organizations? Joskow and Rozanski (1979) identified factors contributing to the productivity gains associated with increasing experience as: routinization of tasks, more efficient production control, improved equipment design, and improved routing and material handling. Hayes and Wheelwright (1984) discussed the following factors as facilitators of organizational learning: individual learning, selection and training, improved methods, enhanced equipment and technology, division of labour and specialization, improved product design, substitution of capital for labour, incentives and leadership. Argote (1993) identified the following factors as contributors to organizational learning curves: improvements in the organization's technology, tooling and layout; improvements in its structure, routines, and methods of coordination; and better understanding of who in the organization is good at what.

How do these discussions of factors responsible for organizational learning curves relate to theoretical discussions of where knowledge is embedded in organizations? Levitt and March (1988) indicate that knowledge is embedded in an organization's routines and standard operating procedures, in its products and processes, in its technologies and equipment, in its layout and structures, and in its culture and norms about how things are generally done. Similarly, Walsh and Ungson (1991) posit five 'retention bins' for organizational memory: individual employees; the organization's culture; its standard operating procedures and practices; roles and organizational structures; and the physical structure of the workplace. According to Starbuck (1992), in knowledge-intensive firms, knowledge is embedded in individuals, in physical capital (including hardware and software), in the organization's routines, and in its culture. Nelson and Winter (1982) focus on routines as repositories of organizational knowledge (see March and Simon 1958; Cyert and March 1963, for discussions of routines at the organizational level of analysis and Gersick and Hackman 1990, for a discussion at the group level of analysis).

Cohen and Bacdayan (1994) demonstrate that knowledge acquired through task performance can be embedded in supra-individual routines. Based on empirical evidence from a laboratory study of dyads playing a card game, the researchers concluded that the behaviour of the dyads was indicative of the operation of routines. In particular, the performance of the dyads became faster and more reliable over time. Different dyads evolved different routines that were stable over time. And dyads persisted in using their idiosyncratic routines, even when more effective routines existed.

Although these discussions of organizational memory differ about whether to include individuals as repositories of knowledge and about the exact number of repositories, the discussions have much in common. Researchers generally agree that organizational knowledge resides in: individuals, including managers, technical support staff, and direct production workers; the organization's technology, including hardware and software; and in the organization's structure, routines, and methods of coordination.[1]

1.1. *Knowledge embedded in individuals*

We turn now to evaluating empirical evidence on the extent to which knowledge acquired through learning by doing is embedded in individual workers. As noted previously, most discussions about factors responsible for organizational learning curves include learning by individual employees as a key factor. Similarly, most discussions of organizational memory cite individuals as a key repository of organizational knowledge (e.g. see Walsh and Ungson 1991). Simon (1991) and Huber (1991) have both suggested that turnover is harmful for organizational memory. If knowledge is embedded in individuals, then their turnover should affect organizational learning.

What does the evidence say about the relationship between turnover and organizational learning? One study investigated the effect of turnover of direct production workers in World War II shipyards (Argote *et al.* 1990). Results indicated that the rate of new hires and the rate of separations did not appear to affect the productivity of the yards. The shipyards were large organizations with formalized and specialized structures and jobs that were generally low in skill requirements (Lane 1951). Argote *et al.* (1990) speculated that perhaps these conditions mitigated the effect of turnover.

Argote *et al.* (1995) investigated whether the effect of turnover depended on the performance of departing members. The researchers collected data that contained information on the reason employees left a manufacturing plant (e.g. whether employees were discharged for poor performance, promoted for good performance, retired, deceased, quit, 'bumped' due to contractual agreements, and so on). Results indicated that the variable representing the number of employees who were promoted out of the plant to participate in competitive apprenticeship programmes on the basis of their good performance was generally negatively related to the truck plant's productivity. This study suggests that the effect of turnover on productivity may depend on the performance level of departing employees.

Devadas Rao and Argote (1995) examined whether the effect of turnover depended on how organizations were structured. The researchers simulated varying degrees of structure in the laboratory and contrasted the effect of turnover in highly structured groups with the effect in less structured groups. The major finding was an interaction between turnover and work group structure: turnover affected the performance of groups that were high in structure less than that of groups low in structure while the performance of high and low structure groups did not differ when turnover did not occur. Factors contributing to the poor performance of groups in

---

[1] Knowledge may also be embedded in the environment outside the organization. In order to affect organizational productivity, however, the knowledge must be transferred inside the organization.

the low structure, turnover condition were their continual need to keep reorganizing around the skills of new members, the difficulty the groups had accessing knowledge, and the loss of critical knowledge when members left the group.

The results of this laboratory study are generally consistent with simulation results Carley (1992) obtained in her analysis of personnel turnover and organizational learning. Carley compared the effect of turnover on hierarchies and teams and found that while teams learned better and faster than hierarchies, hierarchies were less affected by turnover than teams.

Virany *et al.* (1992) examined turnover of executives as a mechanism for organizational learning and adaptation in a study of minicomputer firms. The researchers suggested that executive change facilitates learning and adaptation by changing the knowledge base and communication processes of the executive team. Results indicated that turnover of the chief executive officer and turnover in the executive team were positively associated with organizational performance.

Taken together, these studies of turnover and organizational learning suggest the conditions under which turnover is most likely to have a significant effect. Results indicate that turnover affects performance gains when: (i) departing members are exceptional performers (e.g. see Argote *et al.* 1995); and (ii) when the organizations, or the positions departing members occupy, are low in structure and constraints (e.g. Carley 1992; Virany *et al.* 1992; Devadas Rao and Argote 1995). While turnover of high-performing direct production workers in a manufacturing plant negatively affected the plant's productivity, turnover of executives in the minicomputer industry had a positive effect on performance. The former effect may have reflected the cost of the loss of individuals who had critical knowledge embedded in them while the latter may have reflected the benefit of incorporating individuals with new knowledge into the organizations.

1.2. Knowledge embedded in organizations

We turn now to an evaluation of the extent to which knowledge is embedded in organizations. An interesting naturally occurring experiment provided an opportunity to analyse the extent to which knowledge acquired through learning by doing became embedded in the organization versus in individual workers (Epple *et al.* 1996). A manufacturing plant added a second shift almost two years after the first shift had been in operation. Researchers analysed the transfer of knowledge that occurred from the period of operating with one shift to the period of operating with two shifts and the ongoing transfer of knowledge between the two shifts once they were both in operation (see Epple *et al.* 1991, for development of the method).

Results indicated that knowledge acquired during the period of operating with one shift carried forward quite rapidly to both shifts of the two-shift period. This finding provides evidence about the extent to which knowledge acquired via learning by doing was embedded in the organization versus in individual workers. Both shifts at the plant used the same technology and operated in the same organizational structure. The second shift, however, was composed of predominantly new employees. The second shift achieved a level of productivity in two weeks that it had taken the first shift many months to achieve. This suggests that knowledge acquired during the period of one-shift operation had been embedded in the organization's structure or technology since both shifts used the same structure and technology, whereas the workers were different.

2. The Franchise Study

We turn now to a discussion of results from an empirical study of learning in fast food franchises. The study analyses whether organizations learn from their own direct experience and from the experience of other organizations (see Levitt and March 1988). Two kinds of knowledge transfer are examined: transfer of knowledge across stores owned by the same franchisee and transfer of knowledge across stores owned by different franchisees in the same geographic area. We also analyse qualitative evidence about where knowledge was embedded in the franchises and discuss the implications of where knowledge was embedded for its persistence and transfer.

All of the pizza stores in the study were franchised from the same parent corporation. The sample included ten different franchisees who owned thirty-six stores in one geographic area. The largest franchisee owned eleven stores, whereas five of the franchisees each owned one store.

Since all of the stores were franchised from the same parent corporation, they all had the opportunity to benefit from procedures developed by the corporation and from communication with the corporation through annual meetings, discussions with the corporation's consultants and the like. We expected stores owned by the same franchisee to have even greater opportunities for knowledge transfer since these stores have more frequent communication and denser social networks than independently owned stores (e.g. Tushman 1977).

The research programme also examines whether knowledge acquired by learning by doing is cumulative, as the conventional learning curve model implies, or whether it decays or depreciates (Argote *et al.* 1990). By studying depreciation in a different production setting one can begin to determine the conditions under which depreciation occurs and factors affecting the rate of depreciation. The research programme also analyses whether the outcome of service timeliness exhibits learning as well as the outcome of productivity. Service timeliness was measured as the frequency of 'late' pizzas.

In this chapter we present qualitative evidence on where knowledge is embedded in the organizations and develop the implications of where knowledge was embedded for its transfer. We will also summarize results on productivity (see Darr *et al.* 1995 for a detailed discussion) and present new results on service timeliness.

Data were collected from records at the corporation's regional office and from interviews with the franchisees. The corporation's regional office provided weekly data for the thirty-six stores in a geographic area centred around Pittsburgh for one and half years. Structured interviews with the franchisees provided information about their organization and the use of various mechanisms such as meetings, phone calls, and the like to transfer information.

Several features of the data set make it particularly attractive for studying transfer. The inputs to the production process at the pizza stores are homogeneous and therefore are controlled for naturally in the sample. Differences in technology across pizza stores are very small so this factor is also controlled for in the sample. Competition between the stores is minimized (e.g. by proscriptions from the parent corporation about how close stores can locate to one another).

2.1. *Qualitative evidence on where knowledge is embedded from the franchise study*

The results of structured open-ended interviews conducted with franchisees and store managers suggested that knowledge gained from production experience at the stores was embedded in individual employees, in the stores' structures, and in their technology. Respondents were asked to describe any innovations to the pizza production process that had occurred in the previous six months. In addition, data about the source of the innovation and outcomes resulting from its use were collected.

The interview process revealed fourteen separate production process innovations across the thirty-six pizza stores. Eight of the innovations were codified, and embedded in either the organization's structure and routines (6) or its technology (2). The remaining six innovations were not codified at the time of the interviews, and remained embedded in individuals. The embedding of knowledge in structures and technology allows the stores to retain knowledge over time even as experienced individuals are lost through turnover. Embedding knowledge in structures and technology may also facilitate knowledge transfer.

2.1.1. Knowledge embedded in technology We turn now to an example of knowledge that was embedded in technology at the stores. Technology in the context of pizza stores includes the equipment (e.g. ovens) and tools (e.g. cheese grater) used to make pizzas, as well as the physical layout of the store (e.g. make-line). The 'cheese spreader' is an example of an innovation developed through production experience which became embedded in technology.

Distributing cheese evenly across a pizza is difficult to achieve. Too much cheese decreases profit margins, whereas too little cheese decreases customer satisfaction. Production experience demonstrated that it was difficult to consistently spread cheese by hand. Each individual did it somewhat differently, using a slightly different amount of cheese on each pizza.

A manager at one of the stores in the sample realized that spreading cheese by hand was not an efficient method. He believed that the problem was analogous to spreading fertilizer on grass lawns and thought that some type of 'spreader' was needed. The manager experimented with various configurations of plastic dishes and metal screens to develop a tool which would help pizza makers use consistent amounts of cheese and achieve an even distribution.

The final version of the 'cheese spreader' tool was a plastic cone with holes which allowed cheese to fall through. The cone sat on plastic feet several inches over the pizza. A pizza maker would pour grated cheese over the cone and the cheese would fall in a consistent pattern over the top of a pizza. The franchisee who owned the store where the cheese spreader experiments occurred liked the tool. He diffused the innovation to all of his stores.

The cheese spreader illustrates how insights gained through the pizza production process can become codified and embedded in technology. Insights and knowledge associated with the cheese-spreading process no longer reside solely in individual memories. The knowledge is now embedded in a tool. Even if the developing manager were to leave the organization, some knowledge would remain in the form of the cheese spreader tool. Further, embedding the knowledge in technology seemed to facilitate transfer of knowledge: the cheese spreader tool diffused very quickly to all stores owned by the same franchisee.

The franchisee had not determined the exact effect on performance of using the cheese spreader tool by the time of the interviews. The tool had only been in use for two months. Managers in the franchise believed that the cheese spreader helped them control food costs and increased customer satisfaction. The tool has not diffused to stores owned by different franchisees. Indeed another franchisee reported not liking the cheese spreader tool since he believed that uneven cheese distribution was a hallmark of handmade pizza.

As we noted previously, two of the fourteen innovations we studied were embedded in technology. Of these two innovations, one transferred to stores within the same franchise and also to stores in different franchises while the other innovation (the cheese spreader tool) transferred to stores within the same franchise. Thus, embedding knowledge in technology appears to facilitate knowledge transfer. Further, the qualitative evidence suggests more transfer may occur within the same franchise than between different franchises since both innovations embedded in technology transferred to stores within the same franchise while only one innovation transferred to stores in different franchises.

2.1.2. Knowledge embedded in structure   Structure refers to recurring patterns of activities (Katz and Kahn 1978). Structure includes routines which guide the pizza production process. A routine for achieving an even distribution of pepperoni on pizzas is described in Darr *et al.* (1995). 'Proofing' is another example of an innovation developed through production experience that became embedded in a routine. The routine used to verify that pizza dough is suitable for use is known as 'proofing'.

The pizza dough used in the stores is made in central corporate facilities and shipped to individual store locations. The dough often sits for one or two days before it is used. Even though the dough was formulated to last (refrigerated) for three days, it often degrades more rapidly because of improper handling or exposure to significant temperature changes. Using dough past its prime results in a 'tough' pizza that tastes like 'leather'.

It is the responsibility of the pizza maker to check the suitability of each dough ball prior to use. Before a 'proofing' routine was established, individual franchisees would set their own standards for checking dough. This resulted in inconsistent quality.

One of the franchisees in the sample realized that a simple and accurate method for checking dough quality was needed. He studied the characteristics of dough at various stages of degradation and also produced finished pizzas from dough at different stages. Based on his experiments and experience, he identified two simple tests that could be used to 'proof' dough. The preferred and more reliable test was to pinch the dough. If it did not spring back into place, it was past its prime.

Initially, the 'proofing' method was passed by word-of-mouth among pizza makers who worked for the franchisee who developed it. At this stage, the innovation was still embedded in individuals. A visiting franchisee noticed pizza makers pinching dough and asked about the practice. He was told that it was a new test for checking the quality of dough balls. The visiting franchisee asked the developing franchisee to write down the 'proofing' tests. At this point the innovation became codified. It was shared to all local franchisees, who adopted it as a standard routine.

The 'proofing' tests illustrate how insights gained through the pizza production process can become codified and embedded in routines. Insights and knowledge associated with checking dough quality no longer reside solely in individual memories. The knowledge is now embedded in a standard routine. The 'proofing' routine will remain in the store even if the franchisee leaves.

The example also illustrates how embedding knowledge in routines can facilitate diffusion across organizations. Prior to embedding the 'proofing' tests in routines, it was necessary to either observe the procedure personally, or talk to someone who had performed it previously in order to learn about it. Embedding knowledge in routines facilitates transfer because improvements can occur without as much need for direct observation or contact.

The franchisees in the sample believed that the 'proofing' procedures had improved pizza quality and consistency. There were no direct analyses that definitely supported their perceptions. Overall customer satisfaction (as indicated on random phone surveys) at two of the organizations using the 'proofing' procedures had increased 30 per cent during the year the procedure was introduced. While identifying the precise cause(s) of the increase in satisfaction was not the focus of our study, the proofing procedure may have been a contributing factor.

Six of the fourteen innovations we studied were embedded in the organization's structure. One of these innovations did not transfer out of the store of origin. Two innovations transferred to stores in the same franchise. The remaining three innovations transferred both to stores within the same franchise and to stores in different franchises. These qualitative results suggest that embedding knowledge in structure is a way to facilitate knowledge transfer. These results also suggest that more transfer occurs within commonly owned than between differently owned stores since five of the six structural innovations transferred within the same franchise while only three transferred to stores in different franchises.

2.1.3. Knowledge embedded in individuals   Individual employees in the pizza stores include the pizza makers, the store managers, and the franchisee who owns the store(s). In most stores, the managers as well as the pizza makers make pizza.

Observations in the pizza stores revealed that the knowledge about how to hand toss pizza dough was stored primarily in individual employees. The corporation had codified knowledge about how pizza dough should look after it was tossed. But, there was no codified knowledge about how to transform a dough ball into a pizza shell. The knowledge about hand-tossing pizza dough is passed from person to person. Interestingly, some pizza makers are able to articulate hand-tossing knowledge. For these people, the knowledge is explicit. Other pizza makers are not able to articulate the steps associated with hand-tossing dough. In these cases, the knowledge remains tacit.

Because hand-tossing knowledge remains embedded individuals, it is vulnerable to employee turnover. Franchisees recognize this situation, and often offer higher pay and greater work flexibility to experienced pizza makers. It is difficult to train hand-tossing, and therefore, franchisees do not want their experienced pizza makers to leave. Additionally, franchisees encourage new employees to work with experienced pizza makers. By observing and practising hand-tossing, new employees can learn even if the knowledge remains tacit. Also, embedding the knowledge in more than one individual reduces the organization's vulnerability to turnover.

Knowledge embedded in individuals is not transferred as much as knowledge embedded in other repositories. Of the six innovations that were embedded in individuals, only in two was there evidence of any transfer. One of these was transferred to commonly owned stores; the other to both commonly and differently owned stores. The remaining four innovations were not transferred outside the store of origin.

2.2. *Quantitative results on productivity*

Quantitative results on knowledge transfer will now be presented. Our analysis strategy is to estimate models in which the unit cost of pizza production or the number of late pizzas per unit depends on store-specific experience, franchisee experience, interfranchisee experience, and other control variables. These additional variables are included to investigate alternative explanations for the findings.

A general model[2] we estimated for unit cost was:

$$\text{Log}(c_{\text{nit}}/q_{\text{nit}}) = b_0 + b_1 \text{Log}K_{\text{nit}-1} + b_2 \text{Log}FK_{\text{nt}-1} + b_3 \text{Log}IK_{t-1} + b_4 t +$$
$$b_5 q_{\text{nit}} + b_6 q_{\text{nit}}^2 + b_7 [\text{Log}(K_{\text{nit}-1})]^2 + b_8 p_{\text{nit}} + b_{\text{ni}} S_{\text{ni}} + u_{\text{nit}}, \text{ where}$$

$$(2)$$

t = calendar time in weeks;
j_{n} = no. of stores in franchise n;

---

[2] The most complex model we estimated included unknown production histories in the knowledge variables. Half of the stores had begun production before the start of data collection. The effect of including entire production histories for each store on the results was investigated using a non-linear model in which pizza production prior to the beginning of the sample was added to the store, franchise, and inter-franchise aggregates. For each of the eighteen stores where we did not have complete production data, production history was treated as an unknown coefficient. Including complete production histories does not change our results (see col. 5 of table 1 in Darr *et al.*, 1995).

q_{nit} = no. of pizzas produced by franchisee n in store i in week t;

c_{nit} = costs (food and labour) for store i in franchisee n in week t;

K_{nit} = knowledge acquired by store i in franchisee n through week t;

FK_{nt} = knowledge acquired by franchisee n through week t;

IK_t = knowledge acquired by all stores in all franchisees through week t (inter-franchisee knowledge);

p_{nit} = percentage pan pizzas produced by franchisee n in store i in week t;

S_{ni} = dummy variables for each store;

u_{nit} = error term.

The model we estimated for service timeliness was:

$$\text{Log}(d_{nit}/q_{nit}) = b_0 + b_1 \text{Log}K_{nit-1} + b_2 \text{Log}FK_{nt-1} + b_3 \text{Log}IK_{t-1} + b_4t +$$

$$b_5 q_{nit} + b_6 q_{nit}^2 + b_7[\text{Log}(K_{nit-1})]^2 + b_8 p_{nit} + b_9 w_{nit} + b_{ni}S_{ni} + u_{nit}, \text{ where}$$

$$(3)$$

d_{nit} = no. of late pizzas for store i in franchisee n in week t;

w_{nit} = labour costs for store i in franchisee n in week t;

all other variables are defined as in Eq. (2).

Thus, the unit cost of production or the fraction of late pizzas is estimated to be a function of store-specific experience (K_{nit}), franchisee experience (FK_{nt}), and inter-franchisee experience (IK_t). Calendar time (t) is included to investigate the possibility that improvements observed in productivity or timeliness are a function of general technological developments in the environment that are correlated with the passage of time. The number of pizzas produced by a particular store (q_{nit}) and its square are included to control for scale effects. We investigate whether the rate of learning slows down (in logarithmic form) by including the square of the knowledge variable $(K_{nit})^2$. The percentage of pan pizzas, P_{nit}, is included to control for product mix. The dummy variables are included to control for unmeasured store-specific factors such as management style or location.

We analysed whether knowledge persisted through time or whether it depreciated by replacing the conventional cumulative output measure with an alternative specification:

$$K_{nit} = \lambda K_{nit-1} + q_{nit} \tag{4}$$

This formulation allows for the possibility that knowledge depreciates over time by including the parameter, λ, to form a geometric weighting of the store's past output. If $\lambda = 1$, the knowledge variable equals lagged cumulative output, the conventional measure. Thus, if $\lambda = 1$, there is no evidence depreciation occurred since knowledge obtained from a unit produced in the distant past is as useful as knowledge obtained from a unit produced yesterday. If $\lambda < 1$, there is evidence depreciation occurred: recent output is a more important predictor of current productivity than past output.

The coefficients on the store-specific knowledge variable, K_{nit}, and on the franchise-specific knowledge variable, FK_{nt}, obtained from estimating Eq. (2) were significant. The inter-franchise transfer variable, IK_t, was not significant. These results suggest that stores learned from their own direct experience and from the experience of other stores owned by the same franchisee but not from stores owned by different franchisees. These results are consistent with the qualitative evidence discussed previously: many innovations such as the cheese spreader technology transferred only to stores within the same franchise.

The parameter value of λ that minimized the sum of squared residuals was 0.80. The estimate of lambda was significantly less than one, indicating that past output received less weight than recent output in predicting the current unit cost of production. Thus, knowledge acquired through learning by doing depreciated.

The calendar time (t) variable was positive and significant, indicating that unit cost rose over the course of the study. The positive coefficient on the time variable is likely to be due to inflation in input costs. The coefficient on current pizza count (q_{nit}) was negative and significant, whereas the coefficient on the variable's square was positive and significant. These two coefficients indicate the classic non-monotonic relationship between the scale of production and unit costs: costs first decline and then rise with increases in the scale of production. The initial decline in unit costs as the scale of production increases is reasonable since labour and operating costs can be spread over a larger volume of production. The increase in unit costs at higher volume levels is associated with increased coordination costs. The difficulties of coordinating a large number of employees at higher volumes is exacerbated by the use of less experienced part-time employees during peak loads.

The coefficient of the square of the store-specific learning variable (K_{nit}) was not significant. Thus, there is no evidence that the rate of learning slowed down (in logarithmic form) over the study's time frame. The percentage of pan pizza was also not significant indicating that product mix did not make a difference here. The dummy variables were significant, indicating that important store-specific effects were present.

2.3. Quantitative results on service timeliness

We also investigated whether service timeliness was a function of store-specific experience, franchisee experience, interfranchisee experience, and other control variables. Service timeliness was operationalized as the frequency of 'late' pizzas. The corporation defines a pizza to be 'late' if the number of minutes between when a customer places an order to when preparation of the pizza is completed exceeds a standard limit.

Eq. (3) was estimated using a maximum-likelihood algorithm that allowed for first-order autocorrelation of the residuals.[3] The result[4] of estimating Eq. (3) is:

$$\text{Log}(d_{nit}/q_{nit}) = b_0 - 0.297\text{Log}K_{nit-1} - 0.173\text{Log}FK_{nt-1} - 0.182\text{Log}IK_{t-1} +$$
$$0.001t + 0.002q_{nit} - 0.0000011q_{nit}^2 - 0.299[\text{Log}(K_{nit-1})]^2 +$$
$$0.081p_{nit} - 0.006w_{nit} + b_{ni}S_{ni} + u_{nit}$$

---

[3] There was no evidence of higher-order autocorrelation.
[4] To protect the confidentiality of the data we do not report the constant term.

The overall model was significant, and explained 36 per cent of the variance associated with service timeliness. The sum of squared residuals was minimized by a λ value of 0.76. The estimate of lambda was again significantly less than one, indicating that knowledge depreciated rapidly over time in the pizza stores.

The significant coefficient on the store-specific knowledge variable ($p < 0.001$) indicates that a 10 per cent increase in the weighted cumulative number of pizzas produced was associated with a 2.97 per cent reduction in their lateness frequency. Additionally, a 10 per cent increase in the weighted cumulative number of pizzas produced aggregated across all stores in a given franchise resulted in a 1.73 per cent reduction in lateness frequency for those stores ($p < 0.05$). The coefficient on the inter-franchise variable (IK_t) was not significant. The results for service timeliness suggest the same pattern of learning as the results for unit cost. The pizza stores learned from their own direct experience and from the experience of other stores owned by the same franchisee, but not from the experience of stores owned by different franchisees.

The calendar time (t) variable was not significant. The coefficient on current pizza count (q_{nit}) was positive and significant ($p < 0.001$), whereas the coefficient on the variable's square was not significant. These results indicate that the fraction of late pizzas increased in a linear manner as pizza production volume increased.

The coefficient on the square of the store-specific learning variable was not significant. Also, the coefficient on the percentage pan pizza (p) was not significant. The coefficient on labour cost (w) was negative and significant. A decrease in late pizza frequency is associated with using more personnel. As with the unit cost model, the dummy variables were significant, indicating that important store-specific effects were present.

Further analyses were performed to determine how sensitive the results were to the model's specifications. Results presented here are quite robust and emerge under alternative specifications.[5]

2.4. Relationship between quantitative and qualitative results: transfer

The modelling estimates demonstrate that knowledge transfers across stores owned by the same franchisee, but not across stores owned by different franchisees. The qualitative results are consistent with this finding. While approximately a third of the innovations we studied did transfer across stores owned by different franchisees, two-thirds of the innovations transferred only to stores owned by the same franchisee.

There are several reasons why transfer is more prevalent within than between franchisees. First, as indicated in Darr *et al.* (1995), there are more transfer mechanisms (i.e. meetings, phone calls, personal acquaintances) across commonly owned

---

[5] A specification test (Hausman 1978), was performed to determine whether there was simultaneity in the prediction of unit cost or service timeliness from current pizza count. This might occur, for example, if stores with a higher fraction of late pizzas use more workers. To test for the possibility of endogeneity of current pizza count, Eqs. (2) and (3) were estimated with a two-stage least-squares procedure developed by Fair (1970). The coefficient estimates obtained from the instrumental variable approach are very similar to those described here. Hausman's specification test was not significant.

stores than across differently owned stores. These mechanisms facilitate knowledge transfer.

Second, the primary focus of attention of franchisees is on a limited set of outcome measures that the franchisor (i.e. parent company) collects and distributes. These measures include delivery and service performance (i.e. the number of late pizzas), product performance (i.e. the percentage of pizzas which meet ten quality points), paperwork completion (i.e. form completion percentage), and management turnover. The outcome measures do not include measures of innovation or knowledge transfer. Thus, the franchisees have fewer incentives to attend to transferring knowledge to other franchisees than to attend to these other outcomes. By contrast, the franchisees have more incentives to transfer knowledge to their own stores since transfer has a positive effect on productivity and other outcomes.

Third, as indicated above, many of the insights gained from the pizza production process are tacit. Researchers have demonstrated that tacit knowledge is difficult to share (Berry and Broadbent 1984, 1987). Direct observation of and/or involvement in the context where the knowledge exists facilitates transfer of tacit knowledge (Nonaka 1991). Opportunities for direct observation are more likely to exist within stores owned by the same franchisee.

2.5. *Relationship between quantitative and qualitative results: depreciation*

As noted previously, knowledge acquired via learning by doing in the pizza stores depreciated rapidly. While further research is needed on this issue, knowledge about service timeliness may have depreciated slightly more rapidly than production knowledge.

Production knowledge concerns the process of making a finished pizza from raw inputs. Service knowledge covers the process from customer order to the beginning of pizza production. Our definition of service knowledge focuses only on in-store activities such as order-taking, order communication, and production-scheduling.

Interviews with the franchisees suggested that service knowledge is embedded primarily in individuals. The interviews revealed four service-related innovations. All four were embedded in individuals. For example, order takers (i.e. people who take pizza orders over the phone) in one franchise prioritized the pizza production schedule for the pizza makers. Rather than follow a simple rule for pizza production scheduling such as 'first ordered, first made', the order takers would prioritize scheduling based on type and size of pizza. This service innovation tried to take advantage of cooking time differences across pizza types and sizes to make better use of the oven. The production scheduling innovation was not codified, and it remained embedded in individual order takers. Thus, the knowledge was more vulnerable to turnover.

This lack of much codified knowledge about service timeliness was also observed at the corporate level. The corporation offered several courses about pizza production. By contrast, it offered no courses in order taking or production scheduling. Production knowledge was embedded in standard training materials by the corporation, whereas service knowledge was not codified.

3. Conclusion

The organizations we studied learned from their own direct experience and from the experience of other stores owned by the same franchisee. The stores did not appear to benefit from the experience of stores owned by different franchisees. Thus, knowledge transferred across stores owned by the same franchisee but not across stores owned by different franchisees. This transfer pattern characterized both knowledge about productivity and knowledge about service timeliness.

The rate of depreciation of knowledge observed in the stores was quite rapid. A value of lambda of 0.80, for example, implies that less than half (0.80^4) of the knowledge at the beginning of the month would remain at the end. Virtually all knowledge would be lost by mid-year, if production does not replenish the stock of knowledge. The rapid rate of depreciation is not surprising given the extraordinarily high turnover experienced by the stores. The modal turnover rate for employees is approximately 300 per cent per year.

How do the stores manage to realize significant productivity gains in the face of such incredibly high turnover? And how do the stores transfer knowledge in the face of such unstable membership? We suggest that the stores retain and transfer knowledge by embedding it in the organization's routines and technology rather than in individual employees.

The qualitative evidence indicates that embedding knowledge in technology and structure is an effective way to facilitate knowledge transfer. Seven of the eight innovations embedded in structure or technology transferred outside the store of origin. By contrast, only two of the six innovations embedded in individuals transferred out of the store of origin. We should note that our study is a naturalistic study rather than an experiment. Innovations were not randomly assigned to repositories. Thus, there may be something about the innovation *per se* that made it more amenable to being embedded technology or structure and made it easier to transfer. It is our view, however, that many of the innovations that remained embedded in individuals (e.g. those about production-scheduling) could have been embedded in routines or technologies. The issue of non-random assignment of innovations to repositories notwithstanding, the qualitative results suggest that embedding knowledge in technology or structure facilitates knowledge transfer.

Several lines of work seem particularly promising for advancing our understanding of the acquisition, depreciation, and transfer of knowledge in organizations. Further research is needed to determine whether knowledge embedded in various repositories depreciates at different rates. And more research is needed to ascertain whether knowledge embedded in different repositories such as routines is easier to transfer. More generally, research is needed on the conditions under which knowledge is retained and transferred in organizations.

References

Adler, P. S. (1990). 'Shared learning', *Management Science*, 36: 939–57.

—— and K. B. Clark (1991). 'Behind the learning curve: A sketch of the learning process', *Management Science*, 37: 267–81.

Argote, L. (1993). 'Group and organizational learning curves: Individual, system and environmental components', *British Journal of Social Psychology*, 32: 31–51.

—— (1999). *Organizational Learning: Creating, Retaining and Transferring Knowledge*. Norwell, Mass.: Kluwer Academic Publishers.

——— S. L. Beckman, and D. Epple (1990). 'The persistence and transfer of learning in industrial settings', *Management Science*, 36: 140–54.

—— and D. Epple (1990). 'Learning curves in manufacturing', *Science* (247): 920–4.

——— R. Devadas Rao, and K. Murphy (1995). 'The acquisition and depreciation of knowledge in manufacturing: Turnover and the learning curve', Paper presented at INFORMS, New Orleans, October 1995.

Baum, J., and P. Ingram (1998). 'Survival-enhancing learning in the Manhatten hotel industry, 1898–1980', *Management Science*, 44: 996–1016.

Berry, D. C., and D. E. Broadbent (1984). 'On the relationship between task performance and associated verbalizable knowledge', *Quarterly Journal of Experimental Psychology*, 364: 209–31.

——— (1987). 'The combination of explicit and implicit learning processes in task control', *Psychological Research*, 49: 7–15.

Carley, K. (1992). 'Organizational learning and personnel turnover', *Organization Science*, 3: 20–46.

Cohen, M. D., and P. Bacdayan (1994). 'Organizational routines are stored as procedural memory: Evidence from a laboratory study', *Organization Science*, 5: 554–68.

Cohen, W. M., and D. A. Levinthal (1990). 'Absorptive capacity: A new perspective on learning and innovation', *Administrative Science Quarterly*, 35: 128–52.

Cyert, R. M., and J. G. March (1963). *A Behavioral Theory of the Firm*. Englewood Cliffs, NJ: Prentice-Hall.

Darr, E., L. Argote, and D. Epple (1995). 'The acquisition, transfer and depreciation of knowledge in service organizations: Productivity in franchises', *Management Science*, 44: 1750–62.

Devadas Rao, R., and L. Argote (1995). 'Collective learning and forgetting: The effects of turnover and group structure'. Paper presented at Midwestern Academy of Management Meetings, Chicago, May 1995.

Dutton, J. M., and A. Thomas (1984). 'Treating progress functions as a managerial opportunity', *Academy of Management Review*, 9: 235–47.

Epple, D., L. Argote, and R. Devadas (1991). 'Organizational learning curves: A method for investigating intra-plant transfer of knowledge acquired through learning by doing', *Organization Science*, 2: 58–70.

——— and K. Murphy (1996). 'An empirical investigation of the micro structure of knowledge acquisition and transfer through learning by doing', *Operations Research*, 44: 77–86.

Fair, R. C. (1970). 'The estimation of simultaneous equation models with lagged endogenous variables and first order serially correlated errors', *Econometrica*, 38: 507–16.

Gersick, C. J. A., and J. R. Hackman (1990). 'Habitual routines in task-performing groups', *Organizational Behavior and Human Decision Processes*, 47: 65–97.

Hausman, J. A. (1978). 'Specification tests in econometrics', *ECTRA*, 46: 125–7.

Hayes, R. H., and K. B. Clark (1986). 'Why some factories are more productive than others', *Harvard Business Review*, 5: 66–73.

——and S. C. Wheelwright (1984). *Restoring our Competitive Edge: Competing through Manufacturing*. New York: Wiley.

Henderson, R., and I. Cockburn (1994). 'Measuring competences: Exploring firm effects in pharmaceutical research', *Strategic Management Journal*, 15: 63–84.

Huber, G. P. (1991). 'Organizational learning: The contributing processes and the literatures', *Organization Science*, 2: 88–115.

Irwin, D. A., and P. J. Klenow (1994). 'Learning-by-doing spillovers in the semiconductor industry', *Journal of Political Economy*, 102: 1200–27.

Joskow, P. L., and N. L. Rose (1985). 'The effects of technological change, experience, and environmental regulation on the construction cost of coal-burning generating units', *Rand Journal of Economics*, 16: 1–27.

——and G. A. Rozanki (1979). 'The effects of learning by doing on nuclear operating reliability', *Review of Economics and Statistics*, 161–8.

Katz, D., and R. L. Kahn (1978). *The Social Psychology of Organizations*, 2nd edn., New York: Wiley.

Lane, F. C. (1951). *Ships for Victory: A History of Shipbuilding under the U.S. Maritime Commission in World War II*. Baltimore, Md.: Johns Hopkins Press.

Levitt, B., and J. G. March (1988). 'Organizational learning', *Annual Review of Sociology*, 14: 319–40.

Lieberman, M. B. (1984). 'The learning curve and pricing in the chemical processing industries', *Rand Journal of Economics*, 15: 213–28.

March, J. G., and H. A. Simon (1958). *Organizations*. New York: Wiley.

Miner, A., and P. Haunschild (1995). 'Population level learning', *Research in Organizational Behavior*, 17: 115–66.

Nelson, R. R., and S. G. Winter (1982). *An Evolutionary Theory of Economic Change*. Boston: Belkman Press.

Nonaka, I. (1991). 'The knowledge-creating company', *Harvard Business Review*, 96–104.

Simon, H. A. (1991). 'Bounded rationality and organizational learning', *Organization Science*, 2: 125–34.

Starbuck, W. H. (1992). 'Learning by knowledge-intensive firms', *Journal of Management Studies*, 29: 713–40.

Szulanski, G. (1996). 'Exploring internal stickiness: Impediments to the transfer of best practices within the firm', *Strategic Management Journal*, 17: 27–43.

Tushman, M. L. (1977). 'Communication across organizational boundaries: Special boundary roles in the innovation process', *Administrative Science Quarterly*, 22: 587–605.

Virany, B., M. L. Tushman, and E. Romanelli (1992). 'Executive succession and organization outcomes in turbulent environments: An organizational learning approach', *Organization Science*, 3: 72–91.

Walsh, J. P., and G. R. Ungson (1991). 'Organizational memory', *Academy of Management Review*, 16: 57–90.

Yelle, L. E. (1979). 'The learning curve: Historical review and comprehensive survey', *Decision Sciences*, 10: 302–28.

Zander, U., and B. Kogut (1995). 'Knowledge and the speed of the transfer and imitation of organizational capabilities: An empirical test', *Organization Science*, 6: 76–92.

Zimmerman, M. B. (1992). 'Learning effects and the commercialization of new energy technologies: The case of nuclear power', *Bell Journal of Economics*, 13: 297–310.

Acknowledgement

Figure 2.1 as reprinted by permission from E. Darr, L. Argote, and D. Epple, *Management Science*, 41(11), November 1995, The Institute of Operations Research and the Management Sciences (INFORMS), 2 Charles Street, Suite 300, Providence, RI 02904, USA.

3

Appropriability and the Challenge of Scope: Banc One Routinizes Replication

GABRIEL SZULANSKI

Students of economic and organizational growth share an intense interest in the ability of organizations to innovate and to appropriate some of the benefit from their innovative effort. From the perspective of evolutionary economics, one of the most valuable products of successful innovation is proven team-embodied knowledge which, if adequately leveraged, could generate economic rent. The process of appropriating those rents involves a substantial component of replication or partial replication—either in existing or in greenfield sites—of those routines that underlie the success of the organization (cf. Winter, 1995). Thus, from an evolutionary economics perspective, appropriability hinges not only on the existence or degree of enforceability of intellectual property law or on the possession of complementary assets but also, and perhaps primarily, on the organizational capability to replicate effectively patterns of action that underlie success.

Through repetition, an organization may learn, i.e. evolve the capability, to leverage productive routines through replication. Under certain conditions, the ability to replicate routines could in itself become routinized, with solutions to common deviations from an ideal replication scenario accommodated through sub-routines (cf. Leidner (1993) discussion of the limits of routinization of fast food counter practices and life insurance selling). New or rare contingencies, however, may require additional deliberation and problem-solving, thus upsetting the smooth functioning of a replication routine.

Just how far the replication of routines could be routinized is a question of great practical import for Banc One—a profitable, technologically advanced US super-regional bank that grows primarily by acquisition. Banc One installs its own systems and operating procedures in the banks it acquires. In approximately eight years, it has performed over 135 such bank conversions. Most, but not all, of them have been smoothly successful.

Because of internal restructuring, Banc One has substantially modified the affiliation process and to a lesser extent also the conversion process since the research reported in this chapter was conducted. Thus, discrepancies may exist between Banc One's current affiliation approach and the reality described in this chapter. The author acknowledges the helpful comments and suggestions from Sidney Winter, Lorna Doucet, and three anonymous referees. The author is especially thankful to Bob Barrett, Jack Compton, and Ann Spence. Financial support for this chapter was partly provided by the University Research Foundation of the University of Pennsylvania. Errors and omissions are solely the author's responsibility. Please do not cite or reproduce without the author's explicit consent.

The robustness of Banc One's conversion methods is constantly put to test by its impressive rate of growth. As Banc One grows, the acquisition targets that are converted using those methods become larger and more complex. Furthermore, more acquisitions occur simultaneously. At the same time, Banc One's systems and operating procedures, the very object of replication, grow more diverse and sophisticated. The combination of these factors creates situations where the limits of otherwise effective methods for conversion are occasionally reached. On those occasions the methods have to be revised and adapted to cope with the increased scope of replication, e.g. to convert larger banks, to convert many banks simultaneously, and to convert banks to increasingly sophisticated and complex systems and operating procedures. Because Banc One's conversion capability is considered best in class in the banking industry, it provides a fascinating exemplar of appropriative capability, i.e. of an organization that has evolved the capability to replicate its own productive routines.

In an attempt to provide rich, systematic primary evidence of appropriative capability, this chapter reports the findings of an in-depth field study of Banc One's conversion capability. It gives a snapshot of the anatomy of that capability, reviews some indications of how it came about, and illustrates some of the challenges that may compromise the smooth functioning and effectiveness of the routines that underlie that capability. The smoothness and effectiveness of a conversion process are so important for Banc One's growth strategy, that acquisitions are treated as a separate line of business, and are monitored by Banc One's president. Hence, most facets of the process are well attended, documented in rich detail, and well remembered by participants. Thanks to the full cooperation of the organization, it was possible to reconstruct faithfully past conversions and follow one closely as it unfolded. The conceptual framework used to structure data collection was the replication of organizational routines (Nelson and Winter 1982).

The next section describes in more detail conceptual and methodological aspects of the study. Banc One's replication routine and how it came about is described next, and a separate section is devoted to illustrating some of the challenges that increased scope creates for the smooth performance of the conversion routine.

1. Studying Replication of Routines

1.1. *Evolutionary economics' view of replication.*[1]

Evolutionary economics treats replication of routines as a *costly, time-consuming process* of copying an existing pattern of productive activity. It starts from the point of view of what can be accomplished from the *status quo of a functioning routine*. The existing routine serves as a template for the new one and the *feasibility of close (let alone perfect) replication is seen as 'quite problematic'*. Exact replication will never be fully achieved in practice and in some cases exact replication may not even be the objective. Rather,

---

[1] This subsection draws extensively on Nelson and Winter (1982) and on Winter (1995).

partial replication could be the ultimate objective, accompanied by adaptive or innovative change in some sub-routines.

The replication assumption in evolutionary models is intended primarily to reflect the advantages that favour the going concern attempting to do more of the same, as contrasted with the difficulties that it would encounter in doing something else or that others would encounter in trying to copy its success. A firm with a profitable routine in hand has an inherent advantage in pursuing this strategy, by virtue of its superior access to the successful 'template' example (Nelson and Winter 1982: 118–24). This advantage is particularly significant when the existing routine involves tacit skills or otherwise resists codification.

Replication of routines is assumed to occur primarily because it makes economic sense. This assumption implies that reinvention *de novo*, i.e. repeating the original learning process underlying the routine is not generally a plausible alternative to replication when the goal is to seize a larger share of an extant profit opportunity successfully exploited by the prevailing routine. It implies also that the benefits obtained must exceed or be expected to exceed the opportunity cost of drawing on the resources of the template to support the replication and also the cost of over-coming potential obstacles to replication (cf. Nelson, 1982: 118–24; Winter, 1995).

Nelson and Winter's analysis of replication draws primarily on studies of the transfer of technology (Hall and Johnson 1967; Teece 1977). These studies, heavily influenced by the thinking of Shannon and Weaver (1949) and Arrow (1971), attribute obstacles to replication to characteristics of the template site, of the recipient site, of the technology or routine being transferred, and also to character-istics of the context where the replication takes place. These obstacles may prevent complete success in replicating faithfully the transferred knowledge.

1.2. Study design considerations

Data collection was guided by Nelson and Winter's view of replication. In line with their view, particular attention was paid to characteristics of the template being replicated, the template site, the recipient site, and the context where the transfer took place. In an attempt to highlight generative mechanisms whereby these char-acteristics may affect the replication process and its outcome, a detailed longitudinal documentation of the process was attempted. The research strategy closely approx-imates what Leonard-Barton (1990) calls a synergistic case-study design—retrospect-ive case studies highlight important features of the process which then receive special attention in a real-time examination of an unfolding one. Seeking the ultimate goal of objectivity (Kirk and Miller 1986), the design aimed to increase the validity and the reliability of the findings.

Validity. Banc One provides an extreme situation, where the process of interest is 'transparently observable' (Eisenhardt, 1989). To gain access, I approached Banc One's public relations office. The PR office provided background material and identified key informants. Key informants were the first persons interviewed. Inter-views lasted from 2.5 to 3.5 hours. After the interview, key informants had a clear idea of what type of information I was seeking and of the design considerations of the study, e.g. how to identify suitable practices. They then set out to identify suitable transfers to study, provided me with relevant documentation about those transfers, and introduced me to other people who had played critical roles in the process of transfer. I then tried to interview every person involved with the transfers to maximize the validity of the explanations. Construct validation was obtained by feeding back a write-up of the findings which interviewees and the organization amended twice and then accepted as faithful documentation of the process of conversion.

Reliability. To increase the reliability of my findings I relied on a systematic protocol and on multiple-data collection methods, such as interviews, observations, and archival sources. The fieldwork protocol consisted of three questions: How did the conversion happen? What were the difficulties during the conversion? Where did those difficulties come from? Using archival data, I sketched the answers to these questions in advance. This permitted me to use the interview time efficiently by estimating in advance the time that should be devoted to each question and by permitting me to detect valuable information and probe respondents for precision and depth. Further, when respondents tended to focus on only a few aspects of the conversion, I used the initial conceptual framework to generate more specific questions to guide the questioning. As I progressed through the interviews, some categories became saturated (Glaser and Strauss 1968; Eisenhardt, 1989). Thus, while interviewing 'snowballed' around the key informant in the initial phase, I selected further interviewees increasingly on the basis of the specific categories where data was still insufficient, e.g. to obtain a balanced perspective on events. Interviews became more and more specialized and sacrificed breadth to explore issues in greater depth. Generous access was granted to documents and participants. Interviewees were allowed to revise written notes from their interview before these could be cited. Data was collected over a period of more than two years, before, during, and after the conversion occurred.

2. Replication of Routines at Banc One

Banc One is a profitable, technologically advanced US super-regional bank that over the past decade has grown primarily by acquisition.[2] Banc One handles the integration of a 'pending affiliate' (a bank that Banc One has agreed to acquire) through the affiliation process. During this process, activity takes place in many areas simultaneously. For example, Marketing and Retail employees map the pending affiliate's products into Banc One's products, Finance maps the accounts on the pending affiliate's general ledger, and the Electronic Banking gauges the volume of the pending affiliate's ATM transactions. During affiliation, a 'sister bank'—a Banc One affiliate with a similar operating environment—is proposed to the pending affiliate as a plausible model of their post-conversion operations.

---

[2] Several case studies have been written about Banc One. See e.g. Kanter (1989) and Uyterhoeven (1994).

One of the most demanding activities of the affiliation process is the conversion of the various systems and operating procedures of the new affiliate to those of Banc One. Banc One's data-processing capabilities are admired by the banking industry and so is their ability to convert new affiliates to operate with those systems. What makes Banc One's conversion capability noteworthy is that, rather than being protracted, the actual transition takes a single weekend. On a Friday evening, the branches of the new affiliate close operating as they normally did before they were acquired. The next Monday, they open their doors operating as a Banc One branch, with new systems, new forms, and new operating procedures.

Banc One's bank conversion process is an ideal setting in which to study the replication of routines because it approximates closely the theoretical premises set forth by evolutionary economics. There exists a working template.[3] Some of the elements in that template are not codified and replicating that template is a worthy but difficult task. The new affiliate has a variety of resources on which it can draw 'very helpfully' during a conversion. The desire on the part of Banc One to achieve as precise a replication as possible, to minimize the risk of repeating past errors, is tempered by the need to secure the new affiliate's cooperation. Conversions make economic sense. They are a profitable undertaking, both because they help the new affiliate boost revenue and control costs and also because they liberate scarce managerial resources of the new affiliate from data-processing worries so that they can concentrate on the business of banking. The cost of using the template's site resources to support the conversion is formally considered part of the template's site responsibility and it is within the template's site reach because most of the burden of the conversion is assumed by an organizational subunit dedicated to conversions. Reinvention of the systems and procedures by the new affiliate has proven unfeasible in the past and is no longer considered a plausible alternative.[4] Finally, there is a rich experience base of conversions. Over the last eight years, Banc One has performed over 135 conversions.

All new affiliates eventually undergo conversion to Banc One systems and operating procedures. Expertise and responsibility for bank conversion is vested in a non-banking subsidiary of Banc One, Banc One Services Corporation (BOSC), which leads and supports the process of conversion. BOSC has also responsibility for implementing and maintaining most Banc One systems.

2.1. Bank conversion

Banks rely extensively on data-processing (DP) systems to deliver products and services to their clients. DP systems are a tool for doing business. Thus, converting

---

[3] Indeed, while the concept of a 'template' as used in evolutionary economics can be taken as metaphorical—a reference to the existing routine wherever instantiated—Banc One's practice of identifying a 'sister bank' makes it quite literal in this context.

[4] In the past, some banks, when acquired, attempted to keep their systems, arguing that these systems were in fact better than Banc One's or arguing that it would be easier for them to adapt their own systems to support Banc One's products than to retrain all their personnel to use Banc One systems. Invariably these attempts have proven unsuccessful.

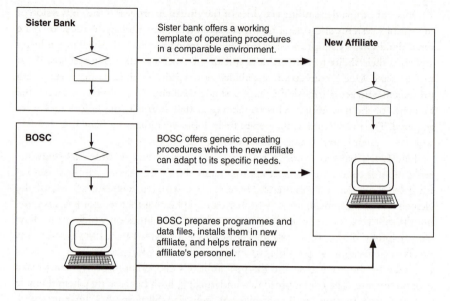

Fig. 3.1 BOSC and sister bank roles

DP systems means that a new affiliate abandons one tool to do business and unlearns the accompanying operating procedures in order to learn new ones that suit the new set of tools. By adopting Banc One's systems and operating procedures, a new affiliate adopts the same tool that all other members of the BO family are using to conduct their business and thus becomes eligible for BOSC's support. BOSC keeps the systems operational and current so as to provide Banc One's affiliates with 'premier data-processing services'.[5]

Essentially, converting a new affiliate means installing new applications[6] in the affiliate's computer system and converting its existing data files on customers to a format which is compatible with the new applications. The new affiliate's personnel are trained and then supported until they can comfortably operate the new systems on their own. Occasionally, a new affiliate may relinquish operating responsibilities to BOSC after a conversion.

Although simple in essence, converting a new affiliate to Banc One systems is a complex and costly endeavour. Decision-making spans five senior management levels within Banc One (President of Banc One, CEO of BOSC, CEO and president

---

[5] Guidelines for Conversion Kick-Off meeting.

[6] The term 'application' means a software program closely associated with a particular financial product and necessary to deliver that product. Applications may be developed by Banc One or supplied by an outside vendor. An example of an application is the Florida Software Mortgage Loan System which provides accounting, on-line processing and reporting for the mortgage loan portfolio. The documentation of another application reads: 'The Demand Deposit Accounting system is the resource used to process checks and deposits for personal and business checking accounts. Processing parameters are established by bank or branch.'

of State Holding Company, CEO of affiliate) and four middle-management levels (BOSC Senior VP of Information Systems, BOSC Vice President of Client Services, BOSC Client Services Conversion Director and a Project Manager responsible for the conversion). All of these levels are active at one time or another during the conversion. Furthermore, just on BOSC's side, about thirty business analysts and technical specialists are involved full time in the conversion effort for a period of about six months. A similar number of specialists support the conversion from the new affiliate's side. The existing operating procedures of the new affiliate have to be adapted to the new systems or new ones have to be developed during the conversion. This requires that most of the personnel in the new affiliate be retrained within a month. Depending on the geographical location and the configuration of the acquired bank, logistics in themselves may be a challenge. Travelling and communications certainly add to the costs of conversion. Together, the cost of man-power, travel, and communication could total more than a million dollars for a large conversion. The new affiliate will typically incur costs comparable to those incurred by BOSC.

2.2. Anatomy of a conversion

Of theoretical interest for the study of replication are characteristics of the template, the recipient site, the template site and, the organizational context where the replication occurs. Accordingly, this subsection reviews some facets—usually attended to before and during a conversion—of Banc One's DP systems and operating procedures, of the pending affiliate's role, of the conversion group and the sister bank, and of the organizational context where the conversion takes place. A special effort is made to provide a rich description of the context.

The template: Banc One operating procedures and common systems   Banc One converts affiliates to what it calls 'common systems', the set of systems that are standard to the corporation at any given time. Although the exact composition of common systems varies, as new applications are developed and old ones discarded, common systems usually cover three groups of applications: Strategic Banking Systems (SBS), Branch Automation systems (BA), and credit (overdraft line of credit) and deposit (chequeing, savings, certificate of deposit) applications. Banc One offers over 75 different credit and deposit products, each supported by its own dedicated application. Branch Automation systems have two separate subsystems: Teller Automation and Platform Automation. Within a single workstation, Teller Automation provides the tellers with all the information and transaction capabilities they need to identify customers and to review account relationships, transactions, activity, and balances. Platform Automation supports sales and service of banking products by allowing service representatives to open accounts on line and by generating automatically the necessary forms. Information common to numerous accounts is entered only once and transferred by the system to the respective application systems. The Strategic Banking System, developed primarily to expedite the introduction of new products and give banks a total and accurate picture of the customer's relationships, acts as an integrating application by providing the capability to process customer information, deposit and credit accounts all in one system.

To operate with BO systems, the branches and the back office of a bank need suitable operating procedures. To address this need, BOSC offers affiliates a set of generic operating procedures, in the form of guidelines or flowcharts, that the new affiliate can customize for their own use by filling in the blanks and expanding some details. For example, such step-by-step procedures instruct tellers on how to handle commercial loans, utilities, instalment loans, money orders, or food stamps. Similarly, they provide instructions that platform operators could follow to open a new savings account, sell loans, stocks, or treasury notes.

A new affiliate may be converted to the three groups of systems simultaneously or in stages, with each group of systems installed in a dedicated conversion. In the latter case, the conversion to Banc One's credit and deposit applications will typically precede the conversion to BA and SBS. A simultaneous conversion is more complex than a staggered one. However, a simultaneous conversion usually takes considerably less time than three successive conversions.

When assessing the effort involved in a conversion, BOSC considers also the complexity of each application. Complexity is typically gauged by the number of exceptions that an application has to handle. The number of exceptions affects both the size of the computer code of that application and the difficulty of understanding and updating it. For example, when converting a complex application, like commercial loans, BOSC's personnel may not understand the new affiliate's existing systems that need to be converted or may not ask the right questions because no two commercial loans are exactly alike. Another example is item capture (e.g. cheques) where there are special features that are not very visible, such as idiosyncratic and often cumbersome account-numbering conventions and special coding schemes that may have evolved over time as the systems were debugged or expanded—but that nobody remembers because the people that developed them have left the bank, or because out of the many thousands of accounts in the new affiliate these modifications affect only a handful.

The age of an application could affect the effort required for its conversion. If an application is too recent, it may not be widely known or understood within Banc One. If it is too old—many of Banc One systems were conceived during the late 1960s, early 1970s—it may impose architectural limitations that are difficult to surmount. Even though the applications may have been enhanced to keep pace with the times, they may not be flexible enough. The number of digits in an account number or in a branch code is a good example. One BO deposit application permits up to nine digits in an account number and some banks work with twelve. Similarly, BO applications permit three digits for a branch code and some of those applications that Banc One supports need four. Sometimes, Banc One will refrain from converting a particular application until a new one that resolves those problems is ready. Sometimes an existing application will be converted to an existing BO application at the cost of sacrificing or grossly simplifying some of its features.

The recipient: a new affiliate   Some characteristics of a new affiliate can affect a conversion effort quite dramatically. Basically, the significant characteristics relate either to the affiliate's willingness to undergo conversion or to the capabilities and structural characteristics of the affiliate that determine the effort to convert it.

When it comes to gauging how committed an affiliate is to conversion, BOSC conversion personnel typically inquire as to whether the management of that affiliate is willing to assign the necessary people, allocate the necessary resources, and seem willing to accept Banc One's uniform product line. An uncommitted affiliate's conversion team will typically be insufficiently staffed with personnel for whom the conversion is part-time duty and not the first priority, and that lack the necessary expertise and/or authority to make important decisions without hierarchical referral. Such an affiliate will typically promise more than it will eventually deliver. If the affiliate is unwilling to spend money on the conversion, it may try to economize by trying to adapt BO systems by itself—a strategy that past experience shows to lead invariably to partial, problematic conversions or even to no conversion at all. Vital for the success of a conversion effort is that a committed affiliate has realistic expectations as to what BOSC will deliver and what is required from them during a conversion.

But regardless of how willing a new affiliate is to convert to BO systems, it may lack some of the necessary capabilities or resources to support the conversion. Turnover may have left the new affiliate without adequate personnel to support the conversion or with insufficient knowledge of their operations because key individuals, responsible for past modifications, left the company without leaving a paper trail of their actions. The introduction of automation in the branches of a new affiliate requires extra training if these branches were not automated before the conversion. Similarly, if the acquired bank owned its data-processing operations before the conversion, it will typically be easier to convert because that bank understands its systems and operations better. If, on the contrary, that bank relied on a data-processing bureau for its systems, it is likely that the bureau assumed also some responsibility for that bank's operations. When that is the case, the new affiliate will have to learn also how to take responsibility for that part of the operations that the bureau used to help with before the conversion. A variant of this situation occurs when the new affiliate's individual banks depended on an in-house services corporation which provided them with systems, operating procedures, and made the operational decisions for them. Finally, a conversion will be smoother the better the controls the affiliate has in place and the better existing procedures, are documented.

Another important capability is the ability to do training in-house. Typically, banks deliver some in-house training through their HR departments, such as stress management or time management workshops, and outsource their other training needs. In some cases they may also have teller training in-house. Banks that lack a training organization may be more difficult to convert because additional training infrastructure will have to be developed during the conversion to deliver technical training; this may require the affiliate to draw from within the ranks for trainers.

Finally, structural characteristics of the new affiliate may affect the effort required for the conversion. A large bank will have typically more complex products and more complex systems. A small bank may be short of resources (money, people) to support the conversion. A large bank may have the necessary resources but it may have to undergo a much more intense training effort and it may also have a greater tendency to internal communication breakdowns.

The complexity of a new affiliate has multiple dimensions. One dimension is the number of services that it provides. A full service organization may use seventy-five applications whereas others may use only fifteen. Another is the number of branches of the new affiliate. The amount of training and post-conversion support needed will increase with the number of branches. Complexity also increases if the bank has multiple corporate identities. Typically each corporation within the bank will have its own back-room operations and separate customer information files. Each back-room has to be trained and their customer information files converted. Also, data coming from different centres may conform to different structures requiring adjustments before it can be used to assemble consolidated reports.

Another aspect of complexity involves the degree of idiosyncrasy of the new affiliate's needs. For example the bank may open to the public during non-standard hours. Some banks open from 7 a.m. to midnight, seven days a week, which requires that the systems be modified to accommodate these special hours. Likewise, the new bank may have large commercial operations which require complex idiosyncratic adaptations for important clients. Banc One may find it difficult to accommodate those special needs within its systems because, being mainly a retail bank, its knowledge base for commercial operations is relatively limited.

Geographic dispersion also adds difficulty to a conversion. The more scattered around are the branches of a bank, the more challenging logistics and coordination are bound to become. Locations that are difficult to access increase significantly the cost of training because the new affiliate's personnel may need to be trained *in situ*.

The template site: Banc One Services Corporation and the sister bank
Characteristics of the template site also affect the unfolding of a conversion. A new affiliate is converted by a dedicated conversion team within BOSC. To help the new affiliate make more informed conversion-related decisions, Banc One recommends a sister bank which is another BO affiliate with a similar operating environment to that of the new affiliate.

The experience level of the conversion team is critical to a smooth conversion. The Conversion Group within BOSC is relatively young and because of Banc One's growth few people have deep experience for a given application. In BO parlance, this limits the 'conversion depth'. Experience is crucial because it helps the conversion team uncover early any discrepancies that may exist between what the new affiliate believes its systems are and what they are in reality. In times of intense conversion activity, experienced personnel may be asked to participate in several conversions simultaneously. This sometimes results in delayed tasks and in lost or unresolved issues. This generates problems that later demand costly attention.

Besides experience, the attitude of the conversion team matters as well. Early in BOSC's growth, conversion personnel became accustomed to diagnosing unilaterally the needs of new affiliates and to proceeding according to their own diagnosis of the affiliate's needs, with little heed paid to the affiliate's own self-assessment. As a consequence, BOSC personnel responsible for building applications or doing conversions developed an attitude of rigidity and inflexibility towards new affiliates, an attitude colourfully described by a conversions member as 'my way or the highway'. Although these norms are rapidly changing towards a more customer-oriented and responsive posture, the change is still not fully reflected in the behaviour of application and conversion personnel within BOSC.

Sister banks are designated to illustrate a realistic scenario for the post-conversion operating environment of the new affiliate. The converted bank can visit them and see how they operate and how they are structured. This will increase the confidence of the new affiliate on the appropriateness of the conversion-related decisions it has to make. This will also reduce the likelihood that the converted bank will repeat avoidable errors. Sister banks can help train a big new affiliate and may even temporarily lend specialists to new affiliates to help them solve transition problems. To select a sister bank, Banc One looks for a bank that has converted to the same systems in the recent past.

Recently Banc One started a project to develop a model bank which consists of a functioning model of a retail bank where corporate standards, procedures, and work flows of a bank's retail front office and a bank's retail back office operations are implemented. Every new system that is made part of Banc One's Common Systems is made also part of the model bank. The goal of the model bank is to complement the sister-bank approach to support conversions before, during, and after they occur. It provides a forum where pilot trials and experiments can be conducted without disrupting the functioning of an actual bank.

The organizational context: culture, structure, affiliation process   Several aspects of Banc One's organizational context affect a conversion. These include facets of BO culture, of its administrative structure, and of the affiliation process by which a pending affiliate is integrated to the BO family.

Banc One's culture   Banc One describes its management philosophy as an 'Uncommon Partnership'. The essence of this philosophy, spelled out on the back of a napkin by the first chairman of Banc One's holding company, is that the affiliates run themselves. This degree of decentralization is uncommon for the banking industry. The purpose of this philosophy was to attract good banks and retain their best people and it meant that the affiliates could run their banks as they saw fit, *as long as they performed*. More recently the 'Uncommon Partnership' idea was refined as follows: 'if it involves people, we do it at the local level; if it involves paper, we centralize it' (cf. Kanter, 1989: 6). Recognizing the benefits of selective centralization, Banc One sought ways to leverage economies of scale on legal services, purchasing, regulatory issues, technology, and also to coordinate investment decisions. This enhances the affiliates' opportunity to devote more time to their customers. Affiliate autonomy encompasses local lending decisions, pricing based on local market conditions, personnel policies and compensation, and responses to community needs.

The revised 'Uncommon Partnership' retains a strong performance orientation. An affiliate's CEO describes what it means for a new affiliate,

In this company, you have almost unlimited authority, as long as you perform. The pressure in this company on new banks to come up to speed is enormous.... They are told the level at which they need to perform, they are given some time to get there and they are offered lots of help.

Even though Banc One has recently broadened its spectrum of performance criteria to include customer satisfaction and societal performance, financial perform-ance is stressed because 'all functions of the bank ultimately manifest themselves in the financial data; up-front attention to these permits superior performance'.[7] Ac-cordingly, the benchmarks for performance improvement, that the holding company sets for the affiliates, are expressed exclusively in financial terms.

Because of the strong emphasis on financial performance, the Chief Financial Officer (CFO) of a BO affiliate has a stronger and more active role than the CFOs of most other banks which typically act as head accounting officers. BO CFOs are heavily involved in the actual operations of their bank and lead and coordinate systems-conversion efforts.

Thanks to a common accounting and financial reporting system, very detailed measures of an affiliate's performance can be compared across affiliates. Financial performance is reported monthly through the Management Information Control System (MICS). MICS produces an elaborate set of reports on an affiliate-by-affiliate basis that are available on-line. Central features of these reports are cost profiles for different bank sizes, branch profitability, and product profitability figures. Among the data reported are dollar figures such as end-of-period assets and net income, and percentages such as equity/assets, ROA, ROE, Net Interest Margin (NIM), and Non-Interest Expense (NIE)/Revenue. Because Banc One enforces a uniform product line in all its affiliates, the performance of different products is comparable across branches and across banks. Affiliates can therefore compare results by month end. Everyone has access to everyone else's numbers.

To facilitate internal benchmarking of performance, the MICS system produces a monthly Peer Comparison report that includes results both for the current period and for the full year. In that report, the affiliates are grouped alphabetically within one of three peer groups. Group membership is determined by asset size. For example the May 1993 Peer Comparison report has three groups: nineteen large banks comprising some 75 per cent of Banc One assets and income; twenty-nine mid-size banks accounting for some 16 per cent of total assets and earnings; and fifty small banks (see Uyterhoeven, 1994).

As a consequence, everyone knows on a monthly basis who is at the top and who is at the bottom. A prolonged stay at the bottom of the scale invites corporate

---

[7] Banc One Corporation, Role of the Chief Financial Officer.

scrutiny, so affiliates have incentives not to stay at the bottom for too long. This generates a climate of friendly competition, which is largely possible because the affiliates serve non-overlapping markets.

This 'compare' facet of BO operations is complemented by norms of knowledge sharing. As the CEO of an affiliate described:

Our network is built by [comparing] results in MICS and lots of talking. I can't imagine how much money this company spends with banks calling each other but it is a good investment. Whatever the number is, it is a good investment. It's got to be a fortune, our banks talk to each other all the time. Its routine, is part of the culture here. They call their counterpart in another bank and ask for information and advice on problems. That's the way we do it which generally became known as 'share and compare' buzzword.

'Share and compare' is a strong element of BO culture. Like comparing, also sharing has been a mainstay of the culture. As a corporate vice-president described:

Sitting around and telling campfire stories, how you do things, is long-standing. What's happened in the last few years [is that] it has become more analytical. New affiliates are firmly socialized into this sharing mode. Disruptive behavior [not sharing] is defined by corporate as out of bounds... [sharing] is not optional.

Besides being required by the corporate office, new affiliates soon find out that sharing is vital to continuously improve performance and thus keep one's job at Banc One. As the same corporate vice-president explains:

You have to improve. In our company it is really how people keep their job. Some banks are going to be good in some lines of business and some in others. So people get together and say: I'm good at this line of business and you are not, and you are good in this line of business and I'm not so why don't we get together and exchange ideas. It is not always one person giving and one person taking. The next time around roles switch. People are most likely to be on both sides of the street. The Fortune 100 of Banc One changes all the time. Always have something to improve and you want to be able to get help when you need help. There are so many banks that do things well that if somebody is going to be Machiavellian and not cooperate, he or she is going to be very much isolated and in this company you are committing career suicide.

Thus, Banc One's *modus operandi* contains both formal and informal elements of internal benchmarking. The MICS enables meaningful real-time comparison of affiliates' performance. An affiliate cannot stay for long at the bottom of the performance distribution without inviting close scrutiny from the corporate office. To escape from the bottom it will often seek help and advice from other affiliates. The monthly Peer Comparison report will help it swiftly identify sources of best practice in the domain it needs to improve. Lots of talking and norms for sharing will make the exchange possible. To prevent this sharing culture from being affected by Banc One's breathtaking rate of growth, acquisition targets are never larger than a third of Banc One's size.

Banc One's administrative structure   Since 1987, Banc One has adopted a state holding company structure, with corporate headquarters and staff offices in Columbus, Ohio. The state holding company structure permits Banc One to accommodate growth by setting up state holding companies in each state that it enters. State holding companies deal with all issues that are best handled at the state level and for which a separate organizational unit may not be justifiable at the level of each affiliate. A newcomer to the Banc One family will be legally owned by a state holding company located in most cases in the same state as the affiliate.

A new affiliate may be a single bank or a holding company grouping many banks. In between the announcement of the acquisition and the actual affiliation, a new affiliate may be restructured. Each bank may have many branches, one or more operation centres and an outside services supplier.

A typical acquisition target for Banc One would be the first, second, or third in share of the relevant market and will permit Banc One to make a difference in that market, to be a price leader, to set the stage. Acquisitions targets could come from a market were Banc One is already present, i.e. 'in-market', or from a new market, i.e. 'out of market'.

During the conversion of a new affiliate to Banc One Common Systems, the corporate office in Columbus, the state holding company, and Banc One Services Corporation play important roles.

The affiliation process   The affiliation process is coordinated by a vice-president from the corporate Affiliation Management area. Sometimes, this vice-president may be assisted by the state holding company. Key premisses and parameters for the conversion process are set during affiliation.

The affiliation process starts in earnest when the new affiliate announces to the press its intent to merge with Banc One, after it has signed a definitive agreement with Banc One's Mergers and Acquisitions unit. During the two months following the announcement, a detailed examination of the pending affiliate's books and records will take place. This examination, called *due diligence*,[8] encompasses Credit, all loan portfolios, Compliance, CRA, Benefits, Facilities, Risk Management, Insurance Sales, Leasing, Accounting, Audit, Operations and Internal Controls, Data Processing, Legal, Funds Management, Trust, Investment Portfolios, Brokerage or Securities sales, deposits, etc. The reports from the due-diligence examination highlight strengths, weaknesses, product differences, and any deal breakers.[9]

After completion of due diligence, an overview of the affiliation process will be given to the senior management of the new affiliate. During the overview, corporate representatives from Finance, Services, Corporate Marketing, and Diversified Services meet with the bank's President and his/her direct reports. Each representative would take a few minutes to explain their functions and their involvement in the affiliation process. The essence of this meeting is described by a vice-president from the Corporate Affiliation office:

---

[8] The exercise of due diligence is a legal prerequisite for defending litigation that may arise from the transaction. It requires that the business or person 'has taken all reasonable precautions or steps and exercised all due diligence to avoid the commission of the offence.'

[9] The affiliation agreement is contingent on the findings of the due diligence process. Affiliation will continue only if no problems are discovered that make the acquisition undesirable from Banc One's viewpoint. Such problems, if discovered, may result in revision or cancellation of the affiliation agreement.

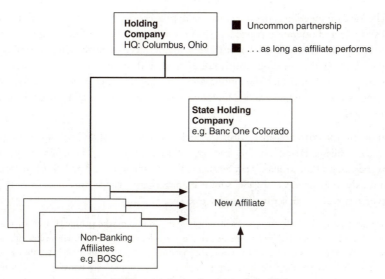

Fig. 3.2 The organizational context of an affiliate

The essence of this meeting is to do for the senior management of the to-be affiliate a dog and pony show on how to save money and expense, to help cut expense. We coordinate and chair the meeting. We develop a list of people that will be doing the things from the affiliate side. People then set appointments and then they turn loose.

At that overview meeting, the senior management of the new affiliate is introduced to the different BO corporate functions and to contact persons at Banc One subsidiaries that handle centralized functions—such as leasing, mortgage origination, mortgage servicing, data processing, electronic banking, item processing, brokerage, credit card, credit life issuance, derivative portfolios, facilities, insurance policies, trust, and investment. They are also introduced to the senior management of a 'sister bank' which will assist them during their affiliation.

Also at that meeting, the senior management of the new affiliate is given a corporate policy manual, an accounting policy manual, and a primer on Banc One's audit processes. They are directed to align product lines and accounting policies with those of Banc One and they are requested to integrate as soon as possible with Banc One's management systems. The responsibility for carrying out these activities is split between corporate headquarters and the state holding company. Occasionally, the new affiliate may be the sole entity responsible for implementing some of these activities.

Finally, during the affiliation overview meeting, the senior management of the new affiliate will schedule the conversion 'kick-off' meeting with BOSC. Even though the conversion may not start until after the actual affiliation and sometimes over a year after, contacts between the new affiliate and BOSC start soon after the affiliation overview meeting because of the critical impact of the data-processing systems on the bank's ability to deliver service.

The kick-off meeting starts the conversion process that brings the new affiliate into BO systems and operating procedures. The conversion kick-off meeting is attended by a group of representatives from every major facet of processing operations at BOSC. During the meeting, information is shared about the new affiliate's data processing which includes the findings of the due-diligence process. A follow-up meeting is then scheduled and a tentative target date for the conversion is usually established.

Preparing for conversion   After the kick-off meeting, BOSC will inspect closely the new affiliate. Based on the findings of this inspection, demands from other conversions, and the affiliate's preferences, BOSC will make a detailed recommendation for the conversion to BOSC senior management. A vice-president from BOSC conversion services described the process:

Immediately after due diligence, we will simply start examining the profile of the bank. How big are they? Is it processed by an outside service provider or have their own service operation in house? What is the situation of the contract? Are they strong operationally? Are they looking for a conversion? Are they weak in terms of feature functions for a conversion? Corporate finance has some input into it. Also, the new affiliate may want to move ahead quickly, or they may want to wait for nine months before really starting anything because their banks are very backward, very conservative and are very nervous about the conversion and there is no real urgency. After we get the general profile of the bank and a vision where the bank will fall in the schedule we will plot that and we will communicate that internally. We believe from a planning horizon this bank will convert at some point in the next 12 months or in the next 18 months. Once we have concurrence, we will then start the planning process in earnest in the conversion group to identify the resources that we are going to need, the conversion manager we are going to need, and looking at the existing schedule, are we going to have enough staff to support the bank, are we going to have any conflicts with management, are there any other significant projects that could potentially impact that conversion and we act from there, identify the issue with management, identify the additional resources that we are going to need, etc. At that point we have a suggestion for a conversion date.

During this process, BOSC staff members may visit the affiliate's facilities to obtain a closer appreciation of what needs to be converted. Also, the sister bank plays an important role by helping the new affiliate to make conversion-related decisions. During these exchanges, BOSC and the affiliate evaluate potential candidates for staffing their conversion teams, most notably the conversion managers. Similarly other aspects of the conversion are discussed. These factors then become parameters for the recommendation for the affiliate's Common Systems conversion process.

Recommending the parameters of the conversion process   The recommendation for that conversion is communicated internally to BOSC top management and to the chairman of the state holding company for the state where the new affiliate is located. The parameters of the conversion are summarized in Table 3.1.

Several factors influence the recommendation. For example, the recommendation for a conversion date will take into consideration the particular circumstances of

T A B L E 3.1. Parameters of conversion

Parameter	Explanation
Conversion date	First day that the new affiliate will operate with BO systems
BOSC Conversion Manager	Conversion project manager on BOSC side
Bank Conversion Director	Conversion project manager on the affiliate's side
Processing Centre location	Location of the bank's Central Processing Unit
No. of banks to be converted	When the new affiliate has more than one bank
Conversion sequence	If conversion spans more than one bank
Cheque capture location	Location of regional processing centre
Application mapping	How the affiliate's existing applications will be replaced by Banc One's

the bank, such as the bank's motivation, involvement, and commitment to be converted, its depth in operations, and the potential impact on customers. Also, the affiliate may have contracts with outside suppliers that have excessively costly buy-out clauses. Rather than incurring the penalty for cancelling these contracts, the bank may elect to synchronize the conversions to the contract's expiration dates. The conversion may be advanced if the affiliate's systems are outmoded, cannot sustain the affiliate's projected growth, impede the bank from offering competitive products, or if the bank, because of the affiliation with Banc One, is losing data-processing staff. The conversion may be advanced also if the new affiliate is in a market already served by Banc One. Conversely, a conversion could be retarded if the affiliate prefers to defer the conversion because they are conservative or are nervous about the conversion. In general, BOSC will do whatever it takes to accommodate the preferences of the affiliate for the conversion date. Occasionally, the choice of a conversion date may respond to other corporate priorities or to conversion issues.

The choice of the conversion manager on BOSC's side depends on the availability of conversion managers and on the importance of the conversion. With respect to the processing centre, in an in-market acquisition, the bank's operations may go to an existing Data-Processing Centre. In an out-of-market acquisition, a new data-processing centre may have to be established. Similar considerations apply for the Regional Processing Centre.

The number of banks to be converted is the number of banks at the time the conversion actually starts. A new affiliate may consist of a group of banks owned by a bank holding company. Even though during the affiliation process the banks of a new affiliate may be consolidated, more than one may still remain after the consolidation. Each bank has its own operating back-room, which has to be converted. If more than one bank is converted, the conversions may be staggered or all the banks may be converted concurrently.

Finally, some or all of the affiliate's existing applications will be mapped into Banc One's applications. The conversion of applications may be staggered or concurrent. Moreover, during the conversion, new applications may be installed in the bank or some existing applications may be discontinued. Because converting applications requires the participation of application specialists, the size of the conversion team will increase with the number of applications converted.

2.3. The conversion process

In six months, BOSC converts the affiliate's product offerings and data-processing systems to the common product and processing systems of Banc One. BOSC's conversion methodology is supported by state-of-the-art project management tools and provides the template for planning and implementing conversion projects. It assists the conversion unit to assess the resources needed for a conversion, how much a conversion can be accelerated, and the impact of other contingencies. The default duration of a conversion process is 180 days. The end of one phase and the beginning of another is marked by project deliverables. The calendar for a specific conversion project is automatically set once the conversion date is chosen.

Conversion in six steps   Banc One's conversion process has six phases: *planning* the project scope and resources; *definition* where the converting bank's and Banc One's environment are defined; *design* where the converting bank's post-conversion environment is defined; *development* where the computer programs and the bank's new work environment is developed; *training* where the bank is prepared for the post-conversion environment; and *support* when the bank begins to operate in its new environment. Each phase has an event that begins and ends the phase; however, different application areas may be in different phases at the same time.[10] Figure 3.3 graphically summarizes the process.

Day 0 is the conversion day. Significant and measurable events during the process are called deliverables. The timing of their delivery is relative to the conversion weekend. Typically, completing a deliverable requires several people, yet only one person will be assigned responsibility for it. Certain deliverables mark the termination of one phase and the beginning of another.

The first phase of the process, the *planning* phase, begins officially at day −170 with a written request for Conversion Team Members from the Bank's Management and from Information Services Management. The primary objective of this phase is to ensure that the key players in the conversion process have been identified and they have a common understanding regarding the bank's current environment, the conversion process, and their role within the project. This phase ends at day −120 when

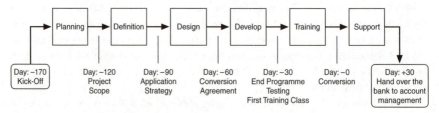

Fig. 3.3 Phases of the conversion process

---

[10] *Banc One Conversion Manual, General Reference.*

the bank returns the affiliation questionnaires and a scope document is generated using this information to describe the application areas being converted.

The *definition* phase begins at day −120 when the questionnaires received from the bank are disbursed to the application areas. The primary objective of this phase is to sketch the bank's future environment, begin mapping to get there, and identify major conversion issues. The phase ends at approximately day −90 when the application strategies are published by the different application areas. Because the application strategy is application area-specific, different applications will end this phase at different times.

The *design* phase begins at day −90 with the delivery of the application strategy to the bank. The primary objective of this phase is to resolve all the outstanding issues in the mapping from the existing bank application to BO applications. The phase ends at day −60 when the conversion agreement is published.

The *development* phase begins at approximately day −60 when the bank has received the Conversion Agreement. Each application area publishes its own Conversion Agreement. The primary objective of this phase is to develop the conversion programmes and to define the post-conversion environment of the bank. This phase ends at day −30 when testing of the conversion programmes is completed and the bank has started its first training class.

The *training* phase begins at approximately day −30 with the first bank training class. The main objective of this phase is to ensure that all preconditions for a successful conversion are met. The *training* phase ends on day 0, the conversion day.

The *support phase* begins the first day after conversion. The objective of the support phase is to ensure the bank has the skills to survive in their new post-conversion environment. The phase ends thirty days after conversion. At this point the converted bank is 'handed over' to performance support, another department within Client Services.

Training   Although most of the training effort occurs during the *Training* phase, preparation for the training activities as well as limited training of selected affiliate personnel may occur also during the other phases of the conversion process. Banc One Services Corporation provides for four kinds of training: Conversion Process, Customer Contact, Back Office, and Post-Conversion Training.

The objective of Conversion Process Training is to explain Banc One's conversion methodology to the new affiliate. It is conducted by BO conversion manager and is attended by the affiliate's president, his or her direct reports, the affiliate's conversion manager, and the affiliate's conversion team. It marks the official beginning of the conversion project (day −170).

Customer Contact Training is attended by all branch personnel. Using generic procedure manuals supplied by Information Services, branch trainers develop customized procedure manuals for hands-on training of the affiliate's personnel, sometimes with the help of computer simulators. Development of the customer contact training starts at about day −90. Branch trainers will be coached by conversion specialists for thirty to sixty hours in 'train-the-trainer' sessions. The customer contact training is delivered during the period from day -15 to day -2. Branch trainers will spend around eight hours training branch managers and customer service representatives reviewing procedures and forms related to new accounts, services, teller documents, maintenance of all types of accounts, procedures, and paper flow. Branch trainers will train teller personnel for five to ten hours on the explanation of procedural changes, introduction to new forms and substitute proof documents, changes in balancing the window and the branch, etc. Branch trainers are designated by the new affiliate.

Back Office Training is attended by people responsible for the daily operation of each application area, the supervisor of the operations department, and occasionally also by customer contact personnel. The training starts around day -45 and goes on until day -5. The applications are divided into the following groups: Demand Deposit, Time Deposit, Certificate of Deposits, Instalment Loan, Commercial Loan, and Customer Information. The training is conducted by the Information Services Applications Coordinator.

Post-conversion training educates the affiliate to survive in the post-conversion environment. Attendance to this training is decided by the affiliate's senior management and by the account manager. It is designed to help the affiliate resolve service problems and accommodate product enhancements. This training starts before the conversion and continues uninterrupted until after the conversion. The Account Manager conducts the training with assistance from the Conversion Manager.

Project control   To ensure the execution of a conversion project plan, several mechanisms have been put in place. Information Systems attempts to develop a plan, manage to the plan and meet everyone's expectations. The conversion plan can be customized for a specific conversion to provide advance warning of impending problems. The project's status is reviewed continually through status meetings and reports. Senior management is informed monthly of the status of key deliverables and of open issues.

Verbal agreements and casual memos are formalized in a set of formal documents or contracts which all parties review and approve to ensure mutual understanding. These documents are the Project Scope, the Application Strategy, and the Conversion Agreement. The Project Scope, issued at day -120, defines the boundaries of the conversion project. An Application Strategy is an initial statement of direction which is published by each application area at day -90 and documents the decisions made to that date and any outstanding issues. The Conversion Agreement, issued at day -60, serves as a binding contract which includes and supersedes any previous memo, telephone conversation, or other pre-existing informal understanding.

Roles and responsibilities   Key roles and their major responsibilities during the conversion process are assigned to personnel on both the converted bank side and on the BOSC Information Services side. Support personnel on both sides assist those performing key roles. There are three key roles on the affiliate's side and four on the Information Services side.

The three key roles on the affiliate's side are: sponsoring the conversion, coordinating conversion-related activities within the affiliate, and managing the conversion of specific application areas. The affiliate's management sponsors the conversion project by setting the direction of the conversion, defining its scope (with Banc One Services Corporation's help) and approving expenditures. The affiliate's Conversion Director, usually a senior manager, coordinates the conversion effort and is highly involved in resolving emerging issues. A team of application area specialists manages the conversion of specific application areas.

The four key roles on BOSC side are approval and monitoring, managing the conversion, converting specific applications, and coordinating across application areas. BOSC IS's management approves the commitments made by Information Services personnel and monitors the progress of the project. A conversion project manager ensures that all the needed resources are brought to the conversion, monitors the progress of the project, and reports its status to BOSC management. Application coordinators provide the primary contact within Information Services for issues related to the conversion of a specific application. Finally, a conversion specialist is responsible for special areas that tend to span multiple applications, such as defining and ordering new forms, training of the bank's personnel that work in direct contact with the customer, and developing customer notifications.

The aftermath of conversion   Overall, a conversion is considered successful if the transition from the existing affiliate's systems to BO systems goes unnoticed for those who have been only indirectly involved with the conversion. In such a case the conversion is said to be a non-event.

From the perspective of BOSC, success in the non-event sense is important but costs matter as well. A conversion is a costly enterprise and a cost overrun in one conversion could mean that another conversion may not be possible for budgetary reasons on that same year or that compromises will have to be made in staffing.

Timing issues are also important. Because the conversion date is fixed, delays in the completion of a key deliverable such as an application strategy may leave less time to complete any task dependent on that deliverable. Thus, for example, if insufficient time is left for testing an application, the application may end up being installed with partial or no testing of modifications made to it during the conversion. Any undetected problem may also lengthen the period of time that elapses before the BOSC conversion team can safely hand over the affiliate to the performance support group.

From the perspective of the customers of the affiliate, things are going to change with the conversion. Some financial products may be discontinued and new ones will come in their place. The notices and reports that customers get may change. In a successful conversion, the bank's customers will have been forewarned in advance of these changes and a promotional campaign will foster a positive attitude among the customers towards Banc One. In a successful conversion the bank should not lose customers because of the conversion.

Finally, from the Banc One's Corporate perspective, it is important that the converted bank's expectations have been met and that the conversion did not negatively impact the ability of BOSC to perform other planned conversions.

2.4. Dilemmas of conversion

Banc One has strong incentives to replicate exactly its systems and operating procedures in each affiliate. As BOSC's CEO explained:

Having the banks on one set of systems, with standard operations, will tremendously increase our affiliates' ability to provide a consistent level of high quality service. It also means we can make changes quickly, introduce new products, and operate at lower cost.

However, the degree of precision exacted in practice is sometimes sacrificed to secure the affiliate's commitment and cooperation. Without the affiliate's commitment, a conversion project is almost certainly doomed. Thus, a very important task for BOSC is to ensure that the affiliate's management is really committed to convert, that it communicates its commitment to all members of the bank, and that the bank is able to deliver on its promises.

During the early conversions, imposing exactness was not problematic. Indeed, the attitude towards the first acquired bank, was that of an inflexible conqueror. As described by a training specialist:

When I first came into Services Corp., that was about eight years ago we used to convert a bank application by application. For example at the time I was working with the commercial loan application group and we would go out and we would install commercial loan systems in a given bank. Without regard to what the other applications were doing and without regard to any client need. We called them up one day and we said we are going to do this this this be ready. We just called them, we said: 'you are on the calendar we are going to convert you in August, be ready. In May we are going to talk what we are going to do to you. And that was the attitude: 'DO TO YOU'.

However as acquired banks became larger, securing an affiliate's collaboration became a delicate task. Most of the banks that Banc One acquires perform reasonably well before the conversion. These banks are not always willing to let go ways of doing business to which they grew accustomed and that served them well. Converting to BO Uniform Products and Common Systems requires them to change at all levels. In some cases, they may even have to discard their own superior products or systems. The larger an affiliate is, the larger the scope of the required change. Thus, the better an affiliate performs before the conversion and the larger that affiliate is the more difficult it generally is to secure its commitment to cooperate with the conversion.

Bound to Banc One corporation by the 'Uncommon Partnership' principle of operational self-determination subject to satisfactory performance, an affiliate could theoretically opt to continue operating with their own information systems and procedures as long as it could make its systems compatible with those of Banc One to support Banc One's products and controls. If they opted so, however, they would need to devote significant attention and resources to keeping their own set of systems and procedures in line with the ever-evolving BO set of products; a very expensive proposition for a bank that needs simultaneously to meet the stiff and constantly rising performance standards of the Banc One family. In practice, few banks continued to operate with their original systems and none for very long.

Yet, many banks did choose nonetheless to invoke a less extreme version of the 'Uncommon Partnership' while negotiating the details of their conversion. As explained by an experienced conversion manager:

The banks are given too much leeway in what they will or will not do. I feel that conversion takes the role of justifying what they should convert in the bank rather than the bank justifying what they will not convert. This creates the need for conversion and then for support to maintain a myriad of different variations. This means that when new products are introduced or when an existing product is upgraded, this needs to be done separately for those that have different sets of products and systems.

This less extreme use of the 'Uncommon Partnership' by affiliates has particularly irksome implications for the conversion group. Affiliates convert to common systems but, rather than use Banc One's templates, they insist in developing their own operating procedures from scratch. They develop procedures that don't work and end up debugging them in real situations during the actual conversion. This learning by trial and error creates an additional burden on the already strained conversion unit during and soon after conversion and also increases demand for support. A substantial part of the errors that such a new affiliate will make could be avoided if the affiliate had been willing to heed the advice of the conversion unit.

The frustration of the conversion group with the 'Uncommon Partnership' stems from the fact that most banks, almost as a reflex, initially reject any advice which is not mandatory under the belief that they know better. Next, they commit avoidable errors. Then, faced with the consequences, the banks admit begrudgingly that they should have followed BOSC's advice. This cycle is described by a training specialist:

A lot of times I can see the problem coming which in hindsight they also see and they don't want to listen to me and that is so typical. We heard you say that to us but we didn't believe you. That's so typical. They understood but they refused to believe. And that happens a lot. In retrospect they say yes, we should have done it your way, but they can't know until they get through the process.

Consequently, many people within BOSC have begun to question openly how applicable is the 'Uncommon Partnership' when it comes to converting a new affiliate. As a vice-president of Operations Support commented:

The 'Uncommon Partnership' is a great philosophy. But we let it go into areas that we never intended to. We are beginning to realize how much this lack of standardization in systems and operations is costing Banc One.

And some sensed a hardening of BOSC's attitude towards new affiliates:

The impression as an organization that I'm getting is that people want us to change toward giving them more guidance, more direction in terms of telling them how we are planning to do that instead of telling them this is how we do it, we'd like you to do that but we really can't force you to do that. That's really moving from kind of middle of the road like it is a suggestion but not a requirement toward something like saying, well . . . this is a requirement.

Indeed, Banc One's senior management was considering the implementation of a new strategy whereby all banks would operate in a standard way, as soon as possible, running on a common set of systems. However, the risk with such a strategy of extreme standardization is that truly superior systems found in new affiliates could be lost.

Banc One has an operating practice called the 'best-of-the-best' designed to reduce that risk. BOSC will systematically look for best practices in a new affiliate during the early phases of a conversion. Practices found superior to those of Banc One are candidates for adoption by the entire BO network. As explained by a conversion vice-president:

Our posture is that we don't have all the best ideas. There are a lot of sharp, creative bankers out there. The banks we acquire are well run profitable banks. They are that way for a reason. They have done something in the product, in their technology or something in their operation that makes sense. So we say let's look at it, let's not just dismiss it out of hand. For example, in a recent conversion, an affiliate had a credit quality reporting system that was far better than anything we had. So not only we decided to keep it in place for them but we are putting together a project to make it available to everybody else.

3. Routinization of Conversion at Banc One

Banc One first converted a bank to its own DP systems in June of 1970 in Mansfield, Ohio. Subsequently, by mid-1993, it had converted over eighty more banks involving a total of over 135 conversions. The early conversions, during the mid- and late 1970s, were of small banks, each with a few hundred million of dollars in assets and a handful of branches.

In 1982, Banc One accelerated its acquisition pace, acquiring larger banks, first within the state of Ohio and later between 1986 and 1990 also in the states of Indiana, Michigan, and Kentucky. During this period, the bank performed many successful conversions. A few however, were problematic. The conversion capability of BOSC emerged both from repeated success and from learning from failed conversion projects. As recounted by a participant:

At first, when a particular bank needed to be converted, all individual departments did it when they wanted. Applications were more independent, we didn't have so much interdependence. People had a tacit process. No written procedures. When somebody left, we had to reinvent the wheel. About 6 years ago conversion management was formed, then they started creating the manual and the docs. Then, when the conversion management group was formed, they started coordinating across application areas. Conversions were done 'in-sync'. It was the first time I met other analysts, and that we started to work together, going to another bank. We began holding biweekly status meetings. In this way we became aware of the interdependencies. Thus we resolved interrelations during the conversion and not after. We became aware of how the system worked together, with a huge benefit to the conversion group. Every time we would run into a problem like that we would generate a task list. Then the problem became a check point and a task.

Thus, interdependencies between the different application groups were slowly recognized and articulated in conversion guidelines. This marked the beginning of the conversion management process. Every problem became first a checkpoint and then a task. As the pace of acquisitions increased the time spent by analysts in conversion activities increased significantly. As recounted by a system analyst:

At that time there were peaks and valleys of small conversions, routine ones, which made it difficult to justify extra people, dedicated fully to conversions. We thought that our primary role was to support existing applications. All of a sudden we had a new priority: to convert. Supporting existing applications went on to the back burner. We had to suspend new releases and deploy the resources to conversion. Suddenly we found ourselves assigned to conversions with deadlines cast in stone. We complained because we thought that our primary role was to support production, but nothing came about.

It was just a matter of time, before a separate group, specialized in bank conversion, was created.

One day I heard a new group was being formed and that they were looking for people. That was a very interesting transition. Then they hired a conversion director. They started to look for people that wanted to transfer. Ninety percent of the people that back then were performing conversions thought they won't be able to set up a conversion group independent from the application groups. The assumption was that they were to recruit from the inside. They went to each area that was already doing conversion. The areas thought it was a bad idea. Some of them reacted childishly saying—you think you can do without me? fine! I won't help. The initiative was triggered mainly by resource contention [system programmers and equipment was necessary to support conversions and application development, GS]. There was also a concern about presenting a coherent look as a corporation to the acquired bank.

The crystallization of the conversion methodology used by BOSC was essentially a reaction to severe problems experienced during a few conversions; most notably the conversion in 1986 of a $650 million bank with thirty-two branches in Lafayette, Indiana, which many within Banc One remember as the worst ever. These problematic conversions were followed shortly after by intense improvement efforts prompted by a visceral impetus to avoid repeating the same painful errors. The learning process is recounted by a training specialist:

Dave Van Lear was then the president of the services corporation and he wanted to get a set of common products supported by a set of common systems. That is where the term 'COMMON SYSTEMS' came from. We wanted to get all of our banks on the same systems. And we were not going to have two DDA systems, we were not going to have three LOAN systems, we were not going to have five this. We were going to have one common product and everybody is going to it. It was kind of an outcropping of the Indianapolis conversion, because when we did their conversions they wanted to keep their own systems and there was this tug of war about which systems they were going to use. So Common Systems became the preferred product that we'll be converting banks to and this group then became the group that was charged with doing the conversion. And Lafayette was our first attempt to do that, and I think we made a lot of mistakes in Lafayette. You'll hear a lot of horror stories about what happened there but it was a good learning experience. We found out what didn't work. And one of the things we found out was that there was no process. It took a process oriented senior executive, the conversion vice president and some other people in that group at that time to create our process, its deliverables and the ways of tracking a conversion. Once we had it on down on paper, other groups began to buy into the conversion management process and at the time the account manager was responsible also for the conversion and each account manager was responsible for a set number of banks and when conversion came up for that bank the account manager was also the conversion manager. Then we started to separate account management from conversion management and a conversion group was hired and this whole thing just mushroomed.

Banc One's conversion capability is admired throughout the banking industry. A well-known story inside the bank recounts a conversation, which took place during a bankers convention, between David Van Lear, technology guru and former CEO of the Services Company, and a banker from another institution. In that conversation, the banker was recounting to Mr Van Lear in great detail and with visible self-satisfaction how they managed to complete successfully the conversion of an acquired bank to their systems after a concerted effort that lasted three years. An unimpressed Van Lear replied: 'Really? we converted four banks over the past weekend.' The difference between the standard industry approach and Banc One's approach to conversion is explained by the training specialist:

We do a hell of a good job in converting organizations into the BO Common Systems. It is not painless but we do a good job of it. I've been in other industries and over the years you hear the horror stories of the months and months of dual systems where in the morning they have to do their work in the old system and in the afternoon they do their work in the new system. People are just astounded when they hear we don't do that. To our way of thinking that is a waste of time. We've got a process in place, we balance to what you had yesterday. You will have the same thing going forward. We pick you up and go forward. We don't do any of this dual stuff. We'll go back and do a conversion over again before we do dual.

4. The Challenge of Scope

BOSC's conversion capability is remarkable. Converting a large bank in a mere 180 days and making the transition from the existing bank's systems to BO Common Systems over a single weekend comes closest to what the word instantaneous could mean in such a setting. Completing a project of such complexity is a non-trivial feat. At full capacity, BOSC can currently complete ten such projects per year, with four to six projects overlapping at any given time.

BOSC capability to convert affiliates is strained by Banc One's accelerating acquisition-based growth.[11] Surpassing the $5 billion-in-assets mark in 1982, Banc One completed in the next ten years about thirty-six affiliations which together with the growth of its own existing affiliates boosted its total assets to a little over

---

[11] *Banc One Corporation: 1991 Annual Report*. See chart on p. 10.

$46 billion. During 1992, Banc One completed the affiliation of seven more banks and two Saving and Loans bringing its total assets to more than $75 billion.[12] Banc One seeks to acquire large market players, provided that these players are smaller than a third of Banc One's size. This, to help preserve the integrity of Banc One's culture. However, as Banc One grows so does the maximum size of a viable acquisition target. Indeed, during 1992 Banc One completed the affiliation of Team Bancshares, Inc. from Dallas, Texas, a bank that with 5.5 billion US$ in assets was larger than the entire BO family ten years before.

As the size of new affiliates increases so does the coordination effort required for their conversion. Because of interdependencies, the intensity of this coordination effort may increase more than proportionately with the affiliate's size. One way to mitigate coordination demands for affiliates that have many banks is to 'divide and conquer' the conversion by scheduling sequential conversions on a bank-by-bank basis. Another way to reduce the coordination effort is to split the conversions, by converting each time only a subset of the applications.

Even though these approaches may reduce the coordination effort required for each conversion, they increase the overall demands on BOSC resources to convert an affiliate; thus limiting the number of conversions that it could attempt simultaneously in a given year. That is because of multiple set-up costs and also because there often is some inevitable duplication of activity in a staggered conversion. Furthermore, because affiliation to Banc One may require substantial and sometimes dramatic changes, an affiliate will typically want to complete the transition in the shortest possible time so as to be able to focus on meeting Banc One's performance standards. Thus, put under pressure to improve performance, once an affiliate starts a conversion, it wants, like BOSC, to compress its duration. This generates a phenomenon akin to a window of opportunity for a conversion to occur before the need to meet BO performance requirements and the problems of day-to-day operation consumes the attention of the affiliate's senior management.

Hence, when time comes to set the parameters of a conversion, both BOSC—eager to perform as many conversions as possible in a given year to satisfy Banc One's appetite for acquisitions—and the affiliate—eager to acquire Banc One's products and capabilities in the shortest possible time—will both have incentives to maximize the scope of the conversion. They will attempt to convert as many systems as possible simultaneously and if the affiliate has many banks they will prefer to convert all banks simultaneously.[13]

This trend to increase scope can be observed in recent conversions. The conversion of a fourteen-bank affiliate in the state of Wisconsin was performed in six steps. Three banks were converted in February, three in April, two in May, two in June, three in July, and one in September 1992. In contrast, in the next conversion, all five banks of an affiliate in the state of Illinois were converted at once in December 1992.

---

[12] Currently, BO assets are a little over $261 billion dollars.
[13] Some services, like reporting a customer's balance in an account located in another bank, can only be offered after all of the affiliate banks have been converted. This provides added incentives to convert all banks simultaneously.

Then, in an even more daring state-wide conversion, all six banks of a new affiliate in the state of Colorado were converted simultaneously.

The demands of the Colorado conversion exceeded the capability of BOSC conversion methodology creating serious difficulties for BOSC and for the Colorado affiliate, difficulties comparable to those experienced during the hitherto 'worst-ever' Lafayette conversion. The Colorado conversion, the most ambitious conversion to that date, 'hit every scenario mankind would know'.[14] The Colorado experience renewed the debate within BOSC as to what should be the largest scope of a conversion attempted with BO methods, or with any method. BO conversion routines were again challenged by the increased scope of conversion.

5. Conclusion

The example of Banc One illustrates just how profitable replicating routines could be. As a rule of thumb, Banc One roughly doubles on average the return on assets (ROA) of the already decently performing banks it acquires.[15] Acquired banks come into the system with a typical ROA of 0.7 per cent and within three to four years most of these banks improve past the 1.5 per cent mark, some surpass 2 per cent. Successful replication is worth to Banc One roughly one ROA percentage point, effectively doubling the affiliate's return on assets. Banc One's systems and operating procedures help increase revenues by supporting a standardized set of products and sparing the new affiliate data-processing-related distractions from the business of banking. Likewise, they help decrease costs by enhancing operational control. These gains from replication do provide support for the assumption that in general replication can make excellent economic sense even when the replication itself is complex and costly.

Banc One's example clearly illustrates just how costly and complex a real-world instance of replication could be. In a recent conversion, the affiliate had forty-three branches spanning the entire state of Colorado, 2,100 employees, and 2.5 billion in assets. The conversion involved about sixty full-time highly skilled professionals during a period of six months and it cost over a million dollars to Banc One.

Banc One's example shows that the replication dilemma, to what extent to strive for exactness in replicating a routine, is a real and rather complex managerial issue for Banc One. Deciding how precisely to replicate their common systems and operating procedures involves trading off economies of scale and flexibility with the need to secure commitment from a new affiliate, which is a necessary ingredient for a successful conversion.

Furthermore Banc One's example suggests that when a practice is replicated in an existing site, the template may be affected by the replication. A portion of the

---

[14] In the words of a manager of the conversion unit.

[15] The banking industry traditional, market independent, measure of performance. A bank with 0.7 % ROA is considered standard. An ROA of 1% is considered good. Banc One's corporate average ROA was 1.5% in 1993.

prevailing practices in the recipient site prior to the replication may find their way into the original template, polluting or improving it.

Finally, the example of Banc One suggests that there may be inherent limits to the routinization of replication. Replication of routines is, in the theoretical world of evolutionary economics as in Banc One example, primarily a mechanism for firm growth. After a replication, however, the firm will be larger. Hence, the routines that underlie the firm's success may have grown larger and possibly more complex. Hence, internal growth by replication may involve routines that themselves create contingencies that institutionalized ways of replicating may not be able to handle. Hence the routinization of replication has a built-in challenge.

This challenge is eloquently described by the conversions vice-president who created the BOSC conversion unit:

When we acquire a bank, we bring it on-board and we take it from less than a 1.0 to a 1.5 or a 1.8 [ROA]. They have a year or two to get there. In a conversion we expect increasingly larger and more sophisticated banks to [abandon their way of doing things and] start operating like a BO bank overnight. To do that they have to change their systems, restructure their operations around those systems and to implement the right controls and procedures. As acquired banks become larger that is becoming a serious issue; a real challenge.

References

Arrow, K. (1971). *Classificatory Notes on the Production and Transmission of Technical Knowledge*. Amsterdam: North Holland.

Eisenhardt, K. (1989). 'Building theories from case study research', *Academy of Management Review*, 14(4): 532–50.

Glaser, B. L., and A. L. Strauss (1968). *The Discovery of Grounded Theory: Strategies for Qualitative Research*. Chicago: Aldine.

Hall, G. R., and R. E. Johnson (1967). *Aircraft Co-Production and Procurement Strategy*. Santa Monica, Calif.: Rand Corporation.

Kanter, R. M. (1989). *Banc One Corporation–1989*. Harvard Business School.

Kirk, J., and M. L. Miller (1986). *Reliability and Validity in Qualitative Research*. London: Sage.

Leidner, R. (1993). *Fast Food, Fast Talk: Service Work and the Routinization of Everyday Life*. Berkeley and Los Angles: University of California Press.

Leonard-Barton, D. (1990). 'A dual methodology for case studies: Synergistic Use of a Longitudinal Single Site with Replicated Multiple Sites', *Organization Science* 1(3): 248–66.

Nelson, R. R., and S. G. Winter (1982). *An Evolutionary Theory of Economic Change*. Cambridge, Mass.: Harvard University Press.

Shannon, C. E., and W. Weaver (1949). *The Mathematical Theory of Communication*. Chicago: University of Illinois Press.

Teece, D. (1977). 'Technology Transfer by Multinational Corporations: The Resource Cost of Transferring Technological Know-How', *Economic Journal*, 87: 242–61.

Uyterhoeven, H. (1994). *Banc One Corporation–1993*. Harvard Business School.

Winter, S. G. (1995). 'Four Rs of Profitability: Rents, Resources, Routines and Replication', in C. A. Montgomery (ed.), *Resource-based and Evolutionary Theories of the Firm: Towards a Synthesis*. Boston, Mass.: Kluwer Academic Publishers, 147–78.

4

Limited Inquiry and Intelligent Adaptation in Semiconductor Manufacturing

M. Thérèse Flaherty

1. Introduction

While plant and animal species adapt through 'natural' processes of selection and variation, businesses are guided in their adaptation by managers who at least try to exercise another powerful evolutionary force: intelligence. The importance of understanding this intelligent adaptation of businesses increased dramatically during the late twentieth century as innovation and technology change accelerated, as knowledge-based services increased, and as competition intensified and globalized. Research on managing the creative and learning processes of firms has often focused on having enough of the necessary human invisible assets[1] and on ensuring that the proper creativity was encouraged by innovative management.[2] These scholars emphasize the importance of intellectual assets, growth, and diversity, allowing that competition performs selection.

In contrast, this chapter examines the possibility that in firms' intelligent adaptation managers actively generate variation through their allocation of assets and encouragement of creativity and, in addition, may limit the ways in which individuals can exercise initiative in accumulating process knowledge in technologically dynamic manufacturing.[3] Some important challenges in managing inquiry in complex tech-

I wrote this chapter in response to several conversations with Sid Winter of the Wharton School, University of Pennsylvania. I am indebted to Sid for his interest, his insightful questions, and his patient editing. The chapter is based on my understandings that have come from years of fieldwork and empirical study of the semiconductor industry and of operations. I am indebted to more practitioners and scholars than I can practically name for teaching me during that long apprenticeship. Roger Bohn and Ramchandran Jaikumar deserve special mention for their development of the theory of stages of knowledge in manufacturing which underlies the conceptual framework of this paper. Of course, the errors and unclear thought that remain in the paper are my responsibility.

[1] See, e.g. Penrose (1959); Itami (1987); Dierickx and Cool (1989); Cohen and Levinthal (1990); Helfat (1997).

[2] Leonard-Barton (1995) and Nonaka and Takeuchi (1995).

[3] This portrays a pattern of management action that differs from the routines that Nelson and Winter (1982) suggest are the basis for continuity and performance in organizations in that they do entail intelligence and creativity. They do, however, have much in common with the Nelson and Winter routines in that the mechanisms do seem to provide a sustainable competence, to be related to specific individuals, to be easier with repetition generally, and to be difficult for other organizations to copy. In the terminology of Winter (in Cohen et al., 1996) they fall under the heading of 'heuristics' rather than 'routines in the narrow sense'.

nologically dynamic manufacturing differ from the challenges of repetitive material-processing operations. This chapter suggests that they can be met by limits to inquiry.

Intuitively, these limits to inquiry reduce the challenges of coordinating a large number of decentralized individual experts who must work together cooperatively and with motivation and at their own initiative in large teams defined by unpredictable problems. When there are far too many opportunities for individuals to take initiative coordination requirements can be formidable. The limits to inquiry commonly observed in semiconductor manufacturing seem to solve that coordination problem—not perfectly, but adequately. They help individuals to limit their unproductive coordination discussion and spend most of their time and attention on productive problem-solving.

The concept of limits is important in management theory whenever bounded rationality is acknowledged.[4] Likewise, limits are important in business strategy where much research and scholarship has suggested that the fit or consistency among the elements of a business is more important to its success than the superlative choice of its goals or the performance of its functional parts.[5] Further, the notion of limits enhancing productivity is familiar in operations where Wickham Skinner suggested that the best-performing factories should be 'focused'.[6] While many meanings have been attributed to Skinner's term 'focus', a simple interpretation is that separating the people who perform two different activities and not allowing them to collaborate will allow both to perform better. This chapter investigates a possible foundation for these limits: the need for managers to bound the ways in which individuals exercise initiative in accumulating process knowledge in technologically dynamic manufacturing.

Section 2 presents a conceptual framework relating quality, process knowledge, and technological change. Here process knowledge is the knowledge workers, managers, and engineers possess regarding why and how particular conditions in the process result in products with particular characteristics. Process knowledge is fundamental to improving operations performance in both quality and product function. Furthermore, Section 3 suggests that the essence of adaptation in manufacturing operations is using current process knowledge to increase process knowledge and then adapting operations to improve their performance. The management challenge described in Section 3 is that managing inquiry in technologically dynamic manufacturing requires not only resources but perhaps new methods of coordination.

Section 4 explains why the semiconductor industry is a good context in which to examine the methods managers in manufacturing have used to solve the coordination challenges of inquiry. Section 5 reports on the characteristics of semiconductor manufacturing that make coordination especially demanding and on a few examples

---

[4] Beginning with Simon (1945), Cyert and March (1963), and going on to Nelson and Winter (1982), limits on behaviour have been important elements in the understanding of administrative behaviour.

[5] See e.g. Dosi *et al.* (1992).

[6] Skinner's (1974) meaning has been interpreted as factories which make fewer products are more productive, factories which make fewer different products are more productive than those which make a wider variety, and there have been many arguments about the basis for the separation and simplicity Skinner argued for.

of how managers of manufacturing in the industry commonly use limits to inquiry to solve coordination challenges during normal times.[7] Section 6 describes several limits on inquiry managers in the industry discovered as they examined their manufacturing during a time of survival stress in the late 1980s. Together these sections suggest that limits to inquiry are just as important to intelligent adaptation in semiconductors as providing resources. Furthermore, they suggest that the kinds of limits imposed can have very important impacts on the direction of adaptation and that therefore they deserve further management attention and study.

Of course, in the evolutionary tradition, this chapter makes no presumption that all managers in semiconductor manufacturing knew perfectly how to manage intelligent adaptation. Nor does it suggest that limits to inquiry are the only important method managers in semiconductors have to do this. Likewise, it does not suggest that all semiconductor managers use limits. It does use common practice in semiconductor manufacturing during the 1980s to generate hypotheses about how managers can solve some of the important coordination challenges of managing adaptation. If this chapter is successful in its goals, limits to inquiry will be examined more closely in this industry and others.

2. A Conceptual Framework for Intelligent Adaptation in Manufacturing

In this section I present a conceptual framework for understanding the relations among process knowledge, quality, and technological progress in manufacturing operations. This framework is based on research by Roger Bohn and Ramchandran Jaikumar on managing stages of knowledge in manufacturing.[8]

2.1. *Quality and the manufacturing process*

Virtually all manufacturing processes generate products[9] that have attributes that are unacceptable to the customer, or in some respect fail to meet specifications established by the producer. Even in apparently stable processes there are recurrent defects: in automobile assembly, for example, recurrent problems with paint flaws are endemic to all companies, even the most advanced Japanese companies.

Disturbances that cause defects in repetitive production processes are practically inevitable. Input materials are not strictly homogeneous over time; equipment and people get fatigued and are changed by the repetitive process itself; the environment changes in ways that managers do not measure; interactions among attributes of products and perceptions of product attributes by customers and managers also change over time. Likewise, customers change and different customers interact with

---

[7] The evidence presented in Section 5 is common knowledge about common practice in semiconductor manufacturing in the early 1980s, and that presented in Section 6 comes from conversations the author had with a number of equipment vendors to the industry during the late 1980s. This evidence was gathered as background for research described in Flaherty (1990): a study of twenty-two semiconductor factories in Japan and the USA.

[8] See e.g. Jaikumar and Bohn (1992) and Bohn (1995).

[9] Or services. For simplicity, I will refer to products, although the framework presented here can be readily applied to service operations.

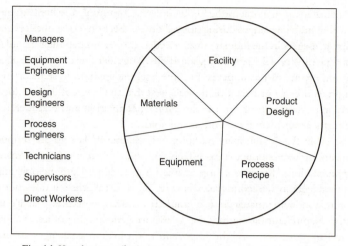

Managers

Equipment
Engineers

Design
Engineers

Process
Engineers

Technicians

Supervisors

Direct Workers

Fig. 4.1 Key elements affecting output in a technologically dynamic factory

manufacturing and service processes differently; people involved in repetitive production processes make mistakes or otherwise behave counter-productively. Figure
4.1 indicates many physical, human, and information elements that interact in
production. Changes in any element can change the distribution of the attributes
of the outputs of the process.

Figure 4.2 illustrates recurrent defects for a single attribute of the product. It
depicts the possibility that the product attribute is understood by the producer well
enough that the factory has established limits for the attribute that indicate acceptability of the product to customers—but is not capable of keeping the process within
those limits consistently. Bohn and Jaikumar call such a production process in the
measurement stage of knowledge. At this stage managers know enough about their
process to measure product attributes in the factory and to determine limits within
which the product will meet the functional standards in use set by the factory
managers. The measured value of the attribute therefore must lie between the upper
and lower control limits in order for a product to be acceptable to customers. In

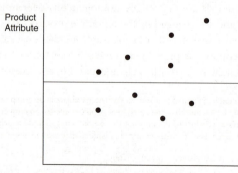

Fig. 4.2 Measured stage of knowledge

addition, the figure reflects the randomness of the process by the scatter of the points representing observations of different products. If the attributes of a product lie outside the control limits, then the product is unacceptable and should not be shipped to customers. Conformance quality is easily measured by the per cent of defects or observations outside the control limits. The term 'quality' is used in this chapter to mean conformance quality.[10]

Figure 4.2 suggests that the distribution of attributes is tending up and to a mean outside the control limits. This, of course, if allowed to continue, means that the product would eventually have a yield of zero. Repetitive production processes appear inevitably to be non-stationary in the sense of having an inherent tendency to drift out of the control limits.

Manufacturing managers use quality control to prevent the distribution of product and service attributes from straying outside the control limits. To do this they must ensure that the root causes of disturbances that would make the distribution move permanently are eliminated from the process; they can ignore transient disturbances.[11] A transient disturbance to handwriting, for example, would be a person bumping the table on which I was writing, while a permanent disturbance would be my changing from writing with my right hand to writing with my left hand. The bump would move a single point or word out of the control limits, while the switch of hands would mean that my process had changed permanently and the handwriting had become much less legible: it had moved permanently out of the control limits.[12]

Two comments are in order about additional issues that complicate the story, but do not fundamentally change it. First, many attributes of most products are important to customers and are considered by producers. If the values of these attributes behave like independent random variables, then the conformance quality is one minus the product of the yields (percentage acceptable) for the various attributes.[13] Thus, it can be very difficult to achieve high yields on a product with many critical attributes. Second, in practice, firms that inspect their products for defects do not accurately identify all the defects. Their inspection procedures identify some false positives and false negatives, leading them to ship some products that are defective even though they passed inspection and to scrap some good products that inspection incorrectly indicates are defective.

2.2. *Quality and stages of process knowledge*

Profitable production systems may initially display distributions like those in Figure 4.2. Figure 4.3 shows a distribution of an attribute of a process that has considerably

---

[10] When the meaning performance quality is intended, in this chapter the full term is used.

[11] Of course, the distinction between 'permanent' and 'transient' disturbances oversimplifies a complex reality. Part of the problem that managers face is to determine which disturbances are permanent enough to demand attention and which will 'take care of themselves'; the disturbances don't come with labels on them. Control limits can be viewed as a practical device for providing labels.

[12] This example comes from a paper on managing quality in hospitals.

[13] More complex interdependencies of defect rates among attributes are of course likely. If there is positive correlation among the defect rates, then the yield of the product is greater than one minus the product of the yields. The precise formula is not of importance here.

M. T. Flaherty

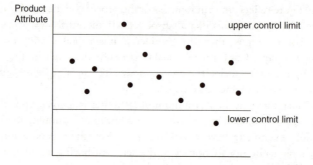

Fig. 4.3 Controlled stage of knowledge

less variance than that in Figure 4.2 and appears to be stationary: furthermore, when observations outside the control limits are encountered, the attributes are subsequently returned to within the control limits by elimination of the proximate causes. This process distribution indicates that the process is 'controlled' or 'in control', in the sense that manufacturing managers know how to change the process in order to return the product attributes to within the control limits.

In some factories, managers go beyond the effort to cope with permanent disturbances as they occur, and they eliminate the root causes of most large disturbances. This suggests that the inevitable disturbances in production processes have been reduced to such an extent that there is very little chance of the products being made by the process having unacceptable attributes. In Figure 4.4 the results of such variance reduction can be seen in a distribution of product attributes that lies entirely within the control limits. The managers of such a process are said to possess another stage of process knowledge, and their manufacturing process is said to be 'capable' of making the product.

Comparisons among three similar processes in the measurement (Figure 4.2), control (Figure 4.3), and capability (Figure 4.4) stages illustrates the reasons for the quality management adage: 'quality is free.' Quality is achieved by discarding defective products in a measurement stage and achieved only through active quality control efforts when the process is in the control stage. In the capability stage, however, the

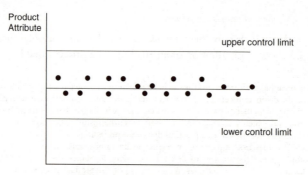

Fig. 4.4 Capability stage of knowledge

factory has little or no need to deploy costly resources for several conformance quality-related knowledge activities: it has no need of inspection, finds no waste, and has none of the confusion in repetitive processes that arises from unforeseen problems due to interactions of multiple disturbances. These savings, the adage says, more than offset the investment costs in permanently higher quality; indeed, the investments pay off so quickly that the 'invest now, returns later' aspect can be overlooked.

Conformance quality, of course, increases dramatically from the measured stage of knowledge (Figure 4.2) through the controlled stage (Figure 4.3) to the capability stage (Figure 4.4). In some products this dramatic increase in conformance quality is so important that it affects not only costs but product performance. In cars, for instance, the attribute of reliability is so highly valued by customers that a big improvement creates something amounting to a new product, not just a lower-cost version of the original product.

2.3. Process knowledge beyond quality

Beyond this increase in quality, there are further possibilities for the increase in the knowledge about the production process. One is what Bohn and Jaikumar say is a new stage of knowledge: characterization. This is illustrated in Figure 4.5 by control limits which are tight and different for two products produced by the same process. The need for characterization arises when a process makes two products, there is a need to change its recipe between the two, and there are often problems that arise when the process conditions are changed: characterization is achieved when the process for both products is well enough understood—when sufficient disturbances are eliminated that no defects are generated when the process attributes are changed between products.[14]

But improvements in process knowledge yield benefits that extend well beyond improvements in conformance quality. As noted above, progress through the knowledge stages brings cost savings because less effort is required for inspection and

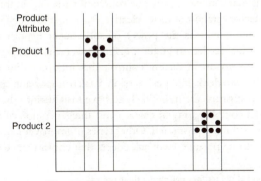

Fig. 4.5 Characterized stage of knowledge

[14] Jaikumar and Bohn (1992) and Bohn (1995) argue that this can be done only after very low process variability within each process has been achieved.

quality control. Also, better process knowledge facilitates improvement in business performance through modifications in process and product design, and through new product introductions. For example, productivity can be increased (without necessarily reducing defects) by changing the process flow and work definition, by substituting new materials or changing the proportions of ingredients in the product recipe.

Additions to process knowledge also enhance the ability to improve the product in terms of new features and better performance. One round of such improvements often enables another round. Management of human resources may also be positively affected by improvements in process knowledge. Adjustments may be made to make work less strenuous; these may be reflected in quality, but they may also be reflected in productivity, labour–management relations, and the willingness of workers to improve operations and to try new things.[15]

The attributes of any product that are measured and monitored at any one time are limited and change over time; managers, because of their bounded rationality, can only track a limited number of attributes. As the variability of one attribute diminishes, managers change the control limits as well as the attributes with which they are concerned. For a given product at one time, different attributes are usually managed at different stages of process knowledge, and the stage of knowledge for one attribute changes over time. For example, as control of one attribute is achieved technological progress in product functionality may require focusing on another attribute where the stage of process knowledge is lower. In a new product generation, for example, the stage of knowledge about many measured attributes can increase during a product generation, but decline between successive generations; such a dynamic is sketched in Figure 4.6.

Quality—defined in terms of low process variability—nevertheless occupies a special place among these dimensions of improvement. This is because as process variability decreases and the stage of knowledge increases, it becomes easier to learn almost anything else about a process. Thus, increasing conformance quality increases the effectiveness of efforts to acquire further process knowledge of all sorts. Intuitively, the reason is that eliminating any one source of variability in the process makes the other causal factors stand out more clearly. The statistical version of this is that the reduced variance increases the power of subsequent hypothesis tests, or reduces the sample size needed to attain a given power. Since experimentation and statistical testing do go on in quality control, this interpretation is more than a metaphor. But the 'Sherlock Holmes' version is also important: as variability decreases, expert investigators are more likely to have insights into the possible causal structures behind a complex array of clues. Thus, the generation of fruitful hypotheses, as well as the testing, is promoted. Other types of improvement do not typically have the sorts of strong positive feedback effects that conformance quality has.[16]

---

[15] I am indebted to Sid Winter for drawing out these points.

[16] Winter (1982) argued that scientific knowledge and 'productive knowledge' are quite different things because the latter, unlike the former, is not directed to causal understanding as an end in itself. In a production setting, understanding is valued only insofar as it makes production more profitable. In this perspective, 'root cause analysis' and related quality management techniques can be seen as a response to

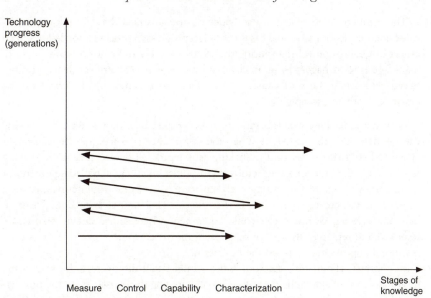

Fig. 4.6 Sketch of the dynamics of stages of knowledge and technological progress

3. Inquiry: Managing Progress within and between Stages of Knowledge

This section extends the framework from Section 2 to explain how managers adapt their manufacturing operations (improve quality and make technological progress) by increasing process knowledge and how management of these inquiry activities must differ from management of traditional manufacturing operations.

3.1. Inquiry as a distinctive activity

Inquiry increases process knowledge within and between stages.[17] Inquiry can decrease process variability and generate ideas for all kinds of improvements in product and process, including quality control. Inquiry activities share some characteristics with traditional material processing operations: they use scarce and productive resources, and they have many alternative uses. Inquiry activities also differ from traditional material processing operations. First, they are not repetitive, and they require intelligence and motivation. Second, the identification of inquiry opportunities must often be done by people closely involved in operations. Third, inquiry activities often require participation by a large, unpredictable network of knowledgeable individuals. Fourth, many individuals who are most valuable in increasing process knowledge acquire their expertise through activities, like production, which create substantial value to the organization.

the hazards of myopia involved in conforming to Winter's characterization: the long-run pay-off to improved understanding may substantially exceed the visible short-run pay-off (66–7).

[17] Bohn (1995) provides more details on how inquiry might be expected to differ among stages of knowledge.

The distinctiveness of inquiry activities can be illustrated by discussion of root-cause analysis. Root-cause analysis is central to progress in process knowledge and an aspect of quality control that during the 1980s was very difficult for many Western manufacturing managers to appreciate and implement. The critical distinction between eliminating the root causes of an effect versus removing the effect can be illustrated with an example.

Consider a machine which begins to shake because its motor shakes, the shaking causing defects in the products. When the disturbance is noted, a technician might arrive and see that the reason the shaking causes product defects is that the shaking has loosened the motor mount; removing the effect might entail replacing the motor mount and perhaps incorporating such replacement in future routine maintenance. This, of course, creates extra costs in the process. This kind of 'bandaiding' is often used in servicing complex electronic equipment where entire circuit boards are removed and replaced (instead of diagnosed) on the customers' premises; it is used because it appears cheaper—in the near term.

In contrast, eliminating the root cause would entail discovering the reason the motor began to shake in the first place and eliminating that reason from the process. Typically, this does not introduce new, *continuing* costs and steps to the process. But it does require more time to diagnose and eliminate the problem; it requires generally a more expert maintenance person; when the system is complex many problems must be addressed by a team with members who are experts in different aspects of the process and product (enumerated in Figure 4.1) to accomplish the diagnosis. Such teams come together for particular projects on an as-needed basis in many quality improvement programmes, hence the subtle scheduling, time-sharing, and team aspects of quality improvement and process knowledge management.

This example shows, for example, how managers face some short- versus long-term trade-offs as they allocate the time of their knowledge workers among problems and opportunities for inquiry. The capacity for knowledge work in most factories is limited and this imposes a trade-off between production and experimentation: some of the very same resources (people, materials, machine time) are used for production, new product introduction, and productivity increase.[18] Facing limits on each resource used in knowledge work and requirements for final product, managers must constantly make trade-offs among the various learning projects and between those projects and actual production. These trade-offs are closely related to the current and future performance of their business.

In part, the limits on the available capacity arise simply from the limited number of individuals available, just as in traditional factory work. But they also result from the need to access particular experts on particular issues at particular points

[18] There are also trade-offs made about which problems or opportunities workers should focus upon. Juran (1979) and Deming (1986) both provide guidance about which ones ought to be addressed first if one is only interested in improving quality or reducing process variability; but, as discussed above, there are many opportunities for knowledge increase that do not reduce process variability and increase quality.

in the investigation process and to have particular data available at other particular points. Specific individuals are needed, at points that cannot be anticipated, to help answer a question, to run a particular machine with an experimental setting, or just to try to remember what happened with a given lot on a given day. These specialized resources are unique, and difficulties in accessing seemingly small details often delay knowledge projects or undermine their effectiveness. In a manufacturing job shop computerized MRP (material requirements scheduling) systems are often required to ensure effective scheduling of complex, multi-purpose machine tools to unique and complex jobs and maximal output. But the need in knowledge-based work like inquiry for a complex and not fully anticipatable network of participants can be a very strong constraint on effective capacity of any organization to do knowledge work because scheduling systems like MRPs require known input requirements.

3.2. Challenges in allocating resources to inquiry

The capacity of knowledge resources cannot be allocated to forthcoming projects simply by assigning resources periodically. First, forecasting the capacity of a particular knowledge worker or group of workers in terms of opportunities is generally impossible and forecasting the opportunities themselves is often difficult. In some inquiry contexts, useful estimates of capacity from comparable projects can be constructed; for example, Brooks[19] cites the several consistent estimates of the hour requirements (inverse of capacity) of typical programmers to do software development, a task requiring a great deal of intellectual talent and ingenuity which might normally be assumed to be incomparable across problems. But in many factories at the measurement or control stages of knowledge, measuring the available capacity for knowledge work like quality control and root-cause analysis is difficult because the defects and their causes cannot be well anticipated. Second, when manufacturing processes are complex, even tracking the resource inputs applied to a particular opportunity is difficult. Further, the problems change—if not from day to day then definitely from week to week.

A third reason for the management difficulty in allocating knowledge workers to opportunities in operations is that real-time indications that the capacity of knowledge workers is insufficient differ from those that a machine has too little capacity for the work assigned to it. The machine, as we well know, works at a constant pace; when that pace is inadequate a pile of inventory awaiting processing appears very quickly in front of it. Professional workers do not provide such obvious signals; they are often reluctant to say that they cannot do something. Instead, they prefer to work overtime, or take on several projects in parallel and stretch out the finishing times of all of them. In some ways, though, people and machines do respond similarly to the strains of inadequate capacity. When machines get over committed, often their operators and managers delay scheduled maintenance; both get fatigued and tend to break down if overcommitted for an extended time.

---

[19] Brooks (1975).

A fourth reason for the management difficulty in allocating workers to knowledge opportunities in operations is that knowledge work requires intelligence, motivation, initiative, and attention, all of which can be difficult to evaluate. In terms of the shaking motor example above, it is difficult for many managers to know exactly how difficult it is to provide a root-cause diagnosis of the shaking motor. The individuals working in the field must think, respond to problems as they arise, and identify the opportunities for valuable work. Clearly, the time required to replace parts is much more predictable (as well as shorter) in this example than the time required to perform a root-cause diagnosis. When the problems encountered are less repetitive, the difficulty in forecasting capacity increases, the requirement for intelligence, expertise, initiative, and motivation on the part of the employees increases. Of course, managing to select intelligent and expert workers, and then to motivate them to work independently is a central challenge in management and especially in the management of inquiry.[20]

3.3. *Effective management of inquiry*

Effective management of inquiry, therefore, can not be pre-programmed.[21] Instead it must involve employees in identifying and deciding the opportunities and problems to which they will allocate their time and attention. It is not clear how to manage such activities. Some suggest creativity and slack resources, but these still leave open the methods by which individuals decide the problems on which they will work in a situation where there are many opportunities and knowledge is distributed unequally through the factory.

In such situations, some suggest that managers promote in all their employees a general understanding of organizational priorities. But this means that individuals must participate and they must not 'leave their heads at the gate'. They need to be somewhat self-regulating and make their own decisions about what matters. Managers often help their employees to understand what are the high-priority projects in the factory, and guide their judgements about where to allocate their time. But they must also stand ready to intervene to ensure that 'the war is not lost for the want of a horseshoe nail'. Such an approach can be highly time-consuming, not to mention frustrating because it would require so many meetings and discussions.

The question posed for fieldwork is whether managers in some technologically dynamic manufacturing industry have devised some other methods to allocate knowledge effort to inquiry—methods which may not achieve the first-best solution, but which economize on coordination.

---

[20] Studies of NUMMI (the GM-Toyota alliance for manufacturing), for example, suggest just this: that the learning factory actually has very few workers who self-determine and participate in inquiry about process knowledge. Instead, the NUMMI workers for the most part are highly directed from above with their inquiry efforts structured by management. See Adler and Cole (1993, 1994) and Berrgren (1994) for instance.

[21] The central challenge of managing inquiry discussed here focuses on the function of the firm as sharing and transferring knowledge of individuals within a group. This aspect of firms is suggested by Kogut and Zander (1992) as a major advantage firms have over markets.

4. Observing Intelligent Adaptation in Semiconductor Manufacturing

Semiconductor manufacturing appears to be an excellent context in which to identify methods managers have devised to coordinate inquiry and intelligent adaptation. The industry has exhibited very rapid product and process change, manufacturing managers struggling with process variability and quality, and firms trading leadership as successive products were introduced.

The industry has, of course, seen tremendous technological progress in its products and processes since the invention of the transistor in the late 1940s. There has been a dramatic increase in volume and functionality of products and a dramatic decrease in their price per transistor. The industry which began in the early 1950s grew in revenue at roughly 30 per cent a year for over forty years. In 1970 the most advanced memory (DRAM) product had a capacity of 1,000 bits; in 1981 it was close to 64,000; in 1990 1 million bits; and in 2000 it is projected to be 256 million bits. In microprocessors, the number of transistors per chip increased from a few hundred in the 4004 Intel microprocessor in 1971 to several million in the Intel Pentium microprocessor by the early 1990s.[22] At the same time, the cost of the products declined rapidly. Gordon Moore was astonishingly accurate for several decades in his prediction at a conference in 1965 that the number of transistors on a chip would double every year.[23]

Manufacturing process knowledge in one product generation often was dependent on the process knowledge achieved in earlier generations, even though the stage of knowledge inevitably decreased as a new product generation began manufacturing as in Figure 4.6. New process equipment must be devised for each product generation. Although some equipment could be used in many generations, photolithography and test equipment often had to be improved dramatically between generations. With each improvement came a higher vulnerability to contamination. A particle landing on a circuit during processing can build in a short circuit if it connects two circuit elements. A particle too small to cause a short in one generation of a circuit might be large enough to do so in the next generation. Smaller particles can 'kill' circuits. The quest for control of contamination problems led to the pursuit of ever-cleaner environments as semiconductor technology advanced. By the mid-1980s clean rooms in which DRAMs were made had become cleaner than hospital operating rooms; workers wore clean suits and masks, took air showers and masks in working in the environment. Many in the industry believe that the ability of the factories to make one generation of product is dependent on the experience of the firm in reducing variability (by root-cause analysis) in the previous generation's factory.

---

[22] Chip is a term used in the industry to denote a single integrated circuit.

[23] A precise statement according to Patterson *et al.* (1989: 371) is the number of transistors on a chip in year T = (number of transistors in 1964) times 2 raised to the power (T minus 1965). The cost of processing a chip is often assumed to be roughly static, so this translates into the cost of a given chip being reduced by half-year. Moore enunciated his 'law' at the conference and did not immediately publish it, so interpretations abound in industry folklore. According to Robert Noyce (1977), Moore first published the law ten years after he announced it in Moore (1975). Hutcheson and Hutcheson (1996) present a graph of technology progress in microprocessors and memory between 1970 and the late 1990s.

Indeed, in many cases process steps developed (using root-cause analysis) in one generation were used directly in the next (when another group of processing steps was the focus of improvement efforts).

The 'normal' processes of competition in the semiconductor industry required managers to struggle continually with these trade-offs as each new product (and therefore process) generation was introduced. Indirect evidence for intelligent adaptation in the firms as the technology progressed comes from the fact that many firms survived through many generations of technology. There was a continuing rise and fall (but not demise) of firms in successive generations of memory, for instance. For example, Toshiba had difficulties in the 256K DRAM generation, but dominated the 1M generation. Likewise, Intel had substantial difficulties during the mid-1980s, but by the end of the decade Intel dominated the industry in the key microprocessor segment.

The 'normal' processes of competition and intelligent adaptation were, however, interrupted during the mid-1980s. The American industry as a whole received a tremendous competitive challenge from Japanese competition, and that challenge related directly to the management of continual improvement in operations. This was a period of environmental stress that called into question the policies of American managers with respect to manufacturing, and the managerial approaches of that period reflect intelligent and successful adaptation to survival-challenging stress.[24] By the early 1990s, American market share had recovered relative to Japanese and many individual firms had regained profitability. To the surprise of many, Japanese firms had not taken over the industry, and Korean and Taiwanese firms were challenging the Japanese companies for dominance in the DRAM business.

One would expect that the management approaches used during such a period would differ from those used during a period of 'normal' continuous improvement or adaptation. Observations of management approaches to inquiry and adaptation in semiconductor manufacturing in these two types of periods are reported in the next two sections of this paper.

5. Limits on Inquiry in 'Normal' Times

This section begins by identifying characteristics of semiconductor manufacturing that make traditional manufacturing approaches to allocating resources ineffective in managing inquiry. Next the section describes a number of administrative limits that appear to be common practice in semiconductor factories for enhancing the effectiveness of inquiry in the factory. Then the section suggests that limits on inquiry can be a useful and effective managerial approach to allocating independent individuals' initiatives to most valuable projects.

---

[24] The importance of manufacturing management was cited as critical to the industry during this period by the National Advisory Council on Semiconductors, the MIT Productivity Study in Dertouzos *et al.* (1989), and in the annual reports of many industry participants. Indeed, the mission of Sematech, established in the mid-1980s, was to help to resurrect the American capital equipment industry; the mission was declared achieved when Sematech stated in the mid-1990s that it had succeeded and would no longer require contributions from the American government.

5.1. Semiconductor manufacturing and inquiry

In semiconductors the knowledge work of introducing products, improving the manufacturing process, and quality control limited the performance of the factory (and often of the business), and became by the early 1980s for many factories the performance-constraining activity. That is, the important leverage on semiconductor manufacturing performance was no longer in capacity costs or direct labour costs; instead it was in the ability and availability of the workers in the factory to identify and solve the important problems. The strategic emphasis in manufacturing went from direct workers and operators to engineers and technicians directing workers—now using their minds—to diagnose and improve. Furthermore, the management of knowledge over the history of a factory put the managers of one fine-tuned for knowledge work in a very different situation from those where volume shipped had been the unchallenged priority.

Semiconductor manufacturing exhibits many characteristics cited above as making the management of inquiry and future-oriented knowledge work much more difficult than managing traditional materials processing manufacturing. First, the manufacturing process is complex, interrelated, and often in a measurement or control stage of process knowledge as a new product generation begins production. No one individual could hope to understand all of the over 200 steps in a typical process, the process technology, the product design, and all of the particular accidents that can happen to any particular product on its path through the factory.

Second, because of the lower stage of knowledge, there are many unanticipatable problems and opportunities for improvement. Product yields themselves testify to this point: in a factory with defective products that were at least 10 per cent of the total products at best and over 50 per cent often, it is clear that there were more problems than engineers and technicians and operators could investigate and eliminate.[25] Third, in these factories productivity was obviously not perfect. Opportunities for improving productivity often presented themselves in terms of equipment that broke down or drifted out of control and therefore required extra maintenance attention: any equipment that was unavailable much of the time was a latent opportunity to improve productivity. In addition, there are the many other opportunities direct operators always see to improve their jobs. These include making their postures more comfortable, making their worksheets and record sheets easier to see, and all the industrial engineering-type ideas of ease and efficiency that were possible in any factory.

The ability of knowledge workers to exploit opportunities for productivity improvement is therefore limited. For example, the knowledge that guides production is fragmented and distributed among many participants. Root-cause analysis, conducted by teams identified in response to problems rather than individuals, is the accepted way to confront this situation and find remedies to problems that actually

---

[25] Indeed, the annals of improvement in factories confirms this. Analog Devices began a programme to have workers spend a few hours a week on improvements to quality in the mid-1980s and found that their workers were responsible for reducing defects in products by half every six months. Stata (1989).

eliminate the causes of defects; but this makes it especially difficult to anticipate the opportunities and problems that should be attended to in the best interests of the factory.

In addition, workers' ability to improve productivity is limited by the requirement to investigate quality control problems as a first priority in every semiconductor fab. Because semiconductor manufacturing is often so close to instability, most semiconductor fabs are especially careful about putting quality control as the highest priority. That is, every engineer and technician and operator must drop interesting projects and investigate the causes of defects or of machines drifting out of control when they occur. Such problems may indicate the onset of permanent disturbances to the production process and these are most easily identified and eliminated soon after they are observed. Quality control is a treadmill and it is necessary to keep running to stay on top of it.

Thus, the trade-offs between short- and long-term benefits of knowledge work are critical to the performance of the semiconductor factory, and they must be made with real-time process knowledge that may be found anywhere in the fab.[26] The managerial challenge of managing inquiry in semiconductor fabs has been managed in part as in traditional manufacturing: the number of technicians and engineers who lead the inquiry is always limited.

But inquiry is also managed in ways that are very different from traditional resource allocation. There are difficult challenges in assigning professionals to work. The very assignment—especially when it must be done in great detail—can limit the willingness of individuals to take initiative and limit their motivation. Furthermore, because no one individual can understand all the process knowledge in a semiconductor factory, it is especially difficult to centralize assignment of individuals to knowledge tasks.

5.2. Limits to inquiry

In semiconductor factories, managers must therefore rely on individuals to think for themselves and many individuals must manage their own time on many different tasks. In addition to general assignments and explanations of the factory's priorities, managers in semiconductor factories apparently use some interesting limits to inquiry to augment their resource allocation, limits that do not threaten the motivation, initiative, and interests of the individuals who are essential to effective knowledge-based work.

The limits that are described here on project choice and on individual autonomy in inquiry work all seem to be understood by those affected as reflecting legitimate short-term versus long-term trade-offs in the interests of the performance of their business. Each one is common practice in the industry, giving extra credence to the possibility that limits are serving a useful purpose in the factories.

---

[26] Deming (1986) and Juran (1979) suggest some approaches for prioritizing among the quality control projects themselves, but they leave to the managers the difficult task of balancing short- and long-term allocation of knowledge workers to the many activities that affect new product introductions and future manufacturing performance.

First, *qualification* by the supplying firm serves to limit inquiry by individuals in the factory. When a product is qualified, the company promises all customers that neither the product design nor its process will be changed in any way that could possibly change its function in a customer's product (even if the change nominally improves the product's features).[27] So after the company qualifies a product to its customers, changes that can be made in the factory are quite limited. There can be no design changes, even though design changes might eliminate the causes of some defects that are found in the process of improving the process. Likewise, there can be no process changes that would potentially improve the performance of a chip or even reduce its selling price: customers' products are calibrated to the original qualified design and performance.

In products where improvements in design or process would give value to customer and manufacturer, changes are instead accumulated for perhaps a year. Periodically, the factory introduces a number of changes that might affect product function, tests them all together to ensure that the product meets acceptability requirements, and then introduces the new product, possibly in addition to the old one. This is often done with 'shrinks' of DRAMs. In a shrink, process control has been improved enough to reduce line-width variation to the point where the control limits can be pulled in and the mean line-width reduced; the entire design of a DRAM can be simply made smaller, shrunk. The result is that the area of silicon on which the chip is built decreases, and the effective cost of manufacturing the chip decreases also.[28]

Although periodic shrinks are certainly motivated by customer requirements rather than learning, qualification seems to be productive for factories in their learning because some of the testing required to certify product changes to customers is combined, with the result that testing costs are economized upon.

Second, there are also *limits on the individuals to whom factory workers can speak* during their inquiry. For example, it is common for factory employees to be told they may not talk to design engineers and change a product design, even if the change would save considerable cost and increase yield. It is also common for operators in factories to be told that they may not speak with equipment engineers who know about how the equipment functions in transforming material; indeed, a number of American factories had no such experts during the early 1980s and depended instead on independent vendors. The first type of limit may help the firm as a whole in its innovative efforts by not allowing highly valuable product design efforts to be delayed by less valuable cost reduction efforts in factories. The second type prohibits making changes to equipment and expending precious attention which could be allocated to

---

[27] Note that changes in the process which could in no way affect the function of the product are often made. For example, reducing the particles allowed in the atmosphere of the fab would not change the function of a product, nor would changing the ways in which wafers are transported.

[28] Costs decrease because the number of chips that can be made on a wafer (the disk of silicon on which the chips are made and which absorbs the majority of variable costs during production) increase and the possibility of a particle 'killing' a chip declines. (Of course, smaller particles then can cause defects on wafers, but the process control improves by the time of a shrink so that the net effect is an improvement in costs.)

higher-value projects on new product introduction, for example. Both limits can be understood to act to deter manufacturing workers from inquiry which may divert resources from valuable long-term projects to less valuable short-term projects and to avoid coordination diseconomies.[29]

Third, the *number of projects* that can be undertaken in a factory at one time is limited. So some factory managers simply limit the number of high-priority projects that can take place simultaneously. One common rule of thumb is that no more than three large projects can go on at one time. This means that other projects—introducing new equipment or improving other equipment can simply not be considered, regardless of who is interested or how potentially valuable the other projects might be. On the one hand, this limit might be seen as non-optimizing; on the other hand, this type of limit can increase the productivity of learning in much the same way that a traffic light that limits vehicle entrants to a highway or a bridge increase in effect the capacity of the bridge relative to letting all the vehicles begin when they arrive. The intuitive reason is that the interference among vehicles increases as the vehicles get closer together; the limits on entrance limit the interference and increase effective capacity. This is also closely related to Skinner's arguments that focus is important to increasing the productivity of factories.[30]

Fourth, the *kinds of projects* that a factory undertakes may systematically differ depending on the state of knowledge in the factory and the expected future of the products affected. That is, the benefits of certain types of projects may differ in known ways and be reflected in these limits. For example, many Japanese factory managers have explained that they derive cost savings and productivity improvements from workers and quality circles, but even more from engineering efforts.[31] Davidson (1982) describes the experience of work groups at Hitachi's Musashi semiconductor facility beginning in the early 1980s. In this factory the first gains were accomplished by engineers alone. Later—and only in the mid-1980s—did the managers decide to enlist the help of workers in quality improvement activities. For another example, some semiconductor factories work at quality control all the time, but they focus on problems of adapting their process to increase yields and productivity only early in the product's life in the factory; once a product or process has passed a certain stage in its life, only quality control is done.

These limits on the types of projects done in different contexts embody short-term versus long-term trade-offs about allocating knowledge resources to projects generating the highest value. So, when a factory is new and expected to live for a long time, the benefits of improving its basic equipment are expected to last a long time. However, when a product is old and close to the end of its life, the benefits of improving its yield may be very limited. Clearly, when the benefits of a project done on a particular product are expected to be transferable to other products, there will be

---

[29] Brooks' (1975) observation that coordination costs are a very large portion of the costs of large software projects is consistent with and reinforces this point.

[30] Skinner (1974).

[31] Karatsu (1981, 1987); Schonberger (1982, 1986); Ishikawa (1985); Gunn (1987); Hall (1987); Hayes *et al.* (1988); Hodges (1990); Smitka (1991); Juran (1995).

a greater expected benefit from a given improvement project than when the project is expected to affect only one product.

All these limits relate to the choices individuals make about the problems to work on and the people to whom they will speak in solving those problems. The underlying problem that motivates these limits is that there is only one factory to work on and one management structure for the activity in it. The problems of coordinating an increasing intensity of effort in one factory seem to mount rapidly. The coordination is required to get individuals to work together on the same problems at the same time and to economize on their deliberations as they share a participative analysis to decide which are the important problems. These limits on inquiry appear meant to ensure that coordination requirements do not swamp the capacity of the factory for improvement and for current production.[32]

6. Limits on Inquiry during Survival-threatening Stress

During the late 1980s, with their survival threatened, managers of American semi-conductor businesses and factories re-examined their conceptualization of manufac-turing, their ways of doing business, and their basic assumptions and strategies. This process was reminiscent of Ashby's[33] account of decision processes cast in terms of cybernetic theory and of Argyris and Schon's learning organizations with 'second-order learning'.[34] Background discussions I had with suppliers to the industry during the late 1980s suggested that an important aspect of the managerial adaptive response to the competitive stress involved reconsidering the very limits to inquiry that appeared to promote learning and a proper balance between current performance and performance improvement in the earlier 'normal' times.

Because the limits on inquiry had been in place for a long time and because the environment had changed, it may not be surprising that stress-induced examination identified many opportunities that seemed to have benefits far outweighing their costs.[35] The limits identified here seem to have prevented inquiry that would have been beneficial during 'normal' times. Indeed, these limits may have become strategic

[32] Sid Winter clarified the point in this paragraph. It is similar to what Derickx and Cool (1989) mean by 'time compression diseconomies'.

[33] Ashby (1970) argues that for an individual to be adaptive to its environment, there must be both a limited model directing most responses and sensing the state of the system and—very important—a review mechanism to examine the first system when performance is unacceptable and change it if necessary.

[34] Argyris and Schon (1978). It is useful to note that Argyris and Schon and many of those who have followed their work have focused on an organizational perspective to change; they have made important contributions to understanding the processes through which organizations and individuals make substan-tial change. Argyris has also proposed some compelling approaches to helping people in organizations recognize their defences and the obstacles they put up to improvement and to change. They rarely, however, consider the substance of the organization and the operations details. In this chapter, I propose some operational clues to help researchers and managers identify and use better adaptation approaches.

[35] Compare e.g. Winter (1994: 476–7): 'While the shelf of potential improvements in a given routine becomes increasingly laden with contributions from new technology, new modes of organization, and observable innovations adopted elsewhere, an organization ... [may not] ... look at the shelf until it suffers a breakdown in that particular routine, or overall performance deteriorates to the point where threats to long-term survival are finally acknowledged and all routines are open to question.'

mistakes since the apparent costs of some of the improvements they prevented were far less than the benefits. Of course, to infer that a limit was bad for a firm, it would be necessary to look at all its opportunity costs and benefits—including other possible improvements, direct coordination costs, other uses for the time of individuals, and possible negative externalities on some individuals who might be expected to participate in the experiment 'for free'. In addition and very subtle, it would be important to consider the long-term costs of coordination under the method of limits to inquiry in comparison with the net costs and benefits of another method.

The main goal of this section is to show by examples that some limits to inquiry that may seem to be highly productive because they limit coordination costs in normal periods may actually have very serious long-term consequences. In particular, this section shows that the limits managers impose on inquiry may be just as important as the magnitude of resources they allocate to it in determining the effectiveness of intelligent adaptation.

First, consider the *diffusion furnace*.[36] In the mid-1980s I asked many American fab managers the following question: what would you do to improve the performance of your fab if I gave you $1 million? The answer I heard several times was: buy a diffusion furnace with better controls. It turned out that the diffusion furnace—whose basic operation had not changed since it was first developed during the early 1960s—was made in many cases by an American company. American fabs could manufacture their advanced products with these furnaces, but the furnaces generated substantial variability in the processes and therefore defects in the products. Indeed, it often took over four months to get a new diffusion furnace calibrated, and then it still drifted out of control every few weeks, requiring another several days of recalibration effort (which meant lost production). In contrast, my informers explained, Japanese companies bought their diffusion furnaces from the same supplier; but their furnaces were readjusted by the Japanese partner of the American supplier. The result was that in Japan the same diffusion furnaces could be calibrated initially in a few days, they remained in control for many months, and they could be readjusted very quickly if they drifted outside acceptable control limits.

The managers from component makers with whom I spoke explained that, despite their frustration, they always had other tasks that were more critical to their ability to produce advanced products. So they had never pressed the issue with the American supplier. Instead, they expended substantial inspection, calibration, and recalibration effort on the diffusion furnaces. The equipment makers alleged that the component makers would not pay for extra calibration. By the mid-1980s, however, these managers and engineers were beginning to think that if they could eliminate the process variability once and for all from the diffusion furnaces, they might not only improve productivity directly but also become much more effective in their other

---

[36] This is a piece of equipment used in semiconductor manufacturing to expose a silicon wafer, on which a patterned mask has been deposited, to a gas of a substance under controlled heat, pressure, and timing conditions to induce a desired concentration of the substance to diffuse into the unmasked parts of the silicon wafer. This is a basic step in the manufacture of most silicon integrated circuits.

learning efforts in the factories. They discussed hiring engineers to negotiate with suppliers; engineers would cost much less than the lost production, and there should be no negative externalities. Likewise, equipment makers by the mid-1980s were losing sales to their Japanese competitors; they began to consider the potential value of collaborating with their customers. For both, their limits on inquiry had simply prevented them from entertaining the question of improving the diffusion furnace.

6.1. Forty-hour a week spare-parts service

Another industry-wide practice that caused problems for semiconductor factories in the early and mid-1980s was the practice of most American equipment manufac-turers to offer spare-parts service only forty hours a week, even though factories often operated around the clock. Factories that were running at capacity would, if a need for a spare part appeared on Saturday morning, stop part of their production for the rest of the weekend and then order the part on Monday morning. This obviously resulted in substantial down-time. Finally, after a few engineers and managers complained in the late 1980s and early 1990s, employees of equipment suppliers began to wear beepers. When a spare part was needed during an off-period, the employee could respond and the factory could receive the part hours earlier, often allowing extra profit of many thousands of dollars. Not surprisingly, this simple innovation took hold: by the mid-1990s, most American equipment companies did offer around-the-clock spare-parts service.

The engineers who discussed this problem during the late 1980s all explained that they had noticed the problem before, but they had felt that they were not supposed to solve problems of this sort or to complain or to ask to spend resources. The reasons that engineers and factory managers gave for not pursuing the improvement possibil-ity before included that they had been busy, that these things were not done, that they had to accept what every other company accepted from their suppliers and what had been negotiated by those who had that responsibility. There were assumptions about what was expected in their jobs.

These managers had incorrect assumptions, at least for the late 1980s. In several cases, I watched a new fab manager ask for beeper service, promise to pay the individual's overtime, and get the service at almost no charge within a few days. Here, too, the limits of inquiry—limits that were well established in the conceptual frame-works with which the individuals worked—had the effect of setting past practices in stone. It was only the environment of wide-open inquiry that came with extreme stress that allowed these engineers throughout the industry to ask for round-the-clock service on spare parts.

6.2. No equipment engineers

During the 1960s, many American factories had equipment engineers capable of designing and fixing equipment in their factories. Subsequently, this practice largely disappeared; most American component manufacturers simply replaced components on failed equipment without determining the root cause of the failure, and relied on independent equipment suppliers to incorporate improvements in the next generation of equipment. As a result, there were few engineers during the 1980s seeking improvements or doing root-cause analysis on equipment used in manufacturing processes. As the above discussion of process knowledge implies, this meant that there were many equipment-related disturbances in the manufacturing processes that remained permanently. There were no equipment engineers with the ability to diagnose the problems and eliminate their causes, and many component manufacturers in the United States simply continued using highly unreliable equipment such as the diffusion furnaces mentioned above. Furthermore, American independent equipment vendors had not worked on perfecting aspects of their equipment related to reliability in manufacturing.

When asked in the late 1980s why they had not hired more expert equipment engineers, some component makers' managers explained that their firms had wanted to concentrate on product advancement and depend on suppliers for equipment development. Equipment suppliers likewise explained that this division of labour had worked for them, that their customers would not pay for improved reliability in manufacturing. As in the previous two examples, it seems that there were cognitive limits on what engineers could recognize as worthy of initiative. The entire argument was known by many people, but the discussion had not taken place.

By the late 1980s both component makers and equipment suppliers recognized that they were at a competitive disadvantage relative to Japanese companies because they had not worked on refining process equipment in the manufacturing facility. During the late 1980s and early 1990s, of course, efforts were made in the American industry to address these equipment problems—efforts marked by improved connections between equipment suppliers and component manufacturers, an increase in process engineers' awareness of equipment engineering, and the efforts of Sematech to improve equipment-manufacturing companies. Some American component makers reintroduced engineers capable of understanding the material-processing function of their equipment to their production facilities, and the American equipment makers which made competitive revivals with the help of Sematech did work collaboratively with manufacturing facilities on issues of reliability.

The examples of limits to inquiry considered here all seem to have harmed the firms whose managers imposed them. Some important questions are left for further research. For example, did the benefits of the limits to inquiry of improved coordination and adaptation performance during normal times outweigh the harm that was discovered during the period of stress? Likewise, are there improvements to the methods of limiting inquiry that could also limit the potential of losses through these limits?

7. Conclusion

The first sections of this chapter were intended to introduce two hypotheses. First, there is a broad hypothesis linking process knowledge, quality, and technological progress. Second, there is a narrow hypothesis: intelligent adaptation works in part because inquiry is effective at unearthing process knowledge that allows fundamental process change, and in part because expedient limits to inquiry helped a complex network of individuals with complementary expertise to focus on a limited set of important opportunities. Evidence consistent with both hypotheses was found in the semiconductor industry both in situations of normal adaptation and in times of stress so great that firms' survival was threatened. In addition, it appears that the limits to inquiry used in semiconductor manufacturing during the early 1980s were strong. They seem to have contributed to learning and intelligent adaptation, but they also may have eventually resulted in strategic mistakes because many fine opportunities were ignored.

Empirical investigations conducted in time series in one industry and set of firms are, as this chapter seeks to illustrate, a powerful method for gathering evidence relevant to such a hypothesis. Of course, an overall assessment of the validity of the hypotheses, as well as examination of new questions raised here, must await the accumulation of evidence from other firm and industry settings.

References

Adler, P. S., and R. E. Cole (1993). 'Designed for Learning: A Tale of Two Auto Plants', *Sloan Management Review* (Spring): 85–94.

———— (1994). 'Rejoinder', *Sloan Management Review* (Winter): 45–9.

Argyris, C., and D. A. Schon (1978). *Organizational Learning: A Theory of Action Perspective*. Reading, Mass.: Addision-Wesley.

Ashby, W. Ross (1970). *Design for a Brain*. London: Chapman & Hall.

Berrgren, C. (1994). 'NUMMI vs. Uddevalla,' *Sloan Management Review* (Winter): 37–45.

Bohn, R. (1995). 'Technological Knowledge: How to Measure, How to Manage', *Sloan Management Review*, 36: 61–73.

Brooks, F. P., Jr. (1975). *The Mythical Man-Month: Essays on Software Engineering*. Reading, Mass.: Addison-Wesley.

Cohen, M. D., R. Burkhart, G. Dosi, M. Egidi, L. Narengo, M. Wanglien, and S. Winter (1995), 'Routines and Other Recurring Action Patterns of Organizations: Contemporary Research Issues', *Industrial and Corporate Change*, 5(3): 653–98.

Cohen, W. M., and D. A. Levinthal (1990). 'Absorptive Capacity: A New Perspective on Learning and Innovation', *Administrative Science Quarterly*, 35: 128–52.

Cyert, R. M., and J. G. March (1963). *A Behavioral Theory of the Firm*. Englewood Cliffs: Prentice-Hall.

Davidson, W. H. (1982). 'Small Group Activities at Musashi Semicondcutor Works', *Sloan Management Review*, 23: 3–14.

Deming, W. E. (1986). *Out of the Crisis*. Cambridge, Mass.: Center for Advanced Engineering Study, MIT.

Dertouzos, M. L., R. K. Lester, and R. M. Solow (1989), *Made in America*. Cambridge, Mass.: MIT Press.

Dierickx, I., and K. Cool (1989). 'Asset Stock Accumulation and Sustainability of Advantage', *Management Science*, 35: 1504–11.

Dosi, G., D. Teece, and S. Winter (1992). 'Toward a theory of corporate coherence: Preliminary remarks', in G. Dosi, R. Gianneti, and P. A. Toninelli (eds.), *Technology and Enterprise in Historical Perspective*. New York: Clarendon Press: 185–211.

Flaherty, M. T. (1990). 'Managing Manufacturing and Engineering in VLSI Fabs', *Proceedings: International Semiconductor Manufacturing Science Symposium* (sponsored by IEEE), May.

———— (1992). 'Manufacturing and Firm Performance in Technology-Intensive Industries: U.S. and Japanese DRAM Experience', *Review of Industrial Organization*, 7: 273–94.

Gunn, T. G. (1987). *Manufacturing for Competitive Advantage: Becoming a World Class Manufacturer*. Boston: Ballinger.

Hall, R. W. (1987). *Attaining Manufacturing Excellence*. Homewood, Ill.: Dow Jones-Irwin.

Hayes, R. H., S. C. Wheelwright, and K. B. Clark (1988). *Dynamic Manufacturing*. New York: Free Press.

Helfat, C. E. (1997). 'Know-How and Asset Complementarity and Dynamic Capability Accumulation: The Case of R&D', *Strategic Management Journal*, 18: 339–60.

Hodges, D. A. (1990). 'VLSI Manufacturing In Japan and the United States', IEEE/SEMI (Institute of Electrical and Electronics Engineers/Semiconductor Equipment and Materials Institute), *Advanced Semiconductor Manufacturing Conference Proceedings*, 1–2.

Hutcheson, G. D., and J. D. Hutcheson (1996). 'Technology and Economics in the Semi-conductor Industry', *Scientific American* (Jan.): 54–62.

Ishikawa, K. (1985). *What Is Total Quality Control? The Japanese Way*, trans. by David J. Lu. Englewood Cliffs, NJ: Prentice-Hall.

Jaikumar, R., and R. E. Bohn (1992). 'A Dynamic Approach to Operations Management: an Alternative to Static Optimization', *International Journal of Production Economics*, 23: 265–82.

Itami, H., with T. W. Roehl (1987). *Mobilizing Invisible Assets*. Cambridge, Mass.: Harvard University Press.

Juran, J. M. (ed.) (1979). *Quality Control Handbook*. New York: McGraw-Hill.

—— (1995). *Managerial Breakthrough*. New York: McGraw-Hill.

Karatsu, H. (1981). *TQC Wisdom of Japan: Managing for Total Quality Control*. Tokyo: JUSE Press. (Trans. by David S. Lu and published by Productivity Press. Norwalk, Conn., 1988).

—— (1987). *Tough Words for American Industry*. Norwalk, Conn.: Productivity Press.

Kogut, B., and U. Zander (1992). 'Knowledge of the Firm, Combinative Capabilities, and the Replication of Technology', *Organization Science*, 3 (Aug.): 383–97.

Leonard-Barton, D. (1995). *Wellsprings of Knowledge: Building and Sustaining the Sources of Innovation*. Boston: Harvard Business School Press.

Moore, G. E. (1975). 'Progress in Digital Integrated Electronics', *Proceedings, IEEE Digital Integrated Electronic Device Meeting*, 11.

Nelson, R. R., and S. G. Winter (1982). *An Evolutionary Theory of Economic Change*. Cambridge, Mass.: Harvard University Press.

Nonaka, I., and H. Takeuchi (1995). *The Knowledge-Creating Company: How Japanese Companies Create the Dynamics of Innovation*. New York: Oxford University Press.

Noyce, Robert (1977). 'Microelectronics', *Scientific American*, 237(9).

Patterson, D. A., D. S. Kiser, and D. N. Smith (1989). *Computing Unbound: Using Computers in the Arts and Sciences*. New York: W. W. Norton & Co.

Penrose, E. T. (1959). *The Theory of the Growth of the Firm*. White Plains: M. E. Sharpe.

Schonberger, R. J. (1982) *Japanese Manufacturing Techniques*. New York: Free Press.

—— (1986). *World Class Manufacturing*. New York: Free Press.

Simon, H. A. (1945). *Administrative Behavior*, 3rd edn. New York: Free Press.

Skinner, W. (1974). 'The Focused Factory', *Harvard Business Review*, May–June: 113–21.

Smitka, Michael J. (1991). *Competitive Ties: Subcontracting in the Japanese Automotive Industry*. New York: Columbia University Press.

Stata, R. (1989). 'Organizational Learning: The Key to Management Innovation', *Sloan Management Review*, 30: 63–74.

Teece, D. J., and G. Pisano (1994). 'The Dynamic Capabilities of Firms: An Introduction', *Industrial and Corporate Change*, 3: 537–56.

Winter, S. G. (1982) 'An Essay on the Theory of Production', in Saul H. Hymans (ed.), *Economics and the World around It*. Ann Arbor: University of Michigan Press.

—— (1982). 'Organizing for Continuous Improvement: Evolutionary Theory Meets the Quantity Revolution', in J. A. C. Baum and J. Singh (eds.), *The Evolutionary Dynamics of Organizations*. New York: Oxford University Press.

PART II

Introduction to Part II

THE DEVELOPMENT OF NEW CAPABILITIES

Each of the three chapters in Part II is concerned with dynamic capabilities. The firms under study are in industries where success in competition requires the capability to continuously introduce new products, and improve older ones, and to develop new production processes to support and accommodate these product changes. The Pisano, and Henderson and Cockburn, chapters are about firms in the pharmaceuticals industry. The chapter by Appleyard, Hatch, and Mowery, is about firms in the semiconductor business. The capabilities studied in these chapters relate to performance in doing R&D, and the ability to learn and to solve problems more generally. Sometimes the orientation is toward the capability to learn how to learn.

Each of the studies looks at several different firms that have varied in their success in developing and implementing key dynamic capabilities. The studies are very much in the tradition of studies in business strategy, in that they have as a principal purpose the identification of factors that have made for successful strategies. But these studies also add to our positive understanding of the key capabilities of firms in industries where innovation is a central aspect of competition. Thus they contribute significantly to the further development of a positive theory of the firm that can fit into an evolutionary theory of industrial competition and development.

In each of the studies, the dynamic capabilities under examination are defined at a relatively broad level: the capability to develop manufacturing processes to produce new pharmaceuticals (Pisano), the R&D capabilities to design profitable new pharmaceutical products (Henderson and Cockburn), the capability to implement new process techniques in the semiconductor business (Appleyard, Hatch, and Mowery). Each of the authors sees the broad capabilities in question as consisting of a collection of more narrowly defined competences, closely overlapping with effective routines, brought together through mechanisms and organizational structures that influence how they work as a whole. Thus Henderson and Cockburn refer specifically to component competences, and architectural competences.

In each of the studies, the authors provide evidence of a combination of explicit and articulated, and tacit and sometimes subconscious, elements. Thus the firms involved are able to articulate broadly the strategies that lie behind the capabilities they are employing, or at least present a theory or a myth about that. On the other hand, in each of the studies it is apparent that the key capabilities involve bundles of routines which are strongly tacit in nature. And we, the editors of this volume, come away from reading these studies with the perception that, in none of the cases, did the firms involved completely understand what they were doing, at least at a relatively fine level of implementation.

The implications are important both for normative analyses of business strategies, and for positive analyses of business behaviour and competition. The studies support the proposition that it is important for a firm to try to think through what it is doing and what it is trying to do, but also warn that managers should not believe in their beliefs or in their articulated strategies too doggedly. And the studies clearly support the basic premises of evolutionary economic theory that firms differ partly by choice, partly by history and partly by chance, and that competition in industries like pharmaceuticals and semiconductors needs to be understood as an evolutionary process, driven by heterogenous learning processes only roughly understood by the firms involved.

5

In Search of Dynamic Capabilities: The Origins of R&D Competence in Biopharmaceuticals

GARY P. PISANO

1. Introduction

The past decade has witnessed a surge of writing on the link between organizational capabilities and competitive performance.[1] Along with this emphasis on capabilities has come renewed interest in the concept of organizational learning. While the concept of organizational learning has long fascinated organizational theorists, the proposition that competitive advantage stems from firm-specific skills and capabilities has made learning a focal point of concern in fields such as competitive strategy, organizational behaviour, and industrial organization economics. Without learning, it is difficult to imagine from where a firm's unique skills and competencies would come, and thus how it might create a competitive advantage. Understanding the processes by which firms learn and how these processes might be better managed has risen to the top of the agenda of both academics and practitioners alike.

Many questions of importance to both researchers and practitioners remain unanswered: How (and, perhaps more important, why) do some firms create unique knowledge bases? Are some organizations better learners than others? If so, why? How can managers promote learning of the skills and knowledge most critical to their firm's competitive advantage? This chapter seeks to shed some light on these issues by reporting the findings of an in-depth, field-based, longitudinal analysis of the evolution of process development capabilities in the pharmaceutical industry. This work is part of a larger study on the factors affecting process development performance across a sample of twenty-three pharmaceutical projects. The sample included projects based on both traditional chemical pharmaceuticals (thirteen projects) and biotechnology-based pharmaceuticals (ten projects). Of these ten biotechnology-based projects, nine were conducted by relatively young biotechnology firms. The youth of these companies makes them an excellent venue in which to study the organizational processes influencing the initial accumulation of capabilities. The projects studied generally represent each firm's first efforts at developing commercial-scale process technologies. Tracking performance differences over these projects allows us to observe organizational learning in action.

---

[1] Among many, see e.g. Teece 1982; Nelson and Winter 1982; Wernerfelt 1984; Hayes *et al.* 1988; Prahalad and Hammel 1990; Chandler 1990; Teece and Pisano 1994.

The focus on *process* development, as opposed to product development, also has some advantages in terms of the main questions of interest. Since biotechnology was a novel approach to drug synthesis, just about every biotechnology firm spent the first few years of their lives undertaking basic product discovery and development. Only once when they had initiated clinical and commercial development of a new drug did the need to develop manufacturing processes arise. Thus, process development confronted these organizations with the challenge of developing a novel set of capabilities early in their lives. Whereas product research began on the very first day of each firm's existence and was often a legacy of basic research begun elsewhere (e.g. a university or teaching hospital), the origins of process development can generally be traced to a very specific point in time (e.g. the hiring of a scientist to undertake process research on a new molecule).

The first section of this chapter presents a simple conceptual framework for learning across development projects that highlights the dual 'outputs' of development projects: the technology that is implemented in a new process (or product design) and the knowledge that becomes available for future projects (see Figure 5.1). In most situations, managerial attention focuses on the first of these outputs— getting a new process or product developed as quickly and efficiently as possible takes precedence over building knowledge for future projects. The literature on innovation has reflected a similar bias, focusing largely on the performance of individual projects or firms at a single point in time rather than on changes in performance over time.[2] Development projects, however, also create technical and organizational learning that become part of a firm's knowledge base and which, in turn, influence the strategies chosen for and performance achieved on future projects. Although many managers would agree that the intellectual by-products of a project lay the critical foundation for upcoming projects, few understand how this learning can be managed or integrated with more immediate goals. In-depth, longitudinal analyses of four biotechnology organizations is then used to explore the managerial and organizational processes associated with capability-building. These cases are to explore the dynamic interaction between the organization's knowledge base, its capability for different development strategies (e.g. learning by doing versus learning before doing), and changes in project performance over time (e.g. lead time). The goal of this chapter is theory-building grounded in detailed first-hand observation rather than hypothesis testing. This approach seems appropriate given the lack of both theoretical and empirical attention given to the formative processes behind organizational capabilities.[3] The chapter concludes with a brief discussion of the implications for theory on organizational learning processes.

---

[2] Exceptions include Iansiti and Clark (1994) and Iansiti (1995).

[3] Iansiti and Clark (1994) provide one of the few empirical analyses of learning across development projects. Henderson (1994) also examines the evolution of product research capabilities in the pharmaceutical industry. But, both of these works were set in the contexts of established organizations where, once again, path dependence seems to play an overwhelmingly important goal.

2. Framework for Learning across Projects

2.1. *Knowledge, competence, and the evolution of search strategies*

There is a long and rich history of literature on organizational learning.[4] The framework presented here builds on the core themes of that literature to explore the specific mechanisms by which organizations learn within the context of process development projects. Although the framework is applied to this specific context, it

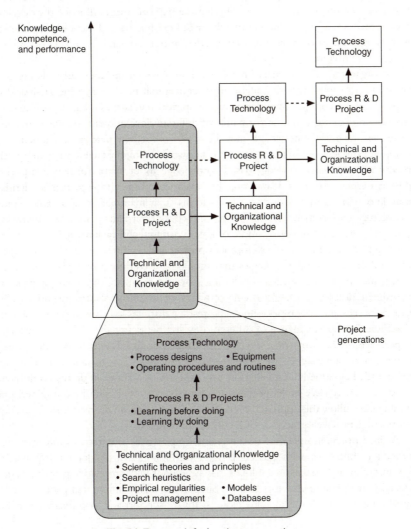

Fig. 5.1 Framework for learning across projects

[4] For a useful review and contribution, see Levitt and March (1988); see also Cyert and March (1963), Levinthal and March (1981), and Nelson and Winter (1982).

is general enough to be applied to product development projects and other problem-solving activities.

Every development project has two potential outputs: the new process or product technology used in the manufacturing environment and the new knowledge that becomes available for future projects (Figure 5.1).[5] The vertical linkages in the figure represent the development processes associated with the creation of a new manufacturing process technology. Each column depicts a project undertaken to develop a generation of process technology. Three potential forces can influence the development process at a given point in time: the firm's existing base of technical knowledge, its existing base of organizational knowledge, and its constraints created by existing process technology.

An organization's technical knowledge base—which includes such elements as scientific principles, theories, algorithms, conceptual models, specific analytical or experimental techniques, heuristics, and empirical regularities—has a profound influence on the choice and performance of different development strategies. In some instances, technical knowledge may be well codified in patents, documents, or computer models, but in many cases it is known to be highly tacit.[6] A key ingredient of a firm's technical knowledge base is knowledge about the performance impact of different types of technical solutions. For instance, a biotechnology firm's scientists may know (from theory or past observations) that mammalian cells grow rapidly between certain temperatures or that certain types of nutrients work well under some process conditions but poorly under others. Existing technical knowledge provides a starting point for any given development project and, as discussed earlier, influences the kind of development strategies that should be used during projects.

Organizational knowledge—including how to organize and manage projects, coordinate different problem-solving activities, determine goals and incentives, allocate resources and assign personnel, and resolve disputes—also is likely to influence the choice and performance of different development strategies. Through repeated experience, some firms may develop specialized competencies in specific project management approaches or development strategies. For instance, a firm that historically has carried out much of its process development work during commercial production may have built specialized competencies in learning by doing and may continue to follow this approach even if the technological environment lends itself to more efficient development through other approaches.

A third potential influence is constraints imposed by the need to integrate new process technologies with existing process technologies or production capabilities. For instance, new process techniques may be at odds with an existing plant's physical capacity or operational competencies. Similarly, a highly automated process would not be a good match for a plant lacking software support and maintenance capabil-

---

[5] Iansiti and Clark (1994) develop a similar perspective. However, their framework focuses on how integration across projects of the same generation influences capabilities for development in future generations. The framework here does not address the issue of cross-project integration, but instead revolves around the impact of individual projects on the knowledge base available for future projects.

[6] On the concept of tacit knowledge, see Polanyi (1958), Teece (1977), and Kogut and Zander (1992).

ities. Even when companies implement new processes at a 'greenfield site', their existing repertoire of plant management skills and operating philosophies can influence choices of process technologies.

The above discussion calls attention to the constraints that existing technical knowledge, organizational knowledge, and process technologies and capabilities may place on process development strategies and performance. This raises a question: where do these constraints arise? A resounding theme in existing literature is that differences in experience account for differences in capabilities across firms.[7] From this perspective, what an organization knows how to do today is a function of what it learned in the course of development yesterday. Thus, referring back to Figure 5.1, the horizontal linkages depict the learning that takes place across projects (or, what are commonly referred to in the literature as 'path dependencies'). Each project not only creates a new process technology but also changes the starting conditions and constraints for the next project. In the course of developing a process technology, the organization engages in problem solving to learn about potential solutions: it conducts experiments, runs simulations, and tests the process at pilot stage and full scale. A component of what is learned becomes embodied in the process flows, equipment designs and settings, process specifications, operating procedures, and other elements of the process design. Moreover, this knowledge— as well as other knowledge generated during the project—becomes available for future projects. For instance, in developing a biotechnology production process, an organization may conduct a series of experiments to determine how temperature affects protein production levels. This knowledge is useful for the current project because it enables developers to specify an optimal temperature; more broadly, such knowledge also is useful for future process development projects with similar technical constraints.

The idea that knowledge from one R&D project lays a foundation for future projects has important implications for both inter-industry and intra-industry differences in development strategies. How the deepening of knowledge across projects influences R&D strategies is the focus of the subsection that follows.

2.2. *Search strategies and the evolution of knowledge*

Search is a relatively common metaphor to describe R&D activities and is also useful to describe the nature of learning across projects. Within an R&D project, a firm engages in search to identify potential problems or gaps between desired and actual performance of a product or process design. It also engages in a search to find and implement solutions to those problems. The idea that R&D is fundamentally about search suggests that learning across R&D projects involves learning how to search more quickly, efficiently, and effectively. Search strategies can take various forms. For instance, Nelson and Winter (1982) model search in terms of total spending on R&D and the allocation of that spending to 'innovative' versus 'imitative' technologies. In a similar vein, Levinthal and March (1981) focus on the distinction between

---

[7] See e.g. Levinthal and March (1981), Nelson and Winter (1982).

'refinement search' and 'innovative search'. Search can also be modelled in terms of the number of distinct technologies or variety of a technology which are tested (see e.g. Evanson and Kislev 1975).

Since experimentation lies at the heart of the innovation process, it can be fruitful to view R&D search strategies in terms of the mode of experimentation. Pisano (1994, 1997) develops a framework that delineates search strategies in terms of how much they rely on inductive versus deductive learning. Both types of learning strategies involve trial-and-error and experimentation. The differences lie in the nature of the experiments conducted. 'Learning-by-doing' represents the classic form of inductive learning. Under a strategy of 'learning-by-doing', a technology is tried under actual commercial operating or usage conditions; performance attributes (and usually problems) are observed; and, the data are then used to iterate the design. An example of a 'learning-by-doing' strategy in the development of a new process technology would be to pilot test a relatively undeveloped process design in an actual commercial production during normal operating hours. The chief advantage of such an approach is that it allows developers to observe the performance under actual operating conditions.

An alternative approach involves conducting laboratory experiments and other simulations designed to model the performance of the technology under some set of expected future operating conditions. With this more deductive approach, the researcher attempts to design an experiment that explicitly attempts to simulate performance and uncover potential problems. Such simulations can take various forms. For example, when a process chemists tests a process in the laboratory, it can be viewed as a representation of the future commercial manufacturing environment. Every element of the experiment has analogies in the factory: each small glass test tube represents the 1,000-gallon stainless-steel reaction tanks found in the factory; the thin glass mixing-rod used to stir the test tube simulates the forces of the automated steel rotators; and the chemist who sets up and watches over the experiment plays the role of both the future factory operators and the computer-based process control system. Although laboratory experiments conjure images of *physical* prototypes, increasingly, such experiments can be conducted via computer-aided simulations. Because such experiments—whether conducted physically or virtually—are attempts to learn about the technology *before* it is put into use under actual operating conditions, they constitute a learning strategy that Pisano (1994, 1997) refers to as 'learning-*before*-doing'.

Any development strategy involves a mixture of learning-before-doing and learning-by-doing. As shown elsewhere (Pisano 1994, 1997), the appropriate balance between the two approaches depends on the nature of underlying knowledge. For learning-before-doing to be effective, researchers, engineers, and other problem-solvers need at their disposal a relatively robust and deep body of theoretical knowledge or heuristics. Without such knowledge, it would be difficult to design an experiment or simulation that would faithfully predict future performance. Moreover, it would be difficult to interpret the results of such an experiment. For example, without detailed knowledge of the first-order and second-order variables affecting process performance, it would be difficult to predict future process performance at a factory from a set of laboratory experimental data. Where the knowledge needed to conduct and interpret high-fidelity experiments or simulations is lacking, it becomes increasingly necessary to engage in learning-by-doing.

The idea that the structure of underlying knowledge influences optimal search strategies has important implications for inter-industry differences in development strategy. In an earlier paper (Pisano 1994), I examined the relationship between a strategy of learning-before-doing and process development lead-time performance. A full description of the models and methods used in that paper are described in the Appendix. To operationalize the concept of 'learning-before-doing', I used the percentage of total project resources expended prior to the first pilot batch of production. This spending is referred to as 'process research' as it takes place solely in the laboratory environment before the process is ever tested at pilot scale. A project in which a high percentage of total resources are expended during process research can be viewed as adopting a 'learning-before-doing' strategy. Alternatively, a firm might chose to spend as little as possible up front and acquire feedback through pilot production and tests in the manufacturing plant. Such a strategy would be more consistent with 'learning-by-doing'. In that paper, it was shown that it was quite possible to learn-before-doing in chemical pharmaceutical projects. A heavier commitment to process research was associated with shorter overall lead times.

But, in biotechnology, a different pictured emerged. There was no statistically consistent relationship between process research and lead time, after holding other factors constant. In biotechnology, it appeared that learning-before-doing was generally not a productive search strategy. This has to do with characteristics of biotechnology process technology compared to chemical synthesis technology: (i) differences in theoretical understanding of the basic processes (ii) ability to precisely fully characterize intermediates and final products, and (iii) knowledge of the second-order effects of scale. Given the difficulty of designing experiments that could faithfully simulate operating conditions at full scale, biotechnology process development relies much more extensively on trial-and-error and iteration of the process design *after* the process is transferred out of the laboratory.

Although there was no clear-cut relationship between learning strategy and learning performance within the biotechnology sample as a whole, a number of interesting firm-level differences appeared.

Figure 5.2 shows the relationship between lead time (adjusted for other factors) and process research in biotechnology. To facilitate analysis of firm-level patterns, individual data points have been labelled sequentially by organization (for example, project A1 preceded project A2). Overall, there was no statistically significant relationship between performance and process research in biotechnology. However, firm-specific analysis reveals some interesting patterns. Organizations A and B seemed to improve their lead-time performance with each project. Organization A, for example, completed its second project about thirty months sooner than its first and Organization B showed an improvement of about fifteen months. Although not formally included as part of this study, follow-up research on A's and B's next

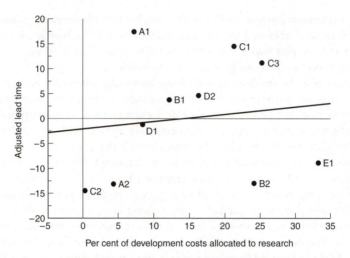

Fig. 5.2 Patterns of lead-time performance in biotechnology

process development projects indicates this pattern of improvement continued. (Both projects were completed well after the time frame for data collection had ended.) Organization A completed its third project in record time with substantial increases in yields versus project A2. Organization B also completed its third project with less lead time than was required for project B2. Beating its own record for B2 was one of Organization B's explicit goals on its third-generation project.

However, improvement was by no means the norm. Organization C demonstrated significant improvement between C1 and C2 and dramatic deterioration between C2 and C3. Likewise, organization D showed no substantial improvement in performance across its projects. Overall, learning appears to be more than simply accumulating experience.

A second noteworthy pattern is that some organizations appear to be better at learning-before-doing than others. For example, Projects E1 and B2 consumed 35 per cent and 25 per cent, respectively, of project resources in research. The lead-time performance of these projects was far superior to that of Project C3 (which involved a similar commitment to research) and was on par with that of C2 and A2 (which relied far more on learning-by-doing). Organizations E (one of the most experienced in the sample) and B (by its second project) appear to have developed capabilities to learn-before-doing.

These observations address one of the questions raised earlier: What might organizations learn to do better across projects? Organizations A and B learned to learn-before-doing. That is, they used knowledge from previous projects to uncover critical parameters and create insights about the process technology that accelerated development. First-generation projects appear to have deepened the organization's reservoir of process knowledge that could be leveraged on second-generation projects. But how did organizations A and B do this? Below, we shed light on this question by digging beneath the regressions to explore detailed patterns of behaviour and organizational processes. Profiles of the improving organizations, A and B, are first presented, followed by profiles of organizations C and D. Unfortunately, because organization E was only able to contribute one project to the sample, there was no way to compare its rate of improvement with the other organizations in the study.

The remainder of this chapter explores these issues with clinical data from a sample of biotechnology projects conducted in four new biotechnology firms. Clinical comparisons across companies are used to shed light on the mechanisms by which organizations learn across projects, the relationship between a firm's approach to managing one project and its approach and performance on its next, and the forces constraining opportunities to exploit learning across projects.

3. Learning to Learn in Biotechnology

The clinical comparisons revolve around four dimensions. One was the framing of technical problems and the level of analysis at which technical understanding was sought. At some organizations, the challenge of process development was viewed in terms of solving basic scientific problems and understanding the behaviour of processes at the molecular level. Others saw the challenge more as solving a specific and narrowly defined engineering problem.

The second dimension was the firm's approach to experimental and analytical methods. Organizations in the study seemed to vary dramatically in the extent to which they placed emphasis on developing high-powered analytical techniques to enhance the quality of feedback from experiments. A third dimension was organizational structure. Although in the broadest terms, all four organizations had similar structures for process development, there were some fundamental differences in how they operated within these structures. Some used teams to integrate process R&D with other parts of the product development project. Others developed a more functionally centred approach.

Finally, and certainly not least important, were differences in how the organizations integrated manufacturing (and, more precisely, the plant) into process development. At some organizations, the plant was viewed as an integral part of the development process and a critical venue for experimentation. Others kept the plant relatively isolated from the development process; preferring instead to do most development in the laboratory and pilot plant. The analysis below illuminates how these decisions shape the accumulation of specific knowledge.

3.1. Organization A

A, a pioneer in the field of biopharmaceuticals, spent its earliest years focused strictly on product research. It followed the common strategy of licensing its first few projects to established pharmaceutical companies for clinical development, manufacturing, and marketing. Although the firm had done some process development on these out-licensed molecules, the bulk of this work was carried out by the licensees responsible for manufacturing. Project A1 represented the firm's first attempt at tackling the entire development process, through manufacturing and marketing.

The challenges facing the firm were both technical and organizational. From a technical standpoint, A1 represented a set of unsolved problems, including media and reactor designs, reaction conditions, purification processes, and analytical methods. Little public scientific knowledge was available; one could not, for example, simply conduct a literature search to determine the best media design for an *e-coli* process. Although many biotechnology firms were developing biochemical processes and solving similar technical problems, they considered this know-how a critical source of competitive advantage and kept it proprietary. Thus, lacking a well-developed knowledge base and access to information at other firms, Organization A found itself literally inventing technology for manufacturing proteins at larger scale.

The second challenge was organizational. Because Organization A had never carried out a complete process development project, it lacked the infrastructure to take a process from research through the factory. On previous projects, process development was undertaken by scientists in the company's product research laboratories. Like many other biotechnology companies, Organization A initially underestimated the value of process development, believing that once an initial process was developed by discovery research, the next step was to transfer it to the plant. After A1, the firm's top management recognized the huge gulf between the interests of research scientists focused on finding novel products and the capabilities required to get a process up and running in an actual plant. Two factors were critical in changing management's thinking on this issue. First, during pilot production runs on earlier projects, management saw that growing genetically engineered bacteria on a larger scale was not a trivial problem, and scale-up involved more than simply transferring the process to larger tanks. Second, through its collaborations with established pharmaceutical companies on earlier projects, the company was exposed to experienced process development and engineering groups.

Organization A began to build a separate process development group and strategy. It created a new position—senior vice-president of process development and manufacturing—and then hired a person with experience in biotechnology process development from one of the company's collaborative partners. An interesting feature of this company's strategy was to integrate process development and manufacturing within the same general organizational structure. The senior vice-president explained:

This organization was set up to avoid specific problems. We wanted to have very close links between process development and manufacturing; we did this by integrating them organizationally and physically. The trade-off is that the links between process R&D and product research are not as strong as they used to be.

This structure seemed to have the desired effect on the way process development was carried out and how the manufacturing plant was used in problem-solving. As one process researcher noted:

Process development and manufacturing were inseparable. Once we did a few small-scale laboratory experiments to find out what unit operations were required, we immediately went into the plant to try it out. Even at a very early stage we used the plant; we did our development work in the manufacturing plant.

Another process researcher added:

From an early phase, we move the process into the pilot plant, which is also our commercial manufacturing plant. There is no distinction between them. It's all one plant, and the same workers do the runs for both. This eliminates the hand-off time lag [between development and manufacturing].

These comments are consistent with Figure 5.2, which shows that firm A spent only about 5 per cent of its project resources before it made its first pilot batches in the plant.

A second noteworthy feature of the company's process development strategy that evolved during the course of the A1 project was its focus on developing a detailed understanding of the process technology at the molecular level. Although the ostensible goal was to develop a commercially viable full-scale manufacturing process, technical problems were framed in terms of understanding, at the most micro-level possible, the structure, behaviour, and characteristics of proteins and the biochemical processes needed to synthesize them. To achieve this level of under-standing, the company focused on building a broad base of scientific capabilities in key process technology disciplines such as microbiology, protein chemistry, bio-chemistry, analytical chemistry, and biophysics. Interestingly, while process develop-ment is sometimes equated with process engineering, the company placed far less emphasis on equipment design, process flows, and other mechanical aspects of the manufacturing system. Thus the company's problem-solving approach might be characterized as 'bottom-up'.

It would be easy to imagine that such a group would lack the capabilities needed to develop manufacturable processes. After all, the traditional domain of the scientist is the laboratory and few scientists have had any exposure to real manufacturing problems or environments. It is the engineers who are supposed to bring a healthy dose of pragmatism to the effort. At Organization A, however, the tight integration between process development and the manufacturing plant appeared to overcome any potential dichotomy. As noted above, development largely took place in the commercial manufacturing environment from an early phase, which forced the scientists to deal with the realities of the plant. They learned how the equipment influenced the process and how production workers actually carried out specific steps, and the factory became their laboratory.[8] Because they experimented using production equipment, the resulting data were far more representative of final out-comes than typical laboratory results.

A third element of the company's development strategy was heavy investment in analytical techniques. Analytical techniques are chemical or physical methods (e.g. SDS gels or chromatography) used to characterize the structure of a protein and detect its presence as well as that of potential impurities. Analytical techniques play a

---

[8] For a discussion of factories as laboratories, see Leonard-Barton (1992).

central role in the development of all pharmaceuticals because of the need to produce the exact molecule at extremely high-purity levels. A critical challenge is to ensure that the process, as it is developed, continues to produce an identical molecule. For instance, a slightly different purification process may filter out the desired form of the protein while leaving in a similar, but biologically inactive, version. Similarly, adding a nutrient to the cell culture process may increase yields but introduce an unwanted impurity. Analytical techniques thus play a critical role in evaluating process R&D experiments.

Such techniques are particularly vital in biotechnology process development because of the sheer complexity of protein molecules and the high potential for biological production processes to generate impurities. Because of their complex structures, proteins are difficult molecules to characterize fully. The 'same' basic protein may come in a variety of forms and even slight differences in structure can have an impact on therapeutic efficacy. In addition, because the desired protein must be isolated and purified from messy fermentation of cell culture broths, analytical techniques are needed to identify potential impurities. Posed in simple terms, high-precision analytical methods allow process researchers to distinguish between good and bad output, a basic requirement for developing or improving any process.[9] With highly sensitive analytical techniques, researchers get better-quality information from each experiment because of reduced observation error. This better information, in turn, allows process researchers to map the impact of changes in specific process parameters to changes in the character of the product. Thus, strong analytical capabilities are an essential part of developing a deeper knowledge base about underlying cause-and-effect relationships.

All biotechnology firms recognize the critical role that analytical techniques play in process development. But Organization A viewed the development of novel analytical techniques as perhaps the most important capability within its process development group. The company's process R&D group took an aggressive posture toward analytical methods development, striving for sensitivity levels that exceeded what was generally perceived to be necessary at the time (although these higher levels of sensitivity became standard practice for the industry some years later).

Organization A's continued emphasis on strong analytical capabilities was an outgrowth of its philosophy that process development problems needed to be framed and solved at the molecular level. Analytical techniques are the 'eyes and ears' of process scientists. The more deeply one wants to probe a process, the more powerful the analytical techniques required. Thus, personnel hired for A's process development group came largely from scientific fields (e.g. protein chemistry, biochemistry, and biophysics), where high-precision techniques are central to research and a part of the tool kit of every Ph.D.

The superior lead-time performance of project A2 compared to A1 suggests that some type of organizational learning took place across projects. But, what was

---

[9] In the 'stages of knowledge' framework developed by Bohn and Jaikumar (1989), the very first stage of knowledge is having the ability to distinguish between good and bad output.

learned and how was it learned? From a purely technical viewpoint, one would not have expected much transfer of knowledge across projects. Scientists interviewed at Organization A, like those at other biotechnology companies in the study, emphasized that each protein molecule is unique and that the process technology must be customized for each. This implies that any 'theories of production' in this setting are local, in the sense that they apply to specific molecules. Indeed, this was learned early by Organization A on project A2. The organization thought it could best leverage development resources by using the basic process technology developed for A1. The initial thinking was that the only difference between A1 and A2 would be the specific genes coding for the protein. But when the genes were inserted into the *e-coli* bacteria cell used to produce A1, the A2 molecule was not biologically active. It was at this point that the company's scientists realized that A2 required a completely different process technology—one that used a mammalian host cell rather than a bacterial cell. Because the physiology of *e-coli* bacterial and mammalian cells is fundamentally different, much of the specific technical knowledge acquired from project A1 was not transferable.

Yet, despite the fact that few technical solutions could be directly transferred, A1 generated technical knowledge and organizational skills that provided a foundation for A2. These capabilities resulted from the firm's three-pronged approach to development: a strong focus on developing basic scientific knowledge at the molecular level, close interaction between process development and the plant, and heavy emphasis on analytical technology. The company's emphasis on developing basic knowledge of biotechnology processes at the molecular level had important implications for the type of knowledge available for use on A2. With A1, the company developed basic know-how about the structure, character, and behaviour of genetically engineered proteins. Thus, while every protein is different, many of the basic principles needed to develop two processes may be the same. Although a new set of technical capabilities was required for A2 to handle the specifics of mammalian cell production, the firm's existing strength in the basic process sciences made it easier to absorb these new capabilities.

In addition, because the problem-solving strategy was to uncover cause-and-effect relationships at the molecular level, A1 generated a set of procedures for measuring and tracking the stability of proteins, characterizing the protein, and identifying impurities. Thus, the company's strong emphasis on analytical techniques complemented its microlevel problem-solving strategy. When development scientists started A2, they had at their disposal a set of powerful analytical techniques that identified impurities at a far more precise level than was possible before A1. On A1, the purification process had to go through multiple iterations simply because as better analytical techniques became available, process researchers found new impurities that needed to be removed. On A2, with a powerful set of analytical techniques in hand, researchers could be much more confident about what constituted good output and how process changes might influence process performance.

The other component contributing to the knowledge base available for A2 was the close interaction between process development and manufacturing on A1. Direct and frequent contact with the plant taught scientists about manufacturing issues such as viral contamination, batch-to-batch variability, and degradation of proteins in larger-scale systems. On the A2 project, process scientists were able to anticipate some of the manufacturing problems and FDA expectations for a process technology. As one process scientists described it, 'We knew what to look out for... and we knew what data and assays would be needed.'

Although process development remained very much an art on A2, Organization A had deepened its knowledge base in a way that allowed process scientists to anticipate problems. Organization A's process know-how was by no means highly codified or theoretical; however, by building basic scientific capabilities and integrating practical knowledge about the actual manufacturing environment, Organization A began to take some of the art out of its biotechnology development. Although learning-by-doing in the actual manufacturing environment was still absolutely necessary and a critical component of the success of A2, the firm had begun to build more global theories of biological production processes that could be used proactively. In this way, the firm began the process of learning to learn-before-doing.

3.2. Organization B

Like Organization A, Organization B initially lacked a formal process development group. The company's process development capability evolved in response to a need to develop a full-scale manufacturing process for its first potential commercial product. To avoid the conclusion that organizational learning takes place only within narrowly prescribed organizational types, it is important to point out some important differences between Organizations A and B. Most noteworthy, whereas Organization A built up a relatively large process development group, B's explicit strategy was to keep the process development group relatively small. The senior manager hired to build the group commented:

The role of process development is to serve as a bridge between basic (product) research and manufacturing. If the group gets too big, it can get in the way. I wanted to avoid a situation where the process development group became a barrier to rapid development. I wanted process development to be a service, not an entity.

Although the formal process development group was small, all the major process development steps—selecting an appropriate clone, defining a basic process architecture, working out detailed process steps and controls, developing appropriate assays, and scaling up—had to be performed to get B1 and B2 on the market. To compensate for its small mass, the process development organization made liberal use of personnel from other organizational functions, including research and manufacturing. Process development projects were performed by integrated teams with members from research, process development, the pilot plant, and commercial manufacturing. Thus, process development in reality was a cross-functional project-level organizational entity.

Despite the organizational differences, Organizations A and B exhibited some striking similarities. Like Organization A, B believed strongly that process development required the firm to be at the leading edge of several basic scientific disciplines. The challenge of process development was viewed in terms of solving basic scientific problems. Also like A, Organization B placed less emphasis on process engineering. As noted by the head of process development, 'Some companies like to build Cadillacs. Our plants are more like Chevys: they're small, but can be easily ratcheted up to meet demand.' Organizational learning at A and B implied building knowledge about the structure and behaviour of proteins, rather than about the physical or mechanical aspects of the process or the broader manufacturing system.

Organizations A and B also were very much alike in their use of manufacturing as a locus of development. Part of the 'keep the process development group small' philosophy was driven by the idea that most process development experiments should be done by the plant. Like Organization A, B carried out its pilot production runs in a commercial manufacturing setting. Thus, the job of manufacturing went well beyond manufacturing the product in compliance with regulatory standards. The plant was expected to play an integral role in process development. To facilitate this interaction, process development and manufacturing were part of the same organization, and the plant was co-located with R&D. A Ph.D.-level scientist who had started in process development and worked on B1 later became head of the manufacturing plant charged with supplying clinical trials. According to process developers, it was helpful to have someone with his background running the plant because he understood how to manage experimentation—there was no hesitancy to change the process technology while products were in clinical trials. A process developer explained:

The key is to be able to show the FDA that the product is exactly the same after you change the process. As long as you can show the data, you're okay. You've got to be able to do good science in the plant. That's where it helps having a scientist run the plant.

As part of 'doing good science' in the plant, the company began to emphasize the analytical techniques needed to characterize proteins and identify impurities. As noted earlier, precise analytical techniques are critical to experimental integrity in biotechnology, and they are particularly important if the company plans to make changes once a process is running in the manufacturing plant.

Tight integration between process development and the manufacturing plant helped deepen the organization's process knowledge in two ways. First, learning did not end with the successful transfer of the process to the factory. Even after the process was up and running, process developers continued to monitor performance. If yields fell outside control limits, process development scientists were called in to investigate the problem and to collaborate with operators in identifying the root cause. Thus, although product B1 was in its eighty-fifth batch, it continued to provide data on the underlying drivers of process performance. Second, close contact with the plant during development and start-up was an educational experience for both parties. As described by the head of process R&D:

What the basic research people here are interested in [is] taking a process all the way from their lab into the factory. Because they get involved in the manufacturing start-up, they see the actual problems and alter their approaches. The guy who cloned the B2 in research was also responsible for developing the commercial purification process. Although he was a researcher, he had learned a lot about manufacturing from his previous process development work on B1.

Tight and ongoing interaction between process development and the plant played a central role in building and diffusing process knowledge. When the company started B2, research scientists and process developers were armed with experience about what worked in the manufacturing of B1. For example, the purification process developed in C1, while commercially viable, was complex and costly to operate. Research scientists and process developers spent more time up front on B2 designing a streamlined purification process before ever testing it in the plant. They also had gained a better understanding of the process parameters that tended to vary under manufacturing conditions, and thus could be more efficient in the design of their laboratory experiments on C2.

At an organizational level, Organizations A and B appear to have followed dissimilar strategies for building process development capabilities. Within Organization A, a large, formally defined process development group was the organizational mechanism for capturing and storing fundamental technical knowledge related to manufacturing processes. Because Organization B lacked the infrastructure to act as a storage mechanism, knowledge tended to diffuse throughout the organization and across functions. Although it might be tempting to think that Organization B would have had greater difficulty capturing knowledge, such was not the case. Organization A's more functional approach and B's more team-oriented approach both appear to have contributed to organizational learning across projects. This contrast suggests that no single strategy holds the key to organizational learning. However, each strategy represents a different approach to solving a more fundamental problem: how to create an integrated body of technical knowledge for developing manufacturing processes.

3.3. Organization C

Organization C is noteworthy for its inconsistency: while significant improvement occurred between C1 and C2, performance deteriorated between C2 and C3. This is all the more surprising given that all three manufacturing processes were very similar—indeed, the same manufacturing plant was used. Some of the discrepancy appears to be a result of the development strategy chosen. On C2, the firm employed learning-by-doing. C1 and C3 represent aberrations from that strategy: the firm undertook more process research (and seems to have paid a price for doing so). Yet there is more here than just a failure to match the project strategy to the imperatives of the technological environment. If we compare C3 and B2, it is clear that firm C did not improve its capability to learn-before-doing, even with the benefit of two previous projects under its belt. Knowledge generated in C1 and C2 was not captured. While A and B made some headway in creating more global theories of biotechnology manufacturing that permitted learning-before-doing, Organization C continues to be heavily reliant on learning-by-doing within each project.

As shown in Figure 5.2, Organization C pursued an extreme version of the learning-by-doing strategy on C2. There was only negligible process research before pilot testing because the same basic technology was used for both C1 and C2. This also accelerated the project's overall lead time. Thus, Organization C was capable of learning across projects, at least during the early phase of the development process. C2's excellent lead-time performance can be partly attributed to this cross-project transfer of technology. Moreover, by moving the process into the pilot production facility, the firm was able to identify process problems quickly and adapt to the manufacturing environment. Finally, a commercial manufacturing plant had been designed and constructed for C1. Knowing the equipment and configuration gave developers a fixed target for developing the process.

With C3, the company appears to have placed more emphasis on laboratory-based process research—primarily for reasons of expedience. Because the pilot and commercial manufacturing plants were completely utilized for clinical and commercial production of C1 and C2, process developers had no choice but to do more of their development work for C3 in the laboratory—that is, they were forced to learn-before-doing. Technically, because C3 used the same basic process technology as C1 and C2, this should not have presented a major problem. In addition, it was expected from the outset that the product would be manufactured in the same plant as the previous two. C3 should have been able to capitalize on knowledge from earlier projects. Process research should have been the phase when the company used experience from prior projects to anticipate and solve problems. Organization B, for example, performed the same relative amount of process research on B2 as Organization C did on C3, yet the lead-time performance of B2 was far superior. To understand why performance deteriorated, we need to examine exactly what was learned (and, perhaps more importantly, not learned) from the C1 and C2 experiences.

The fundamental technical challenge on projects C1 and C2 was framed in terms of fitting the process to the existing plant. As one process developer noted, 'The whole driver of this project was to push productivity to the point where we would not have to use a new plant.' As noted above, having a fixed plant as a target around which to design a process was an advantage in some respects. However, it also led to a narrow problem-solving focus. Only those options which were likely to fit the existing plant configuration and equipment were considered, and process developers were forced to work within a narrower envelope of process possibilities.

For instance, the output of the cell culture process is a function of the scale of the reactors, the density of cell growth (number of cells per litre), and cell-specific productivity (picograms of protein produced per cell). Because the plant was fitted with 1,000-litre reactors, this first process dimension was already fixed. This forced the company's process developers to search for cell lines and other process parameters that met specific targets along the latter two dimensions. These constraints gave process developers less incentive to do exploratory research on a broad range of process options up front. Thus, much of the experimentation that might have yielded greater insight into the molecular biology underlying the production process was precluded by the company's development strategy.

Furthermore, once the process was operating in the plant, senior management was adamant that only minor process changes be made, out of fear that larger-scale changes could cause problems with the regulatory filing. As one process developer noted, 'We didn't understand much about the molecule and we worried how process changes might affect its therapeutic properties.' Compounding this problem was a lack of analytical capabilities needed to characterize the molecule. Senior management worried that if the process were changed significantly, it would be difficult to demonstrate equivalency to regulatory authorities without additional clinical trials. To avoid potential regulatory problems, further experimentation was moved to a separate pilot facility outside the commercial manufacturing plant. Thus, once the process was running in the plant, process developers were largely cut off from further performance feedback.

This approach to development stands in strong contrast to that of A and B, which emphasized understanding the process at the molecular level and using the plant as a locus of experimentation and development. Judged by lead-time performance, firm C's approach on project C2 was a success. By adopting the technology developed for C1, C2 was completed quickly and met its commercial requirements. However, C1 and C2's narrow problem-solving focus constrained opportunities for broader learning. In some ways, this strategy confined the organization to developing and exploiting local theories of the process technology; the deeper technical knowledge that comes from broad exploration and experimentation in the actual manufacturing plant was lost. Organization C learned how to make C1 and C2 work in the factory but did not know at a detailed level *why* it worked.[10] Without a broader theory of how these processes worked, process developers were not well positioned to use laboratory experiments as a means of modelling. Only after they were able to move to the factory did process developers begin to uncover problems.

The inability to lever knowledge from prior projects was further inhibited by a change in project management strategy used by Organization C. On C1 and C2, the company used a functional structure very similar to that described for Organization A: the process development group managed the development and transfer of the process technology. On C3, the firm adopted a project team structure whereby one overall project manager was responsible for coordinating and managing the flow of work across all the development functions. The benefit of such an approach is improved integration across functions. The trade-off is that functional input, including that of process development, is reduced. Technical decisions affecting process development and process development decisions affecting other aspects of development were in the hands of the project team members. Because many members of the project team from other functions had not been involved in prior process development projects, information and technical knowledge from those projects were not well integrated into the C3 project.

Thus, as in Organization A, the process development group at Organization C initially was the repository for technical knowledge. The shift to the team structure

---

[10] The distinction between 'know-how' and 'know-why' has a long history in the literature on process control and manufacturing improvement; see Bohn and Jaikumar (1989) and Leonard-Barton (1995).

destroyed the firm's mechanism for retrieving knowledge. And, unlike Organization B, which used a team structure right from the beginning, technical knowledge regarding processes was not widely diffused at Organization C nor was this knowledge developed and codified in a way that might have permitted rapid diffusion to others within the organization. Process development at Organization C was an art that worked well when the artists were allowed to practise their craft. Because technical knowledge regarding processes was not developed and because people from outside process development (such as research scientists) had not been exposed to process development, the shift to a team-based project management destroyed any opportunities to learn from the prior projects.

3.4. Organization D

In the case of Organization D, lead-time performance deteriorated between the first and second project. As in the case of Organization C, some of this deterioration can be explained by a change in the development strategy. In moving into the pilot plant after only 7 per cent of process R&D resources had been expended, project D1 followed a learning-by-doing strategy. On D2, the firm spent 15 per cent of its process R&D resources prior to the first pilot batch, indicating a shift toward learning-before-doing. However, as in the case of Organization C, we need to ask why D did not improve its capacity to learn-before-doing. Had Organization D captured knowledge, it might have been able to use process research more effectively. At the very least, the increase in process research should not have hurt performance. Again, the lack of improvement is surprising given that D1 and D2 were based on broadly similar classes of process technology. Furthermore, some process development scientists within the firm viewed D1 as more challenging because of the molecule's complex structure and inherent instability.

The patterns of behaviour that inhibited learning at Organization C were also present in D. Again, these can be grouped into two categories: (i) a failure on the first project to develop a deeper technical understanding of the process technology in a way that might offer broader insights for the next project and (ii) a disconnection between process developers and feedback from the manufacturing environment. Because these patterns have already been discussed above, we focus here on the specific ways they played out in Organization D.

On D1, the firm found itself in a competitive race with other biotechnology firms trying to commercialize the same molecule. Speed to market was viewed as absolutely critical. Furthermore, given the molecule's complexity, developing a commercially viable manufacturing process was viewed as the key challenge to rapid launch. However, the original strategy was to use an established pharmaceutical company to both market and manufacture the drug. Organization D was to be responsible only for supplying clinical trials. In order to commence clinical trials as quickly as possible, the company decided to develop the process technology in two stages: it initially would develop a process suitable to start Phase I clinical trials, then, as clinical trials progressed, it would develop a second-generation process capable of producing the product in commercial quantities and at commercially attractive costs.

Almost immediately, it was discovered that the protein had innate characteristics that would cause problems in larger-scale production processes. In particular, the protein tended to stick to the cells from which it was produced and, as a result, it was virtually impossible to isolate and purify. Further manipulations to the cell line solved this sticking problem, but, unfortunately, the new cell line would grow only if cultured in small-scale bottles (where the cells could physically attach themselves to the surface of the bottle). The cell line was completely unsuitable for larger-scale production where cells are typically grown in suspension (that is, floating in the tank rather than attached to the walls of the vessel). Because the first phase of the process development project was focused entirely on getting a small-scale process ready as quickly as possible, the cell-line issue was not dealt with at this time. By using a large number of small bottles, the company would be able to make enough product for Phase I clinical trials. To further expedite the process, the company decided to use a contract manufacturer to make the product for Phase I clinical trials. The view at that time was that once the documentation was transferred, the contractor could begin producing the protein within weeks.

Unfortunately, the transfer of the process was far more complicated than anticipated. The contractor—located three thousand miles away—did not understand the subtleties of the process technology and had difficulty making it work. Organization D was forced to send some of its scientists to the contractor to teach them the process and to leave three people there full time for six months to supervise production and troubleshoot. There were so many problems with production that virtually no further process development was possible back at the company. In the course of this extensive troubleshooting, some process developers involved with the contractors gained in-depth knowledge about the molecule: its robustness (in particular, its tendency to degrade), its toxicity, and other aspects of the process. However, this knowledge was not capitalized on for the second phase of the project, the development of the commercial-scale process. One process developer noted, 'When we returned home, we were not able to use any of the information or learning we acquired at [the contractor]. The company had its own manufacturing people who had their own way of doing things.'

Development of the commercial process involved extensive technical work to find a way to adapt the cell line to a larger-scale production process. At about this time, Organization D's corporate partner decided it wanted Organization D to do the commercial manufacturing. After a year of intensive laboratory work, scientists found a way to genetically alter the cell line so that it could be grown in suspension in a large tank; the process was then tried at large scale. Although it ran, animal tests suggested that the product was not therapeutically active. Further investigation of the process indicated that the protein was being degraded during the production process, and minor changes to cell-culture media resolved the problem.[11] Additional pro-

---

[11] Ironically, degradation of the protein was not the root cause of the problem; in fact, further analysis of the animal test data indicated there never was a problem with the product—it was therapeutically active. One scientist noted that 'this error was fortuitous because it allowed us to identify and solve the degradation problem.'

blems were discovered in the purification end of the process. For example, at larger scale, the filters used for purification tended to clog. Changing the filters solved this problem.

After these start-up problems were solved, the process ran smoothly at commercial scale. At one level, the process development project was a success: an intense burst of development effort in the later phases of the project led to relatively quick development and scale-up of a very complex process. However, scientists associated with the project commented that the intense time pressure late in the project forced them into a reactive mode of problem-solving. According to a key scientist on the project, 'Instead of fully understanding changes before they were made, evaluations were typically done "after the fact" to make sure the product had not been affected as a result of the process change.' Thus, as was the case for Organization C, specific problems were successfully solved but broader opportunities for learning may have been forfeited.

Although projects D1 and D2 overlapped somewhat, project D2 appears not to have benefited from learning in the early phases of D1. Additional emphasis on process research did not expedite development on D2 even though the basic process technologies were similar. There were several reasons for this. First, D2 employed the same two-phase development strategy as D1: first develop a bare-bones process to enable clinical production and then go back and develop a full-scale commercial process. This strategy inherently limited the potential for early-phase process research on D2 to use knowledge from D1. The focus at the early phase was on developing an acceptable process. Because larger-scale manufacturing was a future issue, the scale-up problems of D1 were not considered important information for the early phase of D2. In fact, given intense pressures to make enough product to supply clinical trials, much of the early laboratory work was geared toward supply rather than development.

The second factor that inhibited the transfer of knowledge across projects was a difference in the manufacturing strategies. Although D1 was eventually produced in-house, commercial production of D2 was performed by a corporate partner. The distance between firm D and its corporate partner's plant—more than three thousand miles—inhibited ongoing interaction between process development and manufacturing throughout the project. This made it difficult for process developers to anticipate future manufacturing conditions and constraints. Moreover, experience from D1, which involved the company's own manufacturing plant and people, was essentially useless. The corporate partner's manufacturing environment, operating procedures, skills, and experience were different. When the corporate partner experienced difficulty starting up the process, it blamed the problem on the process technology ('it was unmanufacturable'), while Organization D's scientists blamed it on the plant ('they were incompetent').

Finally, as was the case for Organization C, D was undergoing changes in its approach to project management. On D1, the company used a largely functional structure, while D2 used a team approach that increased cross-functional participation and coordination. Although many of the same scientists were involved in D1 and D2, the management of the project was very different. In particular, senior process development management had far less influence on decisions—even when those decisions had a direct impact on process development activities. For instance, at one point, a decision was made to dramatically increase the size and scope of clinical trials: approximately 50 mg. of the molecule were required. This seemed like a relatively small quantity to most members of the project team and to senior management in the company. However, considering that no one, anywhere in the word, at any time, had ever managed to make more than 1 mg. of the molecule, 50 mg. represented a huge quantity. By the time senior process development managers discovered this, the decision (and contractual commitments) had already been made. Process development scientists then spent several months making hundreds of very small-scale batches of the product and did little technical problem-solving. Thus, as we saw in Organization C, changing the approach to project management disrupted the informal lines of communication that allowed the firm to exploit existing technical and organizational knowledge.

4. Conclusion

Every development project generates two potential outputs: a process technology used to manufacture a particular product or set of products and a technical knowledge about underlying cause-and-effect relationships. Very often, managers and scholars focus their attention on this first dimension of performance. Yet, as discussed above, the 'second-order' knowledge-building effects of projects can have important implication for R&D strategies and performance. The clinical analysis suggest some of the following as themes for future research.

(1) The non-deterministic impact of experience on learning: the limits of path-dependence

As noted earlier, much of the recent literature on organizational capabilities contends that learning is 'path-dependent'. The seeds of today's capabilities are sown in yesterday's experience. There is nothing in the clinical evidence above to refute this compelling principle. However, the clinical analyses also illustrated that the link between 'learning' and 'experience' is not always straightforward. When it comes to learning, not all types of experiences are equal. Some experiences, for example, expose the organization to deeper underlying cause–effect relationships which become applicable on future projects. Experience may provide opportunities for learning, but whether learning takes place from experience, depends on specific organizational actions and management decisions. As discussed in the comparative cases, organizational learning appeared to be far better managed in some firms than others.

(2) Development projects as elements of dynamic capability

In some of the literature on organizational capabilities (Nelson and Winter 1982; Teece *et al.*, forthcoming), a theoretical distinction is made between 'static' routines and 'dynamic' routines. Static routines regulate ongoing operational and commercial activities. Dynamic routines regulate search for improved routines and methods. Process developments are designed to search for, select, and implement superior production routines. In this sense, they constitute part of an organization's dynamic capabilities. However, they are dynamic in another sense as well. As illustrated in the above cases, routines used by organizations to carry out development projects seemed to have an important influence on the evolution of future development capabilities. Development routines themselves evolve over time in response to what has been learned from a previous project.

(3) Integration as a vehicle for learning in novel environments

How do organizations learn when confronted with a novel technical or commercial problem? The answer, as has been well discussed in the literature, is 'by doing'. Yet, as highlighted in the case comparisons, who does what within an organization influences learning. In many companies, there is a sharp distinction between the worlds of R&D and of the plant. Scientists and engineers in R&D engage in problem-solving, learning, and experimentation. Engineers and operators in manufacturing are supposed to focus on meeting supply needs and cost targets and conforming to the process specifications laid down by R&D. This dichotomy was particularly pronounced in Organization C. However, as we saw in A and B, the manufacturing plants were an integral part of process development. This not only had first-order effects in terms of making it easier to identify and solve problems on the current project, but also gave process scientists a much richer understanding of the production environment. This, in turn, enabled better anticipation of problems on future projects. In addition, the experiments conducted in the plants fed higher-quality information back into the firm's knowledge base. A general implication of this finding is that tight integration between development and user or operating environments plays a critical role in learning across projects in novel environments. Once again, whether such integration takes place or not, seemed to depend critically on managerial actions and decisions.

Appendix

Sample and Data-Collection Methods

The sample used in the statistical analyses consisted of twenty-three process development projects, each of which was associated with the launch of a new therapeutic molecular entity. Ten projects involved proteins made through recombinant biotechnology methods, while thirteen involved traditional, chemically synthesized compounds. Five large pharmaceutical companies (including the biotechnology division of one of these companies) and five new entrants into the industry participated. Of the five established pharmaceutical firms, three were headquartered in Europe and two in the United States. Given the proprietary nature of the data used in the study, the names of the companies and the individual projects are not identified. However, the aggregate profile of the companies participating in the study is relatively typical of top-tier firms. All five established companies ranked among the top twenty globally in terms of sales and annual R&D spending; three were among the top ten. All new entrants were based in the United States. Although they all might be considered biotechnology firms, one company's process development project largely involved chemical synthesis, and its project was classified as a chemical-based technology.

Data for each project were collected between mid-1991 and mid-1993 through three methods: in-depth interviews, questionnaire surveys, and internal company documents. In the early phases of the research, a set of unstructured interviews was conducted to identify the relevant managerial and technical issues, generate working hypotheses, and determine the most relevant metrics for examining those hypotheses. The next phase was to collect systematic data across projects. A questionnaire was administered personally during on-site interviews. In virtually every case, my research assistant or a collaborator was also present at these interviews, and we carefully cross-checked notes to ensure consistency. Any discrepancies were resolved through follow-up communications. At least two rounds of interviews were conducted for each company, with later rounds being used to verify or refine data collected earlier. Follow-up telephone and fax communication also was used to fill in missing details. For each project, between five and twenty people—with responsibilities ranging from bench-level scientists and technicians to senior executives—were interviewed. In total, approximately 200 people were interviewed. Internal company documents—including detailed project event reports, technical process information, standard operating procedures, project team charts, accounting reports, and memorandum—were also used to verify information collected through the questionnaire and structured interviews.

Statistical Methods Used to Generate the Data Presented in Figure 5.2

To isolate the impact of learning strategies on lead-time performance, and to determine if there were any differences in this impact between biotechnology- and chemical-based projects, the following regression was estimated:

$$\text{LEAD TIME}_i = \beta_0 + \beta_1 \text{CHEM}_i + \beta_2 \text{PILOT} = 1\ \text{LEAD}_i + \beta_3 \text{INTEGRATED} + \beta_4$$
$$\text{PILOT DEV\%}_i + \beta_5 \text{RESEARCH\%}_i + \beta_6 \text{CHEM}^* \text{RESEARCH\%} + e_i$$

where
   CHEM is a dummy variable $= 1$ if the project was chemical-based;

PILOT-1 LEAD is the number of months between the start of the project and the first attempt to produce a batch of material under pilot plant conditions;

INTEGRATED is a dummy variable set equal to 1 if one organization in the company was responsible for all activities of process R&D (from process research through the successful transfer to the plant);

PILOT DEV% is the percentage of total project hours consumed between the first pilot batch and the start of the transfer to the commercial manufacturing site;

RESEARCH% is the percentage of total project hours spent before the first attempt to produce a batch of materials under pilot plant conditions. *This variable is used as a proxy for the learning strategy.* A higher percentage of total resources expended prior to the first pilot batch of production indicates a relatively greater emphasis on learning-before-doing.

A full presentation of the methods, models, and results is provided in Pisano (1997). The data shown in Figure 5.2 are the residuals of the regression for the ten biotechnology projects in the sample.

References

Bohn, R. E., and R. Jaikumar (1989). 'The Dynamic Approach: An Alternative Paradigm for Operations Management', Harvard Business School Working Paper.

Chandler, A. D. (1990). *Scale and Scope: The Dynamics of Industrial Capitalism*. Cambridge, Mass.: Harvard University Press.

Cyert, R. M., and J. G. March (1963). *A Behavioral Theory of the Firm*. Englewood Cliffs, NJ: Prentice-Hall.

Evanson, R., and Y. Kislev (1975). *Agricultural Research and Productivity*. New Haven, Conn.: Yale University Press.

Hayes, R. H., S. C. Wheelwright, and Kim B. Clark (1988). *Dynamic Manufacturing: Creating the Learning Organization*. New York: Free Press.

Henderson, R. M. (1994). 'The Evolution of Integrative Capability: Innovation in Cardiovascular Drug Discovery', *Industrial and Corporate Change*, 3(3): 607–30.

Iansiti, M. (1995). 'Technology Integration: Managing Technological Evolution in a Complex Environment', *Research Policy*, 24: 521–42.

—— and K. B. Clark (1994). 'Integration and Dynamic Capability: Evidence from Product Development in Automobiles and Mainframe Computers', *Industrial and Corporate Change*, 3(3): 557–606.

Kogut, B., and U. Zander (1992). 'Knowledge of Firm, Combinative Capabilities, and the Replication of Technology', *Organization Science*, 3: 383–97.

Leonard-Barton, D. (1992). 'The Factory as a Learning Laboratory', *Sloan Management Review*, 34(1): 23–38.

—— (1995). *Wellsprings of Knowledge*. Boston, Mass.: Harvard Business School Press.

Levinthal, D., and J. March (1981). 'A Model of Adaptive Organizational Search', *Journal of Economic Behavior and Organization*, 2: 307–33.

Levitt, B., and J. March (1988). 'Organizational Learning', *Annual Review of Sociology*, 14: 319–40.

Nelson, R. R., and S. G. Winter (1982). *An Evolutionary Theory of Economic Change*. Cambridge, Mass.: Harvard University Press.

Pisano, G. (1994). 'Knowledge, Integration, and the Locus of Learning: An Empirical Analysis of Process Development', *Strategic Management Journal*, 15: 85–100.

—— (1997). *The Development Factory: Unlocking the Potential of Process Innovation*. Boston, Mass.: Harvard Business School Press.

Polanyi, M. (1958). *Personal Knowledge: Towards a Post-Critical Philosophy*. Chicago: University of Chicago Press.

Prahalad, C. K., and G. Hammel (1990). 'The Core Competences of the Corporation', *Harvard Business Review* (May–June): 79–91.

Teece, D. J. (1977). 'Technology Transfer by Multinational Firms: The Resource Cost of Transferring Technological Know-How', *Economic Journal*, 87: 242–61.

—— (1982). 'Towards an Economic Theory of the Multi-Product Firm', *Journal of Economic Behavior and Organization*, 3: 39–63.

—— and G. Pisano (1994). 'The Dynamic Capabilities of Firms: An Introduction', *Industrial and Corporate Change*, 3(3): 537–56.

—— —— and A. Shuen (1997), 'Dynamic Capabilities and Strategic Management', *Strategic Management Journal*.

Wernerfelt, B. (1984). 'A Resource-Based View of the Firm', *Strategic Management Journal*, 5: 171–80.

6

Measuring Competence? Exploring Firm Effects in Drug Discovery

REBECCA HENDERSON AND IAIN COCKBURN

1. Introduction

There has recently been a revival of interest in the 'resource-based view of the firm'. Those working within this tradition have drawn inspiration from the work of authors such as Selznick (1957) and Penrose (1959), and have suggested that inimitable firm heterogeneity, or the possession of unique 'competencies' or 'capabilities' may be an important source of enduring strategic advantage (Lippman and Rumelt 1982; Wernerfelt 1984; Barney 1986; Rumelt 1991; Amit and Schoemaker 1993; Dosi and Teece 1993; Peteraf 1993). This perspective promises to be an important complement to the strategic management field's more recent focus on industry structure as a determinant of competitive advantage (Porter 1980).

However, despite the renewed theoretical interest in these ideas, empirical work in the area is still at a preliminary stage. Several studies have shown that heterogeneous firm effects account for a high proportion of the variance of profit rates across firms (Cool and Schendel 1988; Hansen and Wernerfelt 1989; Rumelt 1991), and at the same time an important stream of research has confirmed that idiosyncratic firm capabilities both shape diversification strategy and drive the performance of diversified firms (Hitt and Ireland 1985; Montgomery and Wernerfelt 1988). But in general this work has been forced to rely on measures of competence constructed at such an aggregate level that they cannot capture the richness of the constructs of the theoretical literature. Studies of the evolution of capability at individual firms have greatly enriched our understanding of the nature of particular competencies (Leonard-Barton 1992; Iansiti 1993; Burgelman 1994), but by and large these insights have not been incorporated into studies of aggregate firm behaviour or systematic

This chapter is largely based on material that previously appeared in our article 'Measuring Competence? Exploring Firm Effects in Drug Discovery', *Strategic Management Journal*, 15 (Special Issue 1994): 63–84.

We would like to express our appreciation to the editors of this special issue for their comments on earlier drafts, and to thank seminar participants at the University of British Columbia, Harvard, Stanford, Berkeley, Chicago, Princeton, Michigan, Washington University at St Louis, MIT, and UCLA, and Steven Barley, Bill Barnett, Mauro Guillen, Marco Iansiti, Bruce Kogut, Cynthia Montgomery, William Ocasio, and Birger Wernerfelt for their helpful comments and suggestions. This research was funded by four pharmaceutical companies and by the Sloan Foundation. Their support is gratefully acknowledged. Our thanks also go to all of those firms that contributed data to the study—without their time and trouble this project would not have been possible. The conclusions and opinions expressed remain our own, and any errors or omissions are entirely our responsibility.

studies of competition. With some notable exceptions (see, e.g., work by Mitchell 1989, 1992; Clark and Fujimoto 1991; and Kogut and Kim 1991) relatively little empirical work has attempted to combine the richness of measures of competence derived from fieldwork with large-scale statistical studies of competition.

This chapter explores the role of 'competence' in pharmaceutical research. In 'Scale, Scope and Spillovers: The Determinants of Research Productivity in Drug Discovery' (Henderson and Cockburn (1996), hereafter 'Scale, Scope and Spillovers') we drew upon detailed qualitative and quantitative data obtained from ten major pharmaceutical firms at the programme level to show that large firms were at a significant advantage in the management of research through their ability to exploit economies of scope. But this paper raised a number of puzzling questions. In the first place, we found that a large proportion of the variance in research productivity across firms could be attributed to firm-fixed effects. In the second place, our results suggested that despite the fact that differences in the structure of the research portfolio had very significant effects on research productivity, variations in portfolio structure across firms were both large and persistent. Both findings are consistent with the existence of exactly the kinds of firm-specific, enduring sources of heterogeneity that are highlighted by the resource-based view of the firm.

Here we build on these results to explore the nature of firm effects and the role of 'competence' in pharmaceutical research. While the possession of an unusually productive research effort is only one amongst several possible sources of advantage in the industry,[1] focusing on research as a first step in understanding the role of competence in pharmaceutical competition has a number of advantages. Successful research efforts typically take many years to build and often rely on idiosyncratic search routines that may be very difficult to transfer across organizations (Nelson 1991). Thus a substantial body of theoretical work suggests that idiosyncratic research capabilities are likely to be a particularly important source of strategically significant 'competence' in science- and technology-driven industries (Dierickx and Cool 1989).

We draw on detailed qualitative data about the history of research at each of the ten firms in our sample to construct a variety of measures of 'competence'. These variables account for much of the firm effect identified in our previous work, in both firm-level and research-programme-level data. 'Architectural competence', as captured by our indicators of the firm's ability to knowledge integratively, is positively associated with research productivity. Firms which maintain links to the wider scientific community through the use of publication in the open literature as a criterion for promotion, and firms which manage the allocation of key research

---

[1] While productive research may be a critically important factor in the quest for competitive advantage in the pharmaceutical industry, promising new drug candidates need to be tested in humans, to satisfy a long and complex regulatory process and to capture a share of an increasingly competitive market. Successful pharmaceutical firms may thus be able to sustain themselves through the development of unique competencies in clinical testing, in sales or marketing, or in their ability to work effectively with regulatory authorities (Hirsch 1975; Cool and Schendel 1988).

resources through collaborative rather than dictatorial processes are significantly more productive in drug discovery. This result is robust to controls for variation in technological opportunity and in 'component competence', or possession of skills or assets specific to particular local activities within the firm. We conclude that focusing on 'architectural' or 'integrative' characteristics of organizations can offer valuable insights into the source of enduring differences in firm performance.

We begin with a brief review of the literature as background to the development of some hypotheses. Section 2 describes the estimation methodology and Section 3 the data and the construction of the variables used in the quantitative analysis. Section 4 describes the results and the chapter closes with a discussion of their implications and of some directions for further research.

2. Literature Review and Hypothesis Development

For an organizational 'competence' to be a source of competitive advantage it must meet three conditions: it must be heterogeneously distributed within an industry, it must be impossible to buy or sell in the available factor markets at less than its true marginal value, and it must be difficult or costly to replicate (Wernerfelt, 1984; Barney 1986; Peteraf, 1993). While a wide variety of possible sources of heterogeneity fit these criteria, several authors have suggested that unique capabilities in research and development are particularly plausible sources of competitively important competence (Dierickx and Cool 1989; Nelson 1991), and several studies have confirmed that there are significant and persistent differences across firms in their ability to conduct research and to develop new products (Clark and Fujimoto 1991; Leonard-Barton 1992; Henderson 1993; Tabrizi and Eisenhardt 1994).

To structure our empirical analysis, we draw on the literature to distinguish between two broad classes of capability that might act as sources of idiosyncratic firm advantage in pharmaceutical research: 'component competence' or the local abilities and knowledge that are fundamental to day-to-day problem-solving and 'architectural competence' or the ability to *use* these component competencies—to integrate them effectively and to develop fresh component competencies as they are required. Under 'component competence' we mean to include what others have called 'resources' (Amit and Shoemaker 1993) and 'knowledge and skills' or 'technical systems' (Leonard-Barton 1992; Teece *et al.* 1992), while by using the term 'architectural competence' we mean to include what others have called 'capabilities' (Amit and Schoemaker 1993), 'integrative capabilities' (Lawrence and Lorsch 1967), 'dynamic capabilities' (Teeca *et al.* 1992), 'implicit/social' or 'collective' knowledge (Spender 1994), 'organizational architecture' (Nelson 1991), 'combinative capabilities' (Kogut and Zander 1992), 'managerial systems' and 'values and norms' (Leonard-Barton 1992), and 'invisible assets' (Itami 1987).

2.1. *Component competence*

A number of researchers have suggested that locally embedded knowledge and skills may be a 'competence' for the firm and a source of enduring competitive advantage.

For example, Leonard-Barton (1992) suggests that the tacit knowledge developed by skilled engineers with a particular production process over an extended period of time may become a source of advantage for the firm. Similarly Teece *et al.* (1992) suggest that local capabilities such as proprietary design rules may become so deeply embedded in the knowledge of local groups within the firm that they become strategically important capabilities.

Within the context of pharmaceutical research, there are two dimensions along which firms might develop strategically important local competencies. In the first place, firms may acquire unique disciplinary expertise. Modern drug discovery requires the input of scientists skilled in a very wide range of disciplines, including molecular biology, physiology, biochemistry, analytic and medicinal chemistry, crystallography, and pharmacology. As Peteraf (1993) points out, the employment of a Nobel prize-winning chemist is unlikely, in itself, to be a significant source of competitive advantage since such highly skilled individuals are likely to be both mobile and able to command a wage that reflects their value to the firm. But to the degree that expertise in any one of these disciplines builds on a foundation of experience that is largely tacit, excellence in say, pharmacology, may be a source of enduring competitive advantage. Our qualitative analysis leads us to believe that disciplinary groups embedded within particular firms develop deeply embedded, taken-for-granted knowledge or unique modes of working together that make the group particularly effective and that cannot be easily codified. For example, one of the roots of Merck's recent success may be a legacy of superb medicinal chemistry that dates back to Max Tishler's leadership at the firm.[2] Thus we hypothesize:

H1: Drug discovery productivity is an increasing function of firm-specific expertise in particular disciplinary areas.

The second dimension along which firms may be able to develop strategically important component competence is in particular disease areas. Fundamental science plays an important role in modern pharmaceutical research (see below), but human physiology is enormously complex, and there is still much that is not known about the aetiology of many diseases and the ways in which drugs affect their progress. Thus there is room for groups of disciplinary specialists working together to develop tacit or proprietary knowledge about particular disease areas. For example Eli Lilly has been a leader in the field of diabetic therapy for over a hundred years, and Hoffman-La Roche developed extensive expertise in anti-anxiety drugs following its discovery of the tranquillizer Valium. Our earlier finding that the most important determinant of investment in any given disease area is the previous year's investment (Cockburn and Henderson 1994) is also consistent with the presence of substantial 'local' knowledge and ability in particular areas. Thus we hypothesize:

H2: Drug discovery productivity is an increasing function of component competence in particular disease areas.

---

[2] Our mention of a particular company by name, both here and later in the chapter, does not imply that it is or is not included in the data set.

2.2. Architectural competence

The 'architectural competence' of an organization allows it to make use of its component competencies: to integrate them together in new and flexible ways and to develop new architectural and component competencies as they are required. We include in our definition both the 'architectural knowledge' defined by Henderson and Clark (1990)—the communication channels, information filters, and problem-solving strategies that develop between groups within a problem-solving organization—as well as the other organizational characteristics that structure problem-solving within the firm and that shape the development of new competencies: the control systems and the 'culture' or dominant values of the organization. Several scholars have suggested that these types of assets may be one of the most enduring sources of competitive advantage. Leonard-Barton (1992) points to the role of both managerial systems and the values and norms of the organization in sustaining the ability to use existing skills and to respond to changes in the environment, and Nelson (1991) suggests that the 'organizational architecture' and idiosyncratic search routines that sustain these types of competence develop in an evolutionary way that makes them extraordinarily difficult to replicate. Similarly Kogut and Zander (1992) and Itami (1987) suggest that unique abilities to redeploy existing knowledge may be fundamental to long-term strategic advantage.

Prior research exploring the determinants of effective research organizations and of effective product and process development processes in combination with our qualitative work suggests that two forms of integrative or architectural competence may be particularly important as sources of enduring competitive advantage in pharmaceutical research: the ability to access new knowledge from outside the boundaries of the organization and the ability to integrate knowledge flexibly across disciplinary and therapeutic class boundaries within the organization.

In the 1960s and early 1970s, drug research was largely a matter of the large-scale screening of thousands of compounds in the hope of discovering something new. For example firms injected hundreds of compounds into hypertensive rats in the hopes of finding something that would lower their blood pressure. Medicinal chemists modified compounds that showed signs of positive therapeutic effects in the hope of finding something that might make an effective drug, but in general the 'mechanism of action' of most drugs—the specific biochemical and molecular pathways that were responsible for their therapeutic effects—were not well understood. As long as this mode of drug discovery (popularly but misleadingly known as 'random' drug discovery) was the dominant mode of research, knowledge generated outside the firm was of only limited usefulness, and there was also relatively little need to stimulate rich conversations across disciplinary or disease area boundaries within the firm (Henderson 1994).

But as advances in biomedical science have greatly increased knowledge of both physiology and biochemistry, drug research has moved from a regime of random screening to one of so-called 'rational' drug design. The request 'find me something (anything!) that makes the rat less depressed' has been supplemented with the request 'find me something that inhibits the uptake of serotonin', and the ability to take advantage of scientific advances generated outside the firm—within the public sector and by the competition—as well as elsewhere within the firm, has become increasingly important to productive research.

An extensive body of research that explores the training and management of R&D professionals (Allen 1977; Allen *et al.* 1980; Katz 1988) suggests that in these kinds of highly turbulent science-driven environments, research performance is positively associated with the ability to span the boundaries of the firm. For example this research implies that those firms that nurture the development of 'gatekeepers'—key individuals who bridge the gap between the firm and its environment and that aggressively stimulate the exchange of information between individuals—are likely to outperform those that do not. Similarly Von Hippel's research (1988) suggests that those firms that reach outside the organization for critical knowledge that is generated elsewhere perform more effectively than those that do not. We thus hypothesize:

H3: Firms with the ability to encourage and maintain an extensive flow of information *across* the boundaries of the firm will have significantly more productive drug discovery efforts, all other things equal.

Successful drug discovery also requires the ability to integrate knowledge across both disciplinary and disease area boundaries *within* the firm. For example in 1981 Sankyo halted clinical studies on Compactin, the first HMG CoA reductase inhibitor discovered, in the face of evidence that the drug caused intestinal tumours in dogs. Human testing was only resumed when path-breaking work at Merck in pharmacology, physiology, and biostatistics showed that the mechanisms responsible for these adverse results would not be important in humans (Minsker *et al.*, 1983). Similarly research into the structure and function of alpha and beta receptors originally directed towards the development of superior cardiovascular drugs has since spawned an important stream of research into the workings of the central nervous system.

Recent work exploring the determinants of effective product development under these kinds of conditions suggests that high performance is associated with the use of organizational mechanisms that actively encourage the exchange of information across 'component' boundaries within the firm. For example the work of Hauser and Clausing (1988), Clark and Fujimoto (1991), and Iansiti (1993) suggests that in rapidly changing environments organizations that invest in cross-functional boundary-spanning mechanisms that explicitly focus on the need to rethink the systemic nature of complex products and deepen the flow of information across functional boundaries significantly outperform those that do not. Similarly the work of Henderson and Clark (1990), Christensen (1993), and Iansiti (1993), suggests that in turbulent environments firms that systematically revisit the 'architectural' knowledge of the organization—deeply embedded knowledge about the ways in which the components of the system should be integrated together—are likely to substantially outperform their competitors. We thus hypothesize that:

H4: Firms that encourage and maintain an extensive flow of information across the boundaries between scientific disciplines and therapeutic classes *within* the firm will have significantly more productive drug discovery efforts, all other things equal.

2.3. Prior research on the pharmaceutical industry

These hypotheses are broadly consistent with much of the prior research that has explored the determinants of success in the pharmaceutical industry. For example Koenig (1983) found that the publication of highly cited clinical medical articles is correlated with research productivity, and Roberts and Hauptman (1986) found that new biomedical firms that maintained richer contacts outside the firm developed technologically more advanced products, while Gambardella (1992) found that firms with superior in-house research programmes were better positioned to exploit public science, an ability that was also correlated with research productivity. Similarly in an intriguing study of the use of language as an indicator of technological competence Sapienza (1994) suggests that pharmaceutical firms who make use of boundary-spanning imagery may be more productive than those whose language is dominated by more hierarchical metaphors.

3. Specification of the Econometric Model

The strategic significance of any particular competence is ultimately a matter of its impact on the competitive standing of the firm, or of its role in determining factors such as the long-term survival of the firm, sales, profitability, and market share. Unfortunately the use of these measures to explore the research competencies of pharmaceutical firms is fraught with difficulty. Drug discovery is an exceedingly risky, time-consuming process. On average it takes about seven years to take a promising compound from the laboratory, and for approximately 10,000 compounds synthesized, only about ten will be advanced to clinical development, of which on average only one will be approved for commercial introduction (Sheck *et al.* 1984). Moreover the economic returns to new drugs are highly skewed, with a few 'blockbuster' drugs dominating the portfolios of the major pharmaceutical firms (Grabowski and Vernon 1990).

Thus as a first step towards the exploration of our hypotheses we focus on the productivity of drug discovery as measured by counts of 'important' patents, where we define an 'important' patent as one that was granted in two of the three major jurisdictions: Japan, Europe, and the United States.[3] While patents are clearly only one possible measure of success, and later work will explore the use of Investigational New Drug applications ('INDs'), New Drug Approvals ('NDAs'), as well as sales and market share as alternative measures of research output, patents are critical to competitive advantage in the industry, and all of the firms in our sample described their patenting strategies as highly aggressive. Moreover there is considerable evidence that in science-intensive industries such as pharmaceuticals, patents are closely correlated with profitability and market value (Jaffe 1986; Cockburn and Griliches 1988).

---

[3] We would have preferred to have been able to use citation-weighted patents as our measure of output. Unfortunately since the US patent classifications do not map directly into our definitions of research programmes we would have had to buy citation data directly from Derwent Publications. This proved to be prohibitively expensive.

We hypothesize that patent counts are generated by a production function:

$$Y = f(X, \beta) \tag{1}$$

where Y is patent counts, X is a vector of inputs to the drug discovery process that includes a firm's core competencies, and β is a vector of parameters. Since the dependent variable in this relationship only takes on non-negative integer values, some type of discrete-dependent variable model is dictated, and in the results that follow we assume that patent counts are generated by a Poisson process. We model the single parameter of the Poisson distribution function, λ as a function of some explanatory variables, X, and parameters β in the standard fashion:

$$E[Y_{it}] = \lambda_{it} = \exp(X_{it}\beta) \tag{2}$$

to guarantee non-negativity of λ, and estimate the parameters by maximum likelihood (Hausman *et al.* 1984).

The assumption that the dependent variable is distributed Poisson is quite strong. As our discussion in 'Scale, Scope and Spillovers' suggested, as is the case in most other data of this type, the mean = variance property of the Poisson distribution is violated in our data. In the presence of such overdispersion, although the parameters β will be consistently estimated, their standard errors will typically be underestimated, leading to spuriously high levels of significance. Overdispersion is often interpreted as evidence that the statistical model is misspecified in the sense that there may be unobserved variables in the equation for λ,

$$E[Y_{it}] = \lambda_{it} = \exp(X_{it}\beta + \epsilon_{it}) \tag{3}$$

If ϵ follows the gamma distribution, then it can be integrated out giving Y distributed as a negative binomial variate (Hausman *et al.* 1984). If ϵ is not truly gamma, however, the maximum likelihood estimates of the coefficients of the model will be inconsistent. Gourieroux *et al.* (1984) suggest using a quasi-generalized pseudo-maximum likelihood estimator based on the first two moments of the distribution of Y, which gives consistent estimates for ϵ drawn from a wide variety of distributions. The GMT estimator is just weighted non-linear least-squares estimates of the NLLS model

$$Y_{it} = \exp(X_{it}\beta) + \epsilon_{it} \tag{4}$$

with weights derived from the relation $VAR[Y] = E[Y](1 + \eta^2 E[Y])$ using initial consistent estimates of β. In previous work we have shown that our estimates of the determinants of research productivity were quite robust to these alternative estimation methods, but we continue to explore this issue in the results reported below.

In 'Scale, Scope and Spillovers' we focused on the role of the size and shape of the firm's research portfolio in shaping research productivity, including quantitative measures of firm size and scope, programme size, and intra- and inter-firm spillovers in equation (1). One of the most intriguing findings from this research was that even after controlling for all of these 'visible' factors, we still found surprisingly large and persistent heterogeneities among firms in their research performance. Firm-fixed effects were highly significant in our research productivity regressions, and accounted for a substantial portion of the variance explained. We also found that despite the fact that small changes in the scope and focus of the research portfolio had quite significant impacts on productivity, there was relatively little variance in scope and focus within firms over time.

In this chapter we expand the set of explanatory variables, X, to include variables designed to test the hypotheses that we developed above in the hopes of 'explaining' the firm effects identified in 'Scale, Scope and Spillovers'. Thus one useful way to think about this specification is to divide this specification into three classes: the R&D variables, R, which are entered in logs, a set of control variables, Z (which include measures of competitive activity and measures of scope and scale), and a set of variables designed to capture heterogeneous firm competencies, C. Thus rewriting the equation in logs,

$$\log(\lambda_{it}) = \beta\log(R_{it}) + \delta Z_{it} + \gamma C_{it} \tag{5}$$

where one can interpret the coefficient on *log(R)* directly as the elasticity of Y with respect to R&D, while the elasticities of the control variables, Z, are δZ and the elasticities of the 'capabilities' variables, C, are γC [4].

4. The Data

We use both qualitative and quantitative data drawn from a larger study of research productivity in the pharmaceutical industry. These data were obtained from both public sources and from the internal records of ten major pharmaceutical firms. These ten include both European and American firms and between them account for approximately 28 per cent of US R&D and sales and a somewhat smaller proportion of worldwide sales and research.

4.1. The quantitative data

The quantitative data set matches research inputs and outputs at the level of individual research programmes, where a 'programme' is a level of aggregation somewhere between individual research projects and the level of therapeutic classes—for example 'hypertension' as opposed to 'cardiovascular therapy' or 'compound 12345'. Data were collected by research programme rather than by broad therapeutic class or by individual project since we believe that analysing the problem in this way best reflects the dynamics of pharmaceutical research. A grouping by therapeutic class is too general: 'cardiovascular research', for example, includes research into widely different areas such as hypertension, cardiotonics, anti-arrhythmics, and hyperlipoproteinemia, while at the early stages of research firms fund

---

[4] Note that the choice of whether to use explanatory variables in levels or logs has important implications in this type of model. We report results in levels, but we found little difference in the results when the independent variables were entered in logs. A detailed discussion of this issue is given in our paper 'Scale, Scope and Spillovers'.

programmes, rather than particular projects. Moreover the use of the research programme allows us to be consistent across firms since it corresponds to the level of analysis at which firms organize their internal data and make strategic budgeting decisions.

The database contains up to thirty years of data on each research programme, and up to thirty programmes per firm. However we do not have data from every firm for every year, and not all firms are active in all research areas. After deleting missing values, grossly problematic data, and peripheral classes we are left with 4,930 usable observations in our working sample, indexed by firm, research programme, and year. The number of observations per firm varies from over 1,000 to less than 100, with a mean of 489.8. Since we can only construct organizational variables with any confidence for years following 1975, and because patents grants may lag applications by as much as four years in the United States and six in Japan we only use observations for the years 1975–88. Our final data set contains 3,210 observations. Table 6.1(a) presents some descriptive statistics for the sample. (Full details of the data-collection methodology and of variable construction are given in the appendix.)

4.2. The qualitative data

Our qualitative data are drawn from both primary and secondary sources. We drew on secondary sources including the national press, reference texts, academic textbooks, medical journal articles, and reports by both consultants and the Office of Technology Assessment in order to develop a preliminary understanding of the

TABLE 6.1(a) Descriptive statistics: selected variables at the research-programme level

Variable	Regression sample, 1975–1988 $N = 3120$			
	Mean	Std. Dev.	Minimum	Maximum
Discovery, 1986$m.	1.06	2.31	−3.61	20.18
Stock of discovery	2.987	6.42	−2.21	55.19
SCOPE: No. of programmes with discovery > $500k, 1986$	10.47	4.66	2.00	19.00
SIZE: Total research spending this year	33.54	22.96	4.970	>120
News in own patents	0.44	3.24	−13.60	20.49
News in competitors' patents	9.00	19.62	−91.84	128.3
News in competitors' patents in related programmes	26.66	40.59	−106.6	168.2
KPATS: Stock of own patents	7.76	12.02	0.00	98.18
PROPUB: Publication plays a key role in promotion	3.15	1.49	1.00	5.00
CROSS: Firm sustains a rich information flow across boundaries	2.97	1.28	1.00	5.00
DICTATOR: Single individual makes resource decisions	2.42	1.63	1.00	5.00
GLOBAL: Worldwide research managed as an integrated whole	3.00	1.54	1.00	5.00

organizational and scientific history of the industry. We then conducted in-depth field interviews at the ten firms participating in the study in order to construct a series of narrative histories of the development of cardiovascular drugs within each company.[5] These histories were used to construct our measures of organizational structure and process.

In five of the ten firms we interviewed a wide range of individuals, from the research director and the manager of cardiovascular research to project leaders, bench chemists, and pharmacologists intimately involved with particular projects. In each case, the goal of the interview was to develop a narrative history of cardiovascular drug development at each company as it was experienced by the informant. In the remaining five firms we were able to interview three to four of the most senior scientists in the company, including the chief research scientist or his/her equivalent, and in four of these five to interview a further three to four key individuals who had an in-depth knowledge of the history of cardiovascular drug discovery development inside the firm. In every case these interviews were semi-structured, in that each respondent had been provided with a list of key questions before the interview, and each interview lasted from one to three hours. We supplemented these interviews wherever possible with internal firm documents or academic articles that documented the history that the respondents were describing, and with interviews with a number of industry experts including senior academics in the field. In all, over a hundred and ten individuals were interviewed.

This methodology has both strengths and weaknesses as a means of 'measuring' competence. Perhaps its biggest weakness is that it assumes that the organizational dynamics characteristic of cardiovascular research is characteristic of the firm as a whole. Cardiovascular drugs are one of the largest and most important classes of drugs and thus central to the research programme of nearly every firm in our sample, and we attempted to continually probe the validity of this assumption during our interviews, but we run some risks in applying measures of competence derived from our cardiovascular interviews to the analysis of data describing the full range of programmes. Moreover it introduces a substantial element of subjective judgement into the analysis. This has its advantages—as several authors have suggested, one might expect it to be intrinsically difficult to 'measure' strategically significant organizational competencies since competencies that are easy to describe or measure may be inherently less likely to be an enduring source of competitive advantage (Barney 1991; Nelson 1991) and by relying on in-depth field interviews to construct

---

[5] Since pharmaceutical technology is enormously complex, we thought it unrealistic to attempt to construct a comprehensive history of drug research at each firm. Cardiovascular drugs were chosen as the focus of the study for several reasons. The class includes both extraordinarily powerful agents whose mechanism of action—the precise biochemical means whereby the drug has a physiological effect—is well understood (such as the ACE inhibitors) and less effective agents that have been used for many years and whose mechanism of action is only dimly guessed at (drugs such as digitalis and some of the antiarrhythmic agents fall into this category). Moreover cardiovasculars are one of the largest and most rapidly growing classes of drugs, and in consequence every firm in our sample had a substantial investment in cardiovascular research. In 1978 they were around 16% of all drugs sold in the US and 15% worldwide, while as of 1988, cardiovascular drugs represented just over 22% (by value) of all drugs sold by in the US and around 19% of all drugs sold worldwide (Decision Resources, *World Wide Pharmaceutical Industry*, 1990).

measures of competence one can hope to capture some of the richness and complexity that may be fundamental to the concept. But these measures are inevitably filtered through the investigators' preconceptions and beliefs, and in the case of this study this problem was compounded by the fact that severe confidentiality restrictions made it impossible to share the interview transcripts with other researchers.

Our approach does have a number of strengths. It permits the construction of detailed measures that are rooted in the experience of multiple informants. For example, rather than asking each informant, either in person or by questionnaire: 'Did you use cross-functional teams in 1978, in 1979, in 1980?', we asked 'How was the hypertensive programme organized?', 'How well did that work?', 'When did things change?' We believe that linking our questions about structure and process to particular scientific events in this way offers two significant advantages. Firstly, we believe that it increases the accuracy of our measures. Nearly all of our respondents responded positively to the question 'did you use teams?' for example, but by exploring the pattern of problem-solving around particular scientific discoveries in detail we were able to gain a much richer understanding of the ways in which cross-disciplinary communication was managed inside the firm. Secondly, we believe that the use of a narrative history as a structuring device increased the probability of being able to traces changes in organizational structure or process over time, since in general those we interviewed had very clear memories of the timing of particular scientific events, and these dates could be used to anchor discussions of the changes in the ways in which research was organized within the firm. Thus we hope to be able to capture variation in organizational competence within as well as between firms.

4.3. *Measuring organizational competence*

We constructed a number of measures of organizational competence. Recall that we hypothesized that 'competent competence' in pharmaceutical research might accrue along two dimensions. Firms might develop unique disciplinary skills, or they might develop unique competencies in particular disease areas. Since we do not have comprehensive data about the distribution of disciplinary skills within our sample firms we were unable to test formally the hypothesis that drug discovery productivity is an increasing function of firm-specific expertise in particular disciplinary areas. Examining publications in the open scientific literature, however, suggests that firms do indeed differ in this respect. We can, for example, reject the hypothesis that the proportion of publications in quite broadly defined categories such as pharmacology and medicinal chemistry is constant across firms.

In order to test our second hypothesis, that drug discovery productivity is an increasing function of component competence in particular disease areas, we included KPATS, the stock of patents obtained in each programme, as a dependent variable, where we calculate the stock by assuming a 20 per cent 'depreciation rate' for knowledge, δ. We reasoned that firms with competencies in a particular area are more likely to have obtained patents in that area historically. Notice, however, that the interpretation of the coefficient on this variable is complicated by the fact that it resembles the lagged dependent variable. Although we control for differences in scientific opportunity across programmes by including therapeutic classes in our analysis, KPATS may capture other sources of unobserved heterogeneity across programmes in addition to those introduced by the firm's unique competence in the field.

We constructed a number of variables in an attempt to measure architectural capabilities. In order to test our third hypothesis we included PROPUB as an explanatory variable, where PROPUB was constructed from the interview transcripts using a five-point Likert scale, where the firm was coded 5 if standing in the larger scientific community was a dominant criterion for the promotion of scientific personnel and 1 if an individual's publication record and reputation in the wider community were not significant factors in promotion decisions. We constructed a variety of alternative measures of the degree to which a firm actively promoted the flow of information across its borders, including GEOG, a measure of the closeness of the firm's corporate headquarters to a research university and UNIV, a measure of the degree to which the firm was deeply involved in joint research projects with one or more major research universities. We found, however that the three measures were very highly correlated, and only PROPUB is included in the reported results.

This close correlation highlights an intriguing result of our research. Our qualitative work suggests, for example, that firms that are tightly connected to the larger scientific community invest heavily in a number of related activities: not only do they promote individuals on the basis of their standing in the larger scientific community, but they also tend to be located close to major research universities with whom they have close ties, and to invest heavily in information sources such as libraries and seminar series. This echoes Milgrom and Roberts's (1990) suggestion that organizational competencies are probably composed of several tightly linked complementary activities, and suggests that our measures are best interpreted as 'symptoms' or 'indicators' of the presence of architectural competence, rather than as causal variables. We return to this point in our interpretation of the results.

We constructed three additional variables to test our fourth hypothesis and to explore the degree to which the firm was able to integrate knowledge flexibly across disciplines and disease areas within the firm: CROSS, DICTATOR, and GLOBAL. Clark and Fujimoto (1991) and Tabrizi and Eisenhardt (1994) hypothesize that in complex, turbulent environments firms that make extensive use of cross-functional teams will outperform those that do not. Thus CROSS is measured on a five-point Likert scale, where in any given year a firm scored 5 if problem-solving within the cardiovascular research programmes appeared to be characterized by the frequent exchange of rich, detailed information across disciplinary or disease area boundaries and 1 if there was very little communication within the programme or across programmes within the firm. All of the firms in our sample manage global research activities. Since Westney (1991) has suggested that global research efforts that are organizationally fragmented will be significantly less productive that those that are managed as a coherent whole we included GLOBAL as a dependent variable, where at the extremes for any given year a value of 5 was assigned if global research was managed as a seamless whole under a single director while a value of 1 was assigned if geographically dispersed research units were managed through entirely separate organizations within the firm.

DICTATOR is also scored on a five-point Likert scale, where in any given year a firm scored a 5 if resource allocation within research was entirely controlled by a single individual and a 1 if resource allocation was entirely decentralized and managed through a governing committee. Our qualitative work suggested that the use of a 'dictator' to allocate resources had both advantages and disadvantages. While it permitted the rapid transfer of resources across the firm it also tended to reduce the richness of information flow across programmes since it placed a premium on the transfer of information vertically, to the central decision-maker. Management by committee, on the other hand, while slow, appeared to encourage extensive and sometimes unexpected exchanges of information across programmes. Thus we hypothesize that firms that *do not* use dictators to allocate resources will, all other things equal, be more productive than their rivals as a reflection of an architectural competence in the exchange of information across the firm.

One interesting question about these measures is the extent to which they vary within and between firms. Table 6.1(b) presents ANOVA results for all four variables, decomposing their total variance into 'between' and 'within' components. In all cases there is a statistically significant fixed firm effect, suggesting that these variables will be of some use in accounting for firm-level differences in research productivity. However, most of the variance is between rather than within firms— while these organizational characteristics do change over time, this variation is small compared to the relatively stable differences among firms. Notice that GLOBAL hardly changes at all within firms: the R^2 from regressing it on to firm dummies is over 0.99.

4.4. Control variables

We constructed a variety of variables to control for other factors that might affect research productivity, including the size, shape, and scope of the research portfolio and the effects of internal and external spillovers. A full description of these variables and a discussion of their significance is given in our paper 'Scale, Scope and Spill-overs' and is briefly summarized in the appendix. We also constructed a variety of measures of scientific opportunity. These are described in our paper 'Racing to Invest? The Dynamics of Investment in Ethical Drug Discovery' (Cockburn and Henderson 1994). Since these measures proved generally insignificant they are not

TABLE 6.1(b) ANOVA results

Variable $N = 120$	Between firm mean square d.f. $= 9$	Within firm mean square d.f. $= 110$	*F*-ratio	R^2
DICTATOR	20.78	1.26	16.46	0.57
PROPUB	21.38	0.53	40.18	0.77
CROSS	8.27	1.08	7.67	0.39
GLOBAL	28.60	0.01	2201.88	0.99

reported here, and we rely on our use of therapeutic class dummies to control for differences in opportunity across classes.

5. Results

5.1. *Exploring the roots of firm heterogeneity at the firm level*

We focus first on the analysis of research productivity at the firm level (Table 6.2). Discovery, stock of discovery, scope, and scope-squared are included as control variables. A comparison of models 1 and 2 dramatically demonstrates the importance of firm effects. Introducing dummy variables for each firm into the regression substantially increases the log likelihood function and the R^2 of the model rises from 0.49 to 0.86[6]. This is in line with previous research, and lends credence to a focus on firm-specific competence as a factor in competition. Notice that including firm dummies in the regression results in quite large changes in the coefficients on the control variables, confirming that some important determinants of research productivity are not being captured in the first model.

The firm dummies pick up a variety of effects. As well as the organizational effects with which this chapter is concerned, they also capture factors such as systematic differences across firms in their propensity to patent, accounting practices, and labour market conditions in different countries. Although at the request of the firms supplying the data we do not report the estimated coefficients on these dummies here or in the other tables, they are jointly and separately highly significant in all of the models estimated, and the ranking of firms according to these dummies conforms to our beliefs from our qualitative work about their relative innovative performance.

Since we cannot control for programme-specific competencies in these aggregate data we begin to explore these firm-level effects by testing hypotheses 3 and 4. Model 3 introduces our measures of architectural competence. PROPUB and DICTATOR have the expected sign, but PROPUB is only marginally significant, and CROSS and GLOBAL not only have the 'wrong' sign but are also significant. Including firm dummies in model 4 suggests that these rather puzzling results may be a function of specification error, since when we control for firm effects PROPUB and DICTATOR both become strongly significant with the expected signs while CROSS and GLOBAL are insignificant. In model 5 we introduce the firm's total stock of patents as an additional measure of firm heterogeneity, but it is not significant.[7] We find this unsurprising since aggregation across programmes makes this a very poor measure of competence.

---

[6] R^2 is calculated as the squared correlation between observed values of Y and fitted values of Y from the Poisson regression.

[7] One potential problem with these results is that the Poisson assumption may be inappropriate. Alternative estimation techniques for count data yield essentially similar results, though the standard errors are much larger when we allow for overdispersion, and there are quite large changes in some of the coefficients. However, we are not overly concerned by these results since we have so few observations at this level of aggregation, and the desirable properties of these more general estimators are only obtained asymptotically. We return to this issue in our analysis of the much larger sample of programme-level data.

TABLE 6.2 Determinants of patent output at the firm level. (Poisson regression. Dependent variable = total firm patents, 120 observations)

	1	2	3	4	5
Firm dummies		Sig.		Sig.	Sig.
PROPUB: Publication			0.033	0.132**	0.113**
plays a key role in			(0.017)	(0.034)	(0.036)
promotion.					
CROSS: Firm sustains a			−0.151**	−0.032	−0.021
rich info. flow across			(0.015)	(0.031)	(0.032)
boundaries					
DICTATOR: Single indiv.			−0.112**	−0.096**	−0.091**
makes key resource			(0.015)	(0.020)	(0.020)
decisions					
GLOBAL: Worldwide			−0.037**	1.250	1.271
research managed as an			(0.012)	(1.047)	(1.048)
integrated whole.					
Stock of own patents					0.001
					(0.000)
Intercept	1.356**	1.249**	1.549**	−1.258	−0.834
	(0.344)	(0.368)	(0.364)	(2.118)	(2.133)
Dum78	1.459**	1.171**	1.733**	1.549**	0.988
	(0.351)	(0.375)	(0.369)	(0.389)	(0.516)
Ln(SIZE):	−0.222**	−0.022	0.151*	0.006	0.033
Total firm research	(0.050)	(0.069)	(0.059)	(0.071)	(0.073)
Ln(Total firm stock of	0.860**	0.967**	0.435**	0.853**	0.784**
research)	(0.048)	(0.084)	(0.055)	(0.095)	(0.103)
SCOPE:	0.255**	−0.009	0.256**	−0.017	−0.023
No. programmes	(0.019)	(0.026)	(0.025)	(0.029)	(0.030)
> 500K '86$					
SCOPE * SCOPE	−0.014**	−0.002*	−0.013**	−0.001	−0.001
	(0.001)	(0.001)	(0.001)	(0.001)	(0.001)
Time	−0.049*	−0.082**	0.002	−0.059**	−0.077**
	(0.019)	(0.022)	(0.020)	(0.022)	(0.025)
Time * Dum78	−0.086**	−0.069**	−0.101**	−0.088**	−0.058*
	(0.020)	(0.022)	(0.021)	(0.022)	(0.028)
Log-likelihood	−1195	−623	−974	−608	−607
Pseudo R-squared	0.490	0.859	0.655	0.862	0.863

Notes: Standard errors in parentheses.
In(variable) is set = 0 when variable = 0, and an appropriately coded dummy variable is included in the regression.
** Significant at the 1% level; * Significant at the 5% level.

The standard likelihood ratio tests indicate that our measures of architectural competence are significantly related to research productivity. Comparing the fit of models 1 and 3 we see that the organizational variables explain a substantial amount of the variance in patenting at the firm level. However, these variables only marginally improve the fit of the equation when firm dummies are present. This reflects the fact that the firm dummies and architectural competence variables are not orthogonal. In fact though individual correlation coefficients between the competence variables and the firm dummies are not particularly high, the two sets of variables essentially span the same space. The first three canonical correlation coefficients between PROPUB, CROSS, DICTATOR, and GLOBAL and the firm dummies are greater than 0.9. Bearing this in mind, we interpret these results as suggesting that our measures of competence *are* the firm effect captured by the firm dummies, with the difference in fit between models 3 and 4 attributable to 'noise' such as inter-firm differences in propensity to patent.

Thus the firm-level analysis suggests that heterogeneity across firms plays a significant role in determining variation in research productivity, and provides significant support for our third and fourth hypotheses. Two of our measures of architectural capability are significant and all have the expected sign, suggesting that the ability to integrate knowledge across and within the boundaries of the firm is an important determinant of heterogeneous competence.

5.2. *Exploring firm heterogeneity at the programme level*

The results of Table 6.2 suggest that there are significant and persistent differences in firm productivity, and that these differences may be partly driven by variations in organizational process. However, a number of important effects cannot be adequately controlled for in firm-level data, particularly variation in the mix of technological areas in which the firm is investing and the effects of knowledge spillovers. Controlling for 'composition' effects is important since scientific opportunity varies considerably across programmes, and all other things equal firms that invest in outstandingly fruitful areas will be more productive than those that do not. Similarly, in 'Scale, Scope and Spillovers' we showed that internal and external spillovers of knowledge across research programmes have important implications for productivity. Moreover it is very difficult to operationalize the notion of local competence at an aggregate level in a multiproduct firm. Thus we move next to the analysis of programme-level data (Table 6.3).

The results in Table 6.3 confirm the importance of controlling for therapeutic class effects and spillovers—these variables are strongly significant in all the regressions. Including firm dummies in the regression (model 2) significantly increases both the log likelihood function and the proportion of variance explained, but they are much less important than in the aggregate data. Some part of the firm effect identified in Table 6.2 appears to be a composition effect: in the absence of therapeutic class dummies, fixed-firm effects pick up variation in research productivity across firms arising from their differential specialization in different technological areas. (Note that as in the firm data, because firm dummies, therapeutic class dummies, and other variables in the regression are correlated, we cannot unambiguously partition R-squared into X% = FIRM, Y% = CLASS, etc.)

Model 3 includes our measure of local competence, KPATS, the stock of patents previously obtained in each programme. KPATS has a very significant effect on productivity, increasing the proportion of variance explained from 50 to 68 per cent and significantly increasing the likelihood function. This result gives strong support for our second hypothesis: 'local' competence appears to have a very significant

TABLE 6.3 Determinants of patent output at the research-programme level (Poisson regression. Dependent variable = patents, 3,210 observations)

	1	2	3	4	5
Therapeutic class dummies	Sig.	Sig.	Sig.	Sig.	Sig.
Firm dummies		Sig.			Sig.
Stock own pats in this programme			0.039** (0.001)		0.034** (0.001)
PROPUB: Publication plays a key role in promotion				0.027* (0.017)	0.081** (0.032)
CROSS: Firm sustains a rich info. flow across boundaries				-0.169** (0.016)	0.030 (0.029)
DICTATOR: Single ind. makes resource decisions				-0.111** (0.014)	-0.115** (0.018)
GLOBAL: Worldwide research managed as integrated whole				-0.059** (0.011)	1.531 (1.046)
Intercept	-2.263** (0.144)	-1.517** (0.179)	-1.346** (0.143)	-1.928** (0.167)	-4.059* (2.094)
Dum78	0.184** (0.062)	0.085 (0.071)	-0.216** (0.063)	0.106 (0.067)	-1.289* (0.074)
Ln(Discovery)	0.046** (0.011)	0.046** (0.011)	-0.016 (0.011)	0.072** (0.011)	-0.012 (0.011)
Ln(stock of discovery)	0.075** (0.011)	0.089** (0.011)	0.022** (0.010)	0.055** (0.010)	0.038** (0.010)
Ln(SIZE): Total research spending by firm	0.461** (0.031)	0.229** (0.063)	0.271** (0.032)	0.534** (0.041)	0.219** (0.069)
SCOPE: No. of programmes > 500K '86$	0.208** (0.019)	-0.027 (0.026)	0.164** (0.019)	0.209** (0.024)	-0.018 (0.029)
SCOPE * SCOPE	-0.012** (0.001)	-0.001 (0.001)	-0.009 (0.001)	-0.012** (0.001)	-0.002 (0.001)
News in patents in related programmes	0.033** (0.004)	0.020** (0.004)	0.031** (0.004)	0.031** (0.004)	0.023** (0.004)
News in competitors' patents in this programme	0.009** (0.001)	0.009** (0.001)	0.004** (0.001)	0.009** (0.001)	0.004** (0.001)
News in competitors' patents in related programmes	0.001* (0.001)	0.001* (0.001)	0.003* (0.001)	0.001* (0.001)	0.003* (0.001)
Time	0.037* (0.020)	0.029 (0.021)	0.050** (0.020)	0.050** (0.020)	-0.034 (0.022)
Time * Dum78	-0.115** (0.021)	-0.771** (0.022)	0.004 (0.021)	-0.087** (0.021)	-0.005 (0.023)
Log-likelihood	-6388	-5811	-5366	-6085	-5208
Pseudo R-Squared	0.383	0.503	0.682	0.446	0.693

Notes: see Table 6.2.

impact on research productivity. But while this result is encouraging it must be interpreted with care since KPATS is close to the lagged dependent variable and as such captures a wide variety of unobserved local heterogeneity, including variations in scientific opportunity which are not captured by the fixed therapeutic class effects and differences in local propensities to patent.

Model 4 introduces our measures of architectural competence. As was the case in the aggregate analysis, omitting firm dummies gives puzzling results. CROSS and GLOBAL have the 'wrong' signs and PROPUB is only marginally significant. In model 5, our preferred model, all four variables have the expected sign although again only PROPUB and DICTATOR are significant.

Notice that as in Table 6.2, our measures of architectural competence only marginally improve the overall fit of the equation in the presence of other controls for firm heterogeneity. It is not that these variables are unimportant—in model 4 where they are included in the regression by themselves, they significantly improve the fit of the model. The problem is that a large proportion of the firm effect captured by the firm dummies is precisely the same phenomena that we are modelling with our architectural competence variables. As the ANOVA results above indicate, firm dummies account for much of the variation in the architectural competence variables and canonical correlation analysis indicates that the two sets of variables are very closely associated in a multivariate sense. Thus it is very difficult to separate out their contributions to the explanatory power of the regression.

In Table 6.4 we explore the validity of the Poisson specification. The first column includes model 5 from Table 6.3 for comparison. Model 6 reports the negative binomial results, and models 7 and 8 the non linear least squares and GMT models respectively. The results suggest that our initial conclusions are quite robust. Although these data are clearly overdispersed, with the exception of the NLLS specification the results are quite similar across models. The consistent and efficient GMT estimator gives particularly encouraging results. PROPUB and GLOBAL are highly significant, with a positive impact on research productivity, while DICTATOR is also highly significant and as expected has a negative effect.

Collinearity between the architectural competence variables, the firm dummies, and some of the control variables—particularly SIZE and SCOPE—is such that we hesitate to place too much weight on the relative magnitudes of these coefficients. But the estimated effects of PROPUB and DICTATOR are quite robust to changes in the set of explanatory variables included in the model, and we think that they are capturing important aspects of firm heterogeneity.

6. Conclusions and Directions for Further Research

Our results provide considerable support for the importance of 'competence' as a source of advantage in research productivity. Idiosyncratic firm effects account for a very substantial fraction of the variance in research productivity across the firms in our sample, and we find support for all three of the four hypotheses that we can explore with these data. Research productivity certainly increases with historical

TABLE 6.4 Determinants of patent output at the research-programme level.
(Exploring Econometric Issues. Dependent variable = patents, 3,210 observations)

	(5) Poisson	(6) Neg.Bin.	(7) NLLS	(8) GMT
Therapeutic class dummies	Sig.	Sig.	Sig.	Sig.
Firm dummies	Sig.	Sig.	Sig.	Sig.
Stock own pats in this programme	0.034**	0.049**	0.029**	0.046**
	(0.001)	(0.002)	(0.002)	(0.003)
PROPUB: Publication plays a key	0.081**	0.124**	−0.006	0.399**
role in promotion	(0.032)	(0.046)	(0.062)	(0.074)
CROSS: Firm sustains a rich info.	0.030	0.033	0.009	0.007
flow across boundaries	(0.029)	(0.042)	(0.062)	(0.047)
DICTATOR: Single ind. makes	−0.115**	−0.117**	−0.064*	−0.137**
resource decisions	(0.018)	(0.026)	(0.035)	(0.033)
GLOBAL: Worldwide research	1.531	1.615*	0.999	2.572**
managed as integrated whole	(1.046)	(1.059)	(1.011)	(0.531)
Intercept	−4.059*	−4.345*	−2.693	−6.472**
	(2.094)	(2.124)	(2.035)	(1.113)
Dum78	−1.289*	−0.055	−0.392**	0.103
	(0.074)	(0.114)	(0.170)	(0.165)
Ln(Discovery)	−0.012	0.022	−0.046*	0.053**
	(0.011)	(0.016)	(0.020)	(0.021)
Ln(stock of discovery)	0.038**	0.034*	0.044*	0.064**
	(0.010)	(0.015)	(0.022)	(0.017)
Ln(SIZE): Total research spending	0.219**	0.190*	0.234*	0.216*
by firm	(0.069)	(0.107)	(0.144)	(0.134)
SCOPE: No. of programmes	−0.018	−0.073*	0.025	−0.218**
> 500K '86$	(0.029)	(0.044)	(0.074)	(0.040)
SCOPE * SCOPE	−0.002	0.001	−0.003	0.006**
	(0.001)	(0.002)	(0.003)	(0.002)
News in patents in related	0.023**	0.032**	0.011	0.029**
programmes	(0.004)	(0.007)	(0.007)	(0.009)
News in competitors' patents in	0.004**	0.008**	0.001	0.003
this programme	(0.001)	(0.001)	(0.002)	(0.001)
News in competitors' patents in	0.003*	0.002*	0.003*	0.004**
related programmes	(0.001)	(0.001)	(0.001)	(0.001)
Time	−0.034	−0.033	−0.083*	0.023
	(0.022)	(0.035)	(0.045)	(0.054)
Time * Dum78	−0.005	−0.007	0.057	−0.076
	(0.023)	(0.036)	(0.049)	(0.055)
Log-likelihood	−5208	−4721	−7020	−4576
Alpha		2.367		

Notes: see Table 6.2.

success, and to the degree that cumulative success is a reasonable proxy for the kinds of 'local competence' identified in the literature, our results suggest that differences in local capabilities may play an important role in shaping enduring differences between firms. We also find that two of the measures that we constructed to measure architectural competence are significantly correlated with research productivity. Firms in which publication records are an important criteria for promotion appear to be more productive than their rivals, as are firms which use committees to allocated resources rather than relying on a single 'dictator'.

Our results suggest that a focus on 'architectural', 'integrative', or 'combinative' capabilities as a source of enduring competitive advantage may provide useful insights into the sources of enduring differences in firm performance, but they have challenging implications on two fronts.

In the first place, they highlight the methodological problems inherent in attempting to measure 'organizational competence'. A comparison of the results of our analysis conducted at the firm level with that conducted at the programme level suggests that a significant fraction of any firm effect in research productivity identified at the aggregate level may simply reflect a failure to control for the structure of the research portfolio. To the degree that firms in a wide variety of seemingly homogeneous industries also differ in the composition of their research or product portfolios any interpretation of heterogeneity at the firm level in terms of competence must be treated with caution.

Similarly, despite the fact that we have been able to collect unusually detailed data, we cannot convincingly separate the effects of local competence in a particular field from other sources of unobserved heterogeneity. Our results suggest that there are important, long-lived sources of heterogeneity in research productivity across programmes. While this finding is consistent with the presence of important local capabilities, there are other possible explanations: for example the result may just reflect differences in the nature of the work being undertaken across programmes or in local propensities to patent. Our qualitative work leads us to believe that there are indeed important local capabilities, but their presence is hard to prove convincingly in these data.

Our measures of architectural competence are also subject to problems of interpretation. Recall, for example, that PROPUB is closely correlated with several other measures of the degree to which the firm is linked to its wider scientific context, particularly to indicators of its geographical location and of its degree of involvement with academic science. Similarly our variable DICTATOR proxies for a complex set of organizational behaviours. These variables may be measures of symptoms as much as they are measures of causes: firms that can manage the organizational strains inherent in using a committee to allocate research resources have typically developed a repertoire of behaviours that together support a rich flow of information within the firm. Firms that promote leading scientists on the basis of their publication records are also likely to be located close to important centres of medical research and to be deeply involved with the academic medical establishment.

In the second place, our analysis highlights the importance of exploring the *sources* of organizational competence and their implications for the strategic choices made by the firm. One of our most interesting results is that small changes in the ways in which research is managed inside the firm appear to have major implications for its productivity. Our estimated coefficients imply, for example, that the research efforts of firms which score the highest on the use of publication records as an important criterion in promotion are 38 per cent more productive than those at the bottom end of the scale, all else equal. Similarly, firms that allocate resources through a process of consensus appear to be as much as 55 per cent—more productive than those which use a 'dictator'. These effects may be confounded with other unobserved determinants of research productivity, and thus their magnitudes may be mis-estimated, but nonetheless we find them surprisingly large. Given the apparently large pay-off to changing the organization and management of this crucial function, it is puzzling that there are such large and persistent differences across firms in these dimensions.

There are a number of possible explanations for this observation. The first is that the capabilities we have measured are fundamentally inimitable, in the sense described by Peteraf (1993). Although there might be widespread agreement within the firm that moving to a resource allocation system based around internal peer review is inherently desirable, it might still be difficult to do, partly because such a system must be supported by a complex set of organizational routines that are difficult to replicate and observe (Milgrom and Roberts 1990).

The second is that the failure to adopt efficient techniques for managing research reflects agency problems in the firms which would have benefited from these changes. Several of the firms in our sample were very successful in the early 1960s, and it may be the case that well-known difficulties in monitoring the productivity of research (Holmstrom 1989) together with failures in the market for corporate control permitted them to continue running inefficient research organizations. A third possibility is that our measures reflect the quality of the scientists recruited by our sample companies, rather than any fundamental difference in the quality of the information flow within the organization. To the degree that world-class scientists insist on being able to publish in the open literature, and on control of their own research budgets through peer reviewed committees, it may be the case that our measures describe the conditions necessary to recruit the best-possible scientists. Research within the tradition of human resource management, for example, has begun to explore the differential effects of organizational mechanisms such as teams on performance, and has insisted on the importance of controlling for heterogeneous labour quality in such an analysis (Greenan *et al.* 1993; Ichniovski *et al.* 1993). Lastly, of course, it may simply be the case that our measure of innovative output is not capturing all of the relevant dimensions of innovative success. Firms that are less productive in generating 'important patents' may, in fact, still be strategically or economically very successful. We are actively pursing these questions in our ongoing research.

To the degree that our results are generalizable beyond the pharmaceutical industry to other research intensive settings, they support the view that the ability to integrate knowledge both across the boundaries of the firm and across disciplines and product areas within the firm is an important source of strategic advantage. While our analysis offers insight into the organizational determinants of research productivity, it also raises a number of intriguing questions. Attempts to quantify the nature and effects of organizational competence empirically offer a fruitful avenue for further research.

Appendix: Data Sources and Construction

The data set used in this study are based on detailed data on R&D inputs and outputs at the research-programme-level for ten ethical pharmaceutical manufacturers.

Inputs
Our data on inputs to the drug research process are taken from the internal records of participating companies, and consist primarily of annual expenditures on exploratory research and research by research programme. Several issues arise in dealing with these data.

(a) Research vs. development
We define resources devoted to research (or 'discovery', in the terminology of the industry) as all pre-clinical expenditures within a therapeutic class, and development as all expenses incurred after a compound has been identified as a development candidate. We attributed exploratory research to a particular programme wherever possible, but exploratory research that could not be so assigned was included in overheads. Clinical grants are included in the figures for development, and grants to external researchers for exploratory research are included in the total for research. In some cases, the companies supplied us with data already broken down by research versus development by research programme. In others, we had to classify budget line items for projects/programmes into the appropriate category. This was done based on the description of each item in the original sources, and the location of items within the structure of the company's reporting procedure.

(b) Overheads
In order to maintain as much consistency in the data collection process as possible, we tried to include appropriate overhead charges directly related to research activities, such as computing, R&D administration, and finance, etc., but to exclude charges relating to allocation of central office overheads, etc. The overheads also include some expenditures on discipline-based exploratory research such as 'molecular biology' which appeared not to be oriented towards specific therapies. Overheads were allocated across therapeutic classes according to their fraction of total spending.

(c) Licensing
We treat up-front, lump-sum payments in respect of in-licensing of compounds, or participation in joint programmes with other pharmaceutical companies, universities or research institutes, as expenditure on research. Royalty fees and contingent payments are excluded. Though increasing over time, expenditures on licensing are a vanishingly small fraction of research spending in this sample.

Outputs
In this chapter we use 'important' patent grants as our measure of research output. We count patents by year of application, where we define 'importance' by the fact that the patent was granted in two of the three major markets: the USA, Japan, and the European Community. These data were provided by Derwent Publications Inc., who used their proprietary classification and search software to produce counts of 'important' patents to us broken down by therapeutic class for twenty-nine US, European, and Japanese pharmaceutical manufacturers for 1961 to 1990. These firms were chosen to include the ten firms that have given us data

together with nineteen other firms chosen on the basis of their absolute R&D expenditures, R&D intensity, and national 'home base' to try to get a representative, rather than exhaustive, assessment of worldwide patenting activity. The nineteen firms have been consistently in the top forty worldwide pharmaceutical firms in terms of R&D dollars and sales.

Note that many of these patents will be 'defensive' patents in that firms may patent compounds they do not intend to develop in the short term but that may have competitive value in the longer term, and that we were not able to exclude process patents. Alternative measures of 'importance' such as citation weighting and more detailed international filing data proved prohibitively expensive to construct.

Classification

Classification of inputs and outputs by therapeutic class is important because this drives our measure of spillovers. There are essentially two choices: to define programmes by physiological mechanisms e.g. 'prostaglandin metabolism', or by 'indications' or disease states e.g. 'arthritis'. We have chosen to classify on the basis of indication, largely because this corresponds well to the internal divisions used by the companies in our sample (which is conceptually correct), but also because classification by mechanism is much more difficult (a practical concern.) We classified both inputs and outputs according to a scheme which closely follows the IMS worldwide classes. This scheme contains two tiers of aggregation: a detailed 'research-programme'-level, and a more aggregated 'therapeutic-class' level which groups related programmes. For example, the therapeutic-class 'cardiovascular' includes the research programmes 'anti-hypertensives', 'cardiotonics', 'antithrombolytics', 'diuretics', etc.

There are some problems with this procedure. Firstly, some projects and compounds are simply very difficult to classify. A particular drug may be indicated for several quite distinct therapies: consider serotonin, which has quite different physiological actions on either side of the blood–brain barrier. As a neurotransmitter it is believed to play important roles in mediating motor functions. As a systemic hormone it has a variety of effects on smooth muscle, for example it functions as a vasoconstrictor. Some companies report expenditures in areas which are very difficult to assign to particular therapeutic classes: a company doing research using rDNA technology might charge expenditure to an accounting category listed as 'Gene Therapy/Molecular Biology' which is actually specific research performed on e.g. cystic fibrosis, but we were forced to include these expenditures in 'overheads'. Secondly, our two-tier classification scheme may not catch all important relationships between different therapeutic areas. We believe that we are undercounting, rather than overcounting spillovers in this respect. Thirdly, where firms supplied us with 'predigested' data, they may have used substantively different conventions in classifying projects. One firm may subsume antiviral research under a wider class of anti-infectives, while another may report antivirals separately. Not surprisingly there are major changes within companies in internal divisional structures, reporting formats, and so forth, which may also introduce classification errors. After working very carefully with these data, we recognize the potential for significant misassignment of outputs to inputs, but we believe that such errors that remain are not serious. Using patents (as opposed to INDs or NDAs) as the output measure should reduce our vulnerability to this problem, since we observe relatively large numbers, and a few misclassifications are unlikely to seriously affect our results.

Matching

Data series on inputs and outputs for each firm were matched at the research-programme level. This procedure appears to successfully match outputs and inputs unambiguously for the great majority of programmes. In a very few cases, however, we ended up with research programmes where patents, INDs, or NDAs were filed, but where there were no recorded expenditures. Of these the majority were obviously coding errors or reflected dilemmas previously encountered in the classification process, and appropriate corrections were made. In other cases, it was clear that these reflected 'spillovers'—research done ostensibly in, for example, hypertension—may generate knowledge about the autonomic nervous system which prompts patenting of compounds which may be useful in treating secretory disorders (e.g. ulcers.) In such cases we set 'own' inputs for the programme equal to zero, and included these observations in the database.

Deflation

Since our data sources span many years, it is important to measure expenditures in constant dollar terms. We used the biomedical research and development price index constructed by James Schuttinga at the National Institutes of Health. The index is calculated using weights that reflect the pattern of NIH expenditures on inputs for biomedical research, and thus in large measure reflects changes in the costs of conducting research at academic institutions. However, since the firms in our sample compete directly with academic research laboratories for scientific talent we believe that this index is likely to the most appropriate publicly available index, and our results proved to be very robust to the use of alternate indices. In a later publication we intend to exploit the information that some companies were able to give us on R&D inputs in units of labour hours to construct an index specifically for research costs in the pharmaceutical industry.

Construction of stock variables

Annual flows of research and expenditures were capitalized following the procedure described by Hall *et al.* (The R&D Masterfile: Documentation, NBER Technical WP 72). In brief, we first assume a depreciation rate for 'knowledge capital', δ, here equal to 20 per cent. (This is consistent with previous studies, and as argued above is not going to be very important in terms of its impact on the regression results since no matter what number we chose, if the flow series is reasonably smooth we would still find it difficult to identify δ separately from the estimated coefficient on the stock variable.) We then calculate a starting stock for each class within firm based on the first observation on the annual flow: assuming that real expenditures have been growing since minus infinity at a rate g, we divide the first observed year's flow by $\delta + g$. Each year, the end-of-year stock is set equal to the beginning-of-year stock net of depreciation, plus that year's flow. For the cases where the annual flow was missing 'within' a series of observations, we set it equal to zero. In almost all instances, these missing values occur after the expenditure flows have been declining towards zero: we are reasonably sure that these are 'real' zeros and not missing data which should be interpolated. We used the same procedure to accumulate 'stocks' of patents, based on the flow variables described above.

References

Allen, T. J. (1977). *Managing the Flow of Technology: Technology Transfer and the Dissemination of Technological Information within the R&D Organization.* Cambridge, Mass.: MIT Press.

——D. Lee, and M. Tushman (1980). 'R&D Performance as a Function of Internal Communication, Project Management and the Nature of Work'. *IEEE Transactions on Engineering Management*, EM-27 (1).

Amit, R., and P. Schoemaker (1993). 'Strategic Assets and Organizational Rent', *The Strategic Management Journal*, 14: 33–46.

Barney, J. (1986). 'Strategy Factor Market: Expectation, Luck and Business Strategy', *Management Science*, 32(10): 1231–41.

——(1991). 'Firm Resources and Sustained Competitive Advantage', *Journal of Management*, 17(1): 99–120.

Burgelman, R. (1994). 'Fading Memories: A Process Study of Strategic Business Exit in Dynamic Environments', *Administrative Science Quarterly*, 39(1): 24–56.

Clark, K., and T. Fujimoto (1991). *Product Development in the World Automobile Industry.* Boston: Harvard Business School Press.

Christensen, C. (1993). 'Exploring the Limits of the Technology S-Curve, Parts I and II', *Production and Operations Management.*

Cockburn, I., and Z. Griliches (1998) 'Industry Effects and Appropriability Measures in the Stock Market's Valuation of R&D and Patents', *American Economic Review Papers and Proceedings*, 78(2): 419–23.

——and R. Henderson (1994) 'Racing to Invest: The Dynamics of Competition in Ethical Drug Discovery', *Journal of Economics and Management Strategy*, 3(3).

Cool, K., and D. Schendel (1988). 'Performance Differences among Strategic Group Members', *Strategic Management Journal*, 9: 207–23.

Dierickx, I., and K. Cool (1989). 'Asset Stock Accumulation and Sustainability of Competitive Advantage', *Management Science*, 35(12): 1504–13.

Dosi, G., and D. J. Teece (1993). 'Organizational Competencies and the Boundaries of the Firm', University of California at Berkeley, Consortium on Competitiveness and Cooperation, Working Paper 93-11, Feb.

Gambardella, A. (1992). 'Competitive Advantage from in-house scientific research: The US pharmaceutical industry in the 1980s', *Research Policy*, 21(1): 1–17.

Gourieroux, C., A. Monfort, and A. Trognon (1984). 'Pseudo-Maximum Likelihood Methods: Applications to Poisson Models', *Econometrica*, 52(3): 701–20.

Grabowski, H. G., and J. M. Vernon (1990). 'A New Look at the Returns and Risks to Pharmaceutical R&D', *Management Science*, 36(7): 804–21.

Greenan, N., D. Guellec, G. Broussaudier, and L. Miotti (1993). 'Firm Organization, Technology and Performance: An Empirical Study', Working Paper, INSEF Department of Economic Studies, France.

Hansen, G. S., and B. Wernerfelt (1989). 'Determinants of Firm Performance: The Relative Importance of Economic and Organizational Factors', *Strategic Management Journal*, 10: 399–411.

Hauser, J., and D. Clausing (1988). 'The House of Quality', *Harvard Business Review* (May–June): 63–73.

Hausman, J., B. H. Hall, and Z. Griliches (1984). 'Econometric Models for Count Data with an Application to the Patents–R&D Relationship', *Econometrica*, 52(4): 909–38.

Henderson, R. (1998). 'Underinvestment and Incompetence as Responses to Radical Innovation: Evidence from the Semiconductor Photolithographic Alignment Equipment Industry', *Rand Journal of Economics*, 24(2): 248–70.

—— (1994). 'The Evolution of Integrative Capability: Innovation in Cardiovascular Drug Discovery', *Industrial and Corporate Change*, 3(3).

—— and K. B. Clark (1990). 'Architectural Innovation: The Reconfiguration of Existing Product Technologies and the Failure of Established Firms', *Administrative Science Quarterly*, 35: 9–30.

—— and I. Cockburn (1996). 'Scale, Scope and Spillovers: The Determinants of Research Productivity in Drug Discovery', *Rand Journal of Economics*, 27(1): 32–59.

Hirsch, P. (1975). 'Organizational Effectiveness and the Institutional Environment', *Administrative Science Quarterly*, 20: 327–43.

Hitt, M. A., and R. D. Ireland (1985). 'Corporate Distinctive Competence, Strategy, Industry and Performance', *Strategic Management Journal*, 6: 273–93.

Holmstrom, B. (1989). 'Agency Costs and Innovation', *Journal of Economic Behavior and Organization*, 12(3): 305–27.

Iansiti, M. (1993). 'Science-Based Product Development: An Empirical Study of the Mainframe Computer Industry', Harvard Business School Working Paper 92-083.

Ichniowski, C., K. Shaw, and G. Prennushi (1993). 'The Effects of Human Resource Management on Productivity', mimeo.

Itami, H., with T. Roehl (1987). *Mobilizing Invisible Assets*. Cambridge, Mass.: Harvard University Press.

Jaffe, A. (1986). 'Technological Opportunity and Spillovers of R&D: Evidence from Firms' Patents, Profits and Market Value', *American Economic Review*.

Katz, R. (ed.) (1988). *Managing Professionals in Innovative Organizations: A Collection of Readings*. New York: Harper Business.

Koenig, M. (1993). 'A Bibliometric Analysis of Pharmaceutical Research', *Research Policy*, 12: 15–36.

Kogut, B., and D.-J. Kim (1991). 'Technological Accumulation, Growth Options, and the Sequence of Entry', mimeo, Wharton School. Presented at the Wharton Conference on the Evolution of Firm Capabilities, May.

—— and U. Zander (1992). 'Knowledge of the Firm, Combinative Capabilities, and the Replication of Technology', *Organization Science*, 3(3).

Lawrence, P. R., and J. W. Lorsch (1967). *Organization and Environment: Managing Differentiation and Integration*. Homewood, Ill.: Irwin.

Leonard-Barton, D. (1992). 'Core Capabilities and Core Rigidities: A Paradox in Managing New Product Development', *Strategic Management Journal*, 13: 111–26.

Lippman, S. A. and R. P. Rumelt (1982). 'Uncertain Imitability: An Analysis of Interfirm Difference in Efficiency under Competition', *Bell Journal of Economics*, 13(2): 418–38.

Milgrom, P., and J. Roberts (1990). 'The Economics of Modern Manufacturing: Technology, Strategy and Organization', *American Economic Review*.

Minsker, D. H., J. S. MacDonald, R. T. Robertson, and D. L Bokelman (1983). 'Mevalonate supplementation in pregnant rats suppresses the teratogenicity of mevinolinic acid, an inhibitor of 3-hydroxy-3-methylglutarly-coenzyme a reductase', *Teratology*, 28(3): 449–56.

Mitchell, W. (1989). 'Whether and When? Probability and Timing of Incumbent's Entry into Emerging Industrial Subfields', *Administrative Science Quarterly*, 34: 208–30.

——(1992). 'Are More Good Things Better: Or will Technical and Market Capabilities Conflict when a Firm Expands?', *Industrial and Corporate Change*, 1(2).

Montgomery, C. A., and B. Wernerfelt (1988). 'Diversification, Ricardian rents, and Tobin's q', *Rand Journal of Economics*, 19: 623–32.

Nelson, R. (1991). 'Why do Firms Differ and How Does it Matter?', *Strategic Management Journal*, 12: 61–74.

Penrose, E. T. (1959). *The Theory of the Growth of the Firm*. New York: Wiley.

Peteraf, M. (1993). 'The Cornerstones of Competitive Advantage: A Resource-Based View', *Strategic Management Journal*, 14: 179–91.

Porter, M. (1990). *Competitive Strategy*. New York: Free Press.

Roberts, E., and O. Hauptman (1986). 'The Process of Technology Transfer to the New Biomedical and Pharmaceutical Firm', *Research Policy*, 15: 107–19.

Rumelt, R. P. (1991). 'How Much Does Industry Matter?' *Strategic Management Journal*, 12: 167–85.

Sapienza, A. (1994). 'Measuring Organizational Knowledge', mimeo, Graduate School for Health Studies, Simmons College, Boston.

Selznick, P. (1957). *Leadership in Administration: A Sociological Interpretation*. New York: Harper & Row.

Sheck, L. *et al.* (1984). 'Success Rates in the U. S. Drug Development System', *Clinical Pharmacology and Therapeutics*, 36(5): 574–83.

Spender, J. C. (1994). 'The Geographies of Strategic Competence', mimeo, Rutgers University. Presented at the Price Bertil Symposium on the Dynamic Firm, Stockholm, June.

Tabrizi, B., and K. Eisenhardt (1994). 'Accelerating Product Development', mimeo, Stanford University, Dept. of Industrial Engineering.

Teece, D. J., G. Pisano, and A. Shuen (1992). 'Dynamic Capabilities and Strategic Management', mimeo, Haas School of Business.

Wernerfelt, B. (1984). 'A Resource-based View of the Firm', *Strategic Management Journal*, 5: 171–80.

Westney, E. (1991). 'Country Patterns in R&D Organization: The United States and Japan', in Bruce Kogut (ed.), *Country Competitiveness and the Organization of Work*. Oxford: Oxford University Press.

Von Hippel, E. (1988). *The Sources of Innovation*. Oxford: Oxford University Press.

7

Managing the Development and Transfer of Process Technologies in the Semiconductor Manufacturing Industry

MELISSA M. APPLEYARD, NILE W. HATCH, AND DAVID C. MOWERY

1. Introduction

The resource-based theory of the firm suggests that a business enterprise is best viewed as a collection of sticky and difficult-to-imitate resources and capabilities that enable it to compete against other firms (Penrose 1959; Wernerfelt 1984; Barney 1986).[1] Rather than optimizing subject to some web of external constraints, the resource-based view argues, firms should seek to create rents through creating new capabilities that effectively relax such external constraints. Of particular importance is the specificity inherent in such capabilities: the same characteristics that enable a firm to extract a sustainable rent stream from these assets often make it difficult for the firm to 'transplant' them and utilize them effectively in a new context. Thus, a firm that has developed an advantageous position is protected to the extent that its capabilities are specific and therefore difficult for others to imitate, but this very specificity may constrain the firm's ability to transfer these resources to new uses, to apply them in unrelated lines of business, or to sell them in market transactions.

One of the most frequently cited categories of firm-specific capabilities concerns the firm's technological capabilities. Since these frequently rest on tacit knowledge and are often subject to considerable uncertainty concerning their characteristics and performance, they often cannot be purchased through arm's-length, conventional contracts (Mowery 1983). Other forms of firm-specific capabilities include knowledge of specific markets or user needs; idiosyncratic, firm-specific 'routines', such as decision-making and problem-solving techniques; management information systems;[2] and complex networks for handling the marketing and distribution of

The research for this chapter was supported by the Alfred P. Sloan Foundation and the US Air Force Office of Scientific Research. The support and advice of Dean David Hodges and Professor Robert Leachman of the UC Berkeley College of Engineering, Professor Clair Brown of the UC Berkeley Economics Department, and Professor Neil Berglund of the Oregon Graduate Institute were invaluable in this project. The chapter has also benefited from comments on earlier drafts from Rebecca Henderson and Richard Nelson. The cooperation of managers from firms throughout the global semiconductor industry was also essential to this research project, and we appreciate their willingness to provide data and insights.

[1] 'The capabilities approach sees value implementing strategic change as being difficult and costly. Moreover, it can generally only occur incrementally' (Teece *et al.* 1994: 34).

[2] The point-of-sale data collection and distribution systems of the US discount store chain Wal-Mart is one example of an organizationally embedded system that has proven to be very difficult for competitors to imitate.

products that include procedures for the systematic capture and analysis of user feedback. But empirical evaluation of the influence of these factors on firms' behaviour requires more detailed characterization of firm-specific knowledge, rather than measures that rely solely on inputs, such as R&D or marketing expenditures.

A considerable literature on firm-level differences in capabilities deals with product innovation. Intra-firm management of process innovation, however, has received less attention (an important exception is Pisano 1997).[3] This chapter analyses the management of new process technologies in the semiconductor industry. Successful development and introduction of new process technologies relies on the replication of complex 'routines' within a firm, since in many cases a new manufacturing process is developed in an R&D facility and then transferred to a manufacturing site. Firm-specific differences in the management and organization of process innovation appear to be significant and influence performance.

Immediately below, we discuss the importance of successful development and introduction of new manufacturing processes for competitive performance in the semiconductor industry, and present data that characterize some of the consequences of poor performance in this activity. The case studies in Section 3 provide a more detailed firm-level view of the activities that underpin the development and introduction of new manufacturing processes in this industry. The case studies suggest managerial and organizational reasons for differential performance that complement the findings of other empirical models of new process introduction in semiconductor manufacturing. In Section 4, we summarize the important themes that emerge from these case studies for the 'capabilities view' of the firm and discuss possibilities for further research.

2. New Process Introduction in Semiconductor Manufacturing

The speed and effectiveness with which new products are developed and introduced into large-volume production influences competitive performance in a number of manufacturing industries. For example, new product development figured prominently in recent studies of international competitiveness in automobiles (Womack *et al.* 1990; Clark and Fujimoto 1991*a*, 1991*b*). There are good reasons, however, to suspect that the management of new process introduction is if anything even more important to competitive performance in semiconductors than is true in automobiles or other manufacturing industries.[4] Semiconductor manufacturing processes are

---

[3] Although Clark and Fujimoto (1991), along with other scholars of the Japanese automobile industry, note the complementary relationship of process and product innovation, the bulk of their analysis concerns product innovation.

[4] Pisano and Wheelwright (1995) argue that '... manufacturing-process innovation is becoming an increasingly critical capability for production innovation.' Although these authors assert that 'Few managers of high-technology companies view manufacturing as a primary source of competitive advantage', we found no evidence to support this statement in our fieldwork. Indeed, virtually all of the corporate managers in the US and non-US firms included in our study were deeply concerned with improving their management of the development and transfer of manufacturing process technologies, and devoted considerable resources to these activities.

among the most complex commercial production processes in industry. The fabrication of an integrated circuit with feature sizes and line-widths of less than three-quarters of one micron requires more than one hundred steps (e.g. patterning, coating, baking, etching, cleaning, etc.). Underpinning the principal steps are hundreds of individual manufacturing operations. The development of many of these steps is based on art and know-how rather than science; they are not well understood and easily replicated on different equipment or in different facilities; and they impose demanding requirements for a particle-free manufacturing environment.

Product innovation in semiconductors depends on process innovation to a much greater extent than is true of automobiles. The introduction of a new automobile requires substantial time and investment in the production of dies and tooling for stamping and forming body parts and components, but a new model rarely demands significant change in the overall manufacturing process. Semiconductor product innovations, on the other hand, often require major changes in manufacturing processes, because of the tight link between process and product characteristics that typifies semiconductors. Moreover, imperfect scientific understanding of semiconductor manufacturing means that the performance of new process technologies is very hard to predict. New equipment, with operating characteristics that are not well understood, often must be introduced along with a new 'recipe', also not well understood, in order to manufacture a new product. The complexity of the manufacturing process also means that isolating and identifying the causes of yield failures requires considerable time and effort.

The nature of competition in the semiconductor industry also makes effective management of process technology critical to firm strategy. Particularly in 'commodity product' segments of the industry like memory chips, a new product commands a price premium for a relatively brief period, and being first to market is important to profitability. Rapid 'ramping' (growth in production volume) of a new product affects the returns to the large investments in product development and manufacturing facilities.[5]

Although the intensity of competition and the brevity of product life-cycles arguably are greatest in the memory segment of the industry, the semiconductor industry overall faces shorter product life-cycles and greater threats to individual firms' dominance from the entry of producers of close substitutes (e.g. the 'cloners' of Intel's successful 80386 microprocessor) than is true of automobiles. According to Alvarez (1994), the shrinkage of these product cycles means that rapid and smooth introduction of new manufacturing processes is becoming more and more important to competitive performance.[6]

---

[5] Flaherty (1992) presents a model of capacity expansion races in the production of 64K DRAM memory chips that includes firm-specific constraints on capacity expansion and argues for the importance of such capacity expansion in the decisions of US semiconductor firms to cease production of memory chips. Although Flaherty identifies firm-specific differences in the 'ramping' of new product volumes, she does not attempt to explain them.

[6] According to A. R. Alvarez, the vice-president for R&D of Cypress Semiconductor, 'Industrial success in the year 2001 will depend as much on the methods by which process development is conducted as it will on the results of process development' (Alvarez, 1994: 1).

Indeed, in the lucrative microprocessor market, poor performance in new process introduction by would-be challengers to Intel has severely undercut their prospects. The failure of the PowerPC's challenge to Intel's dominance of desktop computers was directly affected by Motorola's inability to expand output of the PowerPC microprocessor more quickly. Simultaneously, Intel has relied on rapid development and 'ramping' of new manufacturing processes to accelerate its introduction of a succession of improved versions of the Pentium and 'Pentium Pro' microprocessors, making Motorola's challenge even greater.[7] Competition between Intel's Pentium II and the 'K6' microprocessor developed by Advanced Micro Devices also was affected by AMD's inability to increase production rapidly (Takahashi 1997). Rather than a 'capacity race', which was hypothesized to characterize US–Japan competition in DRAM manufacture (e.g. Steinmueller 1988), this competition between architectures is driven by capacity utilization, which in turn is a function of success in new process introduction.

2.1. *Semiconductor manufacturing technology*

A brief overview of the technology of semiconductor manufacturing processes will illustrate the complexities and importance of careful management of new process development and transfer. Semiconductor chips are produced on wafers of silicon by constructing layers of insulating and conductive materials in intricate patterns that define the function of the integrated circuit. Each wafer contains from dozens to thousands of identical chips with features as small as 0.35 μm.[8] Manufacturing facilities ('fabs') house ultra-clean manufacturing environments, called clean rooms, that limit particle contamination.

The microscopic dimensions of their features and their complex designs mean that particle contamination can impair the functionality of finished chips, leading to scrapping, which in turn affects the yield of the manufacturing process. There are two measures of yield in semiconductor manufacturing: line yield is the fraction of wafers that survive the manufacturing process; die yield refers to the fraction of chips on surviving wafers that pass tests for functionality and performance at the end of the manufacturing process. In some cases, as when a wafer contains a number of very costly dies that are produced through a large number of complex steps, manufacturers will aggressively pursue wafer scrapping, which reduces line yield, in order to achieve higher die yield and reduce the number of expensive processing steps carried out on non-functional wafers.[9]

---

[7] See Carlton (1995: B3), who notes that 'the PowerPC initiative has been hampered' by 'Motorola's inability to quickly produce PowerPC chips in volume quantities', while 'Intel has been making such advances in its Pentium technology that it has all but erased the advantage PowerPC was supposed to have in terms of lower price and greater performance.'

[8] To provide some sense of the size of these features, the average human hair is about 100 μm in width.

[9] Among other things, this means that line yield is determined in part by the economic and market characteristics of the device. Moreover, line and die yield are jointly, rather than separately, determined, and may be inversely correlated for reasons that have nothing to do with different sources and characteristics of learning by operators and engineers within a fab.

The manufacturing process for semiconductor devices consists of hundreds of operations that are undertaken on many different types of processing equipment. These operations are categorized into broader categories, known as modules, that correspond to a particular set of steps used to perform the manufacturing activities in each area of the fab, such as photolithography, implantation, and metallization. The modules currently or previously used in the fab represent its manufacturing know-how and define its technical capabilities.

Although the firms in our study have organized their new process development activities in different ways, all of them employ the same general modules, and development and introduction of a new manufacturing process requires a common set of steps. Design of new process modules typically begins before the design of the new product that will use them, because a firm's existing process capabilities limit the nature of the new product designs that it can produce. In this phase of the development of a new process, new steps are designed and refined until they are consistently reproducible. Eventually, the new process steps are integrated into a complete process flow, and the interactions among steps create new challenges for the development team. Before the new product can be introduced to the market, it has to undergo a battery of performance and endurance tests collectively called qualification. Qualification is followed by a period of 'ramping' output to commercial volumes.

Development of a new process requires three types of process modules: existing modules, new modules using existing equipment, and new modules using new equipment. All of these modules must be integrated to support the new process flow. Although the incorporation of existing modules into a new process appears to be the simplest of the development activities needed for a new process, even this task can be complicated by the interaction of existing and new process modules. Developing and integrating new modules is even more difficult. One of the most difficult activities is the development of a new module that uses new equipment. In this case, the problems of learning the physical parameters of the process are heightened by the need to learn the peculiar characteristics and parameters of the new equipment.

The challenges associated with developing new modules and incorporating existing modules into new processes require careful planning and coordinated development of product and process technologies. For example, if a new process technology is introduced for the manufacture of modifications of existing product designs, rather than for an entirely new product design, the introduction of the new process technology is simplified. Effective technology planning should also result in a new process that will accommodate as many future product generations as possible, using modules that can be incorporated into as many future processes and products as possible. This is especially important for modules that require new equipment; their high development costs need to be amortized by use in the manufacture of many subsequent product generations. Finally, the relationship depicted in Figure 7.1 indicates that new processes that incorporate a high percentage of new steps require more time for their development. Shorter development cycles therefore require better planning for the introduction of new products and processes over several

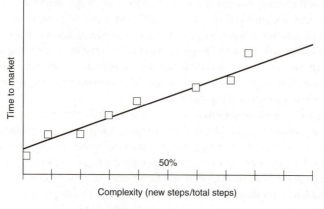

Fig. 7.1 Time to market vs. complexity

generations, so that each new process utilizes a substantial share of the steps and modules associated with its predecessor.

2.2. *Elements of 'best practice' in new process development and implementation*

Our field research led us to distinguish at least three general approaches to managing new process introduction. In our sample, one group of firms introduces new processes that are well understood, exhibiting relatively low defect densities at their inception. A second group of firms introduces new processes that are less well characterized,[10] and attempts to improve their performance through learning-by-doing in the manufacturing fab. A third group of firms focuses on the incremental development and modification of manufacturing processes, frequently introducing new processes and constraining the development of new products to conform to the constraints imposed by the development of their manufacturing process technologies. This last group of firms consists mainly of producers of application-specific integrated circuits (ASICs) that operate as 'foundries'.

The uncertainties of many aspects of semiconductor manufacturing mean that most non-ASIC producers employ a dedicated development fabrication facility for new process development. The 'development fab' serves a function in this industry that resembles that of the 'pilot plant' in the chemicals industry. Development and 'debugging' a new process in a development fab is more effective when the development environment resembles the manufacturing environment in as many aspects as possible, particularly in the equipment and materials used. Many firms that use a development fab transfer significant numbers of technical personnel with the new process technology to the manufacturing fab, in order to improve the speed and effectiveness of the implementation of the new process technology in the manufacturing facility.

---

[10] Process characterization refers to the degree to which the firm understands the physical parameters and their interactions in the process. A process that is highly characterized is well understood and has reproducible manufacturing results in all steps.

Reflecting the complexity of semiconductor manufacturing, as well as the frequent need to alter production equipment as part of new process introduction, differences between the development facility and the manufacturing facility in their equipment sets and configurations can impede new process introduction. In response to this, a number of semiconductor firms have adopted policies that require that the receiving fab have an equipment set that is identical to that on which a new process is developed in the development facility. Even stringent requirements for equipment duplication, however, cannot eliminate all significant differences between the manufacturing environment and that of the development fab for some products or processes. In the case of DRAM products, the differences in manufacturing volumes between the development and manufacturing facilities of leading producers are so great that development fabs cannot fully replicate manufacturing conditions. This factor has contributed to the efforts of some DRAM manufacturers to move new processes out of their development fabs and into manufacturing more rapidly and at lower levels of process characterization.

2.3. Modelling performance in new process introduction

Despite its importance in the semiconductor industry, semiconductor process technology development has received little scholarly attention. In a recent empirical analysis, Hatch and Mowery (1998) use data on 'defect densities' of new semiconductor manufacturing processes to model performance in new process introductions.[11] Longitudinal data on defect densities in new manufacturing processes in the UC Berkeley Competitive Semiconductor Manufacturing (CSM) database (a group that includes producers of DRAMs and other memory products, logic, and ASIC products) point out several interesting characteristics of the learning processes that lead to improvement over time (i.e. declines) in defect densities. First, consistent with the views of scholars who emphasize the importance of firm-level differences in capabilities, Table 7.1 reveals substantial performance differences among manufacturing facilities. Measured as either the initial defect density for a new manufacturing process (the defect density reported for the first quarter of operation of a process in the manufacturing facility) or the average quarterly rate of improvement of defect density, these indicators display enormous variation among individual production sites. Second, the penalties associated with a 'poor start', a high defect density, appear to be difficult to overcome. The data in Figures 7.2 and 7.3 suggest that manufacturing facilities that began with very high defect densities in new manufacturing processes have difficulty in closing the gap with the facilities that began with much lower defect densities. Third, manufacturing processes that are closer to the 'technological frontier', which in this case are associated with smaller line-widths on semiconductor chips, display an even more pronounced 'poor start' penalty. The data summarized in Figures 7.2 and 7.3 suggest that firms that begin with poor defect densities in submicron line-width semiconductor manufacturing processes find it

---

[11] The defect density of a new manufacturing process is simply the number of defects per cm^2 on the silicon wafer from which individual semiconductor chips are cut; it is inversely correlated with die yield.

much harder to close the performance gap with the leaders through learning-by-doing. This result, of course, is precisely what one would expect—labour turnover, technical journals, and other sources of inter-firm spillovers take time to transmit know-how among competitors, and a superior starting point in the most advanced manufacturing processes therefore yields more enduring competitive advantages.

TABLE 7.1 Performance measures for new processes

Fab	Initial defect density (per cm^2)	Average quarterly rate of reduction in defect density (%)
Submicron processes		
O	0.16	11.89
E	0.38	0.32
L	0.40	−25.46
I	0.52	18.51
C	0.57	10.59
N	0.61	2.09
J	0.67	2.13
E	0.70	8.03
D	0.75	−0.55
B	0.77	14.16
I	0.80	16.16
F	1.01	−1.39
M	1.11	3.95
D	1.19	9.72
A	1.29	−3.82
D	2.45	14.65
M	2.60	30.27
H	2.92	25.50
I	3.09	39.62
K	3.53	17.02
G	4.92	30.05
O	6.09	59.45
K	6.52	18.81
G	8.41	53.81
1.0–1.2 μm processes		
N	0.50	3.22
D	0.56	−6.69
H	0.65	5.14
D	0.74	3.64
M	0.82	2.93
M	0.83	8.27
D	0.92	−3.82
C	1.12	19.37
Q	1.31	11.66
R	1.43	18.21
M	1.47	9.59
P	2.08	2.60

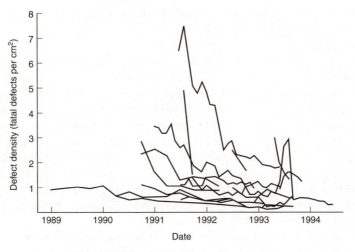

Fig. 7.2 Defect densities of submicron process

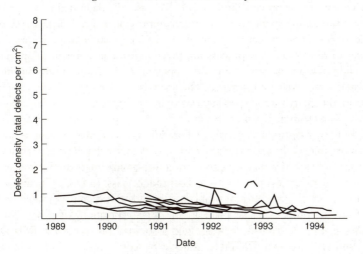

Fig. 7.3 Defect densities of 1.0–1.2 μm processes

Statistical analysis of these performance differences in new process introduction (Hatch and Mowery 1998) revealed several interesting findings. The rate of improvement or learning associated with a new manufacturing process was not solely determined by expansion in volume, but could be increased by allocating more engineering resources to the experiments and organized problem-solving activities that are necessary to reduce 'parametric' defect densities.[12] These results suggest that

---

[12] Defects that cause die yield losses can generally be categorized as coming from unwanted particles or from exceeding the physical tolerance limits of a manufacturing step. The latter type of defects are commonly referred to as parametric processing errors and are a more serious problem in new processes whose parameters are not as well understood as mature processes.

in semiconductor manufacturing, learning-by-doing is not exogenous, but can be increased by management decisions or by firm-level 'routines' that affect the allocation of engineering resources.

Since new semiconductor manufacturing processes frequently are introduced into facilities that are simultaneously operating other, more mature processes, a poorly managed new process introduction can have broader effects on a firm's competitive performance. Committing engineering resources to problem-solving activities for a new process may impede the rate of improvement in other manufacturing processes being operated within the same facility. Yields and output of both a new product and existing products manufactured with more mature processes may all be reduced by an unsuccessful new process introduction. The negative effects of a new process introduction on performance in the manufacture of existing products thus may increase the costs associated with the introduction of a poorly characterized manufacturing process into a commercial-volume fab.

The analysis of management techniques for new process introduction in Hatch and Mowery (1998) yielded other insights into firm specific differences in the management of new process introduction. The use of a dedicated development fab was associated with superior performance in improving defect densities, and locating this development facility on the same site as the high-volume manufacturing facility that was to receive the new process improved performance. Finally, duplication of production equipment sets in the development and manufacturing facilities was associated with better performance. The analysis further suggests the existence of important differences among product classes in the management and learning behaviour associated with new process technologies. As we noted earlier, ASIC producers are more likely to introduce incremental modifications of their process technologies much more frequently, and they frequently do not utilize development facilities. The 'management' variables that are important in explaining interfirm differences in the CSM data are much less powerful for this product class. In DRAM manufacturing, we find that most of the critical problem-solving and learning associated with new manufacturing processes take place in the 'first generation' of a new family of DRAMs, e.g. the first product design and associated process for a 4MB DRAM. Later 'shrinks'[13] of that DRAM product experience fewer problems in process development and transfer.

These statistical results are consistent with a view of new process introduction that emphasizes inter-firm differences in performance, especially in the most advanced products, and that stresses the role of management techniques in improving or degrading the smoothness of the transfer and the rate of learning. Semi-scale development facilities improve firms' performance in products other than ASICs, while significant differences among product classes affect firms' new process introduction. But considerable firm-specific variance remains unexplained (a fixed-effects model revealed significant unexplained firm-level variance), and requires a more

---

[13] A 'shrink' refers to a redesigned chip with a smaller area, which increases die yields and may improve chip performance.

detailed examination. In order to examine the sources of these interfirm differences in management and performance in greater detail, we undertook case studies of new process introduction in two firms in the CSM sample.

3. Case studies of the management of new process introduction

This section compares the management by two semiconductor companies of new process development and transfer to a commercial-volume production facility. The comparison of new process introduction strategies provides a sense of the similarities and differences among semiconductor firms in the capabilities and routines used to manage new process introduction. The firms are disguised as Supreme Technologies (ST) and Multiplex Electronics (ME). We focus on the introduction of one process flow for each company—memory for ST and logic for ME.

The contrasting product markets faced by ST and ME may produce different approaches to management of new process introduction. Nevertheless, the technical challenges, and therefore, the metrics used to evaluate the success of new process introduction, such as defect densities, are consistent across the products of the firms in our sample. Furthermore, both firms participate in a number of product markets and neither company suggested that its strategy for new process introduction varied markedly across its product families. The differences in management of new process introduction between these firms thus appear to be largely the result of firm-level, rather than product-level, differences in technology and competitive strategies.

Both of these firms sought to follow the 'best practices' for new process development and introduction that are highlighted in our statistical analysis—both used a development fab, and both firms sought to attain high levels of equipment duplication and personnel rotation between the development and manufacturing facilities. The considerable inter-firm differences in performance that these case studies highlight therefore are not the result of divergent goals. Instead, they reflect differences between these firms in the underlying capabilities or resources available to achieve these goals. The first firm, ST, chose an ambitious development strategy that proved infeasible, given its internal technical and engineering resources. Moreover, the firm maintained its commitment to a technically demanding project, despite senior managers' awareness of the near-impossibility of attaining its technical goals in a realistic time frame, in large part because of the difficulty of renegotiating the goals and scope of the project among the various groups within the firm. In the course of the project, the firm was forced to abrogate its commitment to the practices noted above, and the project's completion was delayed significantly. By contrast, ME had sufficient internal capabilities and financial resources to follow a 'best-practice' approach.

In the wake of the project discussed below, ST has significantly shifted its strategy, and now seeks to develop process technologies that represent incremental, rather than radical, advances on the state of the art. In addition, the firm has expanded its process development organization considerably. ST's new approach to process development seeks to reduce the demands of individual projects on its internal capabilities and resources, while simultaneously expanding these resources to meet the technical challenges, cycle-time requirements, and other demands of process technology development and transfer.

3.1. Supreme Technologies

Our first case study examined Supreme Technologies' introduction of a new process for a new memory product. The new process presented numerous technical and organizational challenges to ST, since it included a very high proportion of new steps and was eventually transferred to a recipient fab that used wafers of a different diameter from those used by the development fab. Prior to undertaking the development and transfer of this process technology, ST had conducted an internal study of previous process transfers, and adopted policies to improve its performance and to impose greater discipline on modifications in the recipient fab following process transfer. But these reforms in ST's new process introduction policies did not produce a smooth process development and transfer because ST failed to integrate its plans for new process development with its product planning. The result was an overly ambitious project to develop a process technology that encountered serious delays, impeding the timely introduction of a commercially attractive product.

Among the new practices adopted by ST in the wake of its internal study were the assignment of a full-time leader to the project; the scheduling of regular meetings among project team members and between the team and representatives from other divisions in the company; the decomposition of the new process into modules to make easier transfer to the volume manufacturing as each module was completed; the designation of a team in the recipient fab dedicated to the process hand-off; and the maintenance of a baseline process that would continue to run in the development fab for a year or two after the transfer to a volume fab. ST also attempted to align the incentives of engineers in its development fab more closely with those of engineers and managers in the recipient fab, recognizing that this could bring about a smoother transfer of the process technology. The firm sought to create such alignment by rewarding its manufacturing fab for accepting the new process, rather than penalizing it for declines in performance or capacity utilization in the operation of existing processes. ST brought engineers from the recipient fab to the development site in the weeks prior to hand-off, encouraging them to learn the new process and accept responsibility for its successful transfer.[14] By comparison with ME, however, fewer representatives from ST's recipient fab were rotated to its development fab, and they visited the development site for shorter periods of time.

The process that ST sought to develop differed dramatically from that associated with its previous advanced manufacturing process for memory chips. Of the more than one hundred process steps involved in the new manufacturing process, approximately 90 per cent were new, compared with a more typical share of 50-60 per cent in

---

[14] Volume fabs often resist the introduction of new semiconductor processes, since they can cause major upheavals, as people are trained on the new process and new equipment is calibrated and deployed. In some process steps, technical improvements contained in a new process are 'backward compatible' and can improve yields of the existing process flow. The initial net effect nevertheless is negative, with the volume fab experiencing yield declines as it 'ramps up' the new process to high volume.

a new process. Moreover, several of these new steps and modules, particularly the new etch module, had not previously been used in commercial-volume manufacturing and presented serious technical challenges. ST needed the new etch operations to pack more transistors into a smaller die area, but this module required new chemical and thermal specifications, as well as modifications in the equipment that exceeded the capabilities of currently available technology.

ST's development schedule assumed that the firm would have a baseline process running in the development fab two years after top management approved the process development project. Eighteen months after the project's inception, however, ST had to reorganize the core development team. The reorganized team retained only one person from the original team, and another year and a half was required to 'qualify' the new process in the development fab.[15] The project thus was delayed by roughly one year. These delays in the process development project ultimately imposed serious commercial penalties on ST.

In retrospect, ST management acknowledged that the decision to pursue such an ambitious new process technology for this particular product was a mistake. Rather than developing a technically demanding new process and new product simultaneously, managers argued that a 'shrink' of an existing product should have been the focus of a less ambitious process development project, enabling the manufacture of a new product with a process that used fewer radically new steps.[16] Some of the new steps thus could have been incorporated into ST's volume-manufacturing operations before the development of this new product began, and ST would have entered the market sooner.

The ambitious scope of the ST's development project also placed great demands on the capacity of its development facility, which slowed learning and debugging of the new process. Since its development facility was small, with no more than one of several critical pieces of equipment, capacity constraints were significant and often increased the cycle time for completion of a manufacturing lot or an experiment, slowing the evaluation of new process steps. The need to send chips to foreign facilities for packaging[17] produced other delays, which slowed reliability and 'burn-in' testing of packaged chips.

---

[15] Within ST, 'qualification' of the process meant that the process was meeting its die and line yield targets. It also indicated that all modules were characterized sufficiently to facilitate the operation of the process within the development fab as a benchmark and to support its transfer to the manufacturing site.

[16] The internal politics of this very ambitious technical goal for the ST development project merit a study in themselves. Various observers within and outside of the firm suggested that if the firm were to maintain its long-standing position as a 'fast follower' in its segment of the semiconductor industry, ST had little choice but to undertake a very ambitious project that effectively sought to compensate for previous failures to keep up with technical advances. Senior managers within ST and project personnel were well aware at an early point in the project that its technical goals would be difficult to attain and that the project was going to encounter cost overruns and serious delays. Either these and other individuals felt that the firm had little choice, or a decision to cancel the project would have unravelled far too many political agreements and coalitions within the firm. These project goals themselves thus served as a sort of organizational truce.

[17] 'Packaging' refers to the insertion of a die into a casing, usually made of plastic or ceramic, that can be inserted into a 'motherboard' or some other board-level assembly for incorporation into an electronic systems product.

Development fab capacity was also constrained by the decision of ST senior management during the third year of the project to rely on this facility for production of small volumes for sale of the product that relied on the new process. ST sought through this policy to overcome some of the commercial penalties resulting from the delays in the development of the new process. This policy nevertheless produced further delays, since the new process had not yet been fully characterized, and the installation of new equipment in the development fab diverted engineering effort, as new operators were hired and trained.

Although its internal study of previous new process development projects did not prevent the firm from pursuing a project that was technically too ambitious, ST used the study's findings to impose discipline over equipment selection and problem-solving within its process development activities. But here too, the implementation of these policies was incomplete. Despite its emphasis on discipline in its equipment selection and duplication of equipment sets between development and manufacturing facilities, ST switched the recipient fab only six months before transfer of the process technology began. Schedule delays contributed to this decision, which was especially risky in view of the fact that the newly chosen recipient fab was equipped to process wafers of a different diameter from those of the development fab. The shift in recipient fab contributed to a delay of almost a full year in characterizing the manufacturing process in the production facility and expanding output with acceptable yields.

In response to the problems associated with this project, which combined to produce a delay in process development of roughly eighteen months and a delay in the manufacturing 'ramp' (expansion of production to capacity) of about twelve months, ST has again revised its procedures for process technology development and transfer. Assuming that the new procedures are successfully implemented (and our earlier discussion pointed out ST's difficulties in adhering to new policies in the management of new process development and transfer), ST's policies toward process development and transfer will incorporate some elements of the management approaches used by ASIC 'foundries'. The two most important elements of this new approach are (i) locating a substantial number of development engineers, who report to ST's vice-president for R&D, at the firm's manufacturing fabs; and (ii) assigning greater responsibility for development of new process technology modules to the development engineers in the manufacturing facilities. Rather than ambitious, complex development projects that combine many significantly different modules, ST now seeks to focus its process development efforts on specific process 'competences', and aims to transfer these to the manufacturing environment for complete development. In addition, the firm has expanded its R&D staff considerably and will focus this larger group's efforts on a narrower array of critical process modules. Finally, ST has focused its process development efforts on two new products that require relatively modest advances in process technology.

ST's new approach to process technology development and transfer requires considerable discipline in long-term planning for product development, process development, and equipment procurement. A narrower array of process technologies will be developed to support future 'families' of products. Permanent assignment of a substantial share of the firm's process development staff to the manufacturing fabs also represents an interesting modification of the personnel transfer policies previously adopted by this and other semiconductor firms: rather than temporary rotations of large numbers of engineers, a smaller number of individuals will form a more continuous liaison between the process development staffs at the development and manufacturing sites.

Despite its apparent advantages, however, this new approach will involve significant development activities in the manufacturing facility, which could divert equipment, engineering effort, operator time and attention, etc., from production of revenue-yielding products to experiments with new equipment, techniques, and product designs. Although successful semiconductor foundries have shown that these risks and costs can be managed, other firms have found that process development in the manufacturing fab can impair the operation of existing manufacturing processes. The ultimate success of ST's new approach to process development and transfer also will depend critically on the firm's ability to manage the complex overlaps of new and mature process technologies, products, and equipment sets. As we noted above, a poorly conceived product introduction strategy doomed the firm's efforts to adhere to its previous guidelines for process development and transfer. In addition, the firm's commitment to an 'incremental' approach to new process technology development, keeping the share of new manufacturing steps within the new process to a manageable proportion, has yet to be fully tested. Nevertheless, ST's new approach to process technology development has some interesting similarities to that of the other firm discussed in this chapter, as we note below.

3.2. Multiplex Electronics

A central characteristic of new process introduction at ME is the breadth and depth of the firm's efforts to achieve precise duplication of process and equipment specifications between development and manufacturing and across all sites running a particular process.[18] ME also has overlapped development with manufacturing to the greatest degree of any of the companies whose new process development practices we studied in detail, in order to support more precise duplication between development and production, while cutting the ramp time (the length of time required to increase output to fab capacity) at the volume recipient fab. ME's approach to new process development and transfer appears to have considerable technical and performance advantages, but these are achieved at a high financial cost. The high costs associated with ME's strategy for developing and introducing new process technologies almost certainly precludes reliance on this approach by many other firms, including ST. Nevertheless, as we noted earlier, elements of ST's new approach to process technology development resemble techniques long used by ME.

---

[18] Due to altitude and temperature differences between their fabs, ME permits some variation in the process specifications across its sites.

In at least two areas, ME's management of new process development and introduction exhibits a higher level of discipline and more extensive multigenerational planning than were observed in the ST project discussed earlier. ME's process technology development and introduction procedures extend across multiple generations of a given product and process. The first version of a new product design typically is a relatively large die size, and it is manufactured with a process that has been developed for a prior-generation device. The first 'shrink' of this new product, however, is designed under the supervision of the development staff, and its production relies on a process that incorporates new steps. Thus, an all-new product relies on a process that is relatively well understood, and a substantially new process is used only for the manufacture of a product design whose general performance and manufacturability are relatively well understood. ME also tries to maintain a substantial (at least 70 per cent) overlap in steps and in equipment requirements across process generations.

But ME's approach to new process development contrasts with that of ST in another important dimension that has significant financial implications. ME combines the process development and early-stage, commercial-scale manufacturing activities in a single 'hybrid' facility. The development and early-stage volume production of each successive new product take place within a fab constructed specifically for that process. Rather than developing a new process in a specialized development facility and then transferring it to a volume-manufacturing site, ME develops a new process in the hybrid facility, where it is eventually implemented at commercial scale. No transfer therefore is needed prior to the achievement of commercial production volumes; complete equipment duplication between the development and early-stage volume manufacturing is guaranteed; and several members of the development team for each project typically remain with the process once it is 'ramped up' in this new facility. Eventually, several months after the process has been ramped up in the hybrid facility, it is transferred to a very high-volume production facility. This transfer requires substantial personnel rotation and equipment duplication. The new process remains in operation in the hybrid facility for at least twelve months after the transfer in order to provide a production baseline for the very high-volume facility.

The ME strategy for new process introduction has shifted power and responsibility for a broad range of activities within the firm to its process development group. ME's process development organization now is responsible for designing and constructing new manufacturing capacity both at the development site and the high-volume manufacturing site, and for hiring technicians and engineers to sustain the process baseline. ME's circuit design group finalizes the design rules at an early stage in the development of manufacturing process technology, and the development group is charged with developing a process to meet those rules (responsibility for design of subsequent 'shrinks' of the product is assigned to the process development group). The manufacturing fabs contribute little to changes in design rules, since development and early commercial-scale production occur at the development site. Although the high-volume manufacturing sites eventually do become involved in negotiating with the development group over the transfer, the development group has selected and developed the new modules for a new product well before manufacturing engineers become involved.

For each new process, ME brings production personnel from its very high-volume commercial manufacturing facilities to the development site for six months to a year to assist in 'ramping' the new process in the hybrid fab. The integration engineers from the recipient fab are the first to make the trip, followed by engineers and technicians from each equipment module. Compared with the development fabs at ST, ME's hybrid fab produces up to seven times more wafers per week at the time of the transfer to the production facility. Indeed, the peak capacity of ME's dedicated hybrid fab for some processes is comparable to that of several of ST's commercial-volume facilities.

'Ramping' production volume in its development fab has several advantages for ME. Personnel from the production fabs acquire the experience at the hybrid fab to run a high-volume ramp more efficiently when they return to their very high-volume facility. Requests from the recipient fab for changes in the equipment set or the process recipes are reduced by the involvement of many of the fab's engineering staff on the first ramp of the process. The otherwise detrimental effects of the geographic separation of the very high-volume commercial manufacturing facility from the development site are reduced through rotation of personnel between these sites. In addition, since the first production ramp occurs at the hybrid fab, development engineers stay involved with the new process through output expansion and are able to resolve manufacturing problems that are revealed only at commercial-scale volumes. The high costs of new equipment for the development facility are charged to manufacturing, rather than to development, and purchases of multiple pieces of each type of equipment are amortized across these relatively high production volumes. Development of a new process in the relatively large-volume hybrid facility also reduces many of the capacity constraints that slowed the rate of learning for ST in its process development, and the higher volumes reveal some manufacturing problems that otherwise would remain hidden from the development engineers. Finally, ME's strategy accelerates the achievement of sufficient production volumes of reliable chips that can be marketed to select customers and provided as samples to other purchasers.

ME typically organizes the transfer team responsible for moving a new process from the hybrid to the commercial production fab six to eight months prior to certification of a new process in the hybrid fab. Both the development and recipient fabs contribute members to the team, which has twenty to thirty members. ME has aggressive goals for new process hand-offs: the very high-volume recipient fab is expected to attain yields that are within 1 per cent of the hybrid development fab's last yield at the time of the transfer.[19] Over two hundred test wafers are partially processed by both the source and recipient fabs during the transfer, to verify the process and its transfer.

[19] At the time of release to volume manufacturing, ME wishes to achieve a defect density of 0.2 per cm^2 at its development site.

Once a process has been transferred to the very high-volume manufacturing environment, ME managers are responsible for ensuring that all of its steps, materials, and equipment remain identical across all manufacturing sites. Among other things, this goal requires great discipline in equipment procurement, and occasionally results in the firm choosing equipment that lags behind the technological frontier. ME prefers buying equipment 'off the shelf', and resists modifications in some pieces of equipment that threaten exact duplication among its production sites—in some instances, this policy has delayed adoption of new equipment features. Duplicating its process and equipment specifications across all of its manufacturing facilities took approximately six years. Complementing the efforts of the company-wide equipment group, user groups are formed with membership drawn from ME's production sites. The user group for a particular tool decides on upgrades and negotiates with the vendor on how to implement them.

The hand-off to the high-volume manufacturing fab commences when the hybrid fab has begun increasing its own production volume. During the transfer, the recipient fab can apply for a waiver to a particular 'boundary condition' (e.g. a specific equipment setting), but without compelling data, waivers related to process steps or recipes are not allowed. Equipment changes are rarely allowed under the waiver system, although changes in materials or chemical inputs are allowed more frequently. When the source and the recipient fab reach an impasse regarding the specifications of a step, a corporate oversight committee resolves the conflict. This committee also oversees transfers of process technologies among ME's manufacturing fabs, and enforces a corporate edict that demands precise duplication of manufacturing processes, materials, and equipment among all manufacturing facilities responsible for a given process.

The recipient fab and all of ME's fabs that subsequently receive a new manufacturing process can propose changes resulting from experimentation in the manufacturing facilities, but the process-change committee must approve all changes before their adoption. The committee then disseminates the new process specification to all fabs running the process. The composition of the committee changes over the life of a specific manufacturing process. Initially, the development organization plays a major role, but as the new process migrates to several high-volume manufacturing facilities, one is designated as the custodian of the baseline process and the development organization's role within the committee is reduced.[20] The effort to maintain discipline within new process introduction may discourage creativity and problem-solving activities within ME's manufacturing operations. Although ME permits changes to the process specifications that are approved by the process-change committee, the resulting disincentives for creative problem-solving within the firm's manufacturing fabs may eventually create problems in recruiting and retaining engineering talent in these operations. In addition, differences between even the large-scale development fabs operated by this firm and its production facilities mean

---

[20] The development fab runs the baseline for at least a year after the transfer to the initial high-volume site. Then the process is transferred to an additional very high-volume site, and the initial recipient maintains the baseline process.

that disincentives for experimentation in the manufacturing environment may eventually impair manufacturing performance.

3.3. Comparing ME and ST

As we noted in the introduction to this section, both ME and ST sought to follow broadly similar approaches to developing and introducing process technologies as a part of their innovation strategies. Table 7.2 summarizes the similarities and differences in the various elements of each firm's approach. As we noted, ST's failure to adopt a long-term perspective towards 'multigenerational' planning of process, product, and equipment policies, as well as the firm's adoption of an excessively ambitious (relative to in-house engineering resources and technical capabilities) set of technical milestones for the project examined in our case study, led to violations of other 'best-practice' techniques for new process development and transfer. The firm made too little use of personnel rotation, equipment duplication was too low, and too many significant changes in the process technology occurred late in its development and during its transfer—all of these occurred in spite of ST's adoption of a plan for process technology development and transfer that sought to avoid them. ME, on the other hand, was able to pursue a more disciplined approach to process technology development and implementation that drew on the firm's much greater financial and technical resources.

Although there are significant differences between ST and ME in their approaches to managing the development and introduction of new manufacturing process technologies, the high cost of many of ME's practices makes them infeasible for ST. Nevertheless, successful implementation of ST's recent reforms in its management of new manufacturing process technologies will reduce some of the contrasts between ME and ST. These changes in ST's management of new process development and introduction mean that the final stages of development of the process

TABLE 7.2 Goals and performance in new process introduction by ST and ME

Activity	Goal	Firm performance	
		ST	ME
Time horizon for product-process-equipment planning	Long-run	Short-run	Long-run
Share of new steps in new process	Moderate	Extremely high	Moderate
Overlap of development and manufacturing engineers during transfer	High	Low	High
Overlap of equipment between development site and manufacturing site	High	Low	High
Control over process changes at manufacturing fab	High	High	High
Baseline process at development fab	Yes	Disrupted by push for revenues from dev. fab	Yes
Post-mortem exercise	Yes	Yes	Yes

technology, as well as its characterization, will occur in the manufacturing fab. This approach closely resembles ME's reliance on a 'production ramp' in its hybrid development facility. Like ME, ST also is devoting more attention to maintaining precise duplication in the equipment sets used in its development and manufacturing fabs.

The significant differences that remain in these firms' management of new process technologies are attributable in part to a greater depth and breadth of experience in process technology development within ME. Greater experience, along with more extensive financial and technical resources, appears to have resulted in a more disciplined implementation of policies that individually do not differ greatly from those espoused by senior managers in ST. Although senior ST managers may argue to the contrary, the firm's much shorter history of trial, error, and learning has not yet produced comparable adherence to the policies promulgated by senior management.

4. Conclusion

Students of firm-level capabilities emphasize the persistence of differences in performance, as well as behaviour, among firms in the same industry that are not well addressed by other approaches such as neoclassical economics or the structure-conduct approach to strategy developed by Porter (1980). This view also stresses the 'embedded' nature of such capabilities—they develop out of idiosyncratic investments and processes, and competitors find it difficult to duplicate them through imitation or other types of interfirm 'spillovers'. Although this view of the firm appeals to intuition and casual empiricism, it is difficult to prove or disprove through empirical testing. Measures of firm-specific capabilities are difficult to collect on a large scale, and the performance consequences of differences in such capabilities are not easily determined.

This chapter has examined one of the most important firm-specific capabilities for competition in the semiconductor industry: the ability of firms to develop, introduce, and expand production with new processes. Significant increases in the complexity of this industry's process and product technologies during the past fifteen years have intensified the need for a more systematic approach to new process development and transfer—indeed, the very concept of a separate development facility has become widespread within the industry only since the mid-1970s. In addition, the increasing complexity of manufacturing process technologies has made the maintenance of similarity in process technologies between a development and manufacturing fab, and among multiple manufacturing fabs, a very demanding task for firms in this industry.

The 'pre-scientific' nature of much of the knowledge underpinning manufacturing processes in this industry means that much of the relevant knowledge is tacit, rather than codified, and makes the intra-firm transfer of process technologies a very demanding activity. Despite its legitimate claim to be a high-technology industry, knowledge of the precise details of many semiconductor manufacturing processes is so limited that their performance cannot be predicted without extensive experimentation. This characteristic of the process technology means that firm-level differences in managing new process introduction are likely to persist and will have important consequences for performance.

Like new product development, new process introduction is an element of high-technology competition in which management and organization matter at least as much as basic technological knowledge or even the technical skills of the workforce. The capabilities that are exploited by firms to manage new process introduction cannot be reduced to differences in human capital. The skills seem to be organizational, rather than exclusively individual. One firm's hiring the most skilled process engineers of another firm may be necessary, but it is not sufficient, to 'reverse engineer' and introduce a new manufacturing process.

One of the most important characteristics of firms that are relatively successful in new process introduction is the coordination of new product and new process development strategies. Semiconductor producers need product and equipment 'road maps', which lay out the next several generations of a company's products, detailing plans for alternating between the introduction of 'shrinks' of established products and entirely new product designs. At the same time, such a plan must guide the development and introduction of new generations of process technologies, which in turn impose requirements for equipment purchases that will span multiple generations.[21] Implementing the 'road maps' requires support from senior management, as well as close coordination among integration engineers, module developers, and a company-wide equipment group.

Evaluation of the strategies through which firms strengthen or erode their capabilities in such critical functions as new process introduction merits additional work. Our case studies provide a snapshot, rather than a history of new process development in these firms, but they suggest that one of the most important factors in firms' improvement of their management of new process introduction is the ability to learn through systematic retrospective assessments of previous projects. Both of the firms in our case studies had studied their previous performance, and both attempted, with varying degrees of success, to learn from past successes and failures. ME conducted detailed reviews of each major project and adjusted its policies for management of new process introduction. ST, on the other hand, had undertaken only one comprehensive retrospective study that spanned a number of projects. Although this study led to significant changes and improvements in ST's management of new process introduction, it did not address several fundamental issues, such as the need for the firm to plan its development of product and process technologies over a longer time-horizon. The resulting pressures on ST's process development project contributed to the firm's failure to adhere strictly to the study's guidelines.

ST's more recent reorganization of its process development and transfer policies and routines drew on a number of 'benchmarking' studies, gathering data from other firms in the same geographic region on their process and product development

---

[21] A large share of capital expenditures goes to equipment. Currently, high volume fabs cost at least $1 bn., with 85% of that investment spent on equipment and 15% on facilities.

organization and performance. Although gathering these data took considerable time, and interpreting their implications also required a substantial investment of effort, other firms, some of whom were competitors of ST, were surprisingly cooperative in providing the information, provided that they also had access to summaries of survey results. This sort of informal 'know-how trading' (von Hippel 1987) appears to have been an important impetus to ST's efforts to improve its management of new process introduction. Another important source of information for ST was the firm's interactions with a group of foundries that contracted to manufacture ST-designed products. Some important aspects of ST's reforms, such as the development of more new process technology modules within the manufacturing fab, resemble practices long pursued by foundries. Turnover among senior management, another potentially important source of change in management practices, appears to have played little or no role in ST's policy changes. Most senior managers had relatively long tenures with the firm (especially surprising within the semiconductor industry), and both the problems with the project studied in this chapter and the changes adopted in response to these problems were not associated with significant turnover among senior management.

The increasing importance of effective management of new process introduction appears to be expanding the power and authority of the process development organizations, relative to both product design and manufacturing, within ME and ST. This expansion of the power of the development organization seems particularly noteworthy in the sphere of manufacturing. Engineers at the recipient fabs in both firms are expected to avoid any undocumented 'tweaking' of the process once it has been transferred to their facilities. Moreover, both firms exercise controls of varying degrees of stringency over equipment choices in their recipient fabs. The controls enable the firms to maintain high levels of equipment duplication between the development and recipient fab, and among the various manufacturing facilities that are operating identical pieces of equipment.

The growing authority of the development organizations within these firms has important implications for the organization of the development organization itself. We noted in our earlier discussion that development fab capacity constraints are a serious problem in the development of a new manufacturing process. But the effects of these constraints are intensified by the requirement within many firms that a new process be operated within the development fab as a 'benchmark' for months after its transfer to a volume manufacturing site. Operation of a new manufacturing process as a benchmark in the same facility that has responsibility for developing the next new process requires a substantial investment in equipment and trained operators. The firms in our case studies addressed this requirement in different ways. The ST development fab was ordered to begin to show a positive revenue stream by manufacturing larger quantities of products from the new process in a far more disciplined fashion. But the complexity of this new manufacturing process meant that the development team simultaneously had to complete development of the process while producing commercially viable components. Rather than a benchmark, ST's new process was still under development when it first began producing components for sale, and the rate of learning suffered. ME overcame development fab capacity constraints by developing the new process in a hybrid commercial-scale facility and continued operation of the new process in that facility for some months after its development and transfer to a very high-volume production facility.

Generally, the hand-off between development and manufacturing poses a more difficult problem of acceptance than the hand-off between fundamental research and the development organization. The realities of a high-volume manufacturing fab rarely match those of a small-scale development fab—up to ten times as many wafers run through a volume fab relative to a development fab, requiring possible revisions to the new process, particularly in the equipment calibration and maintenance areas. By bringing manufacturing engineers to the development fab before the new process is frozen for transfer, a company can incorporate the suggestions of the manufacturing personnel and heighten the likelihood that the manufacturing staff will accept ownership of the new process. The complexities of long-distance transfer of a new process from development to recipient fab have led an increasing number of semiconductor firms to co-locate their development and manufacturing facilities; statistical analysis suggests that this policy should improve performance (Hatch and Mowery 1998). If this strategy is widely adopted, centres for semiconductor R&D, such as California's Silicon Valley, could witness the departure of development organizations for the rapidly growing manufacturing sites in Texas, the South-West, or the Pacific North-West.

References

Alvarez, A. R. (1994). 'Process Requirements Through 2001', presented at the Second International Rapid Thermal Processing Conference, Monterey, Calif., 31 Aug.

Bacon, G., S. Beckman, D. C. Mowery, and E. Wilson (1994). 'Managing Product Definition in High-Technology Industries: A Pilot Study', *California Management Review*, 36(3): 32–56.

Barney, J. B. (1986). 'Strategic Factor Markets: Expectations, Luck, and Business Strategy', *Management Science*, 32: 1231–41.

Carlton, J. (1995). 'Apple, IBM, Motorola PowerPC Group Issues Blueprint for a Common Computer', *Wall Street Journal*, 15 Nov.

Clark, K. B., and T. Fujimoto (1991). *Product Development Performance: Strategy, Organization and Management in the World Auto Industry*. Boston: Harvard Business School Press.

Competitive Semiconductor Manufacturing Program (1993). *The Competitive Semiconductor Manufacturing Survey: First Report on Results of the Main Phase*. University of California, Berkeley: Engineering Systems Research Center.

Flaherty, M. T. (1992). 'Manufacturing and Firm Performance in Technology-Intensive Industries: US and Japanese DRAM Experience', unpublished MS.

Grindley, P., D. C. Mowery, and B. Silverman (1994). 'Lessons of SEMATECH for the Design of High-Technology Consortia', *Journal of Policy Analysis and Management*, 35(4): 723–58.

Hatch, N. W., and D. C. Mowery (1995). 'Process Innovation and Learning by Doing in Semiconductor Manufacturing', presented at the American Economic Association meetings, Washington, DC, 4–6 Jan.

Mowery, D. C. (1983). 'Economic Theory and Government Technology Policy', *Policy Sciences*, 16: 27–43.

Penrose, E. T. (1959). *The Theory of the Growth of the Firm*. New York: Wiley.

Pisano, G. P. (1997). *The Development Factory*. Boston: Harvard Business School Press.

——and S. C. Wheelwright (1995). 'The New Logic of High-Tech R&D', *Harvard Business Review*, Sept.–Oct.: 93–105.

Porter, M. E. (1980). *Competitive Strategy*. New York: Free Press.

——and M. B. Fuller (1986). 'Coalitions and Global Strategy', in M. E. Porter (ed.), *Competition in Global Industries*. Boston: Harvard Business School Press.

Rosenberg, N., and W. E. Steinmueller (1980), 'The Economic Implications of the VLSI Revolution', *Futures*, 12: 358–69.

Shuen, A. A. (1997). 'Competence Curves: Dynamics of Learning in Semiconductors', unpublished MS, San Jose State University.

Steinmueller, W. E. (1998). 'Industry Structure and Government Policies in the U.S. and Japanese Integrated Circuit Industries', in J. B. Shoven (ed.), *Government Policy Towards Industry in the United States and Japan*. New York: Cambridge University Press.

Takahashi, D. (1997). 'Intel Plans Deeper Price Cuts on Chips in an Effort to Ward Off Competitors', *Wall Street Journal*, 4 Nov.

Teece, D., G. Pisano, and A. Shuen (1994). 'Dynamic Capabilities and Strategic Management', Working Paper, Center for Research in Management, University of California at Berkeley.

Von Hippel, E. (1987). 'Cooperation between Rivals: Informal Know-How Trading', *Research Policy*, 16: 291–302.

Wernerfelt, B. (1984). 'A Resource-Based View of the Firm', *Strategic Management Journal*, 5: 171–80.

Womack, J. P., D. T. Jones, and D. Roos (1990). *The Machine that Changed the World*. New York: Rawson Associates.

PART III

Introduction to Part III

THE EVOLUTION OF ORGANIZATIONAL CAPABILITIES AND THEIR SOCIAL ROOTS: EVIDENCE FROM THE AUTOMOBILE INDUSTRY

The chapters in Part III are all about competences and practices in automobile manufacture. Two of the chapters contrast Japanese and US practice. They all deal with the routines of governing, and operating, in automobile production, with how the routines they describe came into existence, and with how they have evolved.

Coriat is basically concerned with the differences between Japanese automobile manufacturers and American manufacturers, with the focus largely on the period between the 1950s and 1960s, and the late 1980s and early 1990s. His archetypal Japanese automobile producer is Toyota; his archetypal American automobile manufacturer is the Ford Motor Company (at least as it was until recently). He is interested in the differences in their own right insofar as they reveal two different organizational archetypes but also for the light that examining the differences can shed on the concept of 'routines'.

Coriat emphasizes that prevailing routines, in addition to serving to organize work and problem solving patterns, reflect the governance structures, modes of control, and compromises regarding competing interests, that prevail in an organization. Nelson and Winter have also highlighted this latter function in their proposal that routines define the terms of a 'truce'. As with many other comparative analysts of Japanese and American automobile production 'routines', Coriat emphasizes the less hierarchical and more cooperative structure of Toyota compared with Ford, at least in the 1980s, and that the Toyota system involved and tapped a wider range of a worker's skills and ability to think than was then typical American practice.

Fujimoto's highly complementary chapter is focused on changes that have occurred in the Toyota production system over the last decade, the factors inducing these changes, and the processes of change. Fujimoto proposes that, while foreign observers often had assumed that production workers at Toyota were generally pleased with the work environment that was in place in the late 1980s, this was not completely so. And a tightening of the Japanese labour market provided strong incentives to Toyota to revise their production system.

The heart of Fujimoto's chapter is focused on how changes occur at Toyota. He proposes that the process of change involves a combination of a broadly oriented 'vision', a considerable amount of trial and feedback learning, a considerable amount of discussing in order to get broad agreement on what is desirable and acceptable and what is not, and revision of the vision to provide a rationale for the evolving consensus. He proposes that Toyota has been very good at this process. He associates Toyota's continuing success, in the face of periodic external changes and continuing internal ones, as an indication that it has achieved strong dynamic capabilities, in the sense of Teece, Pisano, and Shuen (cf. Part IV of this book).

The chapter by Florida, Kenney, and Jenkins, focuses on the Japanese experience in 'transplanting' the modes of organization that they had operated effectively in their Japanese plants, to transplants in the USA. They observe that, when the Japanese began trying to do this, many organizational theorists were sceptical about their ability to succeed. To a considerable extent, the conventional wisdom was that successful organizational forms needed to be well tuned to the broader institutional environment within which they operated, and scholars looking at Japanese attempts to transplant proposed that the broader institutional environment was very different in the USA from that in Japan.

However, the authors' detailed study argues that Japanese automobile plants in the United States, indeed, did have 'routines' that were very similar to those employed in Japan. In many cases, the differences in the broader institutional environment appear not to have been a constraint on adopting Japanese modes more or less intact. In other cases, differences in the environment apparently forced the transplant to take somewhat different routes toward Japanese practice, but apparently in many such cases they achieved the substance if not the precise form.

It is interesting that, over the period of time when the Japanese transplants were successfully setting up in the United States, many plants of American-owned companies were themselves trying to imitate Japanese practice, in at least certain respects. The study by Florida, Kenney, and Jenkins, briefly discusses these developments, without going into them in detail.

8

*The 'Abominable Ohno Production System'. Competences, Monitoring, and Routines in Japanese Production Systems**

BENJAMIN CORIAT

1. Introduction

The main aim of this chapter is to analyse some basic features of those organizational competences particularly associated with the emergence and spread of the 'Japanese Production System' as symbolized by all the organizational innovations which have emanated from Toyota. In order to do this, it seems essential to study Japanese methods from two angles. First, we have chosen to present the Japanese production system by stressing its innovations and specificities, in particular by comparing it to two earlier 'American' production systems, namely Taylorism and the Ford systems.[1]

Second, we shall study those Japanese innovations in terms of the specific routines which they entail: in this respect we expand on the preliminary conclusions presented in Coriat and Dosi (1998) concerning the dual nature of routines as both problem-solving devices and governance procedures.

We start by briefly discussing the notion of routines in Nelson and Winter (1982) (Section 2) since this helps in clarifying the nature of organization in general and also the specificities of the case of the Toyota production system (Sections 3–5). As the Toyota case vividly illustrates, a comprehensive account of how a particular organization operates requires a joint understanding of how particular ensembles of routines underlie both organizational competences, *together with*, mechanisms of work-control and governance of conflicting interests (Section 6). Finally, in Section 7, we draw from the Toyota example some more general implications with respect to learning, knowledge-codification, and the nature of routines themselves.

*This work greatly benefited at various stages from the comments and suggestions of several participants to the TED project, IIASA and the *Dynacom* project, TSER, European Union. In particular I want to acknowledge the collaboration with Giovanni Dosi, with whom a few of the ideas explored below were jointly developed. Of course, the usual disclaimers apply.

[1] On this point it should be noted immediately that our thesis is that the innovativeness and specificity of Japanese technologies can be explained by the fact that they constitute a series of appropriate solutions to the production of different and varied products, as opposed to the American production system which used to be particularly well adapted to the large-scale production of standardized products. See Fujimoto (1983), Monden (1983), Womack *et al.* (1990), Coriat (1991, 1992).

2. Routines in the Evolutionist Firm

2.1. *The concept of the routine in Nelson and Winter*

Even if it is possible to find previous references (cf. in particular Cyert and March 1967), the notion of organizational routines only entered the core of the theory of the firm with the publication of Nelson and Winter (1982) (cf. also Cohen *et al.* (1996) for a thorough discussion of this notion).

Let us begin with a summary of their basic propositions.

(1) Routines in organizations are in many respects the equivalent of skills in individuals (cf. e.g. Nelson and Winter 1982: 73). In both cases, however, it is important to note that the notion of a 'skill' is not a simple one and cannot be satisfactorily defined by just listing a series of purely technical tasks which are codified and easily stated—such as those listed in a technical manual.[2] Just as important, the notion of skills includes the understanding of the social usages which accompany the exercise of 'technical' skills in the strict sense of the word. 'Skills' therefore refer both to specific skills as well as to the mastery of the 'social appropriateness' of their use (cf. also March 1994).

(2) Terms like routines and skills tend to be quite broadly defined: 'We use the term "routines" in an extremely flexible way, in the same way as "programme" (or "routine") is used to discuss the programming of a computer' (Nelson and Winter 1982: 92). The authors add also the key observation that: 'This [notion of a routine] refers to a model of repetitive activity for an entire organization as well as to an individual skill.' It should be noted that the element of relatively automatic repetition is essential here. The existence of individual skills as well as organizational routines necessarily implies a certain automaticity in their implementation since it is only on this condition that routines are economically efficient. Once they have been adopted, they may be elicited and applied smoothly and easily, without delay and at little or no additional cost.

(3) Routines with organizations bear the following major properties. *First*, they are a fundamental part of the *organizational memory* of the firm: they consititute the accumulated stock of organizational know-how ensuring the smooth functioning of the firm's operations.

Second, they represent sorts of *behavioural targets* for the organization, meant also to exercise a certain form of *control*, essentially linked to the effective handling of inputs and environmental signals which are more or less heterogeneous: the smooth running of an organization implies that routines be flexible enough to absorb minor changes during their execution and smooth them out.

Third, routines need to be 'replicable' at least in principle, i.e. if introduced successfully in one place they must be transferable to other locations (within the same organization).

---

[2] Indeed, Nelson and Winter's chapter on skills shows how this notion, in order to be correctly understood, calls for all the nuances that terms such as 'know-how', 'aptitude', and 'qualifications' suggest. In this respect, note also that the 'know-how' involved in the notion of skills cannot be reduced to a narrowly defined set of 'technical' operations which agents are able to master.

Fourth, one may expect from an efficient routine that it can be *imitated* (although at some learning cost), that is, transferred from one context to another (in particular, the initial context may be a rival organization, aspects of which one wishes to imitate).

Fifth, they correspond to *truces* among potentially conflicting interests. We will return to the implications of this crucial point later; let us just mention here that whatever the events surrounding the development of routines themselves, they may be analysed as a group of protocols relative to the division of labour and to the coordination of tasks which are relatively stabilized and which can henceforth develop with a certain amount of automaticity[3] in ways quite independent from the conflicts which might have marked their origin.

(4) Loosely speaking, *routines* may be considered as playing the same role within organizations *as genes* in living organisms. This property of routines is related to the fact that the repertoire of responses which characterize them should be understood as consisting both of 'the way of doing things' and 'the way of determining what should be done'. Routines are also devices to gather information from the surrounding environment, process it, and deliver messages necessary for the smooth running of the organization. Ultimately, it is primarily by means of routines that organizations function. As Nelson and Winter put it, 'even the sophisticated problem-solving efforts of an organization fall into quasi-routine patterns, whose general outlines can be anticipated on the basis of experience with previous problem-solving efforts of that organization' (Nelson and Winter 1982: 136).

Notice that, in this path-breaking contribution of Nelson and Winter, most properties attributed to routines correspond to a fundamental vision whereby the formation, implementation, and evolution of routines themselves derive from their inherent nature as 'problem-solving devices' (notwithstanding the mention of 'conflict', an explicit account of the latter is ruled out by the 'truce' hypothesis).[4]

2.2. *Routines and the contemporary theory of the firm*

Nowadays the notion of routines is quickly becoming a key aspect of the theory of organizations. Indeed, if following March and Simon (1993) we accept that an organization consists of a set of coordination procedures which relate a multitude of economic agents with different interests, know-how and information, then routines clearly appear to be an essential part of the organization itself.

The notion of routine also throws a new light on the way in which organizations operate, i.e. a routine is an essential element in the *modus operandi*, of the decision-making process. In this respect 'satisficing' (and often 'non-strategic') action-rules represents a good deal of what an organization does, aimed at fulfilling predefined

---

[3] Relatedly, using a term coined by Leibenstein (1982), we may state that routines essentially correspond to a *convention of efforts* which is stabilized, corresponding to a situation which allows for the reproduction of the organization as it stands as well as the behaviour of its members. (In this way, as far as the firm is concerned, this convention of effort ensures a non-zero profit for the organization, plausibly guarantees for the employment of the members of the organization with rather steady working conditions — salaries and the like — and together guarantees the absence of conflict in the workplace which may disrupt the smooth functioning of the firm or endanger its existence). More on this in Orlean (1994).

[4] For a discussion on this point see Mangolte (1997).

'secondary objectives' (often very far from 'ultimate' objectives such as profitability or growth), undertaken on the basis of codified and semi-automatic procedures.

Moreover, routines are largely 'tacit',[5] and as a bridge between the technological and organizational competences specific to each firm, they vary from firm to firm. Thus, routines contribute to explain how and why firms differ from one another, and why differences persist in their revealed performance (cf. on this point also Coriat and Dosi (1998), Dosi and Marengo (1994) and Coriat and Weinstein (1995)).

Finally, routines are a key to the understanding of how firms evolve, since to a good extent, an organization embodies more or less defined 'meta-rules' to make its own routines evolve. These 'meta-rules' might represent sorts of 'higher-level routines' with varying degrees of tacitness and automaticity, interwined with explicit, purposeful acts of strategic discretionality.

Given all that, a key explanation for phenomena such as the way firms 'hold together', the nature of the decision-making processes, why organizations differ and how they evolve.

However, as already mentioned above, most current analyses of organizational routines, undertaken, loosely speaking, in a Nelson–Winter vein, tend to focus on their problem-solving attributes while largely neglecting their role in terms of conflict resolution and of coordination of diverging interests.

Conversely, a more complete theory of the firm—and relatedly also of organizational routines—is argued at greater length elsewhere (Coriat and Weinstein (1995, 1998); Coriat and Dosi 1998; see also Dosi and Marengo 1994, and as a major source of inspiration March and Simon (1993)), one ought to account for the conditions under which the following three sets of functions are carried out:

(1) The coordination of relations between agents in *information-processing*.
(2) The coordination of *competences* and *know-how*, and, via learning, the task of developing and improving upon both collective and organizational competences.
(3) The management of *conflicting interests*, arising primarily from the creation and distribution of the economic surplus between the economic agents competing for a share of it.

Whereas the notion of routines as defined by Nelson and Winter fully accounts for the first two levels of coordination (information-processing and problem-solving devices), it ignores the third dimension (Coriat and Weinstein 1998).

In our view, it is only by understanding how the three forms of coordination *operate* and *interact*, that it is possible to fully appreciate the nature of routines and also to explain not only how routines work and what they are, but also the market behaviour of firms and the nature of their decisions: the type of competitive positioning they choose, whether they pursue a strategy of innovation, imitation or differentiation, the choice between internal and external growth, and so on.

It is indeed in this perspective that we shall analyse in the following the working methods and routines of the Toyota production system. The analysis of this complex

---

[5] The idea that tacitness is one of the fundamental elements of routines was originally emphasized by Nelson and Winter (1982). For further developments, cf. Cohen *et al.* (1996) and the references cited therein.

and articulate system of productive routines will serve also to redefine and enrich the concept of routines, and show its heuristic power in understanding particular organizational forms and their performances.

3. The Two Pillars of the Toyota Production System: An Initial Overview

In order to analyse the Toyota production system as a relatively coherent ensemble of routines, we must first provide a definition of what such a system is, since in the literature it has often been interpreted in ways which are in conflict with each other.

Here, we shall adopt the presentation of the Toyota production system made by those who conceived this system itself. Undoubtedly, the founder of the system is Taichi Ohno. By adopting his presentation, we have the added advantage of having at our disposal a series of extremely detailed texts (cf. T. Ohno (1988*a*, 1988*b*) as well as Ohno and Mito (1992)) in which the author states what he himself sees as being essential and innovative in the system of production he conceived and set up in the Toyota plants. Building on Ohno's work, our study will be illustrated by a series of empirical studies, including those we were able to carry out ourselves in Japan.

3.1. *The Toyota production system as a two-pillar system*

Following Ohno, the Toyota production system may be defined as being a combination of two 'pillars', or organizing principles, which define the overall structure of the organization.

These two fundamental pillars of his innovation are constituted, on the one hand, by *just-in-time*, and by *auto-activation* (*jidoka*) on the other. In the final analysis, as we shall show, the major innovation of the Toyota production system lay in *the simultaneous implementation of these two pillars*, on condition that *jidoka* precedes just-in-time, the former being an indispensable precondition for the implementation of the latter (something which has been largely overlooked by observers of the Japanese system). As Ohno emphasizes, this holds true both in logical, and historical terms. The first major innovation of the Toyota production system was the introduction of *jidoka*. Once this was firmly in place, just-in-time was implemented.

Let us describe in some detail here the contents of each of these two pillars.

(1) The first pillar, *jidoka*, or *auto-activation*[6] was innovative essentially because its aim was to delegate responsibility to the workers for the quality of products right from the elementary production tasks themselves. In practice this innovation means that line workers not only have the right, but are obliged to take the time which is

---

[6] Recall that the term *auto-activation* was coined by Ohno himself by analogy with that of 'autonomation'. The term 'autonomation' is itself obtained by contracting 'autonomy' and 'automation'. It refers to a principle adopted by Ohno when he worked in the textile division of Toyota (the initial activity of the firm involving the introduction into the machines of devices to stop the machine automatically in case of mechanical failure of any part of the machine itself). The philosophy which arose from this held that it was preferable to stop production rather than to allow it to continue, thereby risking quality defects. Stated otherwise, autonomation chooses not to produce products which do not conform to quality standards. When applied to the motor industry, this principle obliged line workers, as well as giving them the right, to stop production so as to ensure that quality standards were met at each stage of production.

necessary (to the point of stopping the flow of production if need be) in order to carry out the tasks necessary to ensure the maintenance of the highest-quality standards at each stage of production, even whilst production is taking place. In principle, this is an essential difference with the organization of work in Taylorism, which demands the rigorous separation of production tasks and quality control. In this respect, the Ohno system is at least a partial reaggregation of the tasks of production and quality control which were separate under Taylorism. We should note here that, to the extent that every defect must be identified and as far as possible rectified on the spot by allowing the line worker a certain amount of initiative, auto-activation clearly includes an element of 'problem-solving'. Such decentralization is made possible by the authorization given to line workers to stop the assembly line in order to rectify the error.

We should further point out that this reaggregation is all the more important as auto-activation—as practised by Ohno—was accompanied by the implementation of the principles of multispecialization and multifunctionalism[7] of line workers, implying large scope for polyvalence in the execution of tasks.

(2) The second pillar, that of *just-in-time* programming, is better known. In brief, it means programming production from 'downstream' (starting with the orders already placed by clients) in order to put into production step by step only those items corresponding to products which have already been sold. In turn, just-in-time as a method of production programming involves, as we shall see later, a series of innovations in the alimentation and the preparation of the work, more generally in the logistics of production and in the management of the flows and stocks of intermediate and semi-finished goods. These innovations taken together constitute a system of production with very reduced stocks (both of final and semi-finished intermediate goods), made possible by a system of information-processing unique and unprecedented in the history of work organization.

Why were these two pillars introduced? And, once they had been introduced, why were they constantly improved upon over time? What need do they respond to?

3.2. The principal rationale of the Toyota production system: the instant management of product variety

Concerning the first question (why were these two pillars introduced), one may start from some partial and anecdotal answers. In the final analysis, 'auto-activation' is nothing other than the transposition to the motor industry of the practices and know-how ('autonomation') from Toyota's textile plants enabling it to economize on raw materials and to ensure product quality. Similarly, the efforts to produce with the least possible stocks may be directly related to conditions in post-war Japan, which was experiencing a severe shortage of raw materials, a situation which stimulated efforts to save as much as possible on them. In short, therefore, a variety of 'small' events and macro conditions may explain efforts to reorganize working methods.

[7] On this point, cf. below where the theme is taken up again.

On the other hand, the answer to the second question (why were the two pillars constantly improved upon over time, to the point of their becoming a 'model' which would often be copied throughout the world) requires some deeper analysis.

Ohno states some reasons very clearly. In essence the combination of *jidoka* and just-in-time, which was introduced as a result of some contingencies revealed itself over time to be extremely well adapted to the production of short series of varied and differentiated products.

Eventually, as Ohno recalls, the system conceived for a small domestic car market (with vehicle sales of only a few thousand per year), and a very differentiated one revealed itself to be particularly well adapted to handling under ordinary production conditions all the unforeseen occurrences stemming from the variety and uncertainty of demand:

The Toyota system was a response to the particular need in Japan to produce a small quantity of each of a number of models; following this, it developed into a veritable system of production. On account of its origin, this system is particularly efficient in conditions of diversification. (Ohno 1988*a*: 49)

Moreover to the extent that 'consumer tastes became more diverse, more individualized and clients themselves more demanding . . . it became more and more urgent to develop production methods which allowed the individual factory production of unique goods . . . Accepting that . . . it is clear that mass production programming, i.e. the Ford system cannot achieve this objective' (Ohno and Mito 1993: 17).

Ultimately, it is this characteristic which explains the success of the Ohno system: if the new system 'is well adapted to the most difficult conditions of diversification, it is because it was conceived for this purpose' (Ohno 1988*a*).

In other words, the unique feature of the system is that it provides a series of efficient solutions to the problem of the long production series of varied and differentiated products, in contrast to its predecessor (the Ford system) which was only able to manage variety at very high cost. To the extent that it is particularly well adapted to an era in which competition is based on differentiation and variety, Ohno considers that his system will replace the Ford one. As Ohno put it, 'The Ford system of mass production put its stamp on its age, the Toyota system is putting its stamp on its own' (Ohno and Mito 1993: 4).

Naturally, the key innovation, which was the simultaneous implementation of both pillars of the Ohno system, demands the implementation of a variety of organizational protocols, for the most part unique, amongst which one must mention the linearization of manufacturing, the *kanban*, and *Andon* signals (and similar ones) all of which will be analysed below. In practice, the simultaneous implementation of all these complementary organizational innovations gave birth to a complex system of radically new routines.

In order to analyse them, it is useful to consider, in Ohno's system, the double dimension of 'skills' (both individual and collective) and 'programmes'. This implies examining not only the production tasks and their nature, but also the modes of task coordination which are required and implemented, ultimately accounting for the set of routines specific to such a system.

4. From Individual Skills to Collective 'Programmes' in the Toyota Production System

Before showing what was unique about the routines created by the Ohno system, it is first necessary to refute a fairly widespread view, namely that the Ohno system, in terms of concrete labour, that is, the elementary tasks assigned to line workers, did not invent anything that had not already been invented by its prestigious American predecessors. Indeed, taking as their starting point the observation that in both the Ohno system and Taylorism the tasks carried out by the line workers are fragmented, highly repetitive, and carried out at a rapid pace, some analysts have asserted that in this respect there was nothing innovative about the Ohno system. Indeed, it is argued, 'Ohnism' was only a variant of Taylorism (Nomura 1993).

The basis of this argument is the fact that the Ohno system too adopted the time-and-motion protocols of Taylorism, and that—from a point of view of concrete labour—the Ohno system is indistinguishable from Taylorism, or at best just a variant of it.

Indeed, as discussed in more details in Coriat (1994), time-and-motion studies (TMS) are an integral part of the so-called 'socio-technical school' and are shared also by Taylorism and Ohnism. However, note that TMS cannot be considered in any way a *principle* of work organization. Rather, TMS are simply a set of techniques aimed at breaking down operational know-how into elementary tasks linked to standard time units. In turn, quite different principles of work organization can be constructed on the grounds of this breakdown, yielding quite diverse patterns of distribution and coordination of tasks.

Relatedly, even within a common concern for time-saving, one historically observes distinct organizing principles and forms of work rationalization. So, for example, the 'American system' is based on fragmentation of tasks, with monitoring of line workers at their work stations and fixed-rhythm assembly lines. Conversely, as we shall see, the Toyota (or more broadly 'Japanese') system is based on despecialization and on the attribution of multiple tasks to line workers organized in teams on the principle of 'time-sharing' (more on this in Coriat 1991, 1994).

Finally, note that the so-called 'Swedish working methods' (Augren *et al.* 1986; Berggren 1988; Sandberg *et al.* 1993), which organize work in 'autonomous' groups and operate using work cycles which may be very long (in some cases up to several hours) also use TMS as their point of departure. In this system the time allocated to work groups is calculated on the basis of the sum of the standard time units required for each type of elementary labour task (Emery 1969; Emery and Trist 1972).

Let us consider at some length the specificities of the use of TMS within Taylorism, which utilizes it—unlike Ohnism—in conjunction with the principles of 'scientific management'.

4.1. TMS and scientific management: the nature of concrete labour in Taylorism

Starting with Taylorism, the time-and-motion protocols have a dual objective:

● to decompose work as much as possible until one obtains the totally fragmented elementary tasks described at length in the contemporary sociology of work processes, as well as in the manuals of work organization based on Taylorism;

● to normalize and standardize these elementary tasks and give them the status of the famous 'one best way' which is in turn imposed upon line workers who are specially trained to carry out these tasks at a fast pace.

Moreover, on the basis of time-and-motion, the protocols of Taylorism can be applied both to tasks of conception and execution, the aim being to arrive at a strict functional division, and together to break down tasks within each job function.

Indeed, following the recommendations of scientific management, the 'one best way'—composed of a set of fragmented tasks—forms the basis for the conception of each individual work station. Each line worker is only given a very small number of fragmented tasks, the coordination between work stations being carried out by the hierarchical superiors. The line workers responsible for coordination are distinct from those assigned to production, and the former have the power to monitor, reprimand, and command the latter.

These basic principles of scientific management can be summarized as the three-fold specialization by job function, fragmentation, and repetition of tasks for each job.

4.2. Elementary tasks and individual skills in the Ohno system

In the Ohno system, the combination of auto-activation and just-in-time makes use of time-and-motion analysis in a totally different way from that implied by 'scientific management'. This difference is noticeable in the very definition of the elementary task which serves as a basis for the allotment of tasks, and is the first of several other differences.

The Ohno system's unique features in this regard may be summarized by the following propositions:

(1) Unlike Taylorism, an elementary task is not the smallest unit of work, but rather the smallest 'transferable' unit, defined as the smallest practical combination of 'productive units of work' which may be transferred from one line worker to another. It should be recalled here that what Ohno termed 'multifunctionalism', i.e. the fact that line workers are taught to carry out several different tasks (in particular, on different machines), is a basic principle of the Ohno organization, just like the interchangeability of line workers within a team. From this stems the very distinctive definition given by Ohno (distinct from Taylorism, that is) of the elementary task as being a series of transferable 'productive units'[8], unlike the classic tasks in Taylorism.

(2) Further, what also distinguishes the elementary task (the 'transferable productive unit of work') at the basis of the Ohno organizational construction from the

---

[8] In the language of American collective bargaining which is always extremely precise since it determines the different stages of grievance procedures, it is this notion of 'elementary unit of work' and not 'task' which appears in collective bargaining agreements in most transplanted Japanese firms. Cf. Parker and Slaughter (1988), as well as the agreement of NUMMI (the well-known joint venture between Toyota and GM). We will return to this agreement later on in this work.

elementary tasks under Taylorism, is that the former includes both direct and indirect tasks. That the inclusion of these indirect tasks (maintenance, setting and adjustment, retooling, quality control, and the like) has been criticized by American Unions (traditional advocates of the Job Rule and supporters of skilled labour) as an aggravating factor does not alter the fact that in principle, the 'productive unit of work' of Ohno, to the extent that it reaggregates direct and indirect tasks, by no means resembles the classic 'task' in Taylorism.

(3) In the Ohno system, productive units of work are carried out within the context of a team. This team shares all the information and know-how about the productive units of work for which it is responsible. On the importance of team work, to which Taylorism is radically opposed, Ohno emphasizes: 'Even if task *a* can be done by one man, five or six workmen need to be assigned to it to permit team work' (Ohno and Mito 1992: 78).

The reason for stressing this point is the fact that in order to deal with product variety (to produce 'just' as much as the factory has sold, without having to continually reprogramme work stations and assembly lines), it is necessary to have teams composed of polyvalent workers capable of managing by themselves the unforeseen contingencies in quantity and quality (and thus the nature of the parts and models to be manufactured). Such teams therefore seem to be necessary for the efficient management of product variety.

It is in the same spirit that one should appreciate the systematic practice of job rotation within and between teams, another of the underlying features of the Ohno system. Job rotation is indispensable to the creation and development of multi-functionalism. This is another fundamental difference with Taylorism: indeed one could state that it is the team, and not the individual, which is the basic reference in the Ohno organization.

(4) The Ohno system does not contemplate any 'one best way'. This concept is only meaningful in a Taylorist universe where work is strictly repetitive and products are standardized. On the other hand, in the Ohno system whose dynamic principle of rationalization is grounded on highlighting the misfunctions so to speak in 'real time' elementary productive units of work and their sequence are governed by the principle of 'continuous improvement'. Labour tasks and their sequences are therefore in principle seen as capable of evolving, the precondition for this evolution being that it be accepted by or, better still, initiated by the line workers themselves. Industrialists visiting Japan were struck by the fact that:

'In the Toyota production system improvements in operations must come from the line workers themselves ... it is the workman himself who drafts the repertory of standard work methods; in this way, he is made to observe reality more rigorously; they will end up putting a video camera at his disposal to enable him to profit from its forceful images'. (F. Lucas 1981; on this issue cf. also Adler 1991)

This to the point that 'a repertoire of standard work methods which has not been changed for a long time is something a team leader should feel ashamed of' (Lucas ibid.). Hence, the systematic call for 'suggestions' in quality circles and other protocols of 'continuous improvement'. Again, it is the production of a variety of products at the heart of the Ohno system which requires the existence of these protocols.

To sum up, despite the fact that they both make use of TMS, Taylorism and the Ohno system differ both in the definition of elementary tasks (fragmented tasks versus 'transferable productive units of work') and in the way these units of reference are allotted to line workers (individual repetitive work made up of fragmented tasks on the one hand, versus team work displaying flexibility and designed to evolve, and governed by the principle of interchangeable line workers[9] on the other). Going even further, from a dynamic point of view, one could say that just-in-time plays the same (endogenous) role in the rationalization of labour which in Taylorism is performed by scientific management.

4.3. *Some implications: the Ohno line worker as a problem solver*

Let us look at the distributions of skills which are specific to the Ohnist routines.

(1) The Ohno line worker, unlike his counterpart in Taylorism, does not have a clearly defined elementary task assigned to him by a higher authority. He is responsible for a wide range of operations which are *not* entirely defined in advance. These tasks are allotted endogenously as a function of the requirements of the market and the orders received. In this respect the Ohno worker is indeed responsible for managing product variety. More precisely, following the propositions formulated by Koike (1988) later clarified in Koibé and Inoki (1990), the management of product variety has two distinct dimensions.

First, the line worker must be skilled at 'managing change' of several kinds, particularly those related to daily variations in the product mix, the labour mix, and the quantity to produce.

Second, he is a 'problem solver' to the extent that he has to use his initiative to resolve a wide range of 'problems' which may crop up during production. This in turn implies the ability (i) to detect, (ii) to diagnose, and (iii) to take appropriate action in each case. In order to do this, the line worker draws on the memory of the programmes of operations acquired during training specially designed to provide him with a large number of responses to the different types of situations which may arise.

(2) To employ a terminology which has become classic in industrial sociology, one may say that the Ohno line worker makes no distinction between 'assigned tasks' and 'concrete tasks'. Better still, there is actually an inversion between these two notions, since it is the concrete labour which dictates and organizes the nature of the 'pre-defined tasks', and which makes the latter evolve and not the other way around. As we have already pointed out, the repertoire of standard work methods (i.e. the assigned tasks) evolve with the actual work and it is the line worker's

---

[9] In this way, even if there is job 'fragmentation' in the Ohno system, in the sense that the complex work of a professional trade disappears, the fragmented tasks are allotted to operators in a reaggregated form, both 'horizontally' (several different successive tasks) and 'vertically' (quality control at work stations, partial management of the programming on assembly lines, and so on). From an empirical point of view, one finds in Adler (1991) a detailed explanation of the way in which the Toyota production system is used in an American transplant of Toyota, based on a detailed case study conducted at NUMMI.

responsibility to see to it that this is done. In that respect it is possible to argue that a key feature of the Ohno organization here is that 'defensive organizational routines' (Argyris 1992) become impossible. These are defined as 'any actions which save the individual, the group and the intergroup from embarrassment or threat and which at the same time prevent them from identifying and neutralizing its causes' (ibid.), and arise in general from the permanent discrepancy in Taylorism between the assigned tasks and actual work. As soon as 'prescriptions' include the detection and the rectifying of errors, the terrain which allows the formation of defensive routines disappears. 'Get it right the first time', the slogan of Toyota plants, indeed leaves no way out for line workers who are held responsible for quality control.

(3) Koike (1988) suggests that the know-how required by the line worker, in his dual role of being responsible for managing change and product variety and of problem solver, is largely *tacit*. This means that the line worker must transfer his basic knowledge about 'usual' operations, i.e. during normal functioning, to each 'non-usual' situation by modifying his mode of operation and by finding a solution to the malfunction. To equip the line worker with the knowledge needed to carry out his usual and his non-usual tasks, specific techniques are called for. Great importance needs to be given to on-the-job training and a key role is played in this learning process by the instructor, who may be a veteran worker or team leader. By definition, a precise list of 'non-usual' events cannot be drawn up in advance. It is only by substantial direct experience and familiarity with a whole range of 'non-usual' situations that the line worker, supervised by a well-informed instructor, develops his own know-how and repertoire of solutions. But the learning process can only achieve its goals if two other techniques are implemented.

First, a whole range of closely related tasks (within one team but also between teams doing the same work) must be taught. The multifunctionalism so dear to Ohno is conditional upon the fact that a wide range of operations and activities are taught. Second, the progress made by the line worker in mastering these operations must be regularly assessed and rewarded.[10] The system must therefore be broadly incentive-compatible making learning self-reinforcing. Koike states that the most important of these incentives are the promotion prospects and career paths which enable line workers to progress professionally. The system simultaneously allows for the continuous acquisition and consolidation of skills and know-how, an indispensable condition for high productivity under a system of varied production.

Nevertheless, these distinctive features can only acquire full significance when they are placed in the context of the 'programmes' of which they form a part and which they serve.

4.4. Ohno routines as 'programmes'

One may consider Ohno routines as protocols which link together individual acts as well as govern them i.e. as 'programmes' entailing specific forms of coordination between the actions (tasks) entrusted to individual line workers. This is also a crucial

---

[10] These rewards and incentives range from wage increases to the operator's career prospects, based also on mobility along internal *rank-hierarchies* (cf. Aoki 1988).

level of comparison between the Ohno system and the Ford system. Indeed, whilst the Ohno system takes as its starting point the Ford criterion of production based on the principle of continuous flow, it gives it, as we shall see, a totally new dimension and a new content.

Table 8.1 based on Ohno and Mito (1992) contrasts the essential elements of the two systems.

These differences can only be fully understood if one grasps how Ohno inverted the logic of the Ford system, which in turn created a chain reaction leading to further major differentiations. To explain this 'inversion', Ohno opposes a 'push' model of mass production to the 'pull', 'just-in-time programming' he invented.

Notice that special attention should be paid to these basic 'organizational philosophies' since they can be seen as *fundamental heuristics* or *meta-routines* guiding the development of and the search for coherence among 'lower level' routines of the organization.

4.5. The 'push' model of mass production versus the 'pull' or just-in-time model

In one of his last books published while still alive, Ohno (see Ohno and Mito 1992) illustrates the difference between the two systems by examining the techniques of

TABLE 8.1 Main oppositions between the Ford system and the Toyota production system

Toyota system	Ford system
1. *Jidoka* and *just-in-time* are the two basic pillars of a system driven by the market and the consumer demands.	Mass production based on highly specialized division of tasks.
2. Pull system based on products already sold.	Push system based on *ex ante* anticipated demands.
3. Production in small lots of differentiated products.	Production on large scale of standardized products.
4. Rapid retooling (down to around 10 minutes) for frequently changing production batches.	Periodic shut down of production for major retooling. Pressure towards longer production runs.
5. Reduce intermediate input stocks to the minimum by application of *Kaubau* and *just-in-time* principles.	Large intermediate stocks at each work station. The production is not 'flowing' but 'pushed'.
6. Multifunctionality of the workers.	Specialized workers task by task ('job rules')
7. Right to stop the line given to the workers to guarantee the quality of the each product.	The line is never stopped, even when the products are full of faults.
8. The quantity produced is equal to the quantity sold.	The quantity produced is defined by the production engineers based on future expectations on the market.
9. Information is selected and distributed from the market to the production lines by means of the *kanbans*.	Information provided and processed along heirarchical lines

Source: adapted from Ohno and Mito (1992).

work scheduling, which leads us directly to the heart of our investigation of routines as 'programmes', that is to say, the different modes of coordination between tasks and separate activities.

After describing the Ford system as a 'push' model of programmed mass production, Ohno observes that:

The term "programmed" is so rich and complex in meaning that it may lend itself to misunderstanding. I should explain that in the Ford system "programmed" means the obligation to produce as much as possible in a minimum given time. This reduces costs which in turn enables the selling price to be lowered, which gradually spreads the use of the car since sales are made easier. This is the theory behind this plan. (Ohno and Mito 1992: 39)

The point here is that the essential strength of the Ford system lies in its underlying logic of 'the obligation to produce as much as possible in a minimum given time'. Ohno compares this system with that of Toyota which, in his opinion, aims to produce: 'just enough to meet market demand, in the quantities required and to do so just in time' (ibid.).

Unlike the Ford system, the inherent cost savings do not stem from the maximum exploitation of economies of scale but rather from producing an amount exactly equivalent to market demand. This objective and this requirement of 'just-in-time' requires—and this is what concerns us—the implementation of new forms and methods of coordination corresponding to the specific routines of the Ohno system.

Its originality lies in the principle of 'inverse' programming, which is not based on a priori production constraints (as in the Ford system), but on information sent by the market which is converted into instructions and then into operating programmes and production set-ups. The programming (including the coordination of activities) is undertaken using *kanban* signals which convey production orders from downstream to upstream.[11]

Of relevance here is the fact that, in principle, the role of these techniques is to ensure a direct management (among line workers and from one work station to another) of programming without first going through different levels of the hierarchy. The unique feature of this type of coordination is that it allows for the 'direct' conversion of information relating to the market into operating instructions. This is in contrast to the coordination structures in the Ford system, which assigns a specific bureaucracy the task of dealing with 'commercial information', interpreting it and transforming it into 'technical information' and operating instructions which are then given to line workers.

This 'direct' or horizontal conversion itself is only possible, it should be noted, if the line workers have the 'individual skills' to interpret the commercial information reaching them and transform it into operating programmes. It is in this instance that

---

[11] A variant of this enables each work station to manage its available stocks so that the object of the *kanban* is to request the production (from the previous work station) of the quantity required to replenish the stocks needed to meet the order. In the more complex versions (developed as early as the second half of the 1970s) these production and delivery instructions are extended to the principal subcontractors, who are responsible for applying the system to their own suppliers.

the Ohno worker must fully display his qualities as 'one in charge of managing product variety'. At a deeper level, we should note that within Ohnist routines, 'individual skills' and 'programmes' are made coherent with and complementary to each other. The latter, centred around the direct management of product variety (to convert the variety stemming from market demand into operating programmes which may be immediately executed) is only possible by making use of the inherent qualities of individual skills.

In practice, however, such forms of coordination are only feasible because other important innovations were introduced at the level of the 'physical' organization of production (as distinct from work organization) which permitted the implementation of work routines in the strict sense of the word. One of Ohno's essential innovations in this respect was a thorough modification of the layout of the machines in the workshops.

4.6. *Lay-out of machines: 'heavy artillery' versus 'linearization'*

Ohno's key innovation in this area is most often termed 'linearization' to indicate that the machines are placed 'in lines' and not 'in batteries' as in the Ford system.

Linearization involves doing away with workshops composed of specialized machines all executing the same tasks in huge production runs and, conversely, constituting workshops in which the machines are not grouped by specialization but according to the principle of the succession of tasks. This is a major change, in that it enables production to be organized around a principle of continuous flow (even for machining) which links together the different functional departments of the plant. As Ohno emphasized, engineering under the Ford system is, on the contrary based on a group of specialized workshops, each of which is constituted on the basis of the grouping together of identical machines:

Traditionally[12] the lathes were grouped together, as were the milling and the boring machines, all of them designed in such a way as to produce the largest possible quantity of one single item. (Ohno and Mito 1992: 20)

Ohno describes this way of laying out machines as corresponding to the model of *heavy artillery*, a model which he distinguishes from his own as follows:

In the Toyota model, on the contrary, a flow is created by placing the lathes, presses and milling machines one after the other in the same order as the different phases of machining, and in ascending order of value added. In this way it is possible to make the line worker responsible not for one, but for several machines. This results in a considerable gain in productivity. (ibid.)

As we can see, there is a double benefit here. It allows for programming based on the principle of continuous flow, whatever the variety of products which have to be manufactured, and without the interruptions caused by workshops laid out in 'artillery battery' form. Moreover, according to Ohno, it also makes possible 'a

---

[12] 'Traditionally' for Ohno means the Fordist organizational tradition.

considerable gain in productivity', since each line worker is responsible for the operation and supervision of several machines.

5. Information, Competences, Conflicts

Using the analytical tools outlined earlier for examining routines, it is now possible to look at Ohno's innovations in more detail.

5.1. *Information-processing and problem-solving*

Analysed as information-processing and problem-solving devices, the series of protocols implied by the Ohno system have the following salient features.

(1) To repeat, multifunctionalism and interchangeability of line workers between tasks and work stations are *de rigeur* in the Ohno team. Indeed, a variety of tasks to be carried out is the principle governing the distribution of concrete labour. In this way the predefined tasks themselves give line workers a certain scope to take initiative.[13]

Information-processing is consistent with the above principle: the *kanban* signals which circulate amongst the line workers represent a continuous horizontal flow of information; unlike Taylorism, information does not pass from one level of the hierarchy to another (via a superior), but circulates amongst 'equals' in a team and amongst different teams. It must be stressed here that this form of information-processing is by definition also a form of problem-solving. And this is so in two respects.

First, because the wide variety of tasks, corresponding to the variety of products which need to be produced 'just-in-time' and which depend on unforeseen changes in orders, are dealt with 'on time' at work stations themselves. Thus, flexibility in work methods—meaning that choices continually have to be made about which operating 'programme' to apply—is the necessary counterpart to the variety of products to manufacture.

Second, because in the predefined tasks assigned to the Ohno line workers, all the malfunctions—quality defects, broken machines, wear and tear of tools, and so on— must be dealt with by the production team.

The *line worker is therefore* by definition *a problem solver*, and is given a degree of freedom unique in the history of contemporary work organization: the right to stop the assembly line to take the time needed to resolve the problem.

---

[13] In order to appreciate just how different the Ohno system is compared to Taylorism, note that in the protocols of the latter, information-processing is done in such a way as to separate as much as possible whatever is related to conception from whatever is related to execution. One may recall that the ideal operator under Taylorism could be a monkey working automatically and as fast as possible using a range of predetermined gestures for which he had been selected and which he had been trained to do. Any possible defect which arose during production whilst the monkey was performing his elementary gestures would not be his business. A separate department to 'monitor' would be responsible for quality control. In this model, as regards problem-solving, nothing is entrusted to the operator. Everything falls under predefined tasks since everything is reduced to the most fragmented and elementary tasks possible. The spirit of the 'one best way' selected by the Office of Methods rules out the idea of granting any initiative to the workshop when problems crop up. The ideal of Taylorism is to anticipate problems and resolve them beforehand in the Office of Methods.

(2) We should note that these differences in information-processing and problem-solving can ultimately be explained by an even more fundamental difference in the 'principles of efficiency' underlying each school of management. If we accept that Taylorism may be in a first approximation summed up as TMS plus the prescription of work into fragmented and repetitive tasks (see above), its underlying principle of efficiency can be stated as follows: the maximum yield from any operational unit (a workshop, a department, a plant, and so on) is a direct function of the yield of every individual worker at his station. This characterization of Taylorism as a social technology for controlling the individual worker in his job is in clear contrast to the principle of efficiency inherent in the Ohno system, which is based on an economy of time which is essentially *systemic*.

The aim of the different reaggregations in the Ohno system is to reduce production time by drastically reducing *the interface time between operations and sequences*. In this sense, the Ohno system works essentially on what may be called as interface intensity or intensity of work connections[14] as opposed to Taylorism which operates on the direct intensity of the worker's efforts at his station. Shared time and connection intensity are thus closely linked to each other just as the notions of 'time allocated' and 'direct intensity' are in the Taylorist economics of time.

The difference between Taylorism and the Ohno system in this regard may be clarified by saying that it was as if the Ohno system accepted to *'give up' efficiency in direct intensity, in exchange for a greater degree of optimization concerning connection intensity*. At any rate, this is how certain statements by Ohno—surprising to say the least—should be interpreted. Thus, when he makes reference to the famous La Fontaine fable, he notes that 'In order for the Toyota system to function at full capacity, all the workers need to be tortoises' (Ohno and Mito 1992: 72).

Rather than being trite or provocative, he is actually stating the principle that the superior performance of the Toyota system does not reside in the greater intensity of work imposed upon line workers considered individually, but in the techniques which 'smooth out' production hitches and which result from the dual implementation of autonomation and just-in-time.

Indeed, in the implementation of the Ohno economics of time, the individual prescription of tasks—in the sense in which it is used in Taylorism—appears counterproductive. First, this is so because a certain degree of operational polyvalence of the workers is required to meet the varied demands of just-in-time production. Second, the strictly individual allocation of tasks is incompatible with the principle of quality control at work stations.[15]

---

[14] The notion of connection intensity was first introduced by C. du Tertre (1990) in a study of work on sites such as those found in the construction industry (building sites). In principle, this characteristic may be applied to an essential feature of Ohno economics of time.

[15] We should also note here that the Ohno system itself is not entirely capable of resolving the implied trade-offs. It frequently happens that they explode: the adjustment therefore occurs during overtime hours at the end of the day, considered as a permanent regulatory mechanism which enables the implementation of auto-activation.

5.2. The economics of time and conflict resolution

As one can easily imagine, the formidable mechanism constituted by the Toyota production system does not function by pure self-organization. A weighty system of monitoring and command of work progressively came into being in order to back up each of the organizational protocols, ensure continuity and fluidity, and set off warning signals if a breakdown occurs or even threatens.

Here again, when trying to highlight the unique aspects of the monitoring and command of work under the Ohno system, and following the intuition of evolutionary theories of the firm, we must make a distinction between 'steady state' routines, and the conditions which gave rise to their formation and evolution (more on this in Coriat and Dosi (1998) and Cohen *et al.* (1996)).

5.3. Steady-state routines: from the virtues of 'management by visual control' to the shortcomings of 'management by stress'

The general principle of the Ohno system here may be summed up in one simple proposition: one must, says Ohno, advocate 'management by visual control'. Just as in Bentham's 'panoptic', everything—Ohno suggests—should ideally be made physically visible to supervisors. To apply this principle correctly, and guarantee its proper implementation, a whole range of more detailed and specific protocols were developed and put into practice in the workshops.

What follows are some of the protocols indispensable to management by visual control.

The reduction of stocks to their minimum (predetermined levels established by the management) is not only economical (since production is just as much as is required) rather it is also explicitly designed—and this is the essential point—to make visible and transparent for the supervisor the whole workshop as well as the pace of work of the line workers. 'Excess stocks' are a sign that too much time has been allotted to the line worker (who could have used some of it to produce other items). On the contrary, depleted stocks indicate either that the pace of production is too slow, or that not enough time has been allotted. The variations in stocks, in relation to predetermined levels known only to the supervisors, are thus a tool in the monitoring and command of the work of line workers.

Besides its application to the level of stocks which acts as a 'synthetic' indicator of control, Ohno advocates that 'visual control' be applied to the detailed surveillance of the individual work stations. In order to do this he makes the following recommendation.

In each plant the most basic standard should be to write in longhand the series of work methods. These should be posted in each section of production in such a way that everyone can see at a glance which work station is concerned, the volume of production and series of work rules required. This is fundamental, and our method of visual control is also based on this. (Ohno 1988*a*)

The role of *andons* (that is, visual devices signalling interruptions in the work process) also fall within the scope of management by visual control: their purpose is precisely to make apparent to all—and this time directly—which line worker was obliged to shut down the assembly line and for how long. Thus the power granted to the worker to interrupt the flow of production (in order to guarantee product quality and to sort out any potential malfunctions) is only granted under very strict conditions of monitoring and command of work: any interruption is visually indicated by a system of illuminated signals (the *andons* themselves).

Also falling within the scope of the general principle of management by visual control are a variety of *poka yoke* or 'anti-error' devices, whose object is the immediate visual display of any error. In the assembly, for example, these *poka yoke* are placed at the level of supplies. As far as possible supplies of loose parts are avoided. Rather, parts and tools (screws, for example) are laid out in subsets with the right numbers and in the exact order in which they will be fitted or used in such a way that any error (a forgotten screw, for example) becomes immediately apparent from looking at the display shelf.

Last but not least, there is no principle, right up to *kanban*, which does not include strict monitoring exercised by each worker over his upstream or downstream fellows. The worker downstream may not tolerate the slightest defect in the parts passed on to him by workers upstream, since it would then be up to the former to rectify the defects in his own time. The just-in-time principle therefore involves a strong reduction in opportunism in behaviour, since the employee is at the same time a line worker and supervisor of the work of his predecessors—a particularly effective way, most have agreed, to reduce 'moral hazards'.

The list of examples illustrating the variety and ingenuity of the protocols used to implement management by visual control has not been exhausted. We will limit ourselves to those which directly concern the organization protocols which Ohno himself judged to be important since they are linked to the implementation of the basic 'pillars' discussed above. They illustrate how 'auto-activation' and just-in-time can only be implemented concomitantly with a principle of control (management by visual control) whose aim is to display or make visible all the malfunctions and all the interruptions to production flows whatever their nature or their source. The problem-solving devices involved in the implementation of *jidoka*, on the one hand, and the monitoring and control of work on the other, are therefore inextricably linked, and cannot exist independently of one another since they condition each other.

In this sense, if it is (almost) possible to refer to steady-state routines as 'truces', we should also note that these truces do not eliminate the need for complex devices to ensure that the compromises on which they are based—incorporated into *modus operandi* of the routines—are respected by the line workers. A truce can be implemented and function only under the watchful eye of the supervisor who assesses each action which is carried out by the line worker. This truce can only exist on condition that there is permanent monitoring of the respect for it.[16]

---

[16] We should point out the 'truces' and compromises reached in this way are not permanent. Similarly, the contents of the routines which form the basis of these compromises are themselves never indefinitely stable. This is especially so under Ohno's principles whereby workers are continuously exhorted to revise the repertoire of standard work methods which forms the basis of routines. The very principle of

This clarifies Ohno's statement that, for a long time, his system was only referred to by Toyota workers as 'Mr Ohno's abominable system' (Ohno 1988*a*). Furthermore, it is easy to understand why even today, when the system is not functioning normally,[17] it rapidly falls down upon line workers as an unbearable mass of instructions which, moreover, have to be executed without protection (the stock having disappeared) and in full view of the supervisors. In a nutshell, under misfunctioning, the system is transformed into what some American unionists have called a system of *management by stress*. The numerous examples cited in Japanese works (e.g. on the theme of *karaochi*)[18] and American literature (see e.g. Parker and Slaughter 1988) clearly demonstrate that 'soft control' implied by Ohno work methods may easily be transformed into a highly authoritarian system requiring orders, threats, and punishments to ensure the carrying out of the rather complex routines demanded by the system.

Even neglecting these extremes, we hope to have shown that, besides the incentive alignments based on monetary incentives or career prospects (such as rank hierarchies) which are crucial in getting workers to adopt the system and in making it work, devices of a strictly organizational nature directly build principles of control and command into the implementation and coordination of routines themselves.

5.4. *Routines as evolving processes, or the art of Japanese social compromise*

The evolution[19] in the social compromises which form part of routines have been no less important. We would like to illustrate this by briefly looking at both the birth of the Ohno routines and then, at the opposite extreme, by examining some of the changes introduced in the newest Toyota plants.

Historically speaking, linearization, which implied multifunctionalism, was initially *forced* upon line workers who were opposed to it. Ohno is explicit on this point:

The changeover was radical and the resistance from the shopfloor was very strong indeed. This is because the skilled workers at the time still had their craft traditions and therefore forcefully resisted any change...This was understandable. (Ohno 1988*a*)

How come then, that both linearization and, subsequently, just-in-time were successfully introduced and became permanent features of the Ohno system?

There is a lengthy explanation, familiar to those who have studied the conditions under which major innovations in work organization are introduced. The tempestuous story begins with a long strike by Toyota workers which led to thousands of

'continuous improvement' requires that elementary standards be continually improved and implies on-going negotiation.

[17] In the sense of an inadequate coordination between the thousands of protocols necessary for the smooth functioning of the Ohno system.

[18] *Karaochi* literally meaning 'death by exhaustion', has given rise to an entire body of Japanese literature which seeks to prove (by citing examples) that the extremely demanding working methods at Toyota cause exhaustion which in turn may lead to premature death.

[19] We should point out here that we are referring to those changes which concern clearly identifiable ruptures or radical innovations. As for the rest, as we have shown, it is the very nature of the Ohno system to experience slow 'continuous improvement' only made possible by the regular revision of work rules.

lay-offs, the formation of a new company union and the banning of the old one which was antagonistic to the firm. Nearly at the same time, the Korean War brought about major macroeconomic changes which led to the creation of the beginning of a mass market. These events, combined with compromises unprecedented in the history of work such as lifetime employment, salary based on seniority, and so on, created the conditions favourable to the development of the innovations of *jidoka* and just-in-time.[20] Even if much of the story remains to be uncovered and told, we know enough to assert without fear of contradiction, that Ohno routines have been profoundly marked by major social conflict. This explains also why they can be 'held in place' only by using monitoring and command structures, amongst which are the devices of management by visual control, inseparable from the contents of routines themselves.

Let us turn to the very last innovations in Toyota routines, those in their newest plant in Kyuchu: in order to understand them it is necessary to take into account also the state of the relations between labour and management at the end of the 1980s.

At the Kyuchu plant, Toyota has introduced several unexpected innovations. In the first place the teams have been reformed along the lines of 'semi-autonomous' (Swedish) teams and have been allotted homogeneous subsections of car production, each corresponding to a clearly identifiable part of a car. Further—an apparent heresy—buffer stocks have been placed at the end of each line. Certain observers saw in this the beginning of the end of the Toyota production system, and went as far as predicting it (Shimuzu and Nomura 1993).

Nonetheless, I will argue that changes occurred within a stable 'organizational paradigm'. Consider the changes first. At the end of the 1980s, for the first time in its history, Toyota was unable to recruit sufficient manual labour as a result of a record number of workers resigning after just six months in the plant. Something had to be done about the drying up of the pool of young males, the basic resource of Toyota plants. Changes were therefore sought in working conditions, more particularly drawing from the Swedish experience.

Nevertheless, this evolution in work and routines did not modify in any way the subtle mix in the Toyota system between decentralized problem-solving on the one hand, and control and monitoring of work on the other, in a clear demonstration of the continuity of the Ohno system.

Consider the continuity elements. Within the framework of *jidoka* and just-in-time, electronics—extensively used in the above plant to ensure 'just-in-time-information'—also serves to measure and make visible the overall amount of time taken by each team. A paint mark on the ground indicates to the line worker that, when he reaches it, the time allotted for that task in which he is engaged is up. Finally, the buffer stocks at the end of each line—in place of intermediary mini-stocks from work station to work station—were calculated in such a way as to reduce stocks of semi-finished goods as compared to classic Ohno plants (which reputedly carried no stocks!).

[20] Thanks to research jointly carried out with my friend Masanori Hanada, I was partly able to reconstruct this history in Coriat (1991), whilst Gordon and Cusumanos (1985) have reconstituted other aspects.

Thus, innovations to the Ohno method—such as Swedish-style teams responsible for a homogeneous subsection of work, or buffer stocks—remain faithful to the basic principles of Ohno: the economics of time and raw materials, under the surveillance of the management by visual control which has itself evolved and become more complex in different respects. For example, new types of electric signals providing the latest information supplement the classic *andons* and permit an even closer monitoring of the respect of work rules, routines, and allotted time. Ultimately, this symbolizes a new type of compromise: greater attention to working conditions[21] accompanied by new progress in the fight against waste and even more refined control methods.

6. The Toyota Production System as Ensembles of Evolving Routines: A General Assessment

One of the theoretical points of departure of this work has been the challenge of accounting, *together*, for the three levels of coordination which organization in general and organizational routines in particular embody, namely related to information-processing, problem-solving, and control mechanisms.

6.1. *Information, problem-solving, and control: the unity of the three levels of coordination*

Indeed, as the foregoing example of the Toyota system vividly illustrates, these three dimensions of coordination—while fruitfully separable in theory—appear empirically deeply intertwined with each other within single routines and in the overall ensemble which makes up a particular production system.

In order to see that, consider first the relation between information-processing on the one hand, and maintenance and utilization of problem-solving competences on the other. The analytical separation between these two domains has in fact been one of the major contributions of evolutionary theories of corporate organization (cf. among others Nelson and Winter (1982) and Dosi and Marengo (1994)), with their emphasis on more or less tacit problem-solving knowledge and organizational competences, irreducible to sheer 'information'. This distinction partly mirrors the one drawn in Arrow (1996) between 'marketing information', which, in our framework comes under information-processing and 'technical information', which in a language nearer the evolutionary approach falls under the heading of utilization and maintenance of competences. But then, how do organizational routines link one with the other? Let us consider how the Ohno system entails a *quasi-direct conversion process* of one into the other.

As we already mentioned, in the system which Ohno created, everything stems from the market, or more precisely, from the 'marketing information' obtained from products sold. A series of organizational devices collect sales information as carefully as possible, and send it to the 'just necessary' localities in the firm, that is to say, those

---

[21] Indeed we should point out that simultaneously with the reconstitution of teams along the lines of semi-autonomous Swedish ones, self-propelled trolleys were introduced to allow workers to have a more comfortable body posture. In addition, the time allotted to training workers for and adapting them to the work pace of the assembly line was also increased so as to better prepare them for this work.

departments of the firm requiring it and no other. There are many procedures for collecting this information from the market. They range from minutely detailed analyses of orders and seasonal variations in them, categories of buyers, changes in interest rates or promotions for such-and-such a model or such-and-such a period, to opinion surveys of real or potential clients. But the key protocol remains the gathering of information on car sales directly from dealers and the 'just-in-time' transfer of this to the assembly plants.

Here, using established routines, the market information is transformed into instructions to be appropriately handled. These routines must both be automatic if they are to be economically efficient, and include an element of discretion, in order to deal adequately with the treatment of variety which is to some extent unpredictable. Indeed, the art of the Ohno system lies precisely in this unique system of conversion procedures, designed to transform market information 'directly' into technical information which, in turn, is instantaneously transformed into work methods.

The key points of this conversion process are the following. The commercial information (actual sales) is conveyed only to the final assembly plants, or, more precisely, to their final stages. Then, starting from the well-known process of inverse iteration from lower down the line to higher up, and notably by using *kanban* signals for orders and delivery, sales information is converted into technical information or, more precisely, into a series of instructions concerning production and delivery from one work station to the next.

This conversion is instantaneous and does not require an intermediary, since the line workers have been trained and the lines prepared (cf. the linearization process described above) to 'automatically' deal with the variety in the demand, and therefore with production instructions. It is in this sense that routines viewed from the angle of 'individual skills' meet routines viewed as collective programmes. These individual skills are designed to be inserted into the routines regulating production adjustments and ultimately into that 'meta-routine' which is the organizational method of the just-in-time.

We may even say that the organization competences specific to the Ohno system reside in these protocols which 'automatically' convert commercial information into production operations.[22] Notice that it is via one single group of organizational routines that the coordination of 'commercial' information and competence-activation occurs.

Let us move a step further and consider the intimate relation between these processes of conversion and control mechanisms. In this respect, begin by noticing that the process of conversion of commercial information into technical information—based on the principle of production without stocks—is itself entirely conceived to ensure 'management by visual control'. Production without stocks, we have argued, is a powerful and permanent means to analyse the smooth functioning of production, since a byproduct of stocks is to 'conceal' any malfunction in the classic (Fordist) organization. In the Ohno system, on the other hand, any interruption to

---

[22] Which, to repeat, is only made possible by training procedures specific to the Ohno system (see also below).

the assembly line, abnormally high or low stocks, or other malfunctions are immediately made 'visible' to the team leaders.

Moreover, any lengthy break in production is dealt with as a 'crisis' necessitating
the mobilization of everyone, which (hopefully) brings any malfunction under
control. Even the methods used in practice to analyse the causes of the malfunction
(the method of the 'five whys')[23] treats a line worker guilty of negligence harshly,
especially if the negligence is partly 'intentional'.

Finally, as mentioned above, the self-monitoring between work stations is one of
the general features of the Ohno system, since no line worker can accept a faulty
component from the previous work station without risking having to undertake
repairs in the time allotted for his own work.

In conclusion, the method of 'get it right the first time', which sums up Ohno's
innovation, consisting in the decentralization of quality control to work stations, in
turn made possible by the reaggregation of the functions of production and command/
monitoring, is therefore a formidable built-in method bringing coherence among
information-processing, activation of technical capabilities, and exercise of control.

This point is made even clearer when we examine the nature of the learning
process which underlies these routines and their improvements to them over time.

6.2. Routine and learning

As already mentioned, the implementation of Ohno routines appears to be strongly
conditioned by a long and complex learning process, involving training of the line
worker to carry out his 'usual' as well as his 'non-usual' tasks (cf. Koike and Inoki
1990) and which uses methods which combine the benefits of both 'on-the-job' and
'off-the-job' training. But this only concerns individual training. As one knows from
the evolutionary literature, routines have an essential organizational dimension which
does not reside in the memory of the individual (or a group of them), but in the
'memory' of the organization itself. Organizational competences are to a large extent
those which outlast the presence of individuals within the organization. But, in turn,
how is this 'organizational memory' built and maintained? What can we infer about
the nature of organizational learning?

The analysis of NUMMI (the joint venture in California between Toyota and GM
staffed by Japanese managers) and Uddevala (the Swedish plant which is by far the
most advanced in the application of Swedish socio-technical methods) will bring
some hints toward an answer to these questions.

It is useful to start with the distinction between individual and organizational
learning. A priori, it is not difficult to understand what one means by individual
learning. It occurs when the individual acquires new skills or new know-how,
improves his powers of judgement and his ability to diagnose and provide responses
to an ever-growing set of events and problems.

In contrast, we assume here that organizational learning is made of all the know-
how, skills, and the like that an organization as such is able to accumulate, and which

---

[23] See Ohno (1988*b*).

does not disappear with the disappearance of the individuals who make up that organization. The memory of know-how must therefore outlast the individuals who possess it at any given moment. As Argyris (1992: 19) points out: 'In order for organizational learning to occur, learning agents' discoveries, inventions and evaluations must be embedded in organizational memory.' For this to occur, the author stresses that these agents' discoveries 'must be encoded in the individual images and shared maps of theory of use, from which individual members will subsequently act. If this encoding does not occur, individuals will have learned but (the) organization will not have done so' (ibid.), the *encoding of know-how* being the *condition for the constitution of an organizational memory*.

We may go further and say that if the organization does not provide devices for encoding and for collecting 'best practices' (whatever it considers them to be), as well as the procedures by which they are diffused throughout the organization, there is a risk that also learning of individuals themselves will be slowed down and more or less completely held up.

The comparative analysis between the methods of organization of work in NUMMI and Uddevala plants highlights these points on the relationships between individual and organizational learning.

The initial observation is that Uddevala appears to give strong priority to individual learning, while NUMMI makes extensive use of Japanese (Ohno) forms of collective learning. In the case of Uddevala, a central feature of the organization is the extremely long individual work cycles (two hours or more), which maximize the 'autonomy' of individual workers. The theory on which this experimentation is built is around the notion of the 'reflexive' organization. The underlying idea is that the memorization of an exceptionally high number of tasks is possible when the principles of assembly are redesigned according to a basic logic of interlocking 'natural' substructures rather than to 'time and motion'. In such an assembly principle, the potential for individual learning is assumed to be vast and to be manifested in a sharp progress in the learning curve relative to global product assembly.

Moreover, the implicit hypothesis is that progress in individual learning automatically benefits collective learning. In this spirit, no 'encoding' procedures for the 'discoveries' and improvement ideas made during assembly are provided for. In practice, the result is that even when a work cycle gives rise to 'discoveries' and improvement ideas (which often seems to be the case, cf. Berggren (1994)) these belong to the workers who made them. More worrying still, in the absence of a minimum amount of 'encoding', the organization is exposed to the risk that some or all of these 'discoveries' and improvement ideas will be lost with the departure or the redeployment of the line workers. Indeed the absence of 'encoding' not only excludes the possibility for organizational learning but may even hinder individual learning, since each worker is obliged to 'rediscover' his procedures before being able to stabilize them firmly.

In the light of this it is easier to understand the utility of the repertoire of standard work methods so dear to Ohno, since it is one of the centrepieces of the encoding process. Indeed, from one repertoire to another, individual learning is converted into organizational know-how, and is embedded into a memory available to everyone, in turn permitting the whole organization to progress. Thus, individual learning allows new solutions which can be 'locally' explored—thanks to encoding—before they are extended to the organization at large. In this sense, Adler and Cole are perfectly justified in stating that

[T]he Japanese production model explicitly focuses on organizational learning. Standardization of work method is a precondition for achieving this end: 'you cannot identify the sources of problems in a process you have not standardized. Standardization captures best practices and facilitates the diffusion of improvement ideas throughout the organization—you cannot diffuse what you have not standardized.' (Adler and Cole 1993: 92)

6.3. Learning as a means of dispossessing workers of their 'discoveries' and improvement ideas

If we analyse in more detail the techniques used to construct organizational learning, we are forced to note that the process of continually writing and rewriting the repertoire of standard work methods, which is the key to organizational learning, has a dual nature. On the one hand, it is evident that this entails the progressive accumulation of problem-solving procedures considered to be of potential use to the organization. On the other hand, the converse is also true: one is dealing here with the steady, permanent, and systematically organized dispossession of workers of their improvement ideas and know-how and their appropriation by the management of the firm. This view may be further reinforced with the mention of 'quality circles' and the practice of systematically encouraging 'suggestions' on the part of workers. Indeed, both these practices take advantage of the 'discoveries' and improvement ideas of the individual workers in the course of their work, in the first place by eliciting, analysing, and refining them, and then drawing up new work methods. Second, by 'encoding' them, they make them diffusable within the organization as a whole. Third, under these conditions, and by means of these protocols, the 'tacitness' inherent in individual skills need not necessarily act as an insurmountable obstacle to progress in organizational learning. Last, but not least, note that all these practices of codification inherent to organizational learning show, as already noted with respect to routines, an intrinsic double nature. At one level of observation, they can be seen as procedures for the redefinition of knowledge and its intra-organiza- tional transfer. At another level, however, they are in fact mechanisms for the organizational appropriation of workers' knowledge, nested into specific protocols for monitoring and command of work, ultimately yielding asymmetric distribution of power within the organization—in general and with respect in particular to the ability of making claims upon the overall surplus generated by the organization.

   In principle, these 'Japanese' practices are indistinguishable from those of Taylor- ism. All these systems collect and analyse workers' know-how and improvement ideas in order to transform them into the evolving socially imposed code which structure the organization. The difference rests in the way in which authority is exercised during the process through which the individual knowledge of employees is transferred to the hierarchy of the firm to become organizational knowledge. The method used in Taylorism is brutal: time and motion are analysed by specialists; on this basis, the work methods are drawn up, the time is allotted, and these methods are then imposed on line workers under strict supervisory control. The Japanese (and Swedish) methods obtain the participation and involvement of the workers in this process whereby they reveal the content of their newly acquired knowledge. This is only made possible by the fact that a series of subtle and skilful—often implicit—compromises are made during the transfer process, whereby the employees obtain something in return in the short or in the longer term (in either pecuniary or non-pecuniary form). This once again clearly illustrates the dimension of social conflict and compromise inherent in the existence and evolution of routines.

7. Some Conclusions

We started with some theoretical considerations and it might be appropriate to come back to them, summarizing our conclusions through a list of synthetic proportions.

(1) *The content of routines: 'programmes' drawing upon individual skills.*

The analysis of the Toyota system made it abundantly clear that routines as 'programmes' for coordinated action draw upon a set of individual skills whose presence is obviously a necessary condition for their implementation. In turn, the elicitation of particular repertoires of action is constrained and shaped by 'meta-routines' governing information distribution and information-processing, allocations of tasks, and decisional power. To paraphrase Warglien (in Cohen *et al.* 1996), routines have an 'architectural dimension' going all the way from the physical layout of manufacturing artefacts to the allocation of work individually or by teams, vertical or horizontal coordination, just-in-time programmed from downstream or upstream, etc.

(2) *The double nature of routines: 'skills', cooperation and authority*

This study, we hope, has been able to consolidate the hypothesis (first put forward in Coriat and Dosi (1998)) concerning the double nature of routines as both devices for problem-solving and mechanisms for the monitoring and command of work. We believe, for example, we have demonstrated—with regard to the Ohno system—how the devices of monitoring and of 'visual control' are a key element of the routine of the Toyota production system. In this respect, routines necessarily include an element of authority.

The way in which this authority, and the related command and monitoring of work, are exercised may vary greatly from one system of work organization to another. In general, a wide variety of devices, procedures, and protocols are used, alone or in combination, ranging from direct monitoring and command externally by physical persons, to automatic monitoring and command and including the use of mechanical or electronic devices (like *andons* in the Ohno system), all of which enable the heirarchy to check whether the activities are being carried out as expected. The aim of these procedures is not only to ensure that the operations are being carried out as defined a priori, but also to reduce the chances of moral hazard.

(3) *Organizational learning, encoding, monitoring, and command*

Last but not least, we hope to have demonstrated the dual proposition that (a) no effective organizational learning can occur without one form or another of encoding;

(b) these forms of encoding are, in one form or another, a way of dispossessing employees of their individual 'discoveries' and improvement ideas to the benefit the organization as such. In this respect different modes of monitoring and commanding work are not only part of the 'steady-state' implementation of organizational routines but are essential to the processes of organizational learning.

(4) *Cognition and its social dimensions*

As mentioned, one of the purposes of this work was to show the analytical advantages of going beyond the notion of 'routines as truces' advanced by Nelson and Winter (1982) and fully exploring their social dimensions. The point is recently reiterated by Winter suggesting that 'what the observer sees [when studying routines] is therefore the product of cognitive functioning constrained by sensitivity to the sources of conflict' (S. Winter in Cohen *et al.* 1996: 662). However, not much work has been done in this direction.

The present study was meant to begin to fill this gap. By analysing the Toyota production system, in terms of both some 'steady-state' (nearly invariant) properties, and its dynamics, we have tried to show that the 'social dimension'—related also but not exclusively to incentive governance and power exercise—first, is an essential part of the implementation of organizational routines even in their 'steady-state' form; and, second, may be a major driver of their emergence and subsequent evolution.

References

Adler, P. S. (1991). *The 'Learning Bureaucracy': New United Motor Manufacturing Inc.*, Working Paper, School of Business Administration, University of Southern California.

—— and Cole R. E. (1993). 'Designed for Learning: A Tale of Two Auto Plants', *Sloan Management Review*, Spring: 85–94.

Akerlof, G. (1984). 'Gift Exchange and Efficiency Wage Theory: Four Views', *American Economic Review*, Proceedings, 74: 79–83.

Andreasen, L., B. Coriat, F. Den Hertog, and R. Kaplinsky (1995). *Europe's Next Step: Organisational Innovation Competition and Employment*. London: Frank Cass.

Aoki, M. (1988). *Information, Incentives and Bargaining Structure in the Japanese Economy*. Cambridge: Cambridge University Press.

—— (1990). 'Towards an Economic Theory of the Japanese Firm', *Journal of Economic Literature*, 26/1.

Argyris C. (1992). *Organisational Learning*. Cambridge, Mass.: Blackwell Business.

Arrow, K. (1996). 'Technical Information and Industrial Structure', *Industrial and Corporate Change*, 5(2).

Augren, S., *et al.* (1986). *Volvo Kalmar Revisited. Ten Years of Experience*. Stockholm: Arbetsniljö-làboràtoret.

Asanuma, B. (1989). 'Manufacturer–Supplier Relationships in Japan and the Concept of Relation Special Skill', *Journal of the Japanese and International Economies* 1: 1–30.

Baum, J. M. C., and J. V. Singh (1994). *Evolutionary Dynamics of Organisations*. New York: Oxford University Press.

Berggren, C. (1988). 'The Swedish Experience with New Work Concepts in Assembly Operations', in B. Dankbar, U. Jürgens, and T. Malsch, *Die Zukunft der Arbeit in der Automobilindustrie*. Berlin: Sigma Edition.

—— (1994). 'Nummi vs. Uddevalla', *Sloan Management Review*, Winter: 37–49.

Chandler, A. D., P. Hagström, and Ö. Sölvell (eds.) (1998). *The Dynamic Firm. The Role of Technology, Strategy, Organisation and Regions*. Oxford: Oxford University Press.

Cohen, M., R. Burkhart, G. Dosi, M. Egidi, L. Marengo, M. Warglien, S. Winter, and B. Coriat (1996). 'Routines and Other Recurring Action Patterns of Organisations. Contemporary Research Issues', *Industrial and Corporate Change*, 5(3): 653–98.

Coriat, B. (1991). *Penser à l'envers: Travail et organisation dans l'entreprise japonaise*. Paris: Christian Bourgois; 3rd edn. 1994.

—— (1992). 'The Revitalization of Mass Production in the Computer Age', in M. Storper and A. Scott (eds.), *Pathways to Industrialisation and Regional Development*. London: Routledge.

—— (1994). 'Taylor, Ford et Ohno. Nouveaux développements dans l'analyse du Ohnisme', *Japon in Extenso*, 31 (Mar.–Apr.).

—— (1995*a*). 'Incentives, Bargaining and Trust: Alternative Scenario for the Future of Work', in *International Contribution to Labour Studies*, 5. Chicago: Academic Press.

—— (1995*b*). 'Variety, Routines, and Networks: The Metamorphosis of Fordist Firms', *Industrial and Corporate Change*, 4(1): 205–27.

—— and G. Dosi (1998). 'Learning How to Govern and Learning How to Solve Problems: On the Co-evolution of Competences, Conflicts and Organisational Routines', in Chandler *et al.* (originally appeared as a IIASA Working Paper, 1994).

—— and O. Weinstein (1995). *Les Nouvelles Théories de l'Entreprise*. Paris: Livre de Poche.

Coriat, B., and O. Weinstein (1998). *Sur la Théorie Evolutionniste de la Firme, Apports et Apories*, Working Paper, CREI, University of Paris XIII.

Cusumano, M. (1985). *The Japanese Automobile Industry: Technology and Management at Nissan and Toyota*. Cambridge, Mass.: Harvard University Press.

Cyert, R. M., and J. G. March (1967). *A Behavioural Theory of the Firm*. Englewood Cliffs, NJ.: Prentice-Hall.

——— (1988). *The Economic Theory of Organisation and the Firm*. New York: Harvester Wheatsheaf.

Doeringer, P., and M. Piore (1971). *Internal Labour Markets and Manpower Analysis*. Lexington, Mass.: D. C. Heath.

Dosi, G., and L. Marengo (1994). 'Some Elements of an Evolutionary Theory of Corporate Competences', in R. W. England (ed.), *Evolutionary Concepts in Contemporary Economics*. Ann Arbor: University of Michigan Press.

Du Tertre, C. (1990). *Technologie, Flexibilité et Emploi: Une perspective sectorielle*. Paris: Ed. l'Harmattan.

Emery, F. E. (1969). *Systems Thinking*. London: Penguin Books.

—— and E. L. Trist (1972). 'Socio-Technical Systems', in L. E. Davies (ed.), *Design of Jobs*. London: Penguin Books.

England, R. W. (ed.) (1994). *Evolutionary Concepts in Contemporary Economics*. Ann Arbor: University of Michigan Press.

Fujimoto, T. (1996). *An Evolutionary Process of Toyota's Final Assembly Operations: The Role of Export Dynamic Capabilities*. Research Institute for the Japanese Economy, Discussion Paper Series, Faculty of Economics, Tokyo University.

Gordon, A. (1985). *The Evolution of Labor Relations in Japan, 1815–1955*. Cambridge, Mass.: Harvard University Press.

Koike, K. (1988). *Understanding Industrial Relations in Modern Japan*. London: Macmillan.

—— and T. Inoki (eds.) (1990). *Skill Formation in Japan and Southeast Asia*. Tokyo: University of Tokyo Press.

Liebenstein, H. (1982). 'The Prisoner's Dilemma and the Invisible Hand: An Analysis of Intra-Firm Productivity', *American Economic Review*, 72 (May).

Lucas, F. (1987). *Etude du Management de la Production chez Toyota*. Paris: Internal Document of Régie Nationale des Usines Renault.

Mangolte, P. A. (1997). *Le concept de routine organisationnelle: entre cognition et institution*, doctoral thesis, Faculty of Economics, University of Paris XIII.

March, T. G., and H. Simon (1993). *Organization*, 2nd edn. Oxford: Blackwell.

Marengo, L. (1992). 'Coordination and Organisational Learning in the Firm', *Journal of Evolutionary Economics*, 2: 313–26.

Monden, Y. (1983). *Toyoto Production System*. Atlanta: Institute of Industrial Engineers.

Nelson, R., and S. G. Winter (1982). *An Evolutionary Theory of Economic Change*. Cambridge, Mass.: Harvard University Press.

Nomura, M. (1993). 'Farewell to Toyotism', Working Paper, University of Okayama.

Ohno, T. (1988*a*). *Toyota Production System: Beyond Large Scale Production*. Chicago: Productivity Press.

—— (1998*b*). *Work Plan Management*. Chicago: Productivity Press.

—— and S. Mito (1992). *Présent et Avenir du Toyotisme*. Paris: Masson.

Orlean, A. (ed.) (1994). *Analyse Economique des Conventions*. Paris: PUF.

Parker, M., and J. Slaughter (1988). *Choosing Sides. Unions and the Team Concept*. Boston: South End Press.

Sandberg, A., *et al.* (1993). *Technical Change and Co-Determination in Sweden.* Philadelphia: Temple University Press.

Shimizu, K. (1994). 'Rapport salarial toyotien: hier, aujourd'hui et demain', *Japon in Extenso*, (Mar.–Apr.): 68–55.

——— and M. Nomura (1993). 'Trajectoire de Toyota', Rapport Salarial et Systéme de Production, in *Actes du Gerpisa*, University d'Evry, Valle d'Essonne.

Williamson, O. E. (1975). *Markets and Hierarchies.* New York: Free Press.

Winter, S. (1994). 'Organizing for Continuous Improvement: Evolutionary Theory Meets the Quality Revolution', in J. M. C. Baum and J. V. Singh (eds.), *Evolutionary Dynamics of Organizations.* New York: Oxford University Press.

Womack, P., *et al.* (1990). *The Machine that Changed the World.* New York: Macmillan.

9

Evolution of Manufacturing Systems and Ex post *Dynamic Capabilities: A Case of Toyota's Final Assembly Operations*

TAKAHIRO FUJIMOTO

1. Introduction

1.1. Purpose of the chapter

This chapter explores the evolutionary process and dynamic organizational capability by which Toyota Motor Corporation reorganized its assembly operations in response to the changes in product and labour markets since the early 1990s.

Toyota's assembly process designs have been significantly modified since the late 1980s, while maintaining much of its core manufacturing capabilities, known as Toyota production system or lean production system. The new system, which some industry observers call post-lean system, Toyotism II, and so on, tries to improve its attractiveness to the new generation of workers in Japan, where the number of the young workforce is decreasing in the long run, while trying to save its cash flow by making the plant and equipment design simpler and by avoiding excessive automation and capital investment. The authors call it 'lean-on-balance' system, as the system tries to regain the balance between employee satisfaction and customer satisfaction, as well as the balance between lean production process and fat plant and equipment design (Fujimoto 1994*a*; Fujimoto and Takeishi 1994).

In a broader context, most of the Japanese automobile makers, facing the labour shortage and expansion of domestic demand around 1990, built a new generation of 'human friendly' assembly plants, such as Mazda Hofu no. 2 plant (1990), Honda Suzuka no. 3 line, Nissan Kyushu no. 2 plant (1992), Toyota Tahara no. 4 line, and so on, with relatively high assembly automation ratios mainly for ergonomic purposes (Fujimoto 1993). Such plants aimed at balancing customer satisfaction with their products and employee satisfaction with their work conditions. The assembly plants, however, suffered from high fixed costs due partly to assembly automation when Japanese domestic production started to decline due to post-bubble recession and further appreciation of the yen since 1992. It has become clear that the Japanese auto companies have to readjust their basic designs of future assembly factories, automation, and work organizations.

This chapter is an abridged version of Fujimoto (1996). A part of the figures in this chapter were jointly developed by the author and Takashi Matsuo, doctoral student at Division of Economics at the University of Tokyo. The author is grateful to all the executives, managers, engineers, shopfloor people, union leaders, and other staff of Toyota Motor Corporation who cooperated with this research.

In this situation, however, Toyota seems to be the only Japanese company that has articulated and implemented the new concept of final assembly as a coherent system as of the mid-1990s, although it is too early to conclude that it is the best system to handle current problems. Miyata Plant of Toyota Motor Kyushu Inc. (called Kyushu Plant henceforth for simplicity), established in late 1992, is the first factory that materialized Toyota's new assembly process design as a total system. The new assembly concept has been diffused among the subsequent plants such as Motomachi RAV4 assembly line (renovated, 1994) and Toyota Motor Manufacturing no. 2 line in Kentucky, US (TMM II, new 1994). Thus, one of our research questions is why Toyota could establish a coherent assembly process prior to its competitors in Japan. Although Toyota's market power and abundant financial resources might explain a part of the story, certain organizational capabilities, specific to Toyota, might also explain this fact. In other words, we are interested in Toyota's distinctive dynamic capability in the particular case of the new assembly system.

The main theme of the present chapter, however, is not only to demonstrate *ex post* rationality of Toyota's new system, but also to describe and analyse how the new system evolved over time. In this regard, the authors hypothesize that the new system was created not simply by a rational and monolithic strategy planning process, but by a more complicated process of system evolution, which may involve not only *ex ante* rational decision-making but also trial and error, unintended changes, conflicts and coordination between different organizational units, complex organizational learning, and so on: a process of emergent strategy formation (Mintzberg and Waters 1985). As Toyota seems to be the first company to reach apparently feasible manufacturing solutions, we may regard Toyota as having 'evolutionary capabilities', by which a firm can handle a complex process of new system evolution better than the others.

In order to analyse this process, the chapter describes and analyses the recent construction of Toyota's domestic assembly factories, including Tahara no. 4 and Toyota Kyushu Plant. The chapter will try to show that Toyota's distinctive competence in manufacturing includes not only its static capability of high quality, productivity, and delivery performance and continuous improvements, but evolutionary (or dynamic) capability. It will also suggest that fundamental objectives at Toyota's manufacturing operations in recent years include not only customer satisfaction, which Toyota traditionally emphasized, but also employee satisfaction, which has become an explicit criterion in the 1990s. We will also try to challenge a rather stereotypical notion that Toyota is a monolithic organization where changes are made by one-shot rational decision-making.

1.2. *Conceptual framework: three layers of organizational capabilities*

In order to analyse dynamic and evolutionary aspects of the automobile assembly systems, the present chapter applies a modified version of the resource-capability view of the firm (Fujimoto 1994*b*).

Generally speaking, so-called resource-based or capability theories of the firm have attracted much attention among business academics and practitioners in recent years. They illustrated a business firm as a collection of firm-specific resources, organizational routines, capabilities, and competencies, which may explain inter-firm differences in competitiveness, as well as intertemporal dynamics (i.e. evolution) of business enterprise systems.[1]

Although the resource-capability framework has been used mainly for strategic analysis at the company-wide level, it can also be applied to rather detailed analyses of manufacturing issues (Fujimoto 1994*a*, 1994*b*). In this context, production and product development capability of a firm refers to certain firm-specific patterns of productive resources and activities that result in competitive (or other) advantages over its rivals. Assuming that both competitive performance and capabilities change over time, we have to distinguish at least three levels of a firm's capability (Table 9.1; Fujimoto 1994*b*): (i) *static capability*, which affects the level of competitive perform-ance, (ii) *improvement capability*, which affects the pace of performance improvements, and (iii) *evolutionary capability*, which is related to accumulation of the above capabilities themselves.[2] While (ii) and (iii) both can be regarded as dynamic capabilities, they are different in that the latter is a non-routine meta-capability (i.e. capability of capability building).

In the existing literature of Toyota's production system, (i) static and (ii) improve-ment capabilities tended to be emphasized as distinctive strengths of Toyota's manufacturing operations. There has been historical analyses of the origin and evolution of Toyota, but they tended not to analyse it from dynamic capability's point of view. This chapter, by contrast, highlights (iii) evolutionary capability at Toyota. Our view is that Toyota's distinctiveness as a manufacturing form has to be analysed at all three levels. The present chapter is an attempt to apply this framework to the case of Toyota's new assembly system.

TABLE 9.1 Three levels of development-production capability

	Basic nature	Influence on	Components
Static capability	static and routine	level of competitive performance	productivity = efficiency of information transmission throughput time = efficiency of information reception quality = accuracy of information transmission flexibility = redundancy of information stock
Improvement capability	dynamic and routine	change in competitive performance	problem-finding problem-solving retention of solutions
Evolutionary capability	dynamic and non-routine	change in capability	pre-trial capability: *ex ante* rationality entrepreneurial visions post-trial capability: *ex post* rationality retention and institutionalization

[1] For the concepts of resource, organizational routine, capability, and competence, see e.g. Penrose (1959), Nelson and Winter (1982), Chandler (1990, 1992), Praharad and Hamel (1990), Grant (1991), Leonard-Barton (1992), Teece *et al.* (1992), and Teece *et al.* (1994). For evolutionary aspects of the firm and its strategies and technologies, see also Dosi (1982), Nonaka (1985), and Mintzberg (1987).

[2] For further details of this three-level framework, see Fujimoto (1994*b*).

1.3. Background: evolution of the Toyota-style production system

Before starting the analysis of Toyota's new assembly system, let us first outline the background of this study. The author has explored evolutionary patterns of the manufacturing-development system of the Japanese auto makers (Toyota in particular) in recent years (Fujimoto 1994*b*, 1995). The present chapter can be regarded as an extension of this historical analysis, which was motivated by the following basic observations:

- Many of the capabilities were gradually acquired by the competing firms throughout the post-war period, particularly between the 1950s and 1970s. There was apparently no grand strategy on the sequence of capability acquisition. It was rather a long-term evolutionary process.
- Some aspects of the capabilities of the effective development-production systems were found at Japanese makers in general. Some other aspects of the capabilities were found only in certain manufacturers known for their high competitive performance, typically Toyota. Still other aspects of the system were generic, or common with automobile mass producers worldwide, in that they all introduced some elements of the standard Ford system directly or indirectly.

In order to analyse the evolutionary dynamics of the system, the author classified patterns of system changes into several types (Figure 9.1): (i) Random trials (a pure chance); (ii) Rational calculation (an organization deliberately chooses a new course of action that satisfies or maximizes its objective function by examining a feasible set of alternatives based on its understandings of environmental constraints and limits of capabilities); (iii) Environmental constraints (an organization detects certain constraints imposed by objective or perceived environments, and voluntarily prohibits certain sets of actions); (iv) Entrepreneurial vision (a desirable set of activities is directly chosen by entrepreneurs of the organizations based on their visions without much analysis of their capabilities and constraints); and (v) Knowledge transfer (a certain pattern is transferred from another organization (inside or outside of the industry) to the one in question).

Historical analyses on some major components of the system, based on the above framework, revealed that the development-production capability of the effective Japanese auto makers gradually emerged as a result of complex interactions of entrepreneurial visions, historical imperatives, inter-firm and inter-industrial transfer of resources and practices, pure chances, as well as the firms' own evolutionary capability. The study clarified that the Toyota-style manufacturing system of the 1980s was formed not by *ex ante* rational decision-makings of the founder-entrepreneurs of the companies, although the resulting system may have been *ex post* rational. Table 9.2 indicates the complexity of the dynamics in the selected cases. Some of the findings in this historical study are summarized as follows (see Fujimoto 1994*b*, for details):

- *Historical imperatives by forced growth and flexibility*: Some of region-specific imperatives that all the Japanese firms faced during the post-war era almost 'forced' them to

TABLE 9.2 Summary of evolution of selected production-development capabilities

	Just-in-Time	Multi-tasking with product-focus lay-out	Jidoka and flexible equipment	Kaizen and TQC	Black-box parts	Heavyweight product manager
Competitive effect (rationality)	creating pressure for productivity improvement; throughput time; inventory cost	productivity improvement	pressures for quality improvement; flexibility	quality improvement productivity improvement	cost reduction by manufacturability; development lead time and productivity	high product integrity; development lead time and productivity
Entrepreneurial vision	Kiichiro Toyoda, 1930s ('just-in-time' slogan); Taiichi Ohno, 1940–50s (system building)	Kiichiro Toyoda, 1945; (a vision of rapid productivity catch-up without economy of scale)	Kiichiro Toyoda, 1931; (a vision of high productivity with small volume production)			
Transfer from other industry	textile (bench-marking of Nichibo); prewar aircraft production	textile: multi-machine operation in spinning; (through Ohno)	textile: Sakichi Toyoda's automatic loom	TQC was established in other industries (e.g. process industry)	prewar locomotive or aircraft parts supplier	prewar aircraft industry (chief designer system); forced transfer (collapse of aircraft industry)
Transfer from Ford system	the synchronization idea from Ford (invisible conveyer line); Kanban as 'incomplete synchronization'	productivity bench-marking with Ford; modified Taylorism	adoption of Detroit-type automation where feasible; U-shape layout as 'incomplete transfer machine'	suggestion system from Ford Training Within Industry Statistical Quality Control		

Imperative of forced growth with resource shortage	limit of permanent work force after the 1950 strikes; 'forced' productivity increase in the 1960s	shortage of investment fund: low-cost automation had to be pursued	shortage of supervisors replacing craftsmen-foremen = needs for TWI	high production growth and model proliferation created pressures for subcontracting, subassembly, and design	
Imperative of forced flexibility with small and fragmented market		'forced' flexibility of equipment due to small volume		product proliferation of the 1960s created pressures for subcontracting out design jobs	product proliferation with limited engineering resource created pressure for compact projects
Imperative of shortage of technology	lack of computer production control technology in the 1950s and 1960s	lack of adaptive control automation: *jidoka* needs human intervention		lack of electric parts technology at Toyota in 1949 (separation of Nippondenso)	
Ex post capability of the firm	flexible task assignment and flexible revision of work standards to better exploit opportunities of productivity increase		Toyota maintained momentum for TQC by creating organizations for diffusing it to suppliers	Toyota institutionalized a version of black-box parts system that could better exploit competitive advantages	only Toyota adopted heavy-weight product manager system from the aircraft industry as early as 1950s

make certain responses, some of which turned out to contribute to the competitive advantages of those firms. Many such responses were not recognized as competitive weapons when the firms first adopted them. Likewise, the imperative of forced flexibility in the fragmented market also benefited the Japanese firms. This is partly because of the region-specific patterns of industrial growth: a rapid production

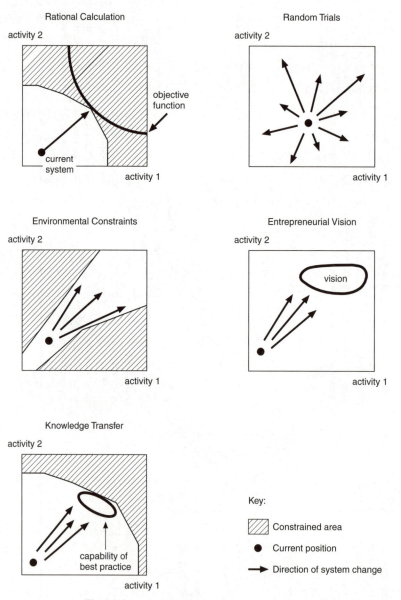

Fig. 9.1 Some generic hypotheses of system emergence

growth accompanied by rapid product proliferation. The flexibility that the firms acquired tended to be recognized as a necessary evil to cope with the fragmented market, rather than a measure for international competition, when the capabilities were first built.

• *Benefits of historical imperatives by lack of technology.* While excessive use of high-tech automation equipment often became an obstacle against productivity improvement, the effective Japanese makers apparently avoided such problems. This may be partly because they consciously rejected the temptation for overspecialization, but it also seems to be partly because high technology was not there in the first place. To the extent that this was caused by certain region-specific technology gaps, the lack of technology may bring about unintended competitive benefits to firms of a region.

• *Knowledge transfer from Ford.* Toyota's capability building was consistently motivated, since the 1930s, by perceived competitive pressures from the US mass producers, particularly Ford. Even with a strongly protected domestic market between the 1930s and 1950s, Toyota's consciousness of the imaginary competitive pressures persisted. Motivated partly by the above consciousness of international competition, Toyota adopted many elements of the Ford system and American mass production system mostly indirectly, including moving conveyers, transfer machines, product and component designs, the Taylor system, supervisor training programmes, and statistical quality control. Pure dichotomy between the Ford system and the Toyota system as the post-Ford paradigm is therefore misleading.

• *Transfer from other industries.* Some of the linkages to other industries, which were technologically advanced in the past, may be firm-specific. For example, Toyota's inherent connection with the textile industry may have facilitated knowledge transfer from it (particularly through Taiichi Ohno) and created its competitive advantages in production control techniques.

• *Unintended transfer.* As in the case of engineers from the pre-war aircraft industry, who were pushed into the auto industry as the former collapsed after the war, knowledge transfer, which the receivers did not intend to make, brought about rapid increase in automobile technologies and product development systems of the post-war automobile industry in Japan.

• *Incomplete transfer.* Although the Japanese auto firms tried to adopt many of the practices and techniques from the US mass producers (i.e. Ford system), some of them were incomplete due to the historical imperatives mentioned above and lack of the firms' absorption capacities. In this sense, *kanban* system may be regarded as an incomplete version of the conveyer system, U-shape machine lay-out as an incomplete transfer machine, and *jidoka* as incomplete adaptive automation. The very incompleteness of the transfer may have facilitated its subsequent diffusion to the entire system. For example, the case of *kanban* system may be regarded as complete diffusion of incomplete synchronization technology.

• *Self-fulfilling visions.* Firm-specific entrepreneurial visions sometimes played an important role in building distinctive development-production capability. This was particularly the case when apparently unrealistic visions that go against common sense triggered self-fulfilling efforts for achieving the bold objectives. Kiichiro

Toyoda in the 1930s and 1940s played a pivotal role in this sense in advocating cost reduction without economy of scale, catch-up with Ford, and just-in-time philosophy. Nissan of those days did not have his counterpart.

• *Ex post dynamic capability.* Even when no firms recognized potential competitive advantages of the new system when they first tried it, some firms could still create firm-specific competitive advantages by exercising post-trial capability: by recognizing the potential competitive advantage of the new system, modifying it to exploit the potentials, institutionalizing it, and retaining it until the advantages were realized. For example, even though all the Japanese auto makers faced similar environmental pressures for adopting the black-box parts system in the 1960s, only Toyota appears to have created a system that could fully exploit potential advantages of this practice. Although all the Japanese auto makers accepted aircraft engineers after the war, Toyota was the only company that institutionalized the heavyweight product manager system that was prevalent in the aircraft industry. Thus, even when all the Japanese firms faced certain historical imperatives that facilitated new practices, only a part of them may have made use of this potential luck by employing firm-specific evolutionary capability.

In summary, an intertwined combination of the logic of system emergence, including historical imperatives, knowledge transfers, entrepreneurial visions, and post-trial capabilities, seemed to be able to explain why firm-specific, region-specific, and universally adopted capabilities coexisted, as well as how they emerged, in the effective product development and production systems in the Japanese auto industry of the 1980s. As for Toyota's firm-specific capabilities, this historical analysis made the author infer that Toyota's distinctive capability included not only static ones, which have been documented in existing literature, but also a dynamic one. Furthermore, the above-mentioned analysis indicated that the company's dynamic capability included not only competence for performing *ex ante* rational problem-solving in a linear manner (e.g. continuous improvements through total quality management) but also competence for managing ill-structured problem-solving, emergent strategies, or complex processes of system evolution. The author called the latter the evolutionary capability, or capability of capability building.

Thus, the previous analysis of the evolution of the Toyota-style manufacturing system up to the 1980s emphasized Toyota's dynamic capabilities, which had not been analysed much in existing literature. However, the study still regarded this dynamic capability itself as more or less a black box. That is, although the previous study inferred the existence of such capabilities from a series of certain historical events and actions, it did not analyse their content. It was difficult to do detailed analyses of the change processes themselves by historical data alone. Also, the author was not sure if such a dynamic capability continued to exist after the 1980s, or if it was a rather temporary phenomenon specific to Japan's high-growth era up to the 1980s.

In order to fill this gap, the present study tries to analyse the more recent process of Toyota's system changes after the 1980s, through which it became possible to gather data on actual change processes inside the organizations. Thus, the key research questions of this chapter include the following:

(1) What are the key components of Toyota's dynamic capabilities? Can this black box be opened?

(2) Did the evolutionary capability that the previous historical analysis identified continue to exist after the 1980s? Can it be regarded as Toyota's robust and distinctive competence?

The subsequent sections of the chapter will try to answer these questions, at least partially.

2. Toyota's New Assembly Factories: Structures and Functions

Section 2 focuses on *ex post* rationality of the emerging Toyota assembly system. It is not the intention of the chapter to demonstrate that this is the best assembly system to handle current competitive and labour problems, compared with alternative assembly process designs (e.g. Volvo's Uddevalla concept). Instead, this section will describe how the new system at Toyota was recognized internally as a rational system after it was established.

2.1. *Conventional Toyota system of production*[3]

Overall patterns in manufacturing Let us start with the Toyota's conventional system of production as an ideal type.

The typical volume production system of effective Japanese makers of the 1980s, particularly at Toyota, consists of various intertwined elements that might lead to competitive advantages. Just-in-time (JIT), *jidoka* (automatic defect detection and machine stop), total quality control (TQC), and continuous improvement (*kaizen*) are often pointed out as its core subsystems. The elements of such a system include inventory-reduction mechanisms by *kanban* system; levelling production volume and product mix (*heijunka*); reduction of '*muda*' (non-value-adding activities), '*mura*' (uneven pace of production), and *muri* (excessive workload); production plans based on dealers' order volume (*genryo seisan*); reduction of die set-up time and lot size in stamping operation; mixed model assembly; piece-by-piece transfer of parts between machines (*ikko-nagashi*); flexible task assignment for volume changes and productivity improvement (*shojinka*); multi-task job assignment along the process flow (*takotei-mochi*); U-shape machine layout that facilitates flexible and multiple-task assignment, on-the-spot inspection by direct workers (*tsukurikomi*); fool-proof prevention of defects (*poka-yoke*); real-time feedback of production troubles (*andon*); assembly line stop cord; emphasis on cleanliness, order, and discipline on the shopfloor (what are referred to as 5-S); frequent revision of standard operating procedures by supervisors; quality control circles; standardized tools for quality improvement (e.g. seven

---

[3] The first half of Section 2.1 was adopted from Fujimoto (1994*b*).

tools for QC, QC story); worker involvement in preventive maintenance (total productive maintenance); low-cost automation or semi-automation with 'just-enough' functions); reduction of process steps for saving of tools and dies, and so on.

The human-resource management factors that back up the above elements include stable employment of core workers (with temporary workers in the periphery); long-term training of multi-skilled (multi-task) workers; wage system based in part on skill accumulation; internal promotion to shopfloor supervisors; cooperative relation-ships with labour unions; inclusion of production supervisors in union members; and generally egalitarian policies for corporate welfare, communication, and worker motivation.[4]

It is important to note that this system was not established by a one-shot rational decision, but evolved gradually through a cumulative process of capability building (Fujimoto 1994*b*). It is largely a product of the post-war history of the Japanese auto industry.

Toyota's assembly process   Let us now focus on the final assembly process at Toyota's conventional factories. We can characterize it as follows:

(1) Toyota's volume factories adopted Ford-style moving assembly lines (typically chain conveyers). Thus there is nothing unique in body transfer mechanisms and basic lay-outs of Toyota's conventional assembly lines, except that Toyota's main assembly lines (typically about 1 km.) tend to be shorter than those of US makers.

(2) The conveyer lines tended to be separated into three line segments: trim, chassis, and final. Different conveyer systems tended to be used among them. However, no buffer body was allowed between the line segments, so the assembly process was operated as if there were one long and continuous line.

(3) Unlike machining or welding, there have been few robots and automated equipment in traditional final assembly lines at Toyota. In fact, Toyota's assembly automation ratio tended to be lower than some European makers that adopted advanced assembly automation systems (VW, FIAT, etc.). In other words, Toyota has achieved world-class productivity in final assembly without relying on high-tech automation (Fujimoto 1993).

(4) In order to achieve a high level of line-balancing, Toyota's assembly lines trained multi-skilled workers who could handle multiple tasks, assigned a set of multiple work elements to each individual worker, and thereby reduced '*muda*' due to line imbalance. While such multiple work assignments raised productivity without increasing work speed, meaningfulness of the assembly jobs tended to be sacrificed: a mutually unrelated set of tasks tended to be assigned to each worker.

(5) One of the unique mechanisms at Toyota's assembly line is the so-called '*andon* cord' (or switch), which assembly workers activate when trouble happens on the assembly line. If the worker and/or team leader cannot fix the problem within the cycle time, the entire assembly line stops. This is said to be an example of Toyota's

---

[4] For existing literature on Toyota's manufacturing systems and human resource management, see Fujimoto (1994*b*, 1996).

kaizen mechanisms, which reveal and dramatize the manufacturing problems and thereby facilitate the shopfloor problem-solving activities.

(6) Performance of Toyota's assembly lines have been traditionally evaluated internally in terms of efficiency and product quality, as well as safety. Quality of work environments had not been equally emphasized, though. There was an evaluation system that identify tasks that are potentially harmful to workers' health, but evaluation criteria for measuring work fatigue had not been developed in the past.

2.2. Toyota's new assembly concept: four main aspects

It is widely known that the basic system of Toyota's manufacturing capabilities had been established by the early 1980s. However, the environments had been changed significantly by the early 1990s. Toyota's assembly system (as well as others) had to adjust itself to the new environments. First, in the labour market, serious labour shortage problems occurred in 1990 and 1991, particularly at assembly shops due to insufficient attractiveness of their work conditions. Second, in product market, the era of continuous production growth in the Japanese auto industry (1950–90) finally ended. Third, international and inter-firm competition, cooperation, and conflicts (trade friction) continued to intensify in the early 1990s (Fujimoto and Takeishi 1994). Toyota and other Japanese auto makers accelerated their expansion of overseas production facilities, including assembly, in response to this situation. Fourth, most of the Japanese auto makers suffered from cash-flow shortage due to domestic recession, appreciation of the yen, depreciation costs of previous plant constructions, continued price competition in domestic market, high-cost product designs (fat design), and so on. Fifth, advancement of production technologies created potential opportunities to automate some or part of the assembly process, one of the least automated operations in today's car manufacturing.[5]

In response to the new challenge from the environment, Toyota has modified its production system since the late 1980s. Final assembly has been the area where the change was most visible and significant. Reflecting the environments of the early 1990s mentioned above, the new assembly concepts aimed at improvements in employee satisfaction, as well as elimination of physically demanding jobs, with minimum capital expenditure. The new process also continued to focus on continuous company-wide improvements (*kaizen*) in quality and productivity. To sum up, the new system attempts to preserve the strength of the conventional Toyota system in QCD (quality, cost, and delivery), while improving attractiveness of the assembly work both physically and psychologically.

The new system, as Toyota itself recognizes, consists of several subsystems, as summarized in Table 9.3: (i) functionally autonomous and complete process; (ii) in-line mechanical assembly automation concept; (iii) ergonomics evaluation system called TVAL (Toyota Verification of Assembly Line); and (iv) low-cost equipment for better work environment and work posture (Kawamura *et al.* 1993; Toyota Motor

---

[5] For further details of the environmental changes, see Fujimoto (1993, 1994*a*, 1996), and Fujimoto and Takeish (1994).

T. Fujimoto

TABLE 9.3 Conventional versus new assembly system at Toyota

Conventional	New	
Continuously moving conveyer line; about 1000 m.	→ Unchanged	
Sort cycle time (1-3 minutes)	→ Unchanged	
Decomposed into three line segments (trim, chassis, final)	→ Decomposed into 5 to 12 line segments (trim, chassis, final)	Autonomous-complete assembly process
No buffer zones between segments	→ Buffer zones between segments	
A new work groups per segments	→ One work group per segment	
Functionally unrelated tasks may be packed into jobs for a worker or a group	→ Functionally related tasks are combined for a worker or a group	
Group leaders play key roles in *kaizen* and line managements	→ Group leaders function was strengthened	
Automation for workload reduction*	→ Unchanged	
Off-line automation: bodies stop*	→ In-line automation: bodies move	In-line mechanical assembly automation
High-tech vision sensing for alignment*	→ Mechanical devices or alignment	
NC (numerical control)*	→ Simple sequence control	
Many industrial robots are used*	→ Compact and simple equipment for assembly automation	
Process evaluation by quality, efficiency, and delivery (QCD)	→ Unchanged	
Posture and weight score to avoid illness	→ Unchanged	TVAL for assembly process evaluation
	→ TVAL for quantitative assessment of workload	
Emphasis on low-cost jigs and power-assist equipment	→ Unchanged	Low-cost equipment for better ergonomics
	→ Anew generation of ergonomic devices: *raku-raku*-seat, wagon carts, body-lifting mechanisms, etc.	
Basic human resource management policies at Toyota	→ Unchanged	
Complete day and night shift	→ Continuous day and night shift	Supporting HRM policies
Informal career plan for multi-skilling	→ Formal career plan for multi-skilling	
	→ Other new HRM policies	

Note: * stands for a relatively recent concept of assembly automation between the late 1980s and the early 1990s, as opposed to Toyota's traditional 'low-cost automation' concept (Fujimoto 1997).

Corporation 1994; Kojima 1994; Ogawa 1994; Shimizu 1995, etc.).[6] Let us now examine the main structures and functions of the above subsystems.

Functionally autonomous and complete process of assembly *Structures.* The autonomous and complete line has been implemented at Toyota Kyushu plant (1992), as well as Toyota's subsequent plant constructions and renovations. It consists of various elements, both physical and organizational, including the following (Figure 9.2): the main assembly line is decomposed into five- to twelve-line segments, each of which is typically 100 metres or twenty work stations; the shape of the assembly area is roughly square, accommodating many short lines, which are linked by a buffer zone, where up to about five bodies can be temporarily stored; a group of functionally related assembly tasks (e.g. piping) are assigned to one segment, so that each subcategory of assembly tasks are completed within a group of workers; a quality check station is located at the end of each line segment; each line segment corresponds to a group (*kumi*) of about twenty workers, within which job rotation and training are conducted; the function and responsibility of group leader are also strengthened (each group leader, now in charge of a semi-independent line segment, enjoys more discretion in managing the group's operations); other supporting equipment for line control (line-speed controllers, switches for planned line stops), information-sharing (monitoring displays, *andon* boards), and self-actualization (*kaizen* shops, training centres, rest areas) are set up for each line segment.

Overall, the autonomous and complete line differs from Toyota's conventional assembly line in that the main line (typically about 1,000 metres) consists of semi-independent segments, each of which is functionally, physically, and organizationally decoupled from the others. Each line segment is a short version of Fordist assembly line equipped with continuously moving conveyers.

Functions. Both quantitative and qualitative results have been reported in terms of initial performance of autonomous complete lines, which are generally consistent with what the process designers aimed at (Niimi *et al.* 1994):

(1) Quality and productivity. As each set of assembly jobs assigned to a work group became more meaningful and easy to understand, and as each group can self-inspect quality more effectively, productivity and quality of the autonomous-complete line were generally higher than conventional assembly lines, particularly at the start-up period (Niimi *et al.* 1994). Period for mastering a job was shortened to about a half. According to a survey of Toyota Kyushu assembly workers, over 70 per cent of the respondents said they became more quality conscious, and that their jobs became easier to understand, compared with previous assembly lines. Also, because the body-buffer areas absorb the impact of line stops at other segments, overall down time decreased (Kawamura *et al.* 1993).

(2) Morale. Also, as the assembly job became more meaningful, morale of the assembly workers increased. In the survey mentioned above, about 70 per cent of

---

[6] Another important aspect in the changes in human resource management policies, which is omitted in this chapter. See Fujimoto (1996) and Fujimoto and Takeishi (1994) for discussions of this aspect.

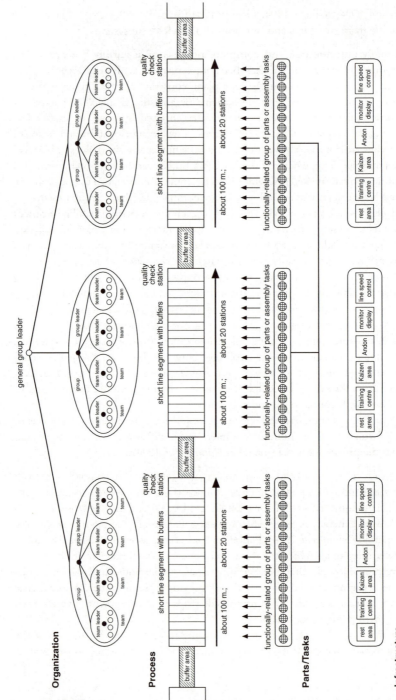

Fig. 9.2 Autonomous and complete assembly-line concept

the respondents found their job more worth doing than before. According to our interview with group leaders and team leaders, they tended to become more proud of their job as instructor and *kaizen* leader, as their tasks shifted from day-to-day trouble-shooting to *kaizen*, supervising, and training. In the past, they tended to be swamped by the complexity and confusion on the line. Some first-line supervisors were feeling psychological pressures due to their increased responsibility, though.

To sum up, the autonomous and complete assembly-line concept aimed at balancing customer satisfaction (quality, cost, and delivery) and employee satisfaction (job meaningfulness, self-esteem, sense of growth) on the assembly lines, has been generally achieved so far. It should be noted, however, the autonomous-complete lines have to carry over both strengths and weaknesses of Fordist conveyer lines with short cycle times.

In-line mechanical assembly automation concept *Structures.* Toyota's new assembly lines adopt the concept of 'in-line mechanical' automation, which consists of several elements. First, both automation equipment and component jig-pallets are synchronized with bodies that move on the conventional continuous conveyers, as opposed to stopping the body for automated assembly. Second, the automation zone and the manual assembly zone coexist on the same assembly line. This contrasts with the idea of separating automated zone and manual zone. Groups of assembly workers on the line, rather than off-line maintenance staff, are in charge of operating the equipment. Third, mechanical methods of alignment between bodies, jigs, equipment, and component, which tend to be inexpensive, simpler, easier to monitor, and easier to fix, are used as much as possible. This contrasts with highly sophisticated and expensive ways of alignment that use electronic vision sensing technologies. Fourth, automation equipment, including robots, tends also to be simple, compact, low power, and easy to maintain so that it can coexist with assembly workers on the continuous conveyers. Jigs are also designed to be compact and inexpensive. Fifth, automated equipment is adopted selectively by taking cost, performance, and ergonomics into account, rather than aiming at the highest assembly automation ratios that are technically possible.

In-line automation is applied to such assembly tasks as engine, transmission, suspension installation, and tire-bolting, which are physically demanding because of the weight of the components, high torque for bolting, and work posture. This concept of assembly automation is significantly different from another type of assembly automation, or 'off-line' automation with visual sensing, which many Western and Japanese auto makers adopted in the late 1980s and early 1990s (Figure 9.3). In such cases (e.g. FIAT Cassino plant, VW Hall 54, Nissan Kyushu no. 2 plant, Toyota Tahara no. 4 line), automation zones equipped with large jigs, sophisticated robots, and electronic vision-sensing devices, are installed separately from conveyer lines, and bodies are stopped for accurate alignment.

Functions. Compared with the off-line type, the in-line mechanical automation tries to reduce negative impacts or side effects of assembly automation, rather than making the operations more sophisticated. The negative side of conventional off-

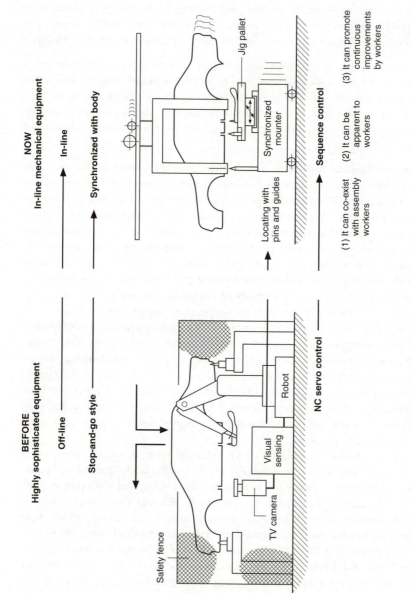

BEFORE
Highly sophisticated equipment

Off-line ⟶ In-line

Stop-and-go style

Synchronized with body

Safety fence

Visual sensing

TV camera

Robot

NC servo control ⟶

NOW
In-line mechanical equipment

In-line

Jig pallet

Synchronized mounter

Locating with pins and guides

Sequence control

(1) It can co-exist with assembly workers

(2) It can be apparent to workers

(3) It can promote continuous improvements by workers

Fig. 9.3 In-line mechanical assembly automation concept

line automation includes the following points (Kawamura *et al.* 1993). First, large automation equipment tends to interfere in the manual assembly area and disjoint the teamwork there. Second, assembly automation in separate areas tends to create 'residual work', which is monotonous and meaningless to the workers in such areas. Third, highly sophisticated equipment tends to become a black box from direct workers' point of view. The job of teaching, operation, and maintenance of such equipment tends to be dominated by maintenance workers and engineers. Fourth, as complete automation tends to alienate human beings, continuous improvements of the process become difficult to attain. Fifth, off-line automation usually needs a large extra space for jigs and robots, as well as buffer stations before and after the process. Sixth, large automation equipment tends not to be flexible enough to model changes.

By alleviating such side effects, in-line mechanical automation for assembly lines aims at reducing manufacturing costs by saving depreciation costs, decreasing machine down time, and promoting continuous improvements (*kaizen*) by workers. It also tries to improve employee satisfaction of assembly workers by letting them control and maintain the equipment as much as possible, promoting a sense of ownership among them, minimizing 'black box', and keeping the assembly process visible from the workers' point of view. In short, in-line mechanical automation, just like the autonomous complete-line concept mentioned above, attempts to balance employee satisfaction and customer satisfaction.

TVAL (Toyota verification of assembly line) *Structures.* TVAL is an indicator that measures the work load of each assembly job quantitatively. Based on existing physiological studies, TVAL score is defined as a specific function of task-duration time, work posture, and weight of parts/tools (Shibata *et al.* 1993). Using these functions, Toyota measured TVAL score of all final assembly jobs in the company.

Function. TVAL was developed by assembly process engineering division in order to help the company make the assembly work friendly to all kinds of people regardless of age, sex, and other individual differences. By using TVAL, assembly process planners can identify physically demanding jobs in an objective manner, prioritize the work stations to be improved, and concentrate efforts for improvements (e.g. automation, power-assist devices, work design changes) on the work stations with high TVAL scores. Thus, TVAL was developed as a tool for improving physiological aspects of employee satisfaction (making assembly jobs less demanding) more efficiently and effectively.

Low-cost equipment for better work environment and work posture *Structures.* There are various tools and equipment designed for making manual assembly jobs physically less demanding and less dangerous. This category includes the following examples: height-adjustable conveyers or platforms with variable body-lifting mechanisms for achieving the best work posture for assembly task; wide floor conveyers that are synchronized with car bodies, so that workers do not have to walk while performing assembly tasks; '*raku-raku*' (comfortable) seats that eliminate crouching (i.e. physically demanding) work posture for assembly tasks inside cabins, by using a seat attached to an arm that can be reached inside the car body;—certain work design changes that aim at shifting in-cabin tasks to those performed outside the car bodies; 'wagon carts' synchronized with car bodies, which carry parts and tools, which reduces walk distance of each worker; simple power-assist equipment that reduces weight of the tools and components that workers carry; easy-to-see job instruction sheets attached to the hood of the car bodies (the instructions are printed out for each segment of the process, so that each sheet is simpler and easier to understand); and better lighting, air-conditioning, low-noise power tools, low-noise roller-friction conveyers, and other equipment for improving work environments.

Functions. These devices and equipment are mostly aimed at physically less demanding assembly work (i.e. achieving low TVAL scores), rather than productivity increase. Some of them need basic process design changes (e.g. choice of conveyer types, doorless methods), while others can be implemented through regular *kaizen* activities (e.g. *raku-raku* seats, wagon carts, power assist). Generally speaking, they are aiming at improving work conditions with reasonably low-cost equipment.

In summary, the foregoing analyses on the content and function of Toyota's new assembly system seem to indicate that the company created a new set of organizational routines that could handle the emerging environment of the 1990s, although the company also maintained and reinforced other parts of its manufacturing-development routines. The author's field studies on the other Japanese firms also indicate that Toyota is the first Japanese auto company which reorganized its assembly routines for the new era in a systematic manner.

3. Evolutionary Process of Toyota's Assembly System

Section 2 described Toyota's new assembly system as a rational response to the changes in the environment. In other words, the foregoing section made '*ex post*' explanation of the functions of the completed system. However, as the evolutionary view of the firms assumes, such *ex post* rationality of a given system does not necessarily mean that the system was built by *ex ante* rational decision-making (Fujimoto 1994*b*). It may be a result of certain trial-and-error processes, pure luck, or, most importantly, *ex post* capability of the firm. In order to assess Toyota's evolutionary capability (capability of capability-building), we have to analyse how the new assembly system emerged since the late 1980s by looking into historical and dynamic aspects of Toyota's assembly organization, but detailed analyses have to be omitted here due to limits on space (see Fujimoto 1996). Thus, this section will directly analyse patterns of evolution in the four main subsystems identified in Section 2.

Following the standard framework of problem-solving, we will first examine the process of problem recognition about the labour issue, then move on to generation and evaluation of alternative plans in several components of the new system (autonomous complete line, in-line, mechanical automation, etc.), and finally summarize the overall patterns.

3.1. Patterns of system evolution

Problem recognition   While the changes in the product market (the end of the growth era) and financial performance after 1990 were obvious to Toyota's organizational members, the changes in the labour market were much more subtle and equivocal. We will therefore focus on organizational problem recognition of the labour issues.

The problem related to attractiveness and employee satisfaction in manufacturing, particularly on the assembly lines, seems to have been recognized first by labour unions in the late 1980s.[7] When Toyota Motor Worker's Union (Toyota Roso) announced its mid-long-term action plan (Chu-choki Katsudo Hoshin) in October 1988, reduction of labour hours, new policies for ageing workers, and absorption of excess labour demand were clearly depicted, but 'attractiveness of work' was not explicitly pointed out.[8] While the quantitative aspect of labour shortage was much emphasized, the concept of assembly automation for a better quality of work environment had not been articulated.

Attractiveness of the company and its shopfloor, particularly in the assembly process, was chosen as an agenda at the Union-Management Meeting (Roshi Kondan-kai) on manufacturing issues in April 1989, which was presumably the first official meeting where the 'assembly line problem' (its attractiveness, work posture, and workload) was explicitly addressed. In the subsequent meetings on 'assembly work improvement' between union and management, the main issue was still labour shortage, but qualitative aspects of job attractiveness became an increasingly important agenda.

Toyota's management became actively involved in the 'job attractiveness' issue by the spring of 1990, when it took the initiative in creating the joint Committee for Improving Attractiveness of Production Work in May 1990. The Committee was coordinated by the Human Resource Division, whereas the Assembly Process Engineering Division was not included in the main Committee.[9] Improvements in the production work environment, as well as desirable assembly process design, were discussed.

Toyota's management side keenly recognized the assembly problem in 1990–1 partly as a result of the alarming result of the opinion surveys that the Human Resource Division had conducted bi-annually since the 1970s, as well as the turn-over record.[10] That is, the turn-over ratio jumped up (particularly at the final

---

[7]   The pressure of labour shortage itself had been recognized as a chronic problem for Toyota during the high-growth era. Also, criticism against Toyota's assembly job is not new (see e.g. Kamata 1973). Thus, it is likely that the problem was recognized by certain organizational members for a long time. This chapter will, however, focus only on the process that such problems became issues to be discussed on a company-wide basis.

[8]   The plan was prepared between 1986 and 1988.

[9]   Production Engineering Administration Dept. was included, instead.

[10]   Some plant managers were apparently recognizing the problem earlier, though. A former assembly dept. head, for example, says he recognized the problem when the number of temporary workers increased in the late 1980s. Relatively low morale of the young temporary workers at that time made him realize that the mind set of the young generation was changing, and that assembly process had to be changed accordingly.

assembly lines), and workers' subjective evaluation of job satisfaction and self-esteem dropped sharply. Thus, the early and qualitative information from the union, as well as subsequent quantitative data that the Human Resource Division collected that were reconfirming the problem, triggered a consensus-building process on the work attractiveness issue.

Also, the Project for Future Assembly Plants, in which the Assembly Process Engineering Division, the Operations Management Consulting Office, the Product Control Division, and the Human Resource Division were involved, may have functioned as the mechanism through which the awareness of the assembly problem was diffused among different divisions. The Assembly-related Division Head meeting was another means for coordinating and exchanging information among different divisions.[11]

Communication between the shopfloor organization and assembly process engineers was also strengthened in the early 1990s, facilitating diffusion of the knowledge from the shopfloor to engineering departments. In 1992, for example, core members (section head level) of the Assembly Process Engineering Division were dispatched to work on the assembly lines to gain direct experiences about the work load and resulting fatigue. This helped the process engineers acquire tacit knowledge on the nature of the assembly work, which was used subsequently for development of TVAL.

To sum up, the problems on assembly lines, which existed at least potentially on the shopfloor for a long time, were recognized as a main issue for the company first by the labour union in the late 1980s, while the management side, interfaced by the Human Resource Division, became increasingly concerned about the problems around 1990. This problem awareness was subsequently diffused to other sections through the Project for Future Assembly Plants, Assembly head meetings, participation of process engineers in direct assembly work, and so on. Also, it should be noted that the focus of the issue shifted from the quantitative aspect of labour shortages to qualitative (and more profound) aspects of the problem. Thus, organizational problem awareness itself evolved over time in both width and depth.

Autonomous complete process: *ex post* synthesis   Detailed historical analyses of the new assembly concept (Fujimoto 1996) indicates that there are various patterns of evolution (Figure 9.4). Let us now examine different patterns in the cases of the autonomous-complete process, in-line automation, TVAL, and ergonomic devices.

The case of the autonomous process may be summarized as '*ex post* synthesis'. That is, the system concept emerged as a result of synthesis of various elements, each of which was developed for various reasons. Some of the elements were not developed as components of the autonomous system, but were reinterpreted and adopted after they were developed. In this sense, the evolution of the autonomous-complete line appears to be '*ex post* synthesis' (Figure 9.4).

---

[11] Assembly Dept. heads of seven factories, as well as heads of the Human Resource Dept., Assembly Process Engineering Dept., Safety and Health Management Dept.., Production Control Dept., and Operations Management Consulting Office were the members of the Assembly-related Division Head Meeting as of 1990.

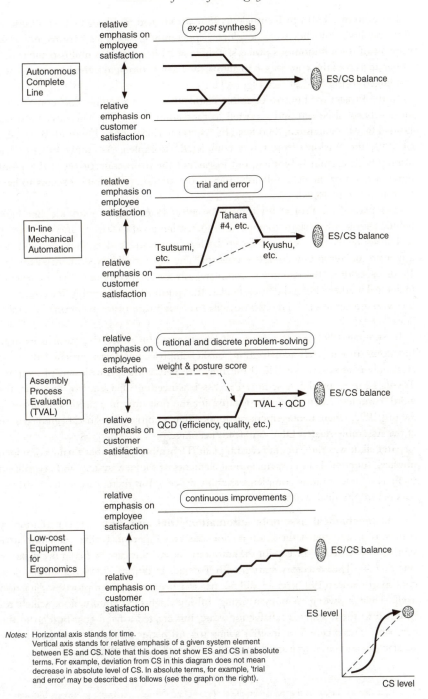

Fig. 9.4 Types of evolutionary paths toward ES/CS balance

For example, TMM in Kentucky (1988) already had multi-segment and buffered assembly lines, but they were developed apparently for logistics reasons, not as an element of the autonomous process. Tahara no. 4 line was also multi-segment with buffer areas, but the concept of an autonomous and complete assembly process was not linked to this lay-out (see Figure 9.5).

In the Project for Future Assembly Plants, the 'short assembly line' concept had already been discussed and reported in the summer of 1990. The discussion was headed by Mr. Shiramizu, then head of Assembly Engineering Division. By the end of 1991, the 'Vision' Project was completed. 'Complete Assembly Process' had already been examined by then, but it was not the main concept yet at this point. Simplification of the assembly jobs to absorb variation proliferation seems to have been more emphasized.

As a part of the Project for Future Assembly Plants, plant A's model line high-lighted simple job designs to cope with increasing product variety and complexity, and it addressed the issue of group leaders and team leaders, but they did not articulate the autonomy-complete concept. The Motomachi experiment in the late 1980s did address the issue of a 'complete' job for each component at the level of individual workers, but it did not articulate the 'autonomous' assembly line concept at the work-group level.[12] The Motomachi trial was made on conventional assembly lines.

By summer 1992, the concept of 'complete assembly process', as well as its main functions (morale, self-actualization, quality improvement) was articulated in the Assembly-related Division Head meetings, as well as the plant design process for Toyota Kyushu by the Assembly Process Engineering Division For example, the word 'complete assembly line' appeared for the first time in a union document in August 1992, where management responded that 'complete line' had been discussed at the Assembly-related Division Head meetings.[13]

After all, it was the Toyota Kyushu plant (December 1992) that finally combined physical, functional, and organizational elements of the new system and crystallized them as an autonomous-complete assembly process. But there were many predecessors before the final synthesis occurred.

In-line mechanical assembly automation: trial and error   The evolutionary pattern of in-line mechanical automation was very different. Unlike the cumulative synthesis observed in the case of the autonomous line, this case looked more dialectic (Figure 9.4). The trajectory started with Toyota's traditional 'low-cost automation' concept (Fujimoto 1997), which did not pay much attention to employee satisfaction itself. Then it swung to human-fitting 'off-line high-tech' automation, which responded to the employee satisfaction issue, but created a fixed-cost burden to the company. Then there was another swing toward better balance between customer satisfaction and employee satisfaction: in-line mechanical automation.

---

[12] Note that the origin of the 'parts-complete' concept and the 'autonomous' concept are different.
[13] Motomachi plant took initiative on this theme.

Takaoka 1

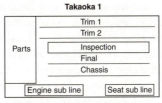

Parts are supplied only from left side.

TMM 1

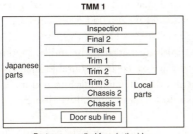

Parts are supplied from both sides.

Tahara 4

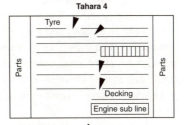

Lines are divided at ➤

Parts are supplied from both sides.

Kyushu Miyata

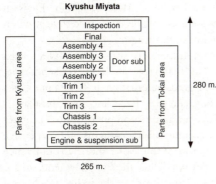

265 m.

Motomachi 2 (new)

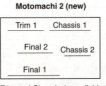

Trim and Chassis 1 are divided.
Inspection process is in other building.

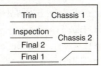

Motomachi 2 (old)

Trim and Chassis 1 are connected.
There is the inspection process in
the building.

TMM 2

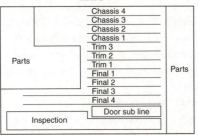

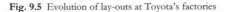

Fig. 9.5 Evolution of lay-outs at Toyota's factories

There were at least two different motivations for the previous off-line automation concept which was pursued in the assembly automation experiment in 1988 to 1991. First, production engineers' desire to develop and implement advanced technologies, stimulated by the European cases of FIAT and VW, is often pointed out. Such a 'technology-push' approach may have also been promoted by the culture of the Tools and Equipment Development group (no. 1 Machine Making Division; now Mechatronics Systems Division), which naturally tends to be equipment-oriented rather than process-oriented.

The second major motivation for drastic assembly automation in the experiment of 1988–91 was to absorb excess labour demand that had been predicted then. In 1989, for example, Toyota predicted that it would need 6,000 more employees in the next five years, and that it would have to absorb a half of this shortage by automation. Thus, the fear of labour shortage, both by management and by union, led to the idea of maximizing automation ratio at any cost. Favourable financial conditions of the bubble era also amplified this mood for maximizing automation. As production volume started to decrease and cash flow shrank, this motivation clearly retreated.

Assembly automation at Tahara no. 4 line has at least three origins: (i) rather small-scale assembly automation developed gradually by Assembly Automation Division (e.g. gas tank, battery, air-conditioner, etc.); (ii) large-scale automation tested for the first time at the off-line automation experiment by no. 1 Machine Making Division (e.g. decking, tire, etc.); (iii) other sources such as foreign auto makers (e.g. wind-screen sealer). Path (ii) tended to be emphasized, though.

As for assembly automation at Tahara no. 4, there are two different views even among production engineers at Toyota. The first view emphasizes discontinuity between Tahara no. 4 and Toyota Kyushu, regards automation at Tahara no. 4 as a deviation from traditional Toyota philosophy, and sees the in-line mechanical auto-mation at Kyushu as return to basics of Toyota's automation philosophy. The cases of engine installation and tire installation, gigantic off-line systems with expensive vision-sensing for alignment, are often cited as examples of the sharp difference between the Tahara concept and Kyushu concept. Thus, the first view tends to see Tahara no. 4 as a 'straw man' while highlighting legitimacy of the in-line mechanical automation.

The second view, by contrast, emphasizes continuity between Tahara and Kyushu, points out that Toyota constantly made trial and error in developing its production systems in the past, sees the above case of engine and tires as just another example of Toyota's trial and error, and insists that the main stream of assembly process designs at Tahara were on the right track of evolution.

In a sense, the first view is a 'paradigm shift' hypothesis, while the second is a 'progressive evolution' hypothesis. Both camps, however, appreciate the value of assembly automation at Tahara Plant no. 4 as precursor of the in-line mechanical automation at Kyushu plant. In other words, even those who criticize Tahara's automation concept normally admit that Tahara's automation experiments enabled the new automation concept at Kyushu and Motomachi.

In any case, the lessons of off-line high-tech automation at Tahara no. 4 line, which had been clear by the spring of 1991, were fully taken into account in the basic design process of Toyota Kyushu's in-line automation by the assembly process engineers. Note also that the experiments for in-line assembly automation were conducted by the Assembly Process Engineering Division, as opposed to no.1 Machine Making Division (Mechatronics Systems Division) that took charge of the off-line automation experiments, which may reflect the shift from the equipment-oriented (technology-push) approach to the process-oriented (demand-pull) approach for assembly automation at Toyota.

TVAL: rational and discrete problem-solving   The case of TVAL shows a smooth pattern of *ex ante* rational problem-solving, rather than *ex post* synthesis (i.e. autonomous line) or dialectic trial and error (i.e. in-line automation). That is, TVAL was developed by engineers in Assembly and Design for the Manufacturing Engineering Division in response to a clearly defined goal of developing a systematic tool for measuring workload from a physiological or ergonomic point of view (Shibata *et al.* 1993).[14] TVAL was also based partly on existing scientific knowledge in the academic community, partly on Toyota's existing measurement system (posture and weight scores), and partly on deliberate experiments that the engineers conducted. Although there may have been trial and error at the microscopic level, it would be possible to regard the development process of TVAL as a cycle of *ex ante* rational problem-solving by process engineers.

In a broader context, development of TVAL may be regarded as an evolutionary path of Toyota's systems for measuring and evaluating assembly processes and tasks. In the past, Toyota's evaluation criteria were concentrated almost exclusively in the domain of customer satisfaction, such as efficiency, quality, delivery, and flexibility, as well as their improvements. It was argued that Toyota system was human-oriented, but this simply meant that value of human activities can be enhanced by reducing non-value activities (*muda*). Thus, reducing *muda* almost automatically meant increasing productivity and increasing human value at the same time in the tradition of Toyota production system. There were no independent criteria that measured employee satisfaction or job attractiveness.

In the final assembly area, also, efficiency was the most important criterion for evaluating shopfloor performance. There was an index that measured workload for each task, called work posture and weight score, developed by the Safety and Health Administration Division, but this was virtually a minimum standard from a safety point of view. In this regard, development of TVAL can be seen as the company's rational effort to balance evaluation criteria for customer satisfaction and those for employee satisfaction in response to the changes in the labour market (Figure 9.4).

---

[14] Mr. Shiramizu, Dept. head and director in charge of assembly process engineering since 1992, took a clear leadership in development of TVAL. He insists that current TVAL, as of 1995, is only 60% complete, as it does not capture full aspects of assembly workload and fatigue. TVAL needs further development, according to him.

Equipment for better work posture: continuous improvements   Finally, let us examine the patterns of various low-cost equipment and tools for better ergonomics, such as '*raku-raku*' seat, wagon carts, power assist tools, etc. The cases of recent human-friendly factories indicate that the framework of continuous and company-wide improvements (i.e. *kaizen*), which is one of Toyota's traditional capabilities, can be directly applicable to such tools and equipment for better work posture, better work environment, and lighter workload. Based on the objective evaluation of each job and each task by TVAL and other measures, workers, team leaders, group leaders, maintenance workers, plant engineers, and so on, individually or collectively create or modify systems for better ergonomics on a continuous basis, just like Toyota's ordinary *kaizen* for quality and productivity.

For example, Toyota Kyushu plant, after its production started in 1992, has continued improvements in this direction. In 1993, the plant started to introduce wagon carts, and solved an alignment problem at the tire automation equipment by *kaizen*. In 1994, it introduced four *raku-raku* seats, and increased the number of wagon carts that are designed mostly for the workers. In 1995, two-hour job rotation was adopted, and a tool was developed for interior parts, both for ergonomic purposes. As a result of these and other efforts, the number of high workload jobs (TVAL score > 35 points) decreased gradually from 95 in 1993 to 89 in 1994, and to 85 in 1995.

In this way, low-cost tools for better ergonomics help the assembly shopfloor achieve a better balance between customer satisfaction and employee satisfaction through a path of incremental improvements (Figure 9.4).

Summary of the evolutionary process   We have analysed the patterns of evolutionary paths from four aspects of Toyota's new assembly system, including the autonomous-complete assembly line concept, in-line mechanical automation, TVAL for measuring workload, and low-cost equipment for better ergonomics. Four different patterns of system evolution were identified, corresponding to the four elements of the system: *ex post* synthesis, trial and error, rational problem-solving, and incremental improvements (Figure 9.4). Thus, we can summarize the foregoing analyses as follows:

(1) *Variety in the evolutionary paths.* The first conclusion is that there is no single pattern that can summarize the emergence of the new assembly system at Toyota. We can infer from this pattern that Toyota's distinctive evolutionary capabilities do not lie in its specific way of controlling system changes. Toyota's dynamic capability may be a more generic ability to harness various evolutionary patterns, including rational and discrete problem-solving, continuous improvements, dialectic paths of trial and error, or more chaotic process of *ex post* synthesis.

(2) *Consistency in ex post rationality.* Despite the variety of the evolutionary trajectories, the function of the resulting system seems to be quite consistent in that all the elements of the new assembly system are aiming at better balance between customer satisfaction and employee satisfaction. In a sense, they are coherent components of what the authors may call a 'lean-on-balance' production system (Fujimoto 1994*a*; Fujimoto and Takeishi 1994).

(3) *Export capability is key.* What follows from the above discussion is that Toyota's evolutionary capability is *ex post* capability (Fujimoto 1994*b*). As explained earlier, by *ex post* capability we mean the ability of an organization to integrate intended or unintended trials that have been already made, refine them or reinterpret them, and make a coherent and *ex post* rational system out of them. The foregoing cases also indicate that Toyota has *ex ante* rational capabilities (i.e. capabilities of making rational choices before it makes trials) in some cases, but it cannot rely on the *ex ante* rationality in all cases. *Ex ante* rationality is not a necessary condition for explaining *ex post* rationality of a system, either. When we observe a variety in the paths of system emergence and consistency in the rationality of the resulting system, what matters is, after all, the *ex post* capability of the firm.

3.2. *Anatomy of Toyota's dynamic capability*

We have so far identified various patterns of the evolution of the system in the case of Toyota's new assembly concept, and argued that what is essential in this case is Toyota's *ex post* dynamic capability. By *ex post* capability we mean a firm-specific ability to build a certain system that is *ex post* rational out of elements of various origins. In the present case, we have illustrated different patterns of evolutionary trajectories (*ex post* synthesis, trial and error, *ex ante* rational problem-solving, etc.) in different elements of the system (autonomous lines, in-line automation, TVAL, etc.).

A question that still remains, however, is what constitutes Toyota's unique and dynamic capability. Although we need further empirical research to answer this question, we propose some preliminary ideas here.

Variety of opinions inside Toyota The foregoing description of the evolution of the system does not fit the stereotyped view that Toyota is always a monolithic organization. In many aspects of environmental perceptions, evaluation of alternatives, and interpretation of solutions, there seem to be significant disagreements inside Toyota. For example, the problem of assembly work attractiveness appears to have been recognized by different organizational units at different times. The problem that assembly line work is not attractive enough (or even boring, tiring, meaningless, and self-alienating) apparently existed at least potentially or partially on the shopfloor, but neither management nor union recognized it as a central issue until the late 1980s, when union leaders did, through their direct channels with their rank-and-file members. The Human Resource Division, through its communications with the union, as well as a result of its own surveys on employee satisfaction and turn-over ratios, recognized it as a critical issue. Most of the managers and engineers in other parts are likely to have lagged behind them.

There have also been disagreements over evaluation of the assembly automation at Tahara no. 4 line, even among production engineers, as described earlier. Some argued that the plant was a symbol of Toyota's mismanagement in production engineering, which was influenced by the atmosphere of the bubble economy. For them, Tahara no. 4 was a temporary, but significant, deviation from Toyota's manufacturing tradition, and was subsequently overcome by a newer assembly concept represented by Kyushu and Motomachi.

Others, however, insist that assembly technologies at Tahara no. 4 essentially belong to the mainstream of Toyota's evolutionary trajectory. They insist that there were only a few cases of obvious over-automation, namely tire and engine and transmission installation, which they think were exaggerated. For them, such trial and error itself is nothing but the tradition of Toyota engineering.

Still another example of disagreement is found in the evaluation of the new assembly line concept itself. For those who emphasize continuity of the Toyota production system (TPS), the new assembly concept is just another variation of TPS. For them, TPS has always pursued both efficiency and human dignity, and so does the new assembly system. For those who emphasize discontinuity, however, the recent trend is a departure from the traditional Toyota production system, in that the new assembly concept identified employee satisfaction as an independent value from efficiency for the first time. One manager described it as an 'amendment of Toyota's constitution'.

Shared views in evaluation of the result   Despite the variety of views on various aspects of decision-making for changing the assembly concept, we also found that the evaluation of the resulting assembly system has been strikingly uniform among different organizational units. All of those whom we interviewed, including production engineers, operations management consulting staff, human resource managers, plant general managers, union leaders, plant general managers, groups leaders and team leaders, said they liked the new assembly system, and evaluated it highly. Some may ascribe this to the Toyota's culture of strong group conformity, but then we cannot explain the existence of significant disagreements in other areas mentioned above.

There is also a striking conformity in the interpretation of the current labour environment among managers, engineers, and union leaders at Toyota: all of those whom we interviewed regarded the need for attractiveness of the workplace as a long-term objective despite recent recession and potential labour surplus. They all explained that the assembly line problem was revealed by the labour shortage in the bubble economy era, but the problem itself exists regardless of economic booms or recessions. Thus, managers, engineers, and union leaders all share the long-term commitment to higher employee satisfaction.

In this regard, what we may have to explain seems to be the paradox that exists between disagreements in the system evolution process and agreement in the results of the process.

Organizational mechanisms for convergence   What is inferred from the above paradox of disagreements and conformity at Toyota is that the company may have an effective convergence mechanism that can quickly convert a variety of organizational elements into a coherent system. Although this chapter cannot present sufficient evidence, we identify at least three elements of this organizational capability: shared basic values, horizontal convergence, and vertical convergence.

(1) *Shared values and evaluation criteria.* Toyota is often said to have basic values shared by its members. Although they are seldom articulated, the basic values may be described as customer-orientation, cost-consciousness, spirit of manufacturing (*mono-zukuri*), and so on. They may be ascribed to the philosophy of Toyota's entrepreneur-founder Sakichi Toyoda or Kichiro Toyoda, or to the heritage of the Ford production system, or they may have been shaped as a result of day-to-day activities in TPS or TQC. In any case, it is likely that Toyota has stable and commonly shared values that are deeply ingrained among many of its members, despite changes and varieties in specific opinions and practices on the surface (Mishina 1995).

(2) *Vertical convergence: quasi-market mechanism inside organization.* Shared values may not be enough to explain Toyota's unique organizational capabilities in system evolution. We suspect that, in addition, there are certain strong 'convergence mechanisms', both vertical and horizontal, at Toyota (Figure 9.6). By vertical convergence we mean a 'quasi-market' of new ideas that appears to exist in the production area. In this case, the shopfloor organizations (*seisan-genba*), whose core part consists of group leaders (*kumi-cho*) and team leaders (*han-cho*), have ultimate legitimacy to choose new production ideas. The analogy that Toyota often uses, 'the downstream process is your customer', is applied to the case of new production ideas.

In the case of new production equipment, for example, production engineers have to 'sell' the new idea embodied in the equipment to the shopfloor organization. Just like customer sovereignty, the shopfloor organization (*genba*) is said to make a final judgement on whether they accept it or reject it. If the equipment does not fit their way of making things, it may be literally discarded or ignored. We have actually heard of some cases in which such scrapping of new equipment happened in the past. This sharply contrasts with many other manufacturers, where plant equipment, once installed is sacred, untouchable, and, of course, un-movable from the shopfloor's point of view.

One important aspect of this quasi-market of new production ideas is that the shopfloor organizations themselves are customer-oriented partly as a result of continuous penetration of the Toyota production system there. The Operations Management Consulting Division, TPS *shusa* at the plant and other educators and promoters of TPS keep on refreshing this concept. In a sense, it may be possible to say that Toyota's shopfloor organization represents both employee's and customer's interests.

Facing this type of shopfloor organization, production engineers tend to become 'customer-oriented' and try harder to develop production technologies that are more friendly to the shopfloor people. The comments of Toyota's engineer the at Vehicle and Design for Manufacturing Division that he is process-design-oriented rather than equipment-oriented, and that he emphasizes shopfloor efficiency over automation ratios, seem to be consistent with the above description of the 'supplier–customer' relations between production engineers and shopfloor organizations. Also, some plant managers say that the cases of the plant people throwing away

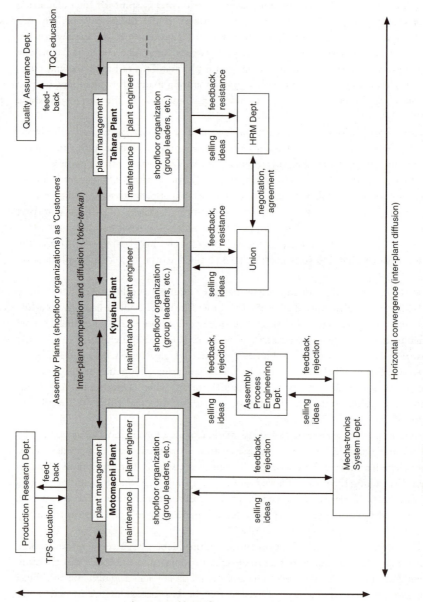

Fig. 9.6 Convergence mechanisms at Toyota's manufacturing organizations (assembly)

new equipment that production engineers installed has become rare in recent years, indicating that production engineers have become shopfloor-oriented.

Another recent example of the shopfloor sovereignty (*genba-shugi*) is the introduction of the continuous two-shift system to Toyota's two-shift factories.[15] The continuous two shifts were introduced to new Toyota Kyushu Inc. in 1992 and were well received as a worker-friendly arrangement. Both union and management at Toyota Motor Corporation, Toyota Kyushu's mother company, quickly agreed that it should also introduce this system. Despite this consensus between both union and management, it took them about two years to finally introduce the continuous two shifts in 1995. This was because the shopfloor people were not persuaded easily. They tended to be afraid of changes in lifestyle, loss of overtime premiums, and other negative aspects of the new system. The union and the Human Resource Division, using their respective channels, approached the shopfloor and tenaciously tried to persuade them. This seems to more than indicate that new systems cannot be introduced without shopfloor consensus (particularly that of group leaders, team leaders, and veteran workers) at Toyota. This kind of shopfloor veto power in the quasi-market inside the company may facilitate the vertical convergence process.

(3) *Horizontal convergence: inter-plant exchange of information.* Promising production ideas, that may be accepted by the management, union, and shopfloor, tend to be quickly disseminated across the plants through various channels, including special projects, management–union meetings, manager meetings at the corporate level (e.g. Assembly Division Head meeting), special projects, rotation of plant general managers (production executives), and so on. At Toyota, horizontal expansion of new ideas, policies, and technologies across the plants is often emphasized as '*yoko-tenkai*' or '*yoko-ten*'.

To sum up, what constitutes Toyota's evolutionary capability is difficult to articulate, but the coexistence of organizational variety and conformity, which is linked by effective convergence mechanisms, both vertical and horizontal, seems to explain at least partially why Toyota historically tended to outperform the other Japanese makers in coming up with coherent, rational, and new systems (Fujimoto 1994*b*). Further empirical and historical research would be needed to confirm this, but the current case of the new assembly automation seems to be at least consistent with this description of Toyota's dynamic capabilities.

Standardization and documentation   Finally, it should be noted that a part of Toyota's dynamic capability may be ascribed to standardization and documentation, which are often regarded as components of bureaucracy and as counteractive. As shown in its *kaizen* activities and company rule systems, Toyota is a company that has highly standardized routine problem-solving processes (e.g. continuous improvements) and developed documentation systems (a kind of organizational memory storage). Although they may sound contradictory to dynamic capability, we would

---

[15] Toyota had adopted a complete day-and-night two-shift system, which included production work after midnight.

argue that standardization of regular problem-solving and systematic documentation of the results are essential components of dynamic capability.

In this sense, we do not follow a stereotyped dichotomy that simply contrasts bureaucracy and innovation. After all, repetition (i.e. standardization) and retention (i.e. organizational memory in the form of documents and others) are basic elements of the evolutionary process.

3.3. Summary: an internal evolutionary mechanism

The above analyses of the organizational process and culture lead us to an idea that this company has an effective *internal evolutionary mechanism* that consists of variation, screening, retention, and diffusion (propagation) of organizational routines inside the company. According to the evolutionary view of the firm, manufacturing companies are facing the external evolutionary mechanisms through which new variants of products, services, jobs, etc., that they offer are constantly evaluated and screened by the changing external environment, and routines are retained and diffused into other firms in the long run. The foregoing case of Toyota seems to indicate that there is an internal process of variety generation, screening, retention, and diffusion, which more or less reflect this external evolutionary process.[16]

In this process, the employees of the company create various short-term solutions to a variety of manufacturing problems in a variety of ways. At this stage the solutions and intentions behind them may be diversified and inconsistent, reflecting diversity of the environment and departmental cultures (Lawrence and Lorsch 1967). In this way, the organizational members bring the external diversity into the organization in the form of various unpolished solutions. When the aggregate of problem findings and tentative solutions lead to a recognition by certain key managers that a company-wide problem has surfaced, various convergence mechanisms are triggered at various levels of the organization, as well as between the company and the union. Different solutions from various areas of the company are brought into the meetings, adjusted to the other solutions, and refined as a part of the total solution. The integrated solution has also to be arranged so that it can pass the informal screen of shopfloor leaders, who themselves are trained to be not only employee-oriented but also customer-oriented. More generally, consciousness of customer satisfaction and competitiveness is prevalent in the entire organization, which functions as a common criterion for screening and refinement. The refined solutions are retained as standards and procedures, and are diffused quickly to the entire plant network. At this stage, we observe a remarkable uniformity and consistency in both solutions and their rationales.

The foregoing case of Toyota's new assembly system seems to be consistent with the above explanation as an internal evolutionary mechanism. The variety of opinions corresponds to internal *variation*; the vertical convergence implies an internal *selection* mechanism that effectively reflects the nature of the external selection

---

[16] For external evolutionary process, see, for example, Nelson (1982). For internal evolutionary process, see Weick (1979), Nonaka (1985), Burgelman (1994), etc.

environments, and shared values would mean consistency of internal selection criteria; the horizontal convergence (*yoko-ten*) is nothing but rapid *diffusion* of selected new routines; and the standardization and documentation bring about a solid *retention* mechanism of organizational routines. Overall, the internal evolutionary process built into the company's organization, which precedes the external selection process, seems to be what lies behind the firm-specific evolutionary capability.

4. Implications

The present chapter explored Toyota's new assembly automation systems that emerged from the environmental changes since the late 1980s. We have identified components of the system, or new organizational routines, including the autonomous-complete assembly line, the in-line mechanical automation concept, TVAL, and low-cost equipment for better ergonomics, and explained its *ex post* rationality in terms of balancing customer satisfaction and employee satisfaction.

Through this analysis of Toyota's recent history in assembly operations, we have reached certain conclusions. First, we argue that Toyota's distinctive capabilities in manufacturing include not only static capability and improvement capability of the existing system (e.g. TPS and TQC), but also dynamic capabilities of making new systems (Fujimoto 1994*b*). In other words, Toyota's capability of facilitating the system evolution process should be emphasized. It can be regarded as a certain problem-solving competence.

Second, the changes do not always result from deliberate and rational problem-solving processes. Trial and error, disagreements, unintended success, and *ex post* synthesis of *ad hoc* elements are quite common in the evolutionary process of manufacturing systems, even when the resulting new system appears rational. In this sense, Toyota's distinctive dynamic capabilities include *ex post* capabilities.

Third, the stereotypical notion that Toyota is always a monolithic organization seems to be a myth. Although there is a striking uniformity in some core values and philosophies, there are also disagreements in other areas, particularly when major system changes occur. This paradox has to be explained in order to understand the essence of Toyota's dynamic capabilities.

Fourth, both vertical and horizontal convergence mechanisms seem to be functioning, bridging the variety and conformity mentioned above. Vertical convergence means a certain quasi-market mechanism, where shopfloor organization has 'consumer sovereignty' for new production ideas (i.e. *genba-shugi*). Horizontal convergence means intense exchange of information across the plants (i.e. *yoko-tenkai*). They may be also regarded as certain intra-organizational mechanisms for selection and diffusion of emerging routines in the context of the evolutionary theory of the firm.

Fifth, we would argue that standardization and documentation are not always enemies of dynamic system changes. They may sometimes be essential elements of dynamic organizational capabilities.

The above propositions are by no means confirmed. Further empirical research is needed. The foregoing analysis nevertheless seems to indicate that the evolutionary capability that the author has identified in the previous historical studies up to the 1980s (Fujimoto 1994*b*, 1995) still exists in the 1990s. Also, the foregoing analysis seems to reveal a part of the organizational processes that are going on inside the black box called the dynamic capability. In this sense, the the emergence of a new assembly system at Toyota seems to be a good first step in this direction.

One of the basic assumptions of the evolutionary perspective in general is that *ex ante* recognition of the system functions by the system builder does not always explain the origin of the system. That is, the *ex post* rationality of a system does not necessarily mean *ex ante* rationality of the system creator. The results of this chapter, an effort to link production and operations management (POM) and the evolutionary theories of the firm, seem to be generally consistent with such an assumption. In this sense, Toyota seems to be a company that has a distinctive capability to handle this complex evolutionary process better than most of its competitors.

References

Burgelman, R. A. (1994). 'Fading Memories: A Process Theory of Strategic Business Exit in Dynamic Environments', *Administrative Science Quarterly*, 39: 24–56.

Chandler, A. D. (1990). *Scale and Scope*. Cambridge, Mass.: Harvard University Press.

—— (1992). 'What Is a Firm?' *European Economic Review*, 36: 483–92.

Dosi, G. (1982). 'Technological Paradigms and Technological Trajectories', *Research Policy*, 11: 147–62.

Fujimoto, T. (1994*a*). 'The Limits of Lean Production', *Politik und Gesellschaft*, Friedrich-Ebert-Stiftung, Germany, Jan.: 40–6.

—— (1994*b*). 'Reinterpreting the Resource-Capability View of the Firm: A Case of the Development-Production Systems of the Japanese Auto Makers', Discussion Paper, Tokyo University Faculty of Economics, 94-F-20. (Presented at Prince Bertil Symposium, Stockholm School of Economics, June.) In *Dynamic Firm*, forthcoming from Oxford University Press.

—— (1995). 'Note on the Origin of the "Black Box Parts" Practice in the Japanese Auto Inudstry', in H. Shiomi and K. Wada (eds.), *Fordism Transformed: The Development of Production Methods in the Automobile Industry*. Oxford: Oxford University Press.

—— (1996). 'An Evolutionary Process of Toyota's Final Assembly Operations: The Role of Ex-post Dynamic Capabilities', Discussion Paper, Tokyo University Faculty of Economics, 96-F-xx. (Presented at Third International Workshop on Assembly Automation, Ca' Foscari University of Venice, Oct. 1995.)

—— (1997). 'Strategies for Assembly Automation in the Automobile Industry', in K. Shimokawa, U. Juergens, and T. Fujimoto (eds.), *Transforming Automobile Assembly*. Springer-Verlag: 211–37.

—— and A. Takeishi (1994). *Jidosha Sangyo 21 Seiki he no Shinario* (The Automobile Industry: A Scenario toward the 21st Century). Tokyo: Seisansei Shuppan.

Grant, R. (1991). 'The Resource-Based Theory of Competitive Advantage: Implications for Strategy Formulation', *California Management Review* (June): 114–35.

Kamata, S. (1973). *Jidoha Zetsubo Kojo* (The Automobile Plant of Desperation). Gendaishi Shuppankai.

Kawamura, T., A. Niimi, N. Hisada, and T. Kuzuhara (1993). 'Korekara no Hito ga Shuyaku no Kumitate Rain Zukuri (Coming Worker Friendly Factory)', *Toyota Technical Review*, 43(2): 86–91.

Kojima, T. (1994). *Cho Lean Kakumei* (The Ultra-Lean Revolution). Tokyo: Nohon Keizai Shinbun-sha (in Japanese).

Lawrence, P. R., and J. W. Lorsh (1967). *Organization and Environment*. Homewood, Ill: Richard D. Irwin.

Leonard-Barton, D. (1992). 'Core Capabilities and Core Rigidities: A Paradox in Managing New Product Development', *Strategic Management Journal*, 13: 111–25.

Mintzberg, H. (1987). 'Crafting Strategy', *Harvard Business Review*, July–Aug.

——and J. A. Waters (1985). 'Of Strategies, Deliberate and Emergent', *Strategic Management Journal*, 6(3): 257–72.

Nelson, R. R., and S. G. Winter (1982). *An Evolutionary Theory of Economic Change*. Cambridge, Mass.: Belknap, Harvard University Press.

Niimi, A., K. Miyoshi, T. Ishii, T. Araki, K. Uchida, and I. Ota (1994). 'Jidoka Kumitate Rain ni Okeru Jiritsu Kanketsu Kotei no Kakuritsu' (Establishment of Autonomous Complete

Process Planning for Automobile Assembly Line), *Toyota Technical Review*, 44(2): 86–91 (in Japanese).

Nonaka, I. (1985). *Kigyo Shinkaron* (The Theory of Corporate Evolution). Tokyo: Nihon Keizai Shinbun-sha (in Japanese).

Ogawa, E. (ed.) (1994). Toyota Seisan Hoshiki no Kenkyu (A Study of Toyota Production System). Tokyo: Nihon Keizai Shinbun-sha (in Japanese).

Penrose, E. T. (1959). *The Theory of the Growth of the Firm*. Oxford: Blackwell.

Prahalad, C. K., and G. Hamel (1990). 'The Core Competence of the Corporation.' *Harvard Business Review* (May): 79–91.

Shibata, F., K. Imayoshi, Y. Eri, and S. Ogata (1993). 'Kumitate Sagyo Futan no Teiryo Hyokaho (TVAL)no Kaihatsu' (Development of Assembly Load Verification), *Toyota Technical Review*, 43(1): 84–9 (in Japanese).

Shimizu, K. (1995). 'La trajectoire de Toyota de 1974 a 1994: Du Toyotisme au nouveau Toyotisme', *Automobile Firms Trajectories The New Industrial Models* (The New Industrial Models). Paris: GERPISA, 15–17 June.

Teece, D. J., Pisano, G., and Shuen, A. (1992). 'Dynamic Capabilities and Strategic Management', revised, June 1992. Working Paper, University of California at Berkeley.

——R. Rumelt, G. Dosi, and S. Winter (1994) 'Understanding Corporate Coherence: Theory and Evidence', *Journal of Economic Behavior and Organization*, 23: 1–30.

Toyota Motor Corporation (1994). 'Atarashii Jidosha Kumitate Rain no Kaihatsu' (Development of New Vehicle Assembly System). *Dai 40-kai Okochi-sho Jusho Gyoseki Hokoku-sho* (Reports of Achievements in Industrialization Awarded the Okochi Memorial Prize 1994), Okochi Memorial Foundation: 99–109.

Weick, K. E. (1979). *The Social Psychology of Organizing*. Reading, Mass.: Addison-Wesley.

10

Transfer and Replication of Organizational Capabilities: Japanese Transplant Organizations in the United States

RICHARD FLORIDA AND MARTIN KENNEY

Abstract

Organizational theory has long held that it is difficult to transfer organizations from one environment to another and that organizations that are transferred will take on characteristics of the new environment. We argue that organizations have the capabilities and the resources to transfer and to some degree replicate key capabilities in a new environment, and further to alter those environments in light of their functional requirements. We explore the question of organizational transfer and replication through the lens of a specific class of transplant organizations—Japanese automotive assembly plants and their suppliers in the United States. We believe that these transplant organizations provide an ideal case to explore such questions because they represent organizations which are being transferred from a supportive to a foreign environment. We find that these Japanese automotive transplants have effectively transferred and to some degree replicated key organizational forms and capabilities at both the intra- and inter-organizational levels.

1. Introduction

The relationship between organizations and their external environment has long been a central issue in organizational theory. Generally speaking, organization theory suggests that organizations are closely tied to their environments, that it is difficult to transfer organizations from one environment to another, and that organizations tend to adapt to and take on characteristics of the surrounding environment.

In this chapter, we explore the transfer and replication of key organizational forms and capabilities. Drawing from a decade-long study of Japanese-affiliated automotive 'transplants' in the USA, we advance the hypothesis that such forms and capabilities can be taken from an original environment and implanted into a new one. Furthermore, we argue that certain types of organizations have sufficient resources and capabilities to alter the new environment in light of their functional requirements.

The research on which this chapter is based was funded by the Alfred P. Sloan Foundation, National Science Foundation, US Department of Agriculture, and the Ohio Board of Regents. Paul Osterman supplied the data from his 1992 survey of US manufacturing establishments. Davis Jenkins directed the 1994 study and Michael Massagli oversaw the survey administration for the 1994 transplant survey. Donald Smith, James Curry, W. Richard Goe, James Gordon, and Mitsumasa Motoya contributed to various phases of the research.

The research examined the transfer of key intra- and inter-organizational practices in light of three related research questions: (i) To what degree can organizations transfer and replicate key practices and capabilities in a new environment? (ii) What strategies do organizations utilize to respond to, and cope with, a new environment? (iii) Do they take on characteristics of the environment, or, if not, how do they act on the new environment to bring it into line with their needs? Our research is based on two major studies of the Japanese transplants in the USA: an initial study of the Japanese automotive transplants and their component parts suppliers conducted in 1988, and a 1994 study of the transfer and adoption of organizational practices by Japanese-affiliated transplants in all manufacturing industries which also included comparison with US manufacturing organizations. Transplants are ideally suited to this study of organizational transfer and replication since they represent organizations that have been transferred from one environment to another.

2. Theoretical Context

Organization theory suggests that organizations that are transferred from one environment to another will take on characteristics of the new environment. While some studies argue for a tight, deterministic connection between environment and organizations, most theorists suggest that organizations gradually take on characteristics of the new environment and/or of organizations with which they interact (Meyer and Rowan 1977; Zucker 1977; DiMaggio and Powell 1983; Granovetter 1985; Hannan and Freeman 1988).

Relatively few theorists focus explicitly on organizational influences on the environment. In his classic studies of innovation in capitalism, Schumpeter (1947) differentiated between *creative* responses that alter social and economic situations and the more typical *adaptive* responses of firms and economic organizations. Pfeffer and Salancik (1978) suggested that while organizations tend to adapt to their environments, they will sometimes alter the environment in line with their needs. Weick (1979) argued that the ability of an organization to influence, construct, or *enact* its environment is a function of size. Young (1988) suggested that organizations can change their environments by strategic use of resources.

The literature on Japanese organizations was generally pessimistic regarding their transfer. It basically argued that Japanese organizations derive from cultural factors such as homogeneity, familism, and group loyalty (Benedict 1946; Nakane 1970). For Abegglen (1958), Japanese organizational characteristics like team-based work organization and long-term tenure reflected a general close alignment between persons and groups. Dore (1973) contrasted the Japanese model of *welfare corporatism* with the Anglo-American model of *market individualism*. Doshe *et al.* (1996) saw Japanese production organization as a more advanced form of Taylorism (see also Kato and Steven 1993). Cole (1971) suggested that Japan's cultural legacy informs unique organizational solutions to general development problems. Until the mid-1980s studies were pessimistic about the transfer of Japanese organization (Cool and Legnick-Hall 1985).

There is, however, another strand of research and theory (Shimada 1986; Shimada and MacDuffie 1986; Aoki 1988; Koike 1988) that suggested that Japanese organizational forms were to some degree autonomous from culture and the environment. Taira (1962, 1964, 1970) documented the emergence of permanent employment from Japanese industrialists' need to cope with high rates of labour mobility and a desire to exert more effective control over the labour force. Gordon (1985) indicated that team-based work organization is the product of post-war industrial unrest over worker control of production (also see Kenney and Florida 1988). Empirical research (Lincoln and Kalleberg 1985, 1990) also noted that Japanese organization rather than culture is the source of workforce motivation, control, and commitment.

The empirical evidence regarding the transfer of Japanese organizational forms and practices is mixed. An early study by Yoshino (1976) suggested that the absence of Japanese socio-cultural conditions in other countries is a serious obstacle to transfer. Cole (1979) was guardedly optimistic:

There are those who would argue that they [quality control circles] have their basis in Japanese cultural and institutional conditions, with their unique group orientation, practice of permanent employment, and strong employee commitment to organizational goals. Consequently they are held not to be applicable to the United States. My own judgement is they may well be applicable if appropriate adaptations are made to accommodate the circles to US conditions. (Cole 1979: 255)

White and Trevor (1983) concluded that Japanese organizational traits were not transferred to Japanese firms operating in the UK. However, Morris (1988), Oliver and Wilkinson (1989), and Kumazawa and Yamada (1989) concluded that the Japanese management system was successfully transferred to Japanese firms in the UK. A study of Nissan in the UK (Crowther and Garrahan 1988) documented the emergence of a Japanese-style automobile production complex comprising a main assembly plant and supplier firms.

There was a considerable amount of research and empirical study of the transfer of Japanese organization to the US beginning in the late 1980s. A series of case studies initially identified the transfer of Japanese organizational practices to the USA (Krafcik 1986; Mair *et al.* 1988; Adler 1993). An MIT study of the global automotive industry found transplants to be important factors in the cross-national diffusion of *lean production* (Krafcik 1989; Womack *et al.* 1990). Research by Florida and Kenney (1991, 1992*a*; Kenney and Florida 1993) found that automotive transplants transferred key practices related to work organization and supplier relations to the USA. They concluded therefore that Japanese work organization represented a set of organizational practices that could be extracted from one environment and replicated in another.

Other studies were pessimistic regarding the ability of transplants to transfer and replicate organizational practices while others were more critical of Japanese work practices in general (Parker and Slaughter 1988; Howes 1993). A study of Japanese transplants in California (Milkman 1991) found little evidence of transfer, and argued that transplants tended to emulate traditional US management practices. That study was criticized, however, for basing its conclusions on a limited sample which was drawn mainly from the transplant electronics industry in Southern California (see Florida 1993; MacDuffie 1993). In a more journalistic exposition based upon off-site interviews with employees and union officials, Fucini and Fucini (1990) argued that the Mazda plant in Flat Rock, Michigan has experienced numerous problems in the transfer of Japanese production methods including high rates of injury, worker discontent, and labour–management conflict.

Still other studies revealed a varied pattern of transfer and adoption. A series of systematic case studies by the University of Tokyo (1990; Abo 1993) found that the transfer of organizational practices differed considerably by industry, with automotive-related transplants exhibiting the greatest propensity to transfer Japanese innovations to the US, while electronics transplants tended to emulate US practices and thus adapt to the US environment. A study of Japanese transplants in the USA and Europe (Fujimoto *et al.* 1994) found evidence of transfer of Japanese-style production process management and quality-control practices, but noted that human-resources practices (particularly those related to labour markets and remuneration) tended to conform to the local environment. A case study of the Subaru-Izusu plant in Indiana by Graham (1993) found that there was considerable resistance to the transfer of Japanese production methods; however, evidence provided in the study indicated that those production methods were still being transferred. Case studies by a team from Michigan (Cutcher-Gershenfeld *et al.* 1995) showed that Japanese transplants differed considerably in the implementation of work teams. The Michigan team attributed these differences to a number of factors, including the nature of the production process, whether the plant was wholly Japanese-owned or a joint venture, and whether it was a new plant or an older acquired facility.

3. Research Design

This chapter draws from the findings of two related research projects on the Japanese transplants in the USA, an initial survey research and field research on Japanese automotive transplants (both assembly plants and suppliers) conducted by Florida and Kenney (1991; Kenney and Florida 1993) in the late 1980s, and a subsequent survey research project on the adoption of advanced production and work practices by Japanese transplants across industries conducted by Florida and Jenkins (1998; Jenkins and Florida 1999) in 1994–5. We defined *transplants* as either wholly Japanese-owned manufacturing establishments or factories which have a significant level of Japanese participation in cross-national joint ventures in the automobile assembly and automotive component parts industries.

The 1988 study included both fieldwork at the automotive assembly transplants and a mail survey of transplant automotive suppliers. The fieldwork was conducted at six of the seven then operating transplant assembly plants in the US and at various supplier firms. More than 100 personal interviews were conducted with Japanese and American executives, managers and engineers; shopfloor workers and trade union officials; and state and local government officials.

The 1988 mail survey was administered to the universe of Japanese-owned or Japanese–US joint venture suppliers in the USA. The sample population was drawn from a database of Japanese transplant assemblers and suppliers from data provided by the Japan Economic Institute, US government sources, industry trade journals, and newspaper reports. Addresses were located for 196 of the 229 suppliers in the original database. Each establishment was then contacted by telephone to identify the appropriate person to complete the survey. The survey resulted in seventy-three completed surveys for a response rate of 37.2 per cent, which is comparable to the rates in other research of this type (see Lincoln and Kalleberg 1985 for example).

The 1994 survey was a survey of all Japanese transplants across industries in the USA, designed to obtain comprehensive information on production work organization, supplier relations, plant characteristics and performance of Japanese manufacturing transplants, and a selected sample of US affiliated manufacturing plants that serve as the suppliers to the Japanese transplant automotive assemblers. The sample of Japanese transplants was based on the 1,695 transplant establishments in the 1993 Japan External Trade Organization (JETRO) database. We supplemented the JETRO list with data on Japanese investment in US manufacturing from other sources, including the list of Japanese-affiliated plants in the USA as of 1990 compiled by the Japan Economic Institute (MacKnight 1992); directories of Japanese-affiliated companies operating in the USA, such as the *Japan Company Handbook*; and various newsletters, news articles, and other publications, resulting in a database of 1,768 transplant manufacturing establishments. Excluding 359 transplants involved in food processing and related industries resulted in a total sample size of 1,409 Japanese transplant manufacturing establishments. The survey was administered to plant managers in these establishments by the Center for Survey Research (CSR) of the University of Massachusetts, Boston. The survey was implemented in 1994 in two phases: the first involving a mail survey and the second relying on telephone interviews. Based on an initial screening, 238 additional plants were eliminated from the sample frame, resulting in a frame of 1,195 Japanese transplants and 338 US suppliers to the transplants. The survey achieved an unadjusted response rate of 40 per cent. In addition, data from a 1992 survey of the adoption of innovative workplace practices conducted by Osterman (1992) were used to compare the transplants to a sample of US-owned manufacturing establishments.

4. Intra-Organizational Factors

4.1. Work and production organization

Table 10.1, which is drawn from the 1988 fieldwork on automotive assembly transplants, summarizes the main characteristics of intra-organizational practices for transplant assemblers and for a representative Big Three automobile companies as of 1988. Table 10.2, based on the 1988 supplier survey, presents similar information for transplant suppliers.

TABLE 10.1 Comparison of organizational practices in the automotive transplants and the Big Three

	Work teams	Rotation	Job classi-fication	Worker QC	Annual wage $US	Hourly wage $US*	Union
Auto Alliance	+	+	2	0	—		
Diamond-Star	+	+	2	0	38,406	16.22	Yes
Honda	+	+	3	0	36,982	17.00	Yes
NUMMI	+	+	4	0	41,545	16.20	No
Nissan	+	+	4	0	36,294	17.85	Yes
Subaru-Isuzu	+	+	3	0	—	15.62	No
Toyota	+	+	3	0	39,582	16.43	No
Big Three	–	–	90	–	—	17.59	Yes

Notes: + = similar to Japan; 0 = modified; – = different from Japan.
However, in the last five years, many Big Three plants are adopting Japanese-style work practices.
* This does not count the cost-of-living wages received in unionized transplants which are calculated separately, but increase worker's pay quarterly.

Source: Author's compilation from various sources.

TABLE 10.2 Percentage of transplant parts suppliers with selected Japanese intra-organizational practices, USA, 1988

Characteristic	Per cent	No. of cases
Work organization		
Work teams	76.7	73
Rotation within teams	87.0	69
Rotation between teams	66.2	68
Just-in-time inventory control	68.5	73
Worker involvement		
Production workers maintain their own machines	79.5	73
Production workers do routine quality control	98.6	73
Production workers help design their own jobs	60.9	69
Division of labour		
No. of job classifications		
1	34.3	67
2	14.9	67
3	16.4	67
4	14.9	67
5	6.0	67

Source: Richard Florida and Martin Kenney, *Survey of Japanese Automotive Transplant Suppliers,* 1988.

Job classifications. The use of a relatively small number of job classifications is a key characteristic of work organization in Japanese automotive factories. This differs from the traditional US system of production organization, particularly in the automotive industry, which was distinguished by large numbers of separate job classifications. A 1986 study by Kochan *et al.* reported that the unionized plants in a multidivisional US manufacturing firm had an average of ninety-six job classifications. Table 10.1 indicates that transplant assemblers in our 1988 study used no more than four job classifications, whereas a representative traditional US Big Three automotive plant had ninety. Furthermore, more than 85 per cent of transplant suppliers that responded to the 1988 survey reported that they had five or fewer job classifications for production workers; and one-third used only one job classification.

Work teams. Another characteristic of the organization of work in Japanese factories is the use of work teams composed of production workers who are responsible for planning and carrying out production tasks (Aoki 1988; Koike 1988). Teams socialize production tasks and assign immediate managerial tasks to shopfloor workers. Table 10.1 indicates that work teams were used at all of the transplant assemblers. Our field research found that teams met daily at Honda, Toyota, and NUMMI to discuss production improvements and redesign of tasks; meetings at the other transplants took place at least once a week. More than three out of four of the transplant suppliers in the 1988 survey reported that they organized production work on the basis of work teams (see Table 10.2).

Rotation. Rotation of workers among tasks within a team is another much cited feature of production in automotive assembly plants in Japan. Rotation functions to train workers in multiple tasks and to reduce the incidence of repetitive motion injuries. While rotation was used by all transplant assemblers in our 1988 study, its frequency varied. Toyota, Honda, and NUMMI reported that workers rotated frequently within their teams. Rotation, however, was less frequent at Mazda, Nissan, and SIA. At the time of our 1988 site visits and interviews, these plants considered rotation a longer-term objective. Mazda workers we interviewed stated that infrequent rotation was a major cause of repetitive motion injury. The findings of the 1988 supplier survey indicated that roughly 87 per cent of suppliers rotated workers within teams, while approximately 66 per cent rotated workers among teams. Field research at Nippondenso's Battle Creek, Michigan plant found that plant rotated workers in high-stress jobs every hour or two and encouraged workers to apply for rotation from team to team.

Quality circles. Quality circles are another element of the organization of production work in Japanese automotive plants (see Cole 1989*a*; Lillrank and Kano 1989). In Japan, quality circles are composed of groups of production workers who devote effort outside regular working hours to improving an element of the production process. According to a 1986 study by Lincoln *et al.* (1986: 354), 76 per cent of employees in a sample of Japanese plants participated in quality circles compared to 27 per cent of workers in US plants. The assembly transplants in our 1988 research varied in the extent and intensiveness with which they employed quality circles. Toyota and Honda reported extensive use of quality circles, Mazda and NUMMI used them moderately, and SIA not at all. Slightly less than half of suppliers in the 1988 survey used quality circles. Transplant assemblers in our 1988 research reported that they paid workers for involvement in quality-circle activity. Of suppliers in the 1988 survey that used quality circles, 83 per cent reported that they paid workers for hours spent working on quality circles. Several transplants in the 1988 study reported that they established competitions between quality-control circles and used prizes, plaques, and cash awards as additional incentives for quality-circle participation. Some transplants reported that they sent American quality circles to Japan to participate in annual company competitions.

Just-in-time inventory control. Production in Japanese automotive assembly plants is organized according to the just-in-time system of inventory control in which materials are forwarded as needed and inventory is kept to a minimum (Cusumano 1985; Sheard 1985). All the transplant assemblers and over two-thirds of suppliers (68.5 per cent) in the 1988 study used a just-in-time system of production control. The 1988 supplier survey asked: 'How similar is your manufacturing process to one that might be found in Japan?' Eighty-six per cent of the respondents said that their US manufacturing practice was either 'exactly the same' or 'very similar' to one that might be found in Japan; only one supplier said that it was not at all similar.

4.2. Change over time: 1994 survey results

The results of the 1994 survey support these earlier findings and shed some additional light on key intra-organizational factors. We were especially interested to see whether or not the transplants have deepened their transfer and adoption of intra-organizational practices and capabilities over time. To shed light on this issue, we compared the findings for the automotive-related transplants in the 1994 survey with the findings of the 1988 survey in Table 10.3. As these data show, there was not a great deal of change over this six-year period. The proportion of plants using teams, job rotation, and few job classifications was relatively stable between 1988 and 1994, although the proportion using quality circles increased substantially. Here, it is important to note that the 1988 survey asked respondents not only if they currently used quality circles but if they planned to do so. A substantial proportion of these plants were just starting up production at the time, and many had not yet fully implemented their human resource and work organization systems. The proportion in the 1988 sample that either used quality circles currently or planned to do so in the near future (73.6 per cent) was closer to the 1994 result (85.7 per cent). Interestingly, the proportion of plants using these practices in combination with one another also remained virtually unchanged. About a third of Japanese automotive supplier transplants used teams, rotation, and quality circles in combination in 1994, compared to 22.2 per cent in 1988. A large part of this difference stemmed from the greater use of quality circles. Furthermore, there was a smaller proportion of plants in the 1994 survey that used none of the practices, providing some limited evidence of increased adoption and diffusion. One explanation is that Japanese automotive transplants originally implanted a fairly advanced set of organizational practices and basically stuck with those practices over time, making little refinement or revision. It is also important to note that our survey documents the level of transfer and adoption of practices, but not worker behaviour under those practices. The field research findings suggest that workers have become more involved in and adept at continuous improvement activities over time.

Our 1994 survey also explored differences in the transfer and adoption of intra-organizational practices for the transplants and US manufacturers in the automotive sector as well as other manufacturing industries. The data on adoption of practices by US-owned manufacturers were provided by Osterman (1994). As Table 10.4 shows, among the US plants, those in transportation equipment were far and away the highest adopters of innovative practices. In fact, US plants in the transportation

TABLE 10.3 Transfer and adoption of innovative work practices by Japanese-affiliated auto-supplier transplants, 1988–94

	1988	1994	1994*
Any teams	76.7	75.3	72.2
Any self-directed teams	71.2	48.4	33.3
Job rotation between work groups	61.6	65.2	66.7
Any quality circles	44.4	85.7	83.3
2 or fewer job classifications	43.0	34.7	58.3
Teams + Rotation + QCs = 3	22.2	33.9	16.7
Teams + Rotation + QCs + few job classifications = 0	9.5	1.8	0.0

Notes: All figures are expressed as the percentage of establishments using the practices indicated.
* These figures are for the 36 plants in the 1994 survey sample that also responded to the 1988 survey by Florida and Kenney.

Sources: Richard Florida and Davis Jenkins, *Japanese Transplant Project* (Carnegie Mellon University, May 1995), and Richard Florida and Martin Kenney, *Survey of Japanese Automotive Transplant Suppliers*, 1998.

TABLE 10.4 Percentage of transplant first-tier suppliers with selected Japanese inter-organizational linkages, USA, 1988

Characteristic	Linkages to assemblers	No. of cases	Linkage to second-tier suppliers	No. of cases
Transit time				
$\frac{1}{2}$ hour	6.9	72	—	—
$\frac{1}{2}$ hour–2 hours	33.9	72	—	—
2–8 hours	38.9	72	—	—
8–24 hours	9.7	72	—	—
Deliver according to just-in-time schedule	80.0	70	43.0	72
Immediate feedback on defective parts	90.2	72	97.2	72
Customers' engineers visit plant site				
For quality control problems	96.8	62	96.9	65
For production problems	74.2	62	83.1	65
Interaction in design				
Close interaction between supplier and customer	50.0	72	33.8	71
Supplier bids on customer design	31.9	72	62.0	71
Supplier can alter customer design	22.2	72	11.3	71
Supplier designs subject to customer approval	15.3	72	11.3	71
Supplier designs but customer can alter	6.9	72	8.5	71

Source: Richard Florida and Martin Kenny, *Survey of Japanese Automotive Transplant Suppliers*, 1988

equipment sector were more likely than their Japanese transplant counterparts to adopt innovative organizational practices. US transportation equipment manufacturers had the highest rates of adoption of teams, job rotation, quality circles, and statistical process control. Sixty-eight per cent of US plants in this sector used teams, rotation, and quality circles in combination.

4.3. Status and hierarchy

The 1988 field research enabled us to probe a series of other factors associated with intra-organizational characteristics including status and hierarchy issues, workforce selection and socialization, and actual behaviour in organizations.

Status. Overt status distinctions between management and blue-collar workers are less evident in Japan than in the US. For example, in Japan workers and managers eat in the same cafeteria; middle-level managers wear the same uniforms as shopfloor workers. Managers typically do not have enclosed offices, but sit at desks on a large open floor adjacent to the production facility. All transplants we visited during our 1988 field research had shared cafeterias. Nissan was the only transplant in our 1988 fieldwork where status distinctions were visible, such as a separate parking lot for top managers' cars and private American-style offices. All the transplant assemblers in our 1988 fieldwork provided uniforms, although some gave workers the option of wearing street clothes. Transplant officials we interviewed suggested that uniforms created an identification between workers and the company. Most top executives wore company uniforms in our 1988 fieldwork, Nissan being the exception. In fact, we were led to conclude on the basis of our 1988 fieldwork that the transplants had greater visible status equality than in Japan where top executives have chauffeured company automobiles and wear suits and ties rather than work uniforms.

Hierarchy. Based on a 1986 survey study, Lincoln *et al.* (1986) indicated that management hierarchies are taller in Japan than in the USA. The findings of our 1988 fieldwork indicated that management hierarchies in the automotive transplants were relatively flat. At Honda, there were nine levels in the internal hierarchy: associate, team leader, coordinator, department manager, plant manager, assistant vice-president, senior vice-president, executive vice-president, and president. This structure was typical of the other transplants as well. At Honda, the various vice-presidents did not form separate levels in the reporting structure, but were part of senior management team, which included the plant manager and the president of Honda America Manufacturing. This senior management team made decisions as a group and thus functioned to some extent as a single reporting level. The president of Honda America was a member of and reported to the board of directors for Honda Japan. We found that a number of shopfloor workers had risen to management ranks at Honda and the company actively encouraged such mobility. Toyota officials reported that shopfloor workers were recruited for middle-level management positions in the factory and the front office. Additional fieldwork we conducted at Toyota during the 1994 study reinforces this earlier finding. Toyota had developed an extensive (three-year) in-house training programme to recruit and develop its next generation of skilled maintenance workers from the ranks of its assembly workforce.

Team leaders. Numerous studies noted the role played by team leaders in automotive assembly plants in Japan. Team leaders are members of shopfloor work-groups but also have managerial responsibility for immediate production activities. In this sense, they replace the more traditional American job category of foreman whose job was to supervise shopfloor workers. Team leaders were used at all the transplant assemblers we visited in the 1988 fieldwork, and 84 per cent of suppliers in the 1988 survey. At some assembly transplants, team leaders were selected by management, while at others, especially the unionized transplants, team leaders were selected by joint labour–management committees. All the transplants reported that they considered the input of workers to be an important criterion for the selection of team leaders.

Job security. Long-term employment tenure is a much discussed feature of Japanese work organization (Abegglen 1958; Taira 1962; Dore 1973; Cole 1979; Lincoln and Kalleberg 1985). In our 1988 fieldwork, we found that the pattern of employment security differed between unionized and non-unionized assembly transplants, and between assemblers and suppliers. Our review of the labour–management agreements for the unionized assembly transplants indicated that all of them had formal contractual agreements stipulating tenure security and guaranteeing jobs except under conditions that jeopardize the financial viability of the company. We also found that NUMMI kept full employment during periods of up to 30 per cent reduction in output by eliminating overtime, slowing the work pace, offering workers voluntary vacation time, placing workers in special training programmes, or transferring them to other jobs. Mazda workers were loaned to local governments during slowdowns. The non-unionized transplants provided informal assurance of tenure security, although this was not reflected in contractual agreements. Nissan and Toyota redeployed workers to other jobs to avoid lay-offs.

Transplant suppliers in our 1988 survey did not offer formal guarantees of tenure security. However, more respondents indicated that the Japanese long-term employment system *should* be transferred to the USA. Nevertheless, they offered a wide range of opinions on this issue—some saw long-term employment as a source of long-run productivity increases, others saw the threat of termination as a way to motivate American workers.

Unionization. Japanese automotive assembly plants are represented by enterprise or company unions (Taira 1962; Shirai 1983). This differs markedly from the prevailing US practice of industrial unionism. The transplants in our 1988 study developed two basic strategies to cope with US labour relations. A number of automobile assembly transplants simply chose to avoid unionization. Furthermore, only four of the seventy-one respondents to the 1988 supplier survey were unionized. The four non-unionized assemblers—Honda, Toyota, Nissan, and SIA—chose rural *greenfield* locations at least in part to avoid unionization. Nissan went to great lengths to defeat a unionization drive. SIA implemented an in-plant video system to communicate messages to workers in anticipation of a unionization campaign. Non-unionized transplants, notably Nissan and Toyota, used employee handbooks that provided plant rules and regulations and formed employee associations to collect employee input and create a stable structure through which work-related grievances were addressed. The unionized transplants, Mazda, NUMMI, and Diamond-Star, established independent agreements with their respective union locals that enlist the union in the implementation of Japanese-like work organization. These agreements made it possible to implement smaller numbers of job classifications and more flexible work rules and to utilize pay systems that differed markedly from typical US automotive industry practice. Related research by Smith and Florida (1994) on the location choices of a large sample of Japanese automotive-related transplants found no statistical evidence that transplant manufacturers were avoiding relatively unionized locations. In fact, transplant manufacturers tended to cluster in manufacturing-intensive areas with relatively higher concentrations of unions.

The 1994 survey also collected data on unionization of Japanese transplant suppliers. The survey results indicated that 15.3 per cent of wholly Japanese-owned suppliers and 17 per cent of Japanese–US joint venture suppliers were unionized. This compared to a 35.4 per cent rate of unionization for US-owned suppliers in our survey that supplied Japanese assembly transplants.

4.4. Socialization

Japanese corporations did not simply impose Japanese production organization and manufacturing practice on their American workforces. Instead, they used a number of selection and socialization mechanisms to ensure effective transfer.

Workforce selection. The transplants used recruitment and selection processes to identify workers who possess initiative, are dedicated to the corporation, work well in teams, and do not miss work. The process differs from the recruitment policies of Japanese corporations in Japan (Rosenbaum and Kariya 1989) but serves a similar function. In Japan, high-school teachers often recommend workers to companies. In this way, they perform a screening functioned that was not available in the USA at the time the transplants were established. This practice differs markedly from the traditional US practice of hiring off the street, though this practice has changed since then and US companies now use similar workforce recruitment and selection practices as the transplants. The transplants in our 1988 study subjected potential workers to cognitive and psychological tests and other screening procedures to identify workers with appropriate characteristics for team-based work and continuous improvement activities. The transplants frequently subcontracted to specialized 'assessment centres' to perform this function. In this process, the transplants examined the previous job records or high-school records for absenteeism and other qualities. Moreover, as much as possible, they hired individuals with no previous factory experience (in this way replicating the Japanese practice of hiring individuals directly out of high schools or universities). Potential employees were put through extensive interviews with personnel officials, managers, and even members of their potential work teams to rate their initiative and group-oriented characteristics. While theorists have generally treated the so-called loyalty of the Japanese workforce as a product of Japanese culture, all Japanese firms, including transplants, make significant conscious efforts to inculcate loyalty in their workforces. Among the transplants, the screening and selection process constitutes an organizational mechanism that selects potentially loyal workers from a large, diverse population.

Prior to start-up, all the assembly transplants sent key employees (e.g. managers and team leaders) to Japanese sister plants for three to six months. There they received both formal training and informal socialization to Japanese practice (e.g. teamwork and *kaizen*). They worked closely with veteran Japanese trainers, who transferred formal and tacit knowledge of production and who functioned as role models to some extent. Workers and trainers also spent time together outside work to continue the socialization process. These trainers then came to the US for periods from three months to two years to work alongside the same US employees and their teams. The 1988 supplier survey indicated that 33 per cent of American managers were sent to Japan for training. According to workers who were interviewed during our 1988 field research at various transplant assembly facilities, trainers provided the most substantial and significant exposure to Japanese practices.

The transplants used ongoing training and socialization programmes to acclimate workers to Japanese production. Most employees began with a six- to eight-week introductory session that included an overview of automotive assembly and fairly rigorous socialization in the Japanese model. After this, workers were assigned to teams where they continued to learn from senior employees. According to the 1988 supplier survey, respondents provided an average of eight days of training for factory workers before they assume shopfloor activities (range = 0–180 days). This was supplemented by an average of sixty-one days additional training on the shopfloor (range = 1–302 days).

4.5. Organizations and behaviour

It is important to distinguish between the form of Japanese organization and its substance, i.e. its effects on worker behaviour. A main objective of the Japanese system of work and production organization is to harness the collective intelligence of workers for continuous product and process improvement. This stands in sharp contrast to traditional intra-organizational practices in American automotive assembly plants, where there were formal and informal organizational barriers and norms inhibiting the use of worker intelligence (Braverman 1974; Edwards 1979; Burawoy 1979, 1983). In Japan, workers are expected to actively participate in company suggestion programmes and quality-control circles as well as informal, everyday *kaizen*, or continuous improvement activities. Here, it is important to note, however, that different Japanese automobile corporations vary in their ability to motivate workers to participate in such practices. In this arena, Toyota is clearly the most effective. Japanese scholars use the term *voluntarism* to explain the extraordinary initiative of workers in Japan. Here again, we note that Japanese automobile companies vary significantly in their ability to generate voluntaristic behaviour—with Toyota being the most effective.

Worker initiative. Transplants encourage worker initiative through the delegation of managerial authority and responsibility to shopfloor workers. Workers at the transplants, especially Honda and Toyota, were found to have significant input into the design of their jobs. More than 60 per cent of respondents to the 1988 supplier survey indicated that production workers were involved in the design of their tasks. Our field research at Toyota and Nippondenso indicated that work teams designed standardized task descriptions for their work units, posting them in the form of drawings and photographs with captions at their work stations. Roughly 80 per cent of suppliers in the 1988 survey reported that production workers were responsible for routine maintenance on their own machines.

Japanese corporations use suggestion systems to harness workers' knowledge and ideas. Our fieldwork indicated that Honda and Toyota established fairly well-developed suggestion systems. Although Mazda had a suggestion system at the time of our original fieldwork, Mazda workers had at times boycotted it to express their dissatisfaction with management policy. The 1988 supplier survey found that 30 per cent of respondents provided cash awards for worker suggestions, and two-thirds reported that 'willingness to suggest new ideas' was a key factor in evaluating production workers.

In our fieldwork, we also asked managers (in this case Japanese managers with experience in Japanese factories and transplant factories) to engage in a comparative exercise and to estimate in a rough sense how much, in percentage terms, Japanese *kaizen* or continuous improvement activity they were able to replicate in their American workforce. While these estimates are rough and certainly subjective, they are nonetheless revealing. Honda managers reported that they had completely replicated Japanese practice in their US plant. A Toyota manager who worked in numerous Toyota plants in Japan as well as at NUMMI and Georgetown, Kentucky, indicated the Georgetown plant was at 60 per cent of Japanese practice and NUMMI at 40 to 50 per cent. Nippondenso managers also reported that they had closely replicated Japanese practice. Officials at Mazda and Nissan reported that they had experienced more difficulty implementing *kaizen* activity, and stood at roughly 50 per cent of Japanese practice. Managers at SIA estimated that the plant was at about 30 per cent of Japanese practice. In our earlier research (Florida and Kenney 1991), we noted that progress of the transplants on this dimension was remarkable, given the time transplant organizations had to socialize American workers to the requirements of Japanese-like work organization. We stand by that assessment today.

Adaptation. The findings from our 1988 fieldwork indicated that while production workers in the USA experienced few problems adapting to Japanese-like organizational forms, management was the source of recurring adaptation problems. Our interviews with NUMMI workers, who previously worked for GM, found that these workers preferred work in the transplant organization to work in the old GM factory. According to one: 'I was at GM and the part I didn't like—which I like now—is that we had a lot of drug and alcohol problems. It was getting to the point, even with me, when it got around lunchtime I had to go out . . . and take down two or three beers.'

Both our 1988 and 1994 fieldwork suggested that management was the source of the most serious adaptation problems. During site visits and interviews, we were told repeatedly that American middle managers, especially those recruited from US automobile corporations, experienced great difficulty adapting to work and production organization at the transplants. A number of transplant automotive assemblers reported that previously formed attitudes and prejudices of US middle managers toward factory workers represented a serious problem. White and Trevor (1983) documented a similar problem in UK transplants. NUMMI workers in the 1988 study complained that American managers were still operating in the 'old GM style'. As one worker put it: 'A lot of things have changed. But see, you hear people talk. You hear them saying once in a while: "Oh, we're going back to the GM ways." I hope not. That was rough. I think to completely bring back the Japanese way, Japan would have to take over the plant completely and have nothing to do with General Motors at all.' Japanese transplant managers indicate that problems with American middle managers encouraged them to promote shopfloor workers to supervisory positions.

5. Inter-Organizational Factors

Inter-organizational relationships are increasingly seen as an important component of organizational forms and capabilities, and as significant mechanisms in the diffusion of new and innovative organizational practices. Nishiguchi (1994) suggested that inter-organizational (e.g. customer–supplier) relations were a powerful mechanism for diffusion of intra-organizational practices. Florida and Kenney (1991) found evidence of an elective affinity between intra- and inter-organizational practices. Using data from a 1993 survey of first-tier automotive parts supplier plants in the US, however, Helper and Levine (1993) found no evidence that having a Japanese customer predicts the presence of employee participation within the plant.

Our fieldwork in the US and Japan found that Japanese assembly transplants initially located facilities in the lower Midwestern region of the USA to take advantage of the indigenous infrastructure of domestic automobile parts suppliers. US-owned supplier firms were unable to adapt to the delivery and quality requirements of the Japanese just-in-time system. Dismayed by the performance of US suppliers, assembly transplants encouraged their first-tier Japanese suppliers to locate in the USA. The Japanese suppliers, in turn, found it in their interest to expand overseas. In effect, the creation of a Japanese-like supplier system in the USA can be understood as a *creative response* (Schumpeter 1947) to the deficiencies of the US environment.

Transplant assemblers played an active role in the creation of this new production environment by financing and helping to set up US branches for key suppliers. For example, Honda encouraged two of its Japanese suppliers to form Bellemar Parts to supply seat sub-assemblies. In another instance, Honda provided technical and financial assistance to a group of Japanese suppliers to form KTH Parts Industries, a company that took over US production of chassis parts that were once produced in-house by Honda at Marysville. By 1988, nearly half of Honda's main suppliers in Japan operated US plants. The 1988 supplier survey found that twelve of seventy-three suppliers were partially owned by the assemblers they supply.

Both our fieldwork and survey research found that Japanese automotive assemblers played the key role in influencing both the original decision of transplant suppliers to relocate production in the USA and their choice of locations in the USA. The 1988 supplier survey found that more than 75 per cent of respondents established US operations to maintain close ties to a major Japanese customer, and 90 per cent chose their specific locations to be close to a major customer. Traditional environmental factors like the local labour market or local labour costs have relatively little impact on locational choices.

5.1. Supplier relations

Table 10.4 summarizes the key findings from the 1988 supplier survey regarding the main characteristics of relations among transplant assemblers and suppliers. This table reports the responses of seventy-three transplant suppliers on their supply relationships with transplant assemblers and with their own second-tier suppliers. Geographic proximity is a basic characteristic of the Japanese supplier relations (Sayer 1986). Among transplant suppliers, 40 per cent reported that they were located within a two-hour shipping radius of end-users, and almost 90 per cent were located within an eight-hour radius. Eighty per cent made just-in-time deliveries. Still, the distances separating end-users from suppliers were somewhat greater in the USA than in Japan. This geographic pattern or *transplant complex* can be thought of as essentially a stretched-out version of Japan's dense just-in-time supplier system, likely to be due to the greater availability of land, well-developed highway systems, larger trucks, and greater storage capacity in the USA.

Interaction and information exchange. Table 10.4 also sheds light on the scope and nature of information exchange between transplant assemblers and suppliers. The 1988 survey found that approximately 97 per cent of transplant suppliers were contacted immediately by phone when they delivered a defective product. Eighty-two per cent of respondents indicated that engineers from their major customer came on-site while they were setting up US operations, three-quarters reported that engineers from their major customer made site visits to deal with production problems, and 97 per cent indicated that engineers from their major customer made site visits to deal with quality-control problems.

Joint product development. Joint participation in design and development is another key characteristic of Japanese supplier relations. Fifty per cent of suppliers in the 1988 survey reported they participated closely with assemblers in the development of new products. This included interaction with US-owned firms as well. Our field research found that Honda engineers, for example, developed new production techniques for a small Ohio plastics firm that became a Honda supplier. Honda, Toyota, and SIA sent teams of engineers and shopfloor workers to consult with suppliers on new product designs and production machinery. Other transplants, particularly Honda, established R&D and technical centres to integrate both transplant and US suppliers into the future design of cars. Based on this we are led to conclude that key elements of Japanese-style supplier relations—e.g. high levels of interaction, joint development, and long-term contracts—which typically have been viewed as a function of Japan's socio-cultural environment, are actually a product of the organizational relation itself and thus reflect the capability to transfer organizational practice between environments.

Supply chain management. In Japan, first-tier suppliers play a critical role in organizing and coordinating supply flows between lower-level suppliers and main assembly plants. They are located close to assemblers, interact frequently with them, and often are at least partially owned by them (Asanuma 1985). First-tier suppliers were, if anything, more important in transplant complexes. For example, our field research found that the windscreens for Honda's American-made vehicles originated at PPG, an American producer. PPG supplied windscreens to a Japanese supplier, AP Technoglass, twice a week. AP Technoglass screened them for defects, cut and ground them, and delivered them to a Honda subsidiary, Bellemar Parts, twice a day. Bellemar, located one mile from the Honda plant, applied rubber seals to the windscreens and made just-in-time deliveries to Honda every two hours. Bellemar also screened for defects, so that Honda received higher quality windscreens than it would without its suppliers. In this way, first-tier suppliers serve as a buffer between assemblers and the environment.

Table 10.4 focuses on relationships across the transplant supply chain. As these data show, second-tier suppliers, who supply to the first-tier suppliers, have less interaction in design or development of new products. The 1988 supplier survey found that one-third of first-tier suppliers integrated second-tier suppliers in new product development. Just 43 per cent of the first-tier suppliers received just-in-time deliveries from their second-tier suppliers, whereas in Japan, tight supplier relations extend to second- and third-tier suppliers. In related field research on the steel industry, we found that such interactive customer–supplier relations were being extended down through the hierarchy to producers of basic inputs like steel and automotive plastics (Florida and Kenney 1992*a*, 1992*b*).

US suppliers to the transplants. The 1988 research explored the role of US-owned suppliers to the transplants. At that time, over half of Mazda's US suppliers were US-owned firms: forty-three of Mazda's ninety-six suppliers were independent US-owned firms, ten were owned by Ford, and forty-three were Japanese-owned or Japanese–US joint ventures *(Automotive News* 1989). Helper (1990) indicated that 41 per cent of 437 US automotive suppliers surveyed supplied at least one component to the transplants.

We found that transplant assemblers developed a variety of linkages to US producers. As in Japan, Toyota established an organization of its Kentucky suppliers, the Bluegrass Automotive Manufacturers Association (BAMA), and has held meetings with US suppliers in both the USA and Japan to encourage diffusion of Japanese practices. NUMMI organized a supplier council of seventy mostly US-owned suppliers to share information-sharing and facilitate product improvement (Krafcik 1986, 1989). SIA has organized teams of engineers, purchasing representatives, and manufacturing experts who work with suppliers to improve quality. Johnson Controls, an American-owned automotive supplier in Georgetown, Kentucky, became the sole source supplier of seats for the Toyota Camry. Toyota worked with the company to implement a full-blown Japanese production system. Johnson Controls delivers completed sub-assemblies to Toyota according to just-in-time requirements every four hours. We visited a ten-person small machine shop in rural Ohio that formerly rebuilt tractor engines, but now rebuilds robot heads for Honda and Honda suppliers.

5.2. Change over time: 1994 findings on inter-organizational relationships

The findings of the 1994 survey reinforce and extend the findings of the earlier fieldwork and survey research (see Tables 10.5 and 10.6). The 1994 findings indicate that inter-organizational factors (e.g. customer–supplier relations) form a catalytic mechanism in the diffusion and transfer of organizational forms and practices. The 1994 fieldwork found that both OEM manufacturers and first-tier supplier were actively engaged in efforts to diffuse innovative organization through supplier networks. Toyota, for example, provided technical assistance to its suppliers through its purchasing departments, and set up a semi-independent operation, the Toyota Supplier Support Center, to work with US-owned suppliers that are committed to adopting core values and practices of the Toyota production system. Toyota also established two US-based supplier associations—associated with its Georgetown, Kentucky, and NUMMI plants, respectively—to accelerate the adoption and diffusion of innovative organizational practices among its suppliers.

TABLE 10.5 Adoption of organizational practices by country of ownership

	Auto parts supplier plants in the USA (1994)			F	Pr>F
	Japanese-owned	US-Japanese joint ventures	US-owned		
Teams: % of plants	75.8	78.0	74.2	—	—
Teams: % of participation	47.6	57.9	44.3	1.7	0.19
Team of authority index	2.2	2.2	2.5	0.9	0.4
Self-directed teams: % of plants	50.2	47.5	56.3	—	—
Self-directed teams: % of participation	32.9	41.1	34.6	0.6	0.55
Quality circles: % of plants	32.9	41.1	34.6	—	—
Quality circles: % of participation	42.6	36.9	37.8	0.6	0.5
Group incentive pay (e.g. gain-sharing): % of plants	11.4	24.0	14.0	—	—
Profit-sharing: % of plants	49.5	58.7	52.9	—	—
Pay for skills: % of plants	50.4	41.1	48.7	—	—

Notes: '% of plants' indicates the percentage of plants in the given sample that use the given practice. '% participation' indicates the percentage of production workers in a plant who are involved in the given practice. For none of these variables is the difference of means among the various ownership types statistically significant by a one-way ANOVA test.

Source: 1994 survey by Richard Florida and Davis Jenkins, Carnegie-Mellon University.

TABLE 10.6 Experience with organizational practices by ownership (in years)

Variable	Japanese-affiliated plants not in auto supply	Japanese-affiliated auto supplier plants	US-owned auto supplier plants	F	Pr>F
Teams	5.0	5.0	5.5	0.1	0.87
Quality circles	4.5	3.8	5.9*	3.9	0.02
TQM: years' experience	3.3	3.3	4.3	1.9	0.15
Tenure of mgmt. regime: years	7.5	6.3	18.2**	76.8	0.0001
Age of plant: years	15.9	15.1	28.2**	19.3	0.00001

* Difference of means statistically significant at p<0.05 by one-way ANOVA test.
** Difference of means statistically significant at p<0.01 by one-way ANOVA test.

Source: 1994 survey by Richard Florida and Davis Jenkins, Carnegie-Mellon University.

We conducted a number of empirical analyses to examine the relationship between innovative organizational systems inside the plant and innovative customer–supplier relations. Basically, we found evidence of a strong connection between intra- and inter-organizational practices. In the automotive sector, in particular, the adoption of innovative intra-organizational practices was linked to a propensity to work closely with suppliers to improve product quality, delivery, and cost. This led us to conclude that customer–supplier relationships reinforce innovative organizational practices and, in the automobile sector at least, provide a mechanism for diffusing innovative work and production organization throughout a tightly linked customer–supplier network (see Jenkins and Florida 1998).

We also examined the effect of certain aspects of customer–supplier relations (such as supplier certification and electronic data interchange) on the adoption of innovative organizational systems (Jenkins and Florida 1998). Here, we found that certification by customer was associated with a greater likelihood of adopting innovative organizational systems only for US-affiliated automotive suppliers to the transplants. Similarly, US-owned automotive supplier plants that certify their suppliers were significantly more likely to adopt innovative organizational systems. It seems that US automotive supplier plants figured out how to integrate supplier certification activities into a strategy that includes the adoption of innovative organizational systems within the plant. Japanese automotive transplant suppliers were more likely to use electronic data interchange (EDI). Furthermore, EDI was associated with the tendency to adopt innovative organizational systems only for the Japanese-affiliated automotive parts suppliers. Japanese-affiliated automotive supplier plants that have EDI with their customers were significantly more likely to adopt innovative intra-organizational practices. Japanese-affiliated automotive suppliers thus appear better able to integrate electronic data interchange into a production system that both emphasizes information-sharing within the factory and rich communications and cooperation with supplier and customer organizations.

Interaction with local organizations. The 1994 study explored the adoption and diffusion of innovative organizational practices among US-affiliated automobile parts plants that serve as first-tier suppliers to Japanese transplant automotive assemblers, focusing on two key questions. Were there differences between the transplants and US-affiliated establishments in the rates of and reasons for adoption of organizational innovations? Did supply relationships with Japanese transplant producers accelerate the adoption of innovative practices by US automotive component suppliers? Cusumano and Takeishi (1991) found some evidence that transplant producers managed to help or at least persuade their suppliers in the USA, both US-affiliated and Japanese-affiliated, to meet Japanese standards for quality and pricing in a survey of purchasing managers at Japanese automotive assembly transplants. However, they concluded that the overall high-quality performance of suppliers to the transplant assemblers reflects more the transfer of Japanese suppliers to the USA than improvement in the capacity of USA-affiliated suppliers through the transfer of managerial skills to those firms.

The findings of the 1994 study indicated that US suppliers to the transplants were quite innovative (see Table 10.5). First, we found little difference in adoption of innovative organizational systems between Japanese-affiliated and US-owned suppliers to the Japanese transplant automobile assemblers. In fact, a slightly higher proportion of US-owned suppliers utilized innovative organizational practices (e.g. teams and so forth), although this difference was not statistically significant. The US-owned supplier sample also included a larger group of traditional or Taylorist establishments. To probe this further, the 1994 study also conducted econometric analyses (multinomial probit models) of the factors that account for the adoption of innovative work and production practices by US automotive suppliers to the transplants and their Japanese counterparts (see Jenkins and Florida 1998). We explored the effects of employment size, capital intensity, wages, education levels, unionization, customer (transplant versus Big Three), and supplier relations on the adoption of innovative work and production practices. The results of this analysis indicated that, for the US-owned automobile suppliers, having a Japanese transplant assembler as a plant's most important customer, was not by itself associated with a greater likelihood that the plant would adopt innovative organizational practices.

We also looked at the timing of adoption of innovative work and production systems for US-owned and transplant suppliers. The results of the 1994 study indicated that US-owned suppliers had on average been using these practices longer than Japanese-affiliated plants—by at least a year for each practice (see Table 10.6). We were especially struck by how recent the adoption of innovative organizational practices was across the entire 1994 sample both Japanese-affiliated or US-owned. The average time that plants were using such practices was 3.5–5 years, with 1989–91 being the peak period for adoption. Plants in the sample were involved with teams the longest on average, followed by quality circles and TQM. The only exception was US supplier plants, which used quality circles for an average of six years compared to only three-and-a-half years for Japanese-affiliated automotive suppliers (Jenkins and Florida 1998).

In short, the 1994 findings reinforce the earlier finding that inter-organizational relationships play a key role in the transfer and adoption of intra-organizational practices (see Jenkins and Florida 1998; Florida and Jenkins 1999). Organizational transfer, in the case of Japanese transplants, is far more likely in industries with tight supplier chains and close interaction across the production chain. Indeed, the high rate of adoption appears to be reinforced by uniquely close and interdependent supplier relations required for integration in the automotive sector. This supports the hypothesis that close inter-organizational relationships affect the adoption of organizational innovations both directly through direct customer requirements and indirectly through learning and emulation. In the automobile sector especially, Japanese transplants have sought to replicate in the USA tightly linked inter-organizational relationships associated with automotive production in Japan. In this sector, there is a strong association between adoption of innovative organizational systems inside the factory and close and interactive inter-organizational relationships. This reinforces the earlier finding from the 1988 study of an isomorphism between intra- and inter-organizational innovations.

6. Conclusion

This chapter has explored the capability of organizations to transfer and replicate practices in different environments, examining the case of Japanese automotive transplants in the USA. Traditionally, organizational theory suggested that such transfer was difficult and that organizations tended to adapt to the conditions of their surrounding environments. To shed light on this issue, we examined the transfer of organizational practices in a large sample of Japanese transplants, reporting the results from two national survey studies as well from detailed field research on the Japanese automotive transplants conducted in 1988 and 1994 respectively.

Generally speaking, the findings from our studies support the view that organizations (in this case Japanese automotive transplants) possess the capabilities to transfer and replicate key practices in a new environment (in this case the USA). Our findings indicate that both transplant assemblers and suppliers have been remarkably successful in the transfer and replication of organizational forms and practices. Key elements of so-called Japanese work organization in the automotive industry have been transferred to transplant organizations in the USA. We also found, however, that there were differences in the extent to which the transplants were able to replicate actual worker behaviour within these organizational forms and practices. Furthermore, we found evidence that other practices such as wage determination and labour relations practices were modified to fit the US context. We also found that the transplants effectively recreated key elements of the inter-organizational practices (e.g. end user–supplier relationships) in the USA.

Our findings thus lend support to the hypothesis that organizations possess the capability to transfer and replicate key organizational forms and practices from one environment to another. Certainly, our analysis of Japanese transplant organizations provides evidence that certain organizational practices were removed from the

Japanese environment and successfully implanted in the USA. However, we do not imply that the process of transfer and replication is somehow natural or automatic. Rather, we found that organizations in this study expended considerable resources to the transfer process, acting purposefully and strategically to select and even to alter the environment to make it conducive to new organizational forms.

Our findings may come as a surprise, given the legacy, conceptual orientation, and predictions of industrial sociology and organization theory. These theories imply that the environment has a determinant effect on organizational form and structure, that it is difficult to transfer and replicate organizational characteristics between dissimilar environments, and that once transferred, organizations take on the characteristics of the new environment. They, thus, minimize the importance of organizational resources and capabilities in this process. The transplants in our sample effectively recreated many of the critical key elements of work organization and supplier relations. Our findings lend considerable support to the view that certain classes of organizations possess the resources and capabilities to transfer and replicate key practices across environments.

Our findings also indicate that there is a symmetry of sorts between intra- and inter-organizational practices. The Japanese transplants have replicated long-term, interactive, participative, and/or mutually dependent relations at both the intra- and inter-organizational levels. These findings are not specific to the transplants but are reflected in comparative institutional research—the US pattern of short-term adversarial labour–management relations was reflected in the short-term arm's length pattern of US supplier relations. We believe that there may be an underlying rationale for such symmetry. Organizational pressures and incentives may lead to increasing continuity in the governance structures inside and outside the firm. Firms that effectively organize intra-organizational activity are likely to replicate it in dealings with external firms as well. More research and theory-building are needed on this crucial issue, using other sectors, industries, and types of organizations.

Our research indicates that organizations can and do shape their environments. Thus, the concept of environmental embeddedness should be revised to incorporate measures of the power, intentions, and purposeful activities of organizations. Transferring organizational practices and forms from one society to another means that they must be uncoupled from the environment in which they are embedded and recreated in the new environment. The transplant organizations examined here provide clear evidence that organizational forms can be effectively lifted from an originally supportive context and transferred to a foreign environment. Furthermore, they show that organizations can shape aspects of the new environment to meet their functional requirements. In general terms, then, we are led to conclude that organizations possess the resources and the capabilities to alter the environment. Acting strategically and purposefully, we conclude that organizations possess the resources and capabilities to transform the social matrix of the environment. Furthermore, we find that successful organizational transfer is neither natural nor automatic; it hinges on the strategic action organizations take to shape the environment to meet their requirements.

References

Abegglen, J. (1958). *The Japanese Factory*. Cambridge, Mass.: MIT University Press.

—— and G. Stalk (1985). *Kaisha: The Japanese Corporation*. New York: Basic Books.

Abo, T. (ed.) (1994). *Hybrid Factory: The Japanese Production System in the United States*. New York: Oxford University Press.

Adler, P. (1993a). 'The "Learning Bureaucracy": New United Motor Manufacturing, Inc.', in Barry M. Staw and Larry L. Cummings (eds.), *Research in Organizational Behavior*. Greenwich, Conn.: JAI Press.

—— (1993b). 'Time-and-motion regained'. *Harvard Business Review*, 71(1): 97–109.

Aiken, M., and G. Hage (1968). 'Organizational Interdependence and Intraorganizational Structure', *American Sociological Review*, 33 (Dec.): 912–30.

Altshuler, A., M. Anderson, D. Jones, D. Roos, and J. Womack (1984). *The Future of the Automobile*. Cambridge, Mass.: MIT Press.

Aoki, M. (1988). *Information Incentives and Bargaining in the Japanese Economy*. Cambridge: Cambridge University Press.

—— 1990. 'Toward an Economic Model of the Japanese Firm', *Journal of Economic Literature*, 28 (Mar.): 1–27.

Asanuma, B. (1985). 'The Organization of Parts Purchases in the Japanese Automotive Industry', *Japanese Economic Studies* (Summer): 32–53.

Benedict, R. (1946). *The Chrysanthemum and the Sword*. Boston: Houghton-Mifflin Publishers.

Braverman, H. (1974). *Labor and Monopoly Capital*. New York: Monthly Review Press.

Brown, C., and M. Reich (1989). 'When Does Union-Management Cooperation Work: A Look at NUMMI and GM-Van Nuys', *California Management Review*, 31(4): 26–44.

Burawoy, M. (1979). *Manufacturing Consent*. Chicago: University of Chicago.

—— (1983). 'Between the Labor Process and the State: The Changing Face of Factory Regimes Under Advanced Capitalism', *American Sociological Review*, 48: 587–605.

Clark, R. (1979). *The Japanese Company*. New Haven, Conn.: Yale University Press.

Cole, R. (1971). *Japanese Blue Collar*. Berkeley: University of California Press.

—— (1979). *Work. Mobility and Participation*. Berkeley: University of California Press.

—— (1989a). *Strategies for Learning*. Berkeley: University of California Press.

—— (1989b). 'Reflections on Japanese Corporate Citizenship: Company Reactions to a Study of Hiring Practices in the United States', *Chuo Koron*, 10: 122–35.

—— (1993). 'Issues in Skill Formation and Training in Japanese Approaches to Automation', in Paul Adler (ed.), *Technology and The Future of Work*. New York: Oxford University Press.

—— (1999). *Managing Quality Fads: How American Business Learned to Play the Quality Game*. New York: Oxford University Press.

—— and D. Deskins (1988). 'Racial Factors in Site Location and Employment Patterns of Japanese Automobile Firms in America', *California Business Review*, 31: 9–22.

Cool, K., and C. Legnick-Hall (1985). 'Second Thoughts on the Transferability of the Japanese Management Style', *Organization Studies*, 6: 1–22.

Crowther, S., and P. Garrahan (1988). 'Invitation to Sunderland: Corporate Power and the Local Economy', *Industrial Relations Journal*, 19(1): 51–9.

Cusumano, M. (1985). *The Japanese Automobile Industry: Technology and Management at Nissan and Toyota*. Cambridge, Mass.: Harvard University Press.

Cusumano, M., and A. Takeishi (1991). 'Supplier Relations and Management: A Study of Japanese, Japanese-Transplant and US Auto Plants', *Strategic Management Journal*, 12: 563–88.

Cutcher-Gershenfeld, J. (1991). 'The Impact of Economic Performance of a Transformation in Workplace Relations', *Industrial and Labor Relations Review*, 44(2): 241–60.

Dillman, D. (1978). *Mail and Telephone Surveys: The Total Design Method.* New York: John Wiley & Sons.

DiMaggio, P., and W. Powell (1983). 'The Iron Cage Revisited: Institutional Isomorphism and Collective Rationality in Organizational Fields', *American Sociological Review*, 48 (Apr.): 147–60.

Dohse, K., U. Jurgens, and T. Malsch (1986). 'From Fordism to Toyotism? The Social Organization of the Labor Process in the Japanese Automobile Industry', *Politics and Society*, 14(2): 45–66.

Dore, R. (1973). *Japanese Factory. British Factory.* Berkeley: University of California Press.

—— (1983). 'Goodwill and the Spirit of Market Capitalism', *British Journal of Sociology*, 34: 459–82.

Drucker, P. (1993). *Post-Capitalist Society.* New York: Random House.

Dunphy, D. (1987). 'Convergence/Divergence: A Temporal Review of the Japanese Enterprise and Its Management', *Academy of Management Review*, 12(3): 445–59.

Edwards, R. (1979). *Contested Terrain.* New York: Basic Books.

Florida, R. (1993). Review of Ruth Milkman, *Japan's California Factories, Contemporary Sociology.*

—— and D. Jenkins (1998). 'The Japanese Transplants in North America: Production Organization, Location and R&D', in Steven Tolliday (ed.), *Between Imitation and Innovation: The Transfer and Hybridization of Production Systems in the International Automobile Industry.* Oxford: Oxford University Press: 189–215.

—— and M. Kenney (1990). *The Breakthrough Illusion.* New York: Basic Books.

—— —— (1991). 'Transplanted organizations: The transfer of Japanese industrial organization to the United States', *American Sociological Review*, 56: 381.

—— —— (1992a). 'The Japanese Transplants, Production Organization and Regional Development', *Journal of the American Planning Association* (Winter): 21–38.

—— —— (1992b). 'Restructuring in Place: Japanese Investment, Production Organization, and the Geography of Steel', *Economic Geography*, 68(2).

—— —— (1994). 'The Globalization of Innovation: The Economic Geography of Japanese R&D in the US', *Economic Geography*, 70(4): 344–69.

Freidman, D. (1988). *The Misunderstood Miracle: Industrial Development and Political Change in Japan.* Ithaca, NY: Cornell University Press.

Fucini, J., and S. Fucini (1990). *Working for the Japanese.* New York: Free Press.

Fruin, W. M. (1992). *The Japanese Enterprise System: Competitive Strategies, Cooperative Structure.* Oxford: Clarendon Press.

Fujimoto, T., T. Nishiguchi, and S. Sei (1994). 'The Strategy and Structure of Japanese Automobile Manufacturers in Europe', in Mark Mason and Dennis Encarnation (eds.), *Does Ownership Matter? Japanese Multinationals in Europe.* Oxford: Oxford University Press.

Gordon, A. (1985). *The Evolution of Labor Relations in Japan: Heavy Industry, 1853–1955.* Cambridge, Mass.: Harvard University Press.

Graham, L. (1993). 'Inside a Japanese Transplant', *Work and Occupations*, 20(2): 147–73.

Granovetter, M. (1985). 'Economic Action and Social Structure: The Problem of Embeddedness', *American Journal of Sociology*, 91(3): 481–510.

—— 1986. 'Labor Mobility, Internal Markets, and Job Matching: A Comparison of the Sociological and Economic Approaches', *Research in Social Stratification and Mobility*, 5: 3–39.

Hannan, M., and J. Freeman (1988). 'The Ecology of Organizational Mortality: American Labor Unions, 1836–1985', *American Journal of Sociology*, 94(1): 25–52.

Helper, S. (1990). 'Selling to Japanese Automobile Assembly Plants: Results of a Survey', working paper, Case Western Reserve University Department of Economics.

—— and D. I. Levine (1993). 'Supplier Participation and Worker Participation: Is There a Linkage?' Case Western Reserve University and University of California, Berkeley.

—— and M. Sako (1993). 'Supplier Relations in the Auto Industry: A Limited Japanese–US Convergence? Results of the 1993 IMVP Supplier Surveys', Case Western Reserve University and London School of Economics.

Hill, R. C., M. Indergaard, and K. Fujita (1988). 'Flat Rock, Home of Mazda: The Social Impact of a Japanese Company on an American Community', Paper presented at the Eighth Annual Automotive Conference, University of Michigan (Mar.).

Howes, C. (1993). *Japanese Automobile Transplants and the US Automobile Industry*. Washington, DC: Economic Policy Institute.

Jacoby, S. (1979). 'The Origins of Internal Labor Markets in Japan', *Industrial Relations*, 18 (Spring): 184–96.

—— (1993). 'Pacific Ties: Industrial Relations and Employment Systems in Japan and the US since 1900', in Howell Harris and Nelson Lichtenstein (eds.), *Industrial Democracy in the Twentieth Century*. New York: Cambridge University Press.

Jenkins, D., and R. Florida (1999). 'Work System Innovation among Japanese Transplants in the United States', in Paul Adler, Mark Fruin, and Jeffery Liker (eds.), *Remade in America: Japanese Transplants and the Diffusion of Japanese Production Systems*. New York: Oxford University Press.

Kagono, T., I. Nonaka, K. Sakakibara, and A. Okumura (1985). *Strategic vs. Evolutionary Management*. Amsterdam: North Holland.

Kalleberg, A., and J. Lincoln (1988). 'The Structure of Earnings Inequality in the United States and Japan', *American Journal of Sociology*, 94: S121–S153.

Kamata, S. (1982). *Japan in the Passing Lane*. New York: Pantheon.

Kato, T., and R. Steven (eds.) (1993). *Is Japanese Management Postfordist? An International Debate*. Tokyo: Madosha Publishers, in Japanese and English.

Katz, H. (1985). *Shifting Gears*. Cambridge, Mass.: MIT Press.

Kenney, M., and R. Florida (1988). 'Beyond Mass Production: Production and the Labor Process in Japan', *Politics and Society*, 16(1): 121–58.

—— —— (1993). *Beyond Mass Production: The Japanese System and Its Transfer to the US*. New York: Oxford University Press.

Kochan, T., and J. Cutcher-Gershenfeld (1988). 'Institutionalizing and Diffusing Innovation in Industrial Relations', Washington DC: US Department of Labor, Bureau of Labor-Management Relations and Cooperative Programs.

—— H. Katz, and R. McKersie (1986). *The Transformation of American Industrial Relations*. New York: Basic Books.

Koike, K. (1988). *Understanding Industrial Relations in Japan*. New York: St Martin's Press.

Krafcik, J. (1989). 'A New Diet for US Manufacturers', *Technology Review*, 92: 28–38.

—— (1986). 'Learning From NUMMI', MIT International Motor Vehicle Program, unpublished manuscript.

Kumazawa, M., and J. Yamada (1989). 'Jobs and Skills Under the Lifelong Nenko Employment Practice', in Stephen Wood (ed.), *The Transformation of Work*. London: Unwin Hyman: 102–26.

Levine, S. (1958). *Industrial Relations in Postwar Japan*. Urbana: University of Illinois Press.

Lillrank, P., and N. Kano (1989). *Continuous Improvement: Quality Control Circles in Japanese Industry*. Ann Arbor: Center for Japanese Studies, University of Michigan.

Lincoln, J., M. Hanada, and K. McBride (1986). 'Organizational Structures in Japanese and US Manufacturing', *Administrative Science Quarterly*, 31: 338–64.

—— and A. Kalleberg (1985). 'Work Organization and Workforce Commitment: A Study of Plants and Employees in the US and Japan', *American Sociological Review*, 50 (Dec.): 738–60.

MacDuffie, J. P. (1993). Review of Japan's California Factories: Labor Relations and Economic Globalization by Ruth Milkman, in *Industrial and Labor Relations Review*, 47(1): 132–3.

—— (1994). 'Human Resource Bundles and Manufacturing Performance: Flexible Production Systems in the World Auto Industry', Wharton School, University of Pennsylvania.

—— and F. Pil (1994). 'Transferring Japanese Human Resource Practices: Japanese Auto Plants in Japan and the US', Paper presented to the International Management Division, Academy of Management.

Mair, A., R. Florida, and M. Kenney (1988). 'The New Geography of Automobile Production: Japanese Transplants in North America', *Economic Geography*, 64: 352–73.

Marsh, R., and M., Hiroshi (1976). *Modernization and the Japanese Factory*. Princeton, NJ: Princeton University Press.

Meyer, J., and B. Rowen (1977). 'Institutionalized Organizations: Formal Structure as Myth and Ceremony', *American Journal of Sociology*, 83(2): 340–63.

Milkman, R. (1991). *Japan's California Factories: Labor Relations and Economic Globalization*. University of California, Los Angeles, Institute of Labor Relations.

Morris, J. (1988). 'The Who, Why and Where of Japanese Manufacturing Investment in the UK', *Industrial Relations Journal*, 19(1): 31–40.

Nakane, C. (1970). *Japanese Society*. Berkeley: University of California Press.

Nishiguchi, T. (1994). *Strategic Industrial Sourcing: The Japanese Advantage*. New York: Oxford University Press.

Nonaka, I., and T. Hirotaki (1995). *The Knowledge Creating Company: How Japanese Companies Create the Dynamics of Innovation*. Oxford: Oxford University Press.

Odaka, K., K. Ono, and F. Adachi (1988). *The Automobile Industry in Japan: A Study of Ancillary Firm Development*. Tokyo: Kinokuniya. Distributed by Oxford University Press.

Oliver, N., and B. Wilkinson (1989). 'Japanese Manufacturing Techniques and Personnel and Industrial Relations Practice in Britain: Evidence and Implications', *British Journal of Industrial Relations*, 27: 73–91.

Osterman, P. (1994). 'How Common is Workplace Transformation and Who Adopts It?' *Industrial and Labor Relations Review*, 47(2).

Ouchi, W. (1980). 'Markets, Bureaucracies and Clans', *Administrative Science Quarterly*, 25 (Mar.): 129–41.

Parker, M., and J. Slaughter (1988). 'Management by Stress', *Technology Review* (Oct.): 36–46.

Pfeffer, J., and G. Slancik (1978). *The External Control of Organizations: A Resource Dependence Perspective*. New York: Harper Row.

Rosenbaum, J., and T. Kariya (1989). 'From High School to Work: Market and Institutional Mechanisms in Japan', *American Journal of Sociology*, 94: 1334–65.

Sayer, A. (1986). 'New Developments in Manufacturing: The Just-in-Time System', *Capital and Class*, 30: 43–72.

Schumpeter, J. (1947). 'The Creative Response in Economic History', *Journal of Economic History*, 7: 149–59.

Sheard, P. (1983). 'Auto Production Systems in Japan: Organizational and Locational Features', *Australian Geographical Studies*, 21 (Apr.): 49–68.

Shimada, H. (1986). 'Japanese Industrial Relations in Transition', MIT Sloan School of Management Work Paper 1854–88.

Shirai, T. (ed.) (1983). *Contemporary Industrial Relations in Japan*. Madison: University of Wisconsin Press: 29–62.

Smitka, M. (1992). *Competitive Ties: Subcontracting in the Japanese Automotive Industry*. New York: Columbia University Press.

Smith, D., and R. Florida (1994). 'Agglomeration and Industrial Location: An Econometric Analysis of Japanese-Affiliated Manufacturers in Automotive-related Industries', *Journal of Urban Economics*, 35: 1–19.

Taira, K. (1962). 'The Characteristics of Japanese Labor Markets', *Economic Development and Cultural Change* (Jan.): 150–68.

University of Tokyo, Institute of Social Science (1990). *Local Production of Japanese Automobile and Electronic Firms in the United States: The 'Application' and 'Adaptation' of Japanese Style Management*. Tokyo: University of Tokyo.

Weick, K. (1979). *The Social Psychology of Organizing*. New York: Random House.

White, M., and M. Trevor (1983). *Under Japanese Management*. London: Heinemann Educational Books.

Wilms, W. (1995). *Reawakening the Spirit*. New York: Times Books.

——A. Hardcastle, and D. Zell (1994). 'A Cultural Transformation: New United Motor Manufacturing Inc.', Paper presented at a conference on The Challenge of Multinational Competition, Stuttgart, Germany, May 1993.

Williamson, O. (1975). *Markets and Hierarchies*. New York: Free Press.

Womack, J., D. Jones, and D. Roos (1990). *The Machine that Changed the World*. New York: Rawson Associates.

Young, R. (1988). 'Is Population Ecology a Useful Paradigm for the Study of Organizations', *American Journal of Sociology*, 94(1): 1–24.

PART IV

Introduction to Part IV

PERSPECTIVES ON CAPABILITIES

The three chapters that follow present significant advancements in the interpretation of the nature and distribution of capabilities within and across firms; their theoretical representation—in particular with reference to the theory of business organization—and their implications to strategic management.

Patel and Pavitt study *technological* capabilities across around 400 of the world's largest technologically active firms, as measured by their patenting activities. They find robust evidence of competences diversified across multiple technological fields, quite inertial—although slowly changing over time—and distinctly different across firms—even if influenced by the sector of principal (production) activity of the firms themselves. Interestingly, these large firms show a range of technologies which they master broader than their production diversification: as such it is an indirect evidence of the profound complementarity between product-embodied technologies, which firms may acquire from outside, and in-house knowledge necessary to utilize them. Moreover, Patel and Pavitt show that most of these firms in addition to *core* (technological) competences possess 'background' competences located in broad ('universal') technologies—such as machinery and chemical process—and 'niche' competences in particular technological sub-fields: these firm-specific technological profiles are proximate predictors of the core activities of the firms.

Teece, Pisano, and Schuen present an ambitious attempt to conceptualize different forms of competence and relate them to both organization theory and strategic management. A general premise, common to the other chapters of this book, is that organizations embody (relatively) coherent structures of tasks and competences, with distinctive governance modes, which do not replicate either pure market arrangements or any 'nexus of contracts'.

Given that, the authors identify the specificities of each firm in terms of (a) *organizational processes* (including their operating routines), (b) *positions* (broadly defined to cover their specific assets, their location along the value chain, and their relationships with suppliers and customers), and (c) *paths* (i.e. their patterns of change in the former two sets of characteristics). A theme which they emphasize—common also to the other two chapters—is the stickiness over time of distinct organizational capabilities and, thus, also the constraints which the past learning history of the organization puts upon the degrees of discretionality of strategic management.

This perspective on organizations and organizational learning clearly shifts the focus of analysis from either product positioning or 'clever strategizing' to the *processes* of problem-solving and organizational governance, and, dynamically, to competence-enhancing strategies.

The chapter by Levinthal broadly shares with the former two the view that organizational capabilities are partly a collective property of ensembles of organizational routines and learning heuristics (and also, 'cultures', 'visions', and strategic orientations), and provides an appealing theoretical framework for their analysis.

Key features here (as well as, more implicitly, in a few other chapters) are the notion of (a) *complementarity* and (b) *interdependence* among organizational routines and complementary assets. A crucial consequence concerns what one could call the '*competitiveness diagnostics*' of corporate performances: precisely because of the (nonlinear) interrelatedness in the contribution of the various organizational traits to overall performances, 'credit assignment' is a difficult exercise. Relatedly, in terms of organizational learning, 'local' exploration and adjustments are likely to be the rule, since otherwise one is likely to lose any grasp on the relationships between causes (i.e. changes in organizational behaviour) and effects (i.e. changes in revealed performances). But a fundamental corollary of all this is also that organizations are likely to end up (*quasi*) stuck into local peaks of the 'fitness landscape', using Levinthal terminology (i.e. roughly speaking the mapping between organizational traits and 'competitiveness'), with low probabilities of exploring radically diverse organizational arrangements.

The three chapters together provide novel insights regarding at least five domains, namely:

(1) The development of knowledge- and learning-based theory of organizations.

(2) A more integrated understanding of the co-evolution of corporate problemsolving capabilities with (potentially conflictual) mechanism of governance (see also the chapter by Coriat) and the institutional settings where firms operate (cf. also the chapters by Fujimoto, and Florida and Kenney).

(3) Much sharper identifications of the different (possibly hierarchically) levels at which 'competences' may be identified, yielding also an easier search for empirical proxies.

(4) The beginning of a challenging endeavour aiming also at formal representations of organizational structures and change (cf. the suggestive hints in Levinthal's chapter, together with the references therein to his own parallel contributions, Marengo's, Warglien's, and others').

(5) The links between *descriptive* interpretations of organizational competences and their *normative* implications regarding in particular those 'strategic management' activities involving delicate balances between the diagnostics of path-dependent organizational irreversibilities and subtle windows of opportunity for organizational reconfigurations, recombination of basic routines, and reorientation of learning procedures.

11

How Technological Competencies Help Define the Core (not the Boundaries) of the Firm

PARI PATEL AND KEITH PAVITT

1. Introduction

1.1. Why firm-specific technological competencies are important

The purpose of this chapter is to show the strong links between what large firms make and sell, and their underlying technological competencies. The subject of 'firm-specific competencies' is of increasing interest to practitioners, and to theorists—and particularly to those in the neo-Schumpeterian tradition, who are seeking to explain why firms provide different ranges of goods and services, why they change at different rates and in different directions over time, and what makes them competitive (Prahalad and Hamel 1990; Dosi *et al.* 1992).

Our main data source is systematic information of US patenting by more than 400 of the world's largest technologically active firms, broken down by each firm's headquarters country and principal product group, and by the technical field and country of origin of the inventor of each patent.[1] Similar data have been used by Hall and her colleagues (1986) to measure lags between R&D and patenting at the firm level, by Narin and his colleagues (1987) for corporate and competitor analysis, by Jaffe (1986) to identify and measure technological 'spillovers', and by Cantwell (1991) to explain patterns of international production.

We concentrate here on systematic comparisons of the level, rates of change, and composition (by technical field) of each firm's patenting activity. We shall show that the technological competencies in large firms are:

- diversified (i.e. multi-technology) and evolving slowly over time, with most firms contributing to improvements in their production machinery and process

This chapter was prepared for the volume on *Nature and Dynamics of Organisational Capabilities*, to be edited by G. Dosi, R. Nelson, and S. Winter, at the International Institute of Applied Systems Analysis (IIASA) in Austria. It is based on research at the Centre for Science, Technology and Energy and Environment Policy (STEEP), funded by the Economic and Social Research Council (ESRC) within the Science Policy Research Unit.

[1] These firms have been chosen from the list of the world's largest firms, published in *Fortune* magazine in 1988. Only those with more than fifty patents granted in the USA in the period 1981–90 have been included. For a detailed description of the characteristics and method of compilation of the database see Patel and Pavitt (1991).

technologies, and an increasing number to improvements in computing, materials, and biotechnology;

● heavily differentiated and stable in their composition and their directions of search, both as a function of the products that they make.

1.2. *Coping with complexity*

Both our questions and our answers are consistent with the neo-Schumpeterian framework of Nelson and Winter (1982), and the more recent analysis of Granstrand and Sjolander (1990) on the 'multi-technology' nature of large firms. Technological artefacts, and the organizational and economic worlds in which they are embedded, are *complex*: in other words, they each comprise so many variables and interactions that it is impossible fully to model, predict, and control their behaviour through explicit and codified theories and guidelines. Certainty about the future, probabilistic risk, and optimization are therefore impossible. The best approach to problem-solving and the management of change is step-by-step experimentation, in which changes are made in one feature or component at a time, and ends and means reinterpreted in the light of the subsequently observed changes. In addition to codified knowledge, experience and tacit knowledge improve the effectiveness of the choices of the feature or component to vary at each stage, and the sub-sequent modifications in means and ends made after observation of the effects of experimentation.

This method is called 'learning', or 'experimentation', or 'trial and error' (and many other things, including 'suck it and see'). Essentially the same approach underlies Lindblom's (1959) prescriptions in public policy, Quinn's (1980) in corporate strategy, and Kline's (1990) in engineering design and development. It explains our results, as follows:

● the complex and multivariate nature of technological artefacts requires the combination and application of advances in many fields of knowledge: hence large firms' competencies are typically *multi-technology*, and increasing over time as new opportunities emerge from the changing knowledge base;

● complexity also constrains firms to search and experiment in and around what they already know and produce: hence firms' competencies are *differentiated*, *stable*, and closely related to their *product mix*.

1.3. *Limitations*

Our chapter has three sets of limitations. First, we measure only technological competence, and thereby neglect many others that are important. Dosi and Teece (1993) have distinguished organizational-economic competencies from technical competencies, and have argued that the latter derive from the former, and are therefore more fundamental to the firm.[2] Our empirical results suggest that this is

---

[2] 'Organizational-economic competence involves: (1) allocative competence—deciding what to produce and how to price it; (2) transactional competence—deciding whether to make or buy, and whether to

only partly correct. A firm's organizational competence does influence its *level* of commitment to technological activities, and its *rate of entry* into fast-growing sub-fields. However, a firm's accumulated technological competence strongly constrains the *directions* in which it searches: even the brightest and the best organizational capabilities will find it difficult (impossible?) to convert a firm making Harris tweed jackets, or Italian high-fashion shoes, into a world class firm in personal computers. The differentiated nature of technical competencies is one the most important factors explaining the coherence and the boundaries of the firm. And a survey of 100 Italian firms by Malerba and Marengo (1993) ranked technological competencies as of greater long-term importance than competencies to respond to either market signals or competitors' strategic actions. The subject therefore deserves analytical and empirical attention, even if it does not cover—and cannot explain—everything.[3]

Our second limitation is that we measure technological competencies only im-perfectly through patent data.[4] In particular, patenting does not fully measure competencies in software technology, since copyright law has until recently been the main means of protection against imitation (see Barton 1993; Samuelson 1993). We have nonetheless been able to identify the growing importance in firms' compet-encies of information technology.

Finally, our third limitation is that we do not assess how differences in the rate and direction of technological accumulation affect firms' economic and competitive performance. Suffice to say that a growing number of studies confirm the competi-tive importance of technological competencies at the level of the firm,[5] which should in principle heighten interest in studies like ours that attempt to describe and explain how they are acquired.

1.4. Structure

We begin in Section 2 by describing the diversity of the technological competencies of our large firms, and in Section 3 show that they are also both stable and differentiated. In Section 4, we examine in more detail the links between specific competencies and specific products, and changes over time, before setting out our conclusions in Section 5.

---

do so alone or in partnership; and (3) administrative competence—how to design organizational structures and policies to enable efficient performance. Technical competence, on the other hand, includes the ability to develop and design products and processes, and to operate facilities effectively...A firm becomes superior in a particular technological domain because it has certain organizational capabilities: it allocates resources to more promising projects, it harnesses experience from prior projects, it hires and upgrades human resources, it integrates new findings from external sources, and it manages a set of problem-solving activities associated with that technology' (Dosi and Teece 1993: 6–7).

[3] In a similar manner (and using the jargon of another academic discipline), we are fully aware that technological competencies in large firms are 'socially constructed' (Bijker *et al.* 1993). But we concentrate here on the important cognitive factors that shape the social construction of technology.

[4] The uses and abuses of patent data have been extensively discussed elsewhere, see e.g. Basber (1987); Pavitt (1988); Grilliches (1990); Patel and Pavitt (1995).

[5] See e.g. Cantwell (1989); Franko (1989); Geroski *et al.* (1993); Oskarsson (1993).

2. Technological Diversity: The Prevalence of the 'Multi-Technology' Firm

2.1. *The extent of technological diversity*

The most striking feature of the technological competencies of large firms is the *diversity* of technological fields in which they are active. This is shown in Table 11.1, which gives the distribution of US patenting of our large firms, in each of the sixteen principal product groups, across four major technological families: chemical, electrical-electronic, non-electrical machinery, and transport.[6] Firms have substantial technological competencies outside what would appear to be their core areas. Thus, electrical and chemical firms have two-thirds or more of their competencies in their obvious core areas, but they also have 15 per cent or more in non-electrical machinery, and automobile firms have less than a third of their competencies in transport technologies, but more than 45 per cent in non-electrical machinery. Only firms principally in pharmaceuticals have less than 10 per cent (on average) of their technological competencies in non-electrical machinery.

TABLE 11.1 Distribution of large firms' technological activities in five broad technological fields, according to their principal product group: 1981–90 (percentage share of the PPG's patents in technology field)

Principal product group (PPG)	Chemical	Non-electrical machinery	Electrical	Transport	Other	Total
Chemicals	71.0	16.9	8.9	0.6	2.6	100.0
Pharmaceuticals	80.2	8.0	2.1	0.0	9.7	100.0
Mining and petroleum	57.1	34.2	6.7	0.9	1.1	100.0
Textiles etc.	52.9	31.7	9.5	0.6	5.3	100.0
Rubber and plastics	43.2	29.3	4.7	20.1	2.7	100.0
Paper and wood	25.4	47.1	12.4	0.4	14.6	100.0
Food	70.6	21.9	3.0	0.1	4.3	100.0
Drink and tobacco	40.8	50.3	4.6	0.3	3.9	100.0
Building materials	30.5	51.3	10.0	0.9	7.3	100.0
Metals	26.8	54.9	13.9	2.1	2.2	100.0
Machinery	7.6	64.9	13.9	10.2	3.3	100.0
Electrical	7.6	21.2	67.0	1.3	2.8	100.0
Computers	5.2	16.3	77.3	0.2	1.0	100.0
Instruments	14.3	18.3	64.2	0.1	3.0	100.0
Motor vehicles	3.8	44.8	20.7	28.8	1.9	100.0
Aircraft	8.1	48.5	31.2	8.3	3.9	100.0
All 440 large firms	28.8	27.9	35.7	4.4	3.1	100.0

Source: Calculated from data supplied to SPRU by the US Patent and Trademark Office.

---

[6] The method for distributing firms' technological activities amongst four technological families is described more fully in Patel and Pavitt (1994). Briefly stated we reclassified the US Patent Classes and subclasses into thirty-four technical fields, and ninety-one sub-fields. On the basis of the ninety-one sub-fields, we recombined patenting into the four technological families shown in Table 11.1. The 'other' category includes traditional manufacturing (e.g. textiles) and non-manufacturing (e.g. construction, medicine, agriculture).

Another measure of technological diversity is the number of technical fields—out of the total of thirty-four used in our analysis[7]—in which our firms have been granted a patent and are therefore technically competent. Only 4 per cent of our firms were active in the 1980s in ten or fewer of these technical fields, whilst 52 per cent were active in between ten and twenty, and 44 per cent in more than twenty—hence the term 'multi-technology' firm (see Archibugi 1988; and Granstrand and Sjolander 1990). More detailed statistical analysis shows that technological diversity increases with firm size and technological intensity (patents per unit sales), and that there are some industry effects: in particular, food firms are significantly less diverse than the average, and aircraft and chemical firms significantly more so. On the other hand, a firm's home country has no significant effects.

2.2. From distinctive core competencies to profiles: a two-dimensional (and measurable) definition of firms' competencies

Given these results, it is difficult to define a firm's technological competencies in terms of a few fields of excellence.[8] It is probably more useful to think in terms of *profiles* of competencies, with varying levels of commitment and competitive advantage in a range of technological fields. With our data, these profiles can have two dimensions:

(1) The *Patent Share* (PS) of the firm's patenting in each of our thirty-four technical fields reflects the relative importance of each field in the firm's total technological portfolio.

(2) The firm's *Revealed Technology Advantage* (RTA) reflects the firm's advantage in each field compared to other firms. It is the firm's share of patenting in the field, divided by the firm's aggregate share of patenting in all fields.

We shall now show that—along both dimensions—firms' technological profiles are highly differentiated, stable over time, and strongly related to the firms' product base.

3. Stability and Differentiation in Firms' Technological Competencies

3.1. Stability in technological profiles

For nearly all our firms, these technological profiles are remarkably stable over time. For each firm, we correlated both the patent shares (PS) and the RTAs for the periods 1969–74 and 1985–90. Table 11.2 shows that, according to both measures, more than 90 per cent of firms have profiles of technological competence that are statistically similar between 1969–74 and 1985–90, at the 1 per cent level of significance. No systematic differences in stability can be detected between firms in different sectors and countries. Large firms clearly do not shift around rapidly in their fields of technological competence.

---

[7] See Tables 11.6 and 11.8 for the name of each of the technical fields.

[8] e.g. 'Few companies are likely to build world leadership in more than five or six fundamental competencies. A company that compiles a list of twenty to thirty capabilities has probably not produced a list of core competencies' (Prahalad and Hamel 1990).

TABLE 11.2 Stability of technological profiles across 34 technical fields, 1969–74 to 1985–90

	No. of firms	Patent shares			Revealed technology advantage		
		Not sig. at 5%	Sig. at 5%	Sig. at 1%	Not sig. at 5%	Sig. at 5%	Sig. at 1%
Chemicals	65	1	1	63	5	7	53
Pharmaceuticals	25	2	3	20	0	0	25
Mining and petroleum	31	7	7	17	5	5	21
Textiles etc.	13	4	6	3	5	6	2
Rubber and plastics	10	0	0	10	1	1	8
Paper and wood	17	1	3	13	4	4	9
Food	16	0	1	15	1	2	13
Drink and tobacco	11	0	1	10	0	2	9
Building materials	17	0	0	17	0	0	17
Metals	44	4	6	34	5	7	32
Machinery	63	2	5	56	5	10	48
Electrical	56	4	5	47	5	8	43
Computers	16	0	0	16	0	1	15
Instruments	19	0	0	19	2	3	14
Motor vehicles	37	0	0	37	2	2	33
Aircraft	19	0	0	19	1	1	17
All sectors	459	25	38	396	41	59	359

This remains true even after taking account of acquisitions and divestments. We have shown elsewhere that, for forty-one of the largest firms in our population, only one had a technological profile statistically different (at the 5 per cent level) in 1987–92 from 1979–84 (Patel and Pavitt 1998). And only in very few of the cases involving substantial technological activities were the technological profiles of the acquired firm different from the acquiring firm, either before or after acquisition.[9]

3.2. Firm-specific constraints on exploiting high opportunity fields

This stability over time in firms' technological profiles is defined by relatively broad technological fields, and does not reflect the more localized processes of search that firms undertake. For this reason, we have identified in US patenting activities the 1,000 (out of a total of around 100,000) technological subclasses of the highest technological opportunity, as measured by their absolute increase in patenting from the 1960s to the late 1980s. In aggregate, their share increased steeply from 3 to 18 per cent of total US patenting. A relatively high proportion of fast-growing fields are to be found in electronics and chemical technologies.[10]

---

[9] Intriguingly, all these cases involved US-owned firms (*Black and Decker's* purchase of *Emhart*, *General Motors of Hughes*, *General Electric* of *RCA*, and *Kodak* of *Sterling Drug*). In contrast, *ATT* and the European firms (*ABB, Alcatel, Philips, Thomson* and *Olivetti*) reinforced their existing profiles through their acquisitions, as did *Hitachi* and *Fujitsu*.

[10] For this reason, we find significant correlations between firms' share of total patenting in fast-growing fields, on the one hand, and their R&D intensity and share of total patenting in science based technologies, on the other.

TABLE 11.3 Correlations of past (1969–84) shares of total patenting on shares of patenting in fast-growing areas in 1985–90

	Chemicals	Mechanical	Electrical	Transport	Other
Share of total chem. 69–84	0.91*	−0.41	−0.61	−0.26	0.00
Share of total mech. 69–84	−0.41	0.68*	−0.10*	0.14*	0.09*
Share of total elec. 69–84	−0.58	−0.12	0.87*	−0.17	−0.17
Share of total trans. 69–84	−0.34	0.18*	−0.13	0.85*	−0.04
Share of total other 69–84	0.06	−0.12	−0.18	−0.07	0.55*

* Denotes a statistically significant coefficient that is greater than zero at the 5% level.

In Table 11.3, we show that firms are in fact heavily constrained by their prior competencies in the extent to which they are capable of accumulating competencies in these fast-growing fields. Their shares of total fast-growing patenting in 1985–90 within the five broad fields of technology used in Table 11.1—chemicals, mechanical, electrical-electronic, transport, and 'other'—are strongly correlated with their prior shares of total patenting in these same fields over the period 1969–84. In other words, firms' capacities to exploit fields of high technological opportunity are strongly constrained by their prior competencies.

3.3. The differentiation of industries' technological competencies

In addition to being very stable, our data also show that large firms' technological competencies are highly differentiated. For the firms in each of our sixteen industries, the distribution of both average patent shares and revealed technology advantage RTAs are in general very different. For patent shares, 23 per cent of the cross-industry correlations are positive and significant at the 5 per cent level; and for RTAs the share is reduced to 5 per cent. In both cases, there are essentially three clusters with similar technological profiles:

- the chemical and chemical-related industries (the first eight listed in Table 11.1);
- machinery and vehicles;
- electrical and computers.

There is also one significantly negative correlation that is important: between the RTAs of firms in chemicals and in electrical products. Although both are often lumped together as 'high technology' or 'science-based' firms, they are clearly based on very different mixes of technological competence.

3.4. Do firms' technological profiles match product groups?

One drawback with this industry-based analysis is that it neglects the possibility of diversity in the profile of technological competencies of firms *within* each industrial sector. For this reason, we summarize in Tables 11.4 and 11.5 our systematic examination of the similarities and differences in profiles of technological competencies individually for all our large firms. Each table shows the percentage of firms' technological profiles, for the period 1981–90, that are similar (that is, positively

TABLE 11.4 Correlations of firms' shares across 34 technical fields by principal product group, 1981–90 (percentage of the total that are positive and significant at 5% level)

	Own PPG	Other PPGs	Phar.	Mini	Text.	Rubb.	Paper	Food	Drink	Buil.	Metal	Mach.	Elec.	Comp.	Inst.	Motor	Airc.
Chemicals	78.6	19.1	60.3	61.8	53.6	49.0	17.8	39.0	9.8	24.9	19.1	4.5	1.7	0.0	8.7	2.4	1.9
Pharmaceuticals	94.3	15.8		28.3	30.8	18.7	6.4	38.3	12.5	4.5	4.1	1.1	0.1	0.0	8.2	0.1	0.0
Mining and petroleum	69.0	19.3			39.0	34.4	15.9	22.1	3.6	17.5	17.7	7.0	1.3	0.2	5.5	4.8	3.4
Textiles etc.	55.6	24.7				35.6	45.0	25.0	17.5	45.6	15.3	14.8	10.5	5.9	13.3	4.6	10.0
Rubber and plastics	72.2	16.9					14.8	14.3	4.2	18.1	8.5	7.3	5.4	1.3	6.3	2.2	5.6
Paper and wood	58.2	13.3						17.1	26.4	34.0	9.6	23.9	5.4	2.6	6.3	4.9	3.4
Food	67.0	14.1							54.5	14.3	4.3	5.2	0.8	0.4	3.4	1.0	1.2
Drink and tobacco	50.0	11.4								18.0	5.9	20.9	3.3	1.5	4.8	7.9	10.4
Building materials	48.3	15.5									25.7	17.1	5.7	0.7	6.5	6.4	15.3
Metals	72.8	12.7										23.0	11.1	4.2	5.9	7.2	18.4
Machinery	45.0	12.8											12.7	5.9	7.6	44.3	30.1
Electrical	61.6	10.4												59.3	30.9	13.7	41.4
Computers	100.0	12.7													34.2	5.9	38.9
Instruments	55.2	12.2														11.6	30.4
Motor vehicles	85.7	12.0															36.8
Aircraft	72.5	18.5															
All sectors	67.3	14.5															

TABLE 11.5 Correlations of firms' RTAs across 34 technical fields by principal product group, 1981–90 (percentage of the total that are positive and significant at 5% level)

	Own PPG	Other PPGs	Phar.	Mini	Text.	Rubb.	Paper	Food	Drink	Buil.	Metal	Mach.	Elec.	Comp.	Inst.	Motor	Airc.
Chemicals	48.7	9.6	26.1	25.2	33.6	26.6	12.0	6.4	2.7	19.1	14.5	3.8	1.3	0.0	2.5	0.8	0.9
Pharmaceuticals	86.7	6.2		3.1	16.8	0.9	3.8	20.6	13.0	0.5	0.0	0.5	0.1	0.0	4.2	0.0	0.0
Mining and petroleum	72.9	7.4			4.2	7.5	9.7	0.2	0.0	4.6	14.2	3.6	0.6	0.0	1.1	1.8	2.9
Textiles etc.	46.7	12.4				33.3	23.3	10.0	10.0	38.1	10.8	4.5	4.8	0.0	3.3	0.3	0.0
Rubber and plastics	86.1	9.0					17.3	0.0	11.1	18.1	1.5	9.0	2.0	0.0	0.5	0.0	9.3
Paper and wood	37.3	7.9						11.9	22.2	29.9	1.6	9.2	2.8	0.7	6.3	1.4	0.0
Food	100.0	5.2							87.5	6.3	0.8	1.8	0.1	0.0	0.0	0.0	0.0
Drink and tobacco	82.1	6.9								10.2	2.0	5.8	1.1	0.0	0.0	1.1	0.0
Building materials	52.5	9.6									10.5	10.0	3.9	0.0	6.0	2.1	1.0
Metals	77.8	7.2										11.4	5.1	0.0	0.9	3.8	3.2
Machinery	21.3	7.4											5.8	2.0	3.1	27.1	7.6
Electrical	45.5	5.7												47.4	15.3	3.6	5.5
Computers	99.3	7.6													16.5	0.0	3.9
Instruments	38.1	4.9														1.8	3.7
Motor vehicles	75.6	5.7															8.6
Aircraft	76.5	3.7															
All sectors	51.5	7.2															

correlated at the 5 per cent level) to firms inside the same product group, and to those in the other product groups: Table 11.4 does this for patent shares, and Table 11.5 for Revealed Technology Advantage. The main patterns that emerge are as follows.

● Firms have significantly different profiles of technological competence from most others: only 27.8 per cent are similar in patent shares, and 15.3 per cent in RTAs.

● In all sectors, firms have a higher probability of finding others with similar technological profiles within their sector than outside: from twice as high for machinery firms, to more than ten times as high for pharmaceutical firms.

● The frequency of technological proximity between firms in different sectors is not evenly spread or random, but reveals distinct groupings, many of which have been anticipated earlier in Section 3.3 above.

4. A Closer Look at Technological Competencies

4.1. What specific technological competencies are needed to make which specific products?

Thus, the similarities and differences in the technological profiles amongst firms are not random, but represent the different bundles of technological knowledge that are necessary for firms to be competent to produce different classes of product. We showed in broad outline what these are in Table 11.1. We shall now explore them in more detail.

For this purpose, we distinguish—as shown in Figure 11.1—two dimensions of any large firms' technological competencies (see Section 2.2 above):

● on the Y-axis, the percentage share of each of our thirty-four technical fields in total patenting (PS), reflecting the relative importance of each field in the firm's total technological portfolio;

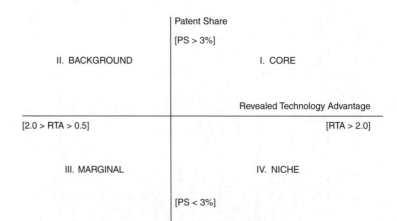

Fig. 11.1 A classification for firms' technological profiles

● on the X-axis, the firm's Revealed Technology Advantage (RTA) in each of the thirty-four technical fields, reflecting the relative importance of the firm for the field.

On this basis:

● the 'distinctive' technical competencies of the firms are those in which the RTA is relatively high: namely in the *first* quadrant, which defines and describes the *core* of its competencies, and in the *fourth* quadrant, where it may have *niche* advantages in relatively small technological fields;
● in the *second* quadrant, the firm may have *background* competencies, in fields where it allocates a relatively high share of its technological resources, but where—given the relatively large size of the field—it does not achieve a relatively high technological advantage compared to its competitors;
● and in the *third* quadrant, it may have *marginal* competencies, where it neither allocates a large share of its own resources, nor achieves a distinctive advantage compared to other firms.

In Table 11.6, we describe the nature of contribution of competencies in each of our thirty-four technical fields to firms in each of the sixteen industrial sectors, according to the fourfold classification shown in Figure 11.1. From this, it emerges that technical fields vary greatly in the nature and extent of their contributions to firm-specific competencies:

● organic chemistry and materials are *core* competencies in five industries; drugs, non-electrical machinery, and image and sound in three each; instruments (in spite of its overall importance) in only one; and five fields in none at all;
● *background* competencies are located mainly in machinery, instrumentation, and chemical processes;
● *niche* competencies are restricted to relatively few fields such as agricultural chemicals, dyestuffs, power plant, and nuclear energy;
● the most prevalent of *marginal* technologies are assembly and materials handling, plastic and rubber, and metallurgical processes;
● computer-related technological competence is so far identifiable beyond the usual 'high-tech' industries only in machinery and vehicles.

It also emerges from Table 11.6 that profiles of competencies vary greatly amongst firms in the different sectors:

● the number of technical fields involved varies from six in pharmaceuticals to twenty-five in aircraft;
● in only four sectors (chemicals, pharmaceuticals, petroleum and mining, and electrical products) do the number of *core* technological fields outnumber the number of *background* fields. More detailed calculations show that, in at least six sectors, competencies in *background* fields account for more than 50 per cent total firms' patenting in all technological fields.

TABLE 11.6 Firms' technical profile according to their principal product group, 1981–90

	Chem.	Phar.	Mini	Text.	Rubb.	Paper	Food	Drink	Buil.	Metal	Mach.	Elec.	Comp.	Inst.	Motor	Airc.
InOrChem	***								*	****	*					*
OrgCh	****	****	****	****	****	**	**	**	*		*	**		**		**
AgrCh	****	***	**	**	**	**	*	**	*		**	**	**	**		***
ChePro	****	**	**	**	**	**	****	**	**	**	**	**	**			
Hydroc	*	***	****	*	*	*				**						
Bleach	***	***	*	****		***	***	**		*						
Drugs	****	****	*	**	****	***	****	*			*					*
Plastic	***		*	***	****	****	*	*	***	****	*	**		**	*	**
Materials	**		*	****	****	***	**	**	****	****	**					
Food&T	*	*		**	**	****	****	****	*	*****	*			**	*	****
Metallu Pro	**		*	**	**	**	**		**	****	***	**		*		
ChemApp			****			**	**		**	**	****			*	****	****
NonElMach			**								****	***			****	
ElEqup				**		****	**	**	**	**	****	****	**			
SpecMach				**	*		**			**	****		**		**	
MetalWEq					**		**		**	****	****	**			**	**
AssHandApp				*	**	*	*	**	*		***	***	*	*		
Nuclear												**				
PowerP					***	***					***		**		***	***
VehiEngi						**	**				****		****		****	*
OthTran										*	**		**		****	
Aircraft			****	***					*		****					****
Mining			****								*****			**		*
Telecoms												****	****	**		
Semicond												****	****			**
ElectrDevi												****	****	****	**	**
Computers						**					*	**	****	****	**	**
Image&Sou												**	*	****		
Photog&C	**													*		
Instrumen			**	*	**	****	**	**	**	**	**	**		****	**	**
MiscMetProd			**	**	**	****	**	**	**						**	**
TextWoodetc.				*		*	*									
Medical	****			**		**								*		

**** Core   *** Niche   ** Background   * Marginal

4.2. *Three large companies*

In Figures 11.2 to 11.4, we exemplify in greater detail the intersectoral trends described above, by reproducing the technological profiles of three large (and well-known) firms, from the chemical, electrical, and automobiles industries.[11] A number of features of firms' profiles emerge from Figure 11.2.

- A relatively large number of technological fields combine to define each firm's technological profile: increasing from eleven in the chemical firm, to eighteen in the electrical firm, and twenty in the automobile firm. In all three firms, these sectors account for more than 90 per cent of the firms' patenting.
- All three firms have at least one *niche* competence.
- However, the *core* competencies are very different:

chemical firm: organic and agricultural chemicals, pharmaceuticals, and photography;
electrical firm: computers, semiconductors, and image and sound;
automobile firm: vehicles, engines, and other transport.

- In addition, the chemical firm has just one *background* competence (chemical processes) accounting for 7 per cent of all its patenting. The electrical and automobile firms are very different, with respectively eight and ten *background* competencies, accounting for 47 per cent of all patenting in the electrical firm, and 64 per cent in the automobile firm. In both cases, instrumentation accounted for about 15 per cent of all patenting activities.

These examples confirm what emerged from the more general analysis in Section 4.1: firms devote a considerable proportion of their technological resources to fields that cannot be called their 'distinctive core competencies'. We shall return to the reasons why in Section 5.2 below.

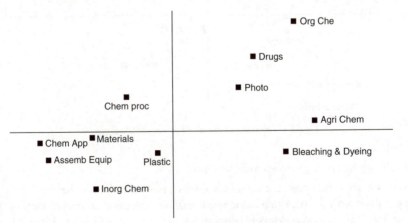

Fig. 11.2 Technological profile of a chemical company

---

[11] Since we are mainly interested in illustrating differences amongst firms from different industries, the RTAs are calculated on the basis of patenting by firms from all sectors. For competitor analysis, they should be calculated on the basis of competitor firms only.

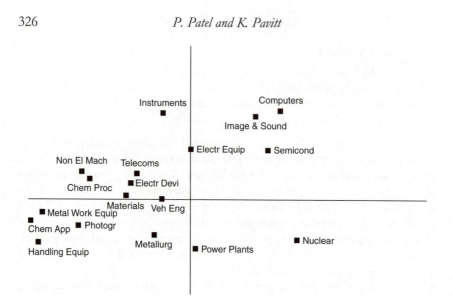

Fig. 11.3 Technological profile of an electrical company

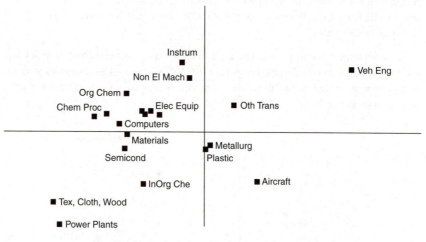

Fig. 11.4 Technological profile of an automobile company

4.3. Changing technological competencies over time

Not only are large firms technologically diverse, but their diversity has been chang-ing—albeit slowly—over time. Our initial analysis suggested an overall increase in our firms' technological diversity between the early 1970s and the late 1980s. How-ever, it also revealed varying patterns of behaviour amongst different groups of firms. This is confirmed in Table 11.7, which shows the numbers of firms (from Europe, Japan, and the USA) whose technological diversity increased, decreased, and re-mained stable over this period.

TABLE 11.7 Changes in firms' technological diversity by product group and region, 1969–74 to 1985–90

	USA			Europe			Japan			Total		
	Dec.	Stab.	Inc.	Dec.	Stab.	Inc.	Dec.	Stab.	Inc.	Dec.	Stab.	Inc.
Chemicals	23	0	3	3	2	10	0	1	23	26	3	36
Pharmaceuticals	3	3	8	2	0	5	0	0	4	5	3	17
Mining and petroleum	10	1	5	2	1	8	0	1	3	12	3	16
Textiles etc.	3	2	1	1	1	1	0	0	4	4	3	6
Rubber and plastics	5	0	0	3	0	0	0	0	2	8	0	2
Paper and wood	7	1	5	1	0	2	0	0	1	8	1	8
Food	8	2	2	0	0	1	0	1	2	8	3	5
Drink and tobacco	2	2	3	1	0	2	0	0	1	3	2	6
Building materials	7	1	1	3	0	1	0	0	4	10	1	6
Metals	8	3	4	7	3	9	0	0	10	15	6	23
Machinery	20	2	8	7	1	12	1	0	11	28	3	31
Electrical	16	4	7	5	3	4	0	0	17	21	7	28
Computers	5	0	5	1	1	2	0	0	2	6	1	9
Instruments	6	2	3	0	1	0	2	0	5	8	3	8
Motor vehicles	6	0	4	5	1	9	0	0	12	11	1	25
Aircraft	10	0	2	2	0	5	0	0	0	12	0	7
All product groups	139	23	61	43	14	72	3	3	101	185	40	234

Notes: Dec.: Firms where there has been a decrease in the number of technical fields (out of 34) of activity.
Stab.: Firms where there has been no change in the number of technical fields (out of 34) of activity.
Inc.: Firms where there has been an increase in the number of technical fields (out of 34) of activity.

It emerges clearly that firms differ markedly according to their country of origin, with most Japanese firms showing increases in technological diversity, and a majority of European firms doing likewise, whilst most US firms show a decrease in the diversity of their patenting. At the sectoral level, technological diversity increased for the majority of US firms in pharmaceuticals, and for the majority of European firms in the chemical and machinery-related sectors.

The meaning of these trends is ambiguous. It is tempting to conclude that the declining technological diversity of US firms reflects their declining technological competitiveness, compared to firms from Japan and Europe.[12] However, the data for US firms reflect domestic patenting, the scope of which is sensitive to its cost; whilst the data for European and Japanese firms also reflect international patenting, the scope of which reflects international technological competitiveness and business strategy. The trends could therefore simply reflect increases in the cost of US patenting (influencing US firms), and the processes of technological catch-up (influencing European and Japanese firms). Suffice to say that, by the 1980s, the US firms were in aggregate still slightly more diversified than European and Japanese firms.

---

[12] Since the late 1960s, business-funded R&D has increased more rapidly in Japan than in Europe, and more rapidly in Europe than in the USA. See Patel and Pavitt (1995).

Stronger conclusions can be reached about the technical fields into (and out of) which firms are moving over time. Table 11.8 shows the total number of large firms that have been active in each of our thirty-four technical fields in 1969–74 and 1985–90. It thereby compares the degree of pervasiveness of technological competencies in different fields, and the changes over time. The technological fields are sorted according to the last column, namely the increase in the number of active firms between the two periods. It emerges that:

- for firms from Japan, Europe, and the USA, the most pervasive competencies are the same: instrumentation and control, production machinery, and chemical

TABLE 11.8 Number of firms that are active in 34 technical fields, 1969–74 to 1985–90

	1969–74	1985–90	Change
Calculators and computers, etc.	215	285	70
Drugs and bioengineering	159	204	45
Materials (inc. glass and ceramics)	321	362	41
Plastic and rubber products	251	287	36
General electrical ind. apparatus	331	367	36
Instruments and controls	373	407	34
Metallurgical and metal treatment proc.	238	270	32
Dentistry and surgery	143	173	30
Miscellaneous metal products	351	380	29
Other—ammunitions and weapons, etc.	314	337	23
Image and sound equipment	209	231	22
Chemical processes	392	413	21
Mining and wells: mach. and proc.	117	137	20
Hydrocarbons, mineral oils, fuels, etc.	135	152	17
General non-electrical ind. equip.	363	377	14
Agricultural chemicals	96	108	12
Semiconductors	154	166	12
Photography and photocopy	137	147	10
App. for chemicals, food, glass, etc.	384	393	9
Assembling and material handling app.	310	319	9
Road vehicles and engines	134	142	8
Electrical devices and systems	259	267	8
Organic chemicals	281	284	3
Non-electrical specialized ind. equip.	391	394	3
Power plants	135	138	3
Inorganic chemicals	181	183	2
Aircraft	71	73	2
Metallurgical and metal-working equip.	366	366	0
Telecommunications	253	252	−1
Bleaching, dyeing, and disinfecting	113	110	−3
Other transport equip. (exc. aircraft)	211	206	−5
Food & tobacco (proc. and prod.)	127	119	−8
Induced nuclear reactions	48	30	−18
Textile, clothing, leather, wood products	119	94	−25

TABLE 11.9 Large firms' production with capabilities, compared to technological capabilities, in the 1980s

Principal product	No. of firms	Technological field	No. of firms
Computers	17	Computing	288
Electrical and electronic	56	Semi-conductors	166
Instruments	21	Instruments	407
Chemicals	66	Organic chemistry	284
Pharmaceuticals	25	Pharmaceuticals	204
Mining and petroleum	31	Chemical processes	413
		Chemical apparatus	393
Non-electrical machinery	58	Gen. non-elect. mach.	377
		Spec. non-elect mach.	394
		MW machine tools	366
Automobiles	35	Road vehic. and engines	142
Aerospace	18	Aerospace	73

processes, in all of which an overwhelming majority of our firms were technologically active;

● the least pervasive competencies were in nuclear energy, aircraft, and textiles;

● over time, the fields in which the number of firms with competencies increased most rapidly were computing, drugs and bio-engineering, and materials; and

● the patterns and trends were similar in all three regions, except for a particularly sharp decline in US firms with competencies in image and sound, and in photography and photocopy.

More generally, Table 11.9 confirms that firms have a much broader range of capabilities in technology than in production. Thus, it is probable that not more than ninety-four of our firms make and sell computers (i.e. those with their principal products in computers, electrical and electronic products, and instruments), yet nearly 300 made world-frontier technological improvements in computing, more than 150 in semiconductors, and 407 in instruments. Similar patterns can be observed in other fields and sectors.

5. Conclusions

A number of conclusions emerge from our empirical findings.

5.1. *Explaining the* core—*rather than the* boundaries—*of the firm*

Notions of firm-specific dynamic competencies provide a convincing empirical explanation of the *core* (not the *boundaries*) of the firm (Dosi *et al.* 1992). In particular, our results in Tables 11.4 and 11.5 suggest that we are able to claim the following: 'Show us a firm's profile of technological competencies, and we shall *probably* be able to predict the range of products it makes, and almost certainly be able to predict what it does *not* make.'

5.2. 'Focusing' on 'core distinctive competencies' is not enough

The importance of *background* competencies is neglected or ignored in the conventional analyses that stress the need to concentrate resources in distinctive *core* and *niche* competencies (Prahalad and Hamel 1990). In sectors making and improving complex products and production systems (e.g. automobiles and aircraft), firms require the broad range of technological competencies that enable them to stimulate and integrate technological improvements by their suppliers of materials, components, subsystems, and production equipment. Technical interdependence means that the notions of 'focus' and 'make or buy', applied in production and marketing activities, do not work in relation to technological competencies.

5.3. Learning costs versus transaction costs

Firms have much broader technological competencies than production activities. The technological fields where firms have been acquiring an in-house capability most vigorously since the early 1970s—computers, biotechnology and pharmaceuticals, and materials—are also those where firms have increased most vigorously their external alliances for technological exchanges and joint developments (see Mowery 1988; Hagedoorn and Schakenraad 1992). This suggests that external alliances are complements to internal learning, and not substitutes reflecting changing transaction costs.

   This is consistent with the conclusions of research by Ove Granstrand and his colleagues at Chalmers in Sweden.[13] In particular, large firms and the products they make depend on many fields of technological competence, the number of which is increasing over time with the widening range of technological opportunities emerging from improvement in computing and other technologies. In order to assimilate this range of emerging technologies, large firms simultaneously increase their internal competencies, form alliances with external sources, and *increase* their overall R&D expenditures, rather than *reduce* them as the results of any increased allocative efficiency from external sourcing.

5.4. Competence-destroying innovations?

Competence-destroying innovations are unlikely in large firms with diversified competencies and R&D programmes (Tushman and Anderson 1987; Utterback and Suarez 1993). Although radical breakthroughs may destroy one part of such a firm's competence, it is unlikely to destroy them all. This can be seen in the new biotechnology, where—in spite of a slow start—established chemical and pharmaceutical firms have succeeded in combining the radical breakthroughs with their established fields of competence (Arora and Gambardella 1992; Galimberti 1993). More generally, the observed rapid spread amongst firms of competencies in computing and other fast-moving technologies suggests that radical breakthroughs could better be described as 'competence augmenting' than as 'competence destroying'.

---

[13] See, in particular, Granstrand and Sjolander (1990), Granstrand *et al.* (1992), Oskarsson (1993), and Jacobsson and Oskarsson (1994).

However, our evidence by itself neither supports nor refutes recent research concluding that established firms find it difficult to maintain an innovative lead when new product design configurations emerge (Henderson and Clark 1993; Utterback 1994)—if only because radically new technologies are not synonymous with radically new product design configurations. However, it does raise questions about the universality of any corporate inability to deal with radically new product configurations. These can best be resolved by widening the range of empirical studies beyond the USA and the electronics industry.

5.5. *What type of variety?*

'Variety' is an often used term in evolutionary economics.[14] Our analysis shows various possible definitions of the term, each of which should be carefully distinguished in any general scheme of things:

- Variety *within* firms in the technological competencies that they embody.
- Variety *between* firms in their mix (or profile) of technological competencies, largely defined by the products they develop and make.
- Once given their profile of competencies and product mix, *lack* of variety in managerial decisions about their *directions* of search, but considerable variety in decisions about their *rate* of search.

5.6. *The red herring of 'optimality'*

Finally, we should avoid trying to answer unanswerable questions, in particular about the optimality of choices of particular firms to combine particular technologies in particular ways to make particular products, from amongst the (almost) infinity of mathematical possibilities that exist. As in nature, firms evolve in a complex and path-dependent world, where history matters. If neither Darwin nor DNA can model and predict the emergence of the elephant and the mouse, we should not be expected to do the equivalent in explaining why firms are what they are and not something else.

---

[14] See e.g. Metcalfe and Gibbons (1989).

References

Archibugi, D. (1988). 'In Search of a Useful Measure of Technological Innovation', *Technological Forecasting and Social Change*, 34.

Arora, A., and A. Gambardella (1992). 'New Trends in Technological Change: the Use of General and Abstract Knowledge in Industrial Research', *Rivista Internazionale di Scienze Sociali*, 3.

Barton, J. (1993). 'Adapting the Intellectual Property System to New Technologies', in Wallerstein *et al.* (1993).

Basberg, B. (1987). 'Patents and the Measurement of Technological Change: a Survey of the Literature', *Research Policy*, 16.

Bijker, W., T. Hughes, and T. Pinch (1993). *The Social Construction of Technological Systems: New Directions in the Sociology and History of Technology*. Cambridge, Mass.: MIT Press.

Cantwell, J. (1989). *Technological Innovation and Multinational Corporations*. Oxford: Blackwell.

—— (1991). 'The Theory of Technological Competence and its Application to International Production', in D. McFetridge (ed.), *Foreign Investment, Technology and Economic Growth*. Calgary: University of Calgary Press.

Dosi, G., D. Teece, and S. Winter (1992), 'Towards a Theory of Corporate Coherence: Preliminary Remarks', in G. Dosi, R. Giannetti, and P. A. Toninelli (eds.), *Technology and Enterprise in a Historical Perspective*. Oxford: Clarendon Press.

—— —— (1993). 'Competencies and the Boundaries of the Firm', Center for Research in Management, CCC Working Paper No. 93-11, University of California at Berkeley.

Franko, L. (1989). 'Global Corporate Competition: who's winning, who's losing, and the R&D factor as one reason why', *Strategic Management Journal*, 10.

Galimberti, I. (1993). *Large Chemical Firms in Biotechnology: Case Studies of Learning in Radically New Technology*, D. Phil. thesis, University of Sussex.

Geroski, P., S. Machin, and J. van Reenen (1993). 'The Profitability of Innovating Firms', *RAND Journal of Economics*, 24.

Granstrand, O., and S. Sjolander (1990). 'Managing Innovation in Multi-technology Corporations', *Research Policy*, 19.

Grilliches, Z. (1990). 'Patent Statistics as Economic Indicators', *Journal of Economic Literature*, 28.

Hagedoorn, J., and J. Schakenraad (1992). 'Leading Companies in Networks of Strategic Alliances in Information Technologies', *Research Policy*, 21.

Hall, B., Z. Grilliches, and A. Pakes (1986). 'Patents and R&D: Is there a Lag', *International Economic Review*, 27.

Henderson, R., and K. Clark (1993). 'Architectural Innovations: the Reconfiguring of Existing Product Technologies and the Failure of Established Firms', *Administrative Science Quarterly*, 35.

Jacobsson, S., and C. Oskarsson (1993). 'Educational Statistics as an Indicator of Technological Activity', *Research Policy*, 24.

Jaffe, A. (1986). 'Technological Opportunity and Spillovers of R&D: Evidence from Firms', Patents, Profits and Market Value', *American Economic Review*, 76.

Kline, S. (1990). 'A Numerical Measure for the Complexity of Systems: the Concept and some Implications', Report INN-5, Dept. of Mechanical Engineering, Stanford University.

Lindblom, C. (1959). 'The Science of Muddling Through', *Public Administration Review*, 19.

Malerba, F., and L. Marengo (1993). 'Competence, Innovative Activities and Economic Performance in Italian High Technology Firms', mimeo, Bocconi University, Milan.

Metcalfe, S., and Gibbons, M. (1989). 'Technology, Variety and Organisation: A Systematic Perspective on the Competitive Process', *Research on Technological Innovation, Management and Policy*, 4.

Mowery, D. (ed.) (1988). *International Collaborative Ventures in US Manufacturing*. Cambridge, Mass.: Ballinger.

Narin, F., E. Noma, and R. Perry (1987). 'Patents as Indicators of Corporate Technological Strength', *Research Policy*, 16.

Nelson, R., and S. Winter (1982). *An Evolutionary Theory of Economic Change*. Cambridge, Mass.: Belknap.

Oskarsson, C. (1993). 'Diversification and Growth in US, Japanese and European Multi-Technology Corporations', mimeo, Dept. of Industrial Management and Economics, Chalmers University of Technology, Gothenburg.

Patel, P., and K. Pavitt (1991). 'Large Firms in the Production of the World's Technology: An Important Case of "non-Globalisation"', *Journal of International Business Studies*, 22: 1–21.

—— —— (1994). 'The Continuing, Widespread (and Neglected) Importance of Improvements in Mechanical Technologies', *Research Policy*, 23.

—— —— (1995). 'Patterns of Technological Activity: Their Measurement and Interpretation', in P. Stoneman (ed.), *Handbook of the Economics of Innovation and Technical Change*. Oxford: Blackwell.

—— —— (1998). 'The Wide (and Increasing) Spread of Technological Competencies in the World's Largest Firms: a Challenge to Conventional Wisdom', prepared for the volume *The Dynamic Firm*, to be edited by A. Chandler, P. Hagstrom, and O. Solvell, to be published by Oxford University Press.

Pavitt, K. (1988). 'Uses and Abuses of Patent Statistics' in van Raan (1988).

Prahalad, C., and G. Hamel (1990). 'The Core Competence of the Corporation', *Harvard Business Review* (Jan.): 79–91.

Quinn, J. (1980). *Strategies for Change: Logical Incrementalism*. Homewood, Ill.: Irwin.

Samuelson, P. (1993). 'A Case Study on Computer Programs', in Wallerstein *et al.* (1993).

Tushman, M., and P. Anderson (1987). 'Technological Discontinuities and Organization Environments', in A. Pettigrew (ed.), *The Management of Strategic Change*. Oxford: Blackwell.

Utterback, J. (1994). *Mastering the Dynamics of Innovation*. Cambridge, Mass.: Harvard Business School Press.

—— and F. Suarez (1993). 'Innovation, Competition and Industrial Structure', *Research Policy*, 22.

van Raan, A. (ed.) (1988). *Handbook of Quantitative Studies of Science and Technology*. Amsterdam: North-Holland.

Wallerstein, M., M. Mogee, and R. Schoen (eds.) (1993). *Global Dimensions of Intellectual Property Rights in Science and Technology*. Washington, DC: National Academy Press.

12

Dynamic Capabilities and Strategic Management

DAVID J. TEECE, GARY PISANO, AND AMY SHUEN

1. Introduction

The fundamental question in the field of strategic management is how do firms achieve and sustain competitive advantage. The position we take here is that, in many industries at least, they do so by developing strong 'dynamic capabilities'. This perspective is especially relevant in a Schumpeterian world of innovation-based competition, price and performance rivalry, increasing returns, and the 'creative destruction' of existing competences. The approach we lay out here is designed both as a start toward a better theory of firm performance in such industries, and as a vehicle for informing managerial practice.

The view of the objectives of firm strategy developed here, and in earlier versions of this chapter (Teece and Pisano 1994; Teece *et al.* 1996) differs significantly from certain other orientations of strategic thinking. In our earlier versions, we spelled out these alternative views in some detail. Here we can be terse.

During the 1980s the dominant view on firm strategy taught in American business schools was the 'competitive forces' theory espoused by Porter. This view focused on the structure of markets and the nature of competition in different industries. It was concerned with identifying what kinds of markets allowed firms to make money, and how firms could position themselves in those markets to be profitable. In the late 1980s, game-theoretic considerations became prominent in the strategic literature. The orientation was towards how firms could gain an advantage over their rivals by a series of strategic moves.

The orientation here, in contrast, is to the kind of capabilities a firm must acquire to be successful in industries where technological advance is relatively rapid.

The view we espouse has a number of things in common with the 'resource-base' perspective on firm strategy that began to get articulated in the late 1980s. However, our perspective on firm strategy is more specifically focused on the resources and the other kinds of factors influencing capabilities that a firm needs to possess in order to be able to cope with an environment in which change is rapid. In the following section, we begin by discussing resource-based theories of firm strategy. Then we go on to develop our point of view on dynamic firm capabilities.

2. Models of Strategy Emphasizing Efficiency

2.1. Resource-based perspective

The resource-based approach sees firms with superior systems and structures being profitable not because they engage in strategic investments that may deter entry and raise prices above long-run costs, but because they have markedly lower costs, or offer markedly higher quality or product performance. This approach focuses on the rents accruing to the owners of scarce firm-specific resources rather than the economic profits from product market positioning. Competitive advantage lies 'upstream' of product markets and rests on the firm's idiosyncratic and difficult to imitate resources.[1]

One can find the resources approach suggested by the earlier pre-analytic strategy literature. A leading text of the 1960s (Learned *et al.* 1969) noted that 'the capability of an organization is its demonstrated and potential ability to accomplish against the opposition of circumstance or competition, whatever it sets out to do. Every organization has actual and potential strengths and weaknesses; it is important to try to determine what they are and to distinguish one from the other.' Thus what a firm can do is not just a function of the opportunities it confronts; it also depends on what the organization can muster.

Learned *et al.* proposed that the real key to a company's success or even to its future development lies in its ability to find or create 'a competence that is truly distinctive'.[2] This literature also recognized the constraints on firm behaviour and, in particular, noted that one should not assume that management 'can rise to any occasion'. These insights do appear to keenly anticipate the resource-based approach that has since emerged, but they did not provide a theory or systematic framework for analysing business strategies. Indeed, Andrews (1987: 46) noted that 'much of what is intuitive in this process is yet to be identified'. Unfortunately, the academic literature on capabilities stalled for a couple of decades.

New impetus has been given to the resource-based approach by recent theoretical developments in organizational economics and in the theory of strategy, as well as by a growing body of anecdotal[3] and empirical literature that highlights the importance of firm-specific factors in explaining firm performance. Cool and Schendel (1988) have shown that there are systematic and significant performance differences among firms which belong to the same strategic group within the US pharmaceutical industry. Rumelt (1991) has shown that intra-industry differences in profits are greater than inter-industry differences in profits, strongly suggesting the importance

---

[1] The strategic conflict literature also tends to focus practitioners on product market positioning rather than on developing the unique assets which make possible superior product market positions (Direickx and Cool 1989).

[2] Elsewhere Andrews (1971: 47) defined a distinctive competence as what an organization can do particularly well.

[3] Studies of the automobile and other industries displayed differences in organization which often underlay differences amongst firms. See e.g. Hayes and Clark (1985); Womack *et al.* (1990); Clark and Fujimoto (1991); Barney *et al.* (1994); Henderson and Cockburn (1994).

of firm-specific factors and the relative unimportance of industry effects.[4] Jacobson (1988) and Hansen and Wernerfelt (1989) made similar findings.

A comparison of the resource-based approach and the competitive forces approach in terms of their implications for the strategy process is revealing. From the first perspective, an entry decision looks roughly as follows: (i) pick an industry (based on its 'structural attractiveness'); (ii) choose an entry strategy based on conjectures about competitors' rational strategies; (iii) if not already possessed, acquire or otherwise obtain the requisite assets to compete in the market. From this perspective, the process of identifying and developing the requisite assets is not particularly problematic. The process involves nothing more than choosing rationally among a well-defined set of investment alternatives. If assets aren't already owned, they can be bought. The resource-based perspective is strongly at odds with this conceptualization.

From the resource-based perspective, firms are heterogeneous with respect to their resources, capabilities, and endowments. Further, resource endowments are 'sticky': at least in the short run, firms are to some degree stuck with what they have and may have to live with what they lack.[5] This stickiness arises for three reasons. First, business development is viewed as an extremely complex process.[6] Quite simply, firms lack the organizational capacity to develop new competences quickly (Dierickx and Cool 1989). Secondly, some assets are simply not readily tradeable, for example, tacit know-how (Teece 1976, 1980) and reputation (Dierickx and Cool 1989). Thus, resource endowments cannot equilibrate through factor input markets. Finally, even when an asset can be purchased, firms may stand to gain little by doing so. As Barney (1986) argues, unless a firm is lucky, possesses superior information, or both, the price it pays in a competitive factor market will fully capitalize the rents from the asset.

Given that in the resources perspective firms possess heterogeneous and sticky resource bundles, the entry decision process suggested by this approach is as follows: (i) identify your firm's unique resources; (ii) decide in which markets those resources can earn the highest rents; and (iii) decide whether the rents from those assets are most effectively utilized by (a) integrating into related market(s), (b) selling the relevant intermediate output to related firms, or (c) selling the assets themselves to a firm in related businesses (Teece 1980, 1982).

The resource-based perspective puts both vertical integration and diversification into a new strategic light. Both can be viewed as ways of capturing rents on scarce, firm-specific assets whose services are difficult to sell in intermediate markets (Penrose 1959; Williamson, 1975; Teece 1980, 1982, 1986; Wernerfelt 1984). Empirical work on the relationship between performance and diversification by

---

[4] Using FTC line of business data, Rumelt showed that stable industry effects account for only 8% of the variance in business-unit returns. Furthermore, only about 40% of the dispersion in industry returns is due to stable industry effects.

[5] In this regard, this approach has much in common with recent work on organizational ecology (e.g. Freeman and Boeker 1984) and also on commitment (Ghemawat 1991: 17-25).

[6] Capability development, however, is not really analysed.

Wernerfelt and Montgomery (1988) provides evidence for this proposition. It is evident that the resource-based perspective focuses on strategies for exploiting existing firm-specific assets.

However, the resource-based perspective also invites consideration of managerial strategies for developing new capabilities (Wernerfelt 1984). Indeed, if control over scarce resources is the source of economic profits, then it follows that such issues as skill acquisition, the management of intangible assets (Shuen 1994), and learning become fundamental strategic issues. It is in this second dimension, encompassing skill acquisition, learning, and accumulation of organizational and intangible or 'invisible' assets (Itami and Roehl 1987) that we believe lies the greatest potential for contributions to strategy.

2.2. *The dynamic capabilities approach: overview*

The global competitive battles in high-technology industries such as semiconductors, information services, and software have demonstrated the need for an expanded paradigm to understand how competitive advantage is achieved. Well-known companies like IBM, Texas Instruments, Phillips, and others appear to have followed a 'resource-based strategy' of accumulating valuable technology assets, often guarded by an aggressive intellectual property stance. However, this strategy is often not enough to support a significant competitive advantage. Winners in the global market place have been firms that can demonstrate timely responsiveness and rapid and flexible product innovation, coupled with the management capability to effectively coordinate and redeploy internal and external competences. Not surprisingly, industry observers have remarked that companies can accumulate a large stock of valuable technology assets and still not have many useful capabilities.

We refer to this ability to achieve new forms of competitive advantage as 'dynamic capabilities' to emphasize two key aspects which were not the main focus of attention in previous strategy perspectives. The term 'dynamic' refers to the capacity to renew competences so as to achieve congruence with changing environment; certain innovative responses are required when time-to-market is critical, the rate of technological change is rapid, and the nature of future competition and markets difficult to determine. The term 'capabilities' emphasizes the key role of strategic management in appropriately adapting, integrating, and reconfiguring internal and external organizational skills, resources, and functional competences to match the requirements of a changing environment.

One aspect of the strategic problem facing an innovating firm in a world of Schumpeterian competition is to identify difficult-to-imitate internal and external competences most likely to support valuable products and services. Thus, as argued by Dierickx and Cool (1989), choices about how much to spend (invest) on different possible areas are central to the firm's strategy. However, choices about domains of competence are influenced by past choices. At any given point in time, firms must follow a certain trajectory or path of competence development. This path not only defines what choices are open to the firm today, but it also puts bounds around what its internal repertoire is likely to be in the future. Thus, firms, at various points in time, make *long-term*, *quasi-irreversible* commitments to certain domains of competence.[7]

The notion that competitive advantage requires both the exploitation of existing internal and external firm-specific capabilities and of developing new ones is partially developed in Penrose (1959), Teece (1982), and Wernerfelt (1984). However, only recently have researchers begun to focus on the specifics of how some organizations first develop firm-specific capabilities and how they renew competences to respond to shifts in the business environment.[8] These issues are intimately tied to the firm's business processes, market positions, and expansion paths. Several writers have recently offered insights and evidence on how firms can develop their capability to adapt and even capitalize on rapidly changing environments.[9] The dynamic capabilities approach provides a coherent framework which can both integrate existing conceptual and empirical knowledge, and facilitate prescription. In doing so, it builds upon the theoretical foundations provided by Schumpeter (1934), Penrose (1959), Williamson (1975, 1985), Nelson and Winter (1982), Barney (1986), Teece (1988), and Teece *et al.* (1994).

3. Toward a Dynamic Capabilities Framework

3.1. *Terminology*

In order to facilitate theory development and intellectual dialogue, some acceptable definitions are desirable. We propose the following:

Factors of production. These are 'undifferentiated' inputs available in disaggregate form in factor markets. By undifferentiated we mean that they lack a firm-specific component. Land, unskilled labour, and capital are typical examples. Some factors may be available for the taking, such as public knowledge. In the language of Arrow, such resources must be non-'fugitive'.[10]

Resources.[11] Resources are firm-specific assets that are difficult if not impossible to imitate. Patents, trademarks, and certain specialized production facilities and experienced engineers are examples. Such assets are difficult to transfer among firms because of transaction costs and because the assets may contain tacit knowledge.

Organizational routines/competences. When firm-specific assets are assembled in integrated clusters spanning individuals and groups so that they enable distinctive activities to be performed, these activities constitute organizational routines and

---

[7] Deciding, under significant uncertainty about future states of the world, which long-term paths to commit to and when to change paths is the central strategic problem confronting the firm. In this regard, the work of Ghemawat (1991) is highly germane to the dynamic capabilities approach to strategy.

[8] See e.g. Iansiti and Clark (1994), and R. Henderson (1994).

[9] See Hayes *et al.* (1988), Direrickx and Cool (1989), Prahalad and Hamel (1990), Chandler (1990), and Teece (1993).

[10] Arrow (1996) defines fugitive resources as ones that can move cheaply amongst individuals and firms.

[11] We do not like the term 'resource' and believe it is misleading. We prefer to use the term firm-specific asset. We use it here to try and maintain links to the literature on the resource-based approach which we believe is important.

processes. Examples include quality, miniaturization, and systems integration. Such competences are typically viable across multiple product lines. Successful external 'integration' can result in inter-firm routines and processes.

Core competences. We define those competences that define a firm's fundamental business as core. Core competences must accordingly be derived by looking across the range of a firm's (and its competitors') products and services.[12] The value of core competences can be enhanced by combination with the appropriate complementary assets. The degree to which a core competence is distinctive depends on how well endowed the firm is relative to its competitors, and how difficult it is for competitors to replicate its competences.

Dynamic capabilities. Dynamic capabilities are the ability to reconfigure, redirect, transform, and appropriately shape and integrate existing core competences with external resources and strategic and complementary assets to meet the challenges of a time-pressured, rapidly changing Schumpeterian world of competition and imitation. Dynamic capabilities thus reflect an organization's ability to achieve new and innovative forms of competitive advantage despite path dependencies and core rigidities in the firm's organizational and technological processes.

Products. End products are the final goods and services produced by the firm based on utilizing the competences that it possesses. The performance (price, quality, etc.) of a firm's products relative to its competitors will depend upon its competences (which over time depend on its capabilities), assuming competitors source in the same factor markets.

3.2. Markets and strategic capabilities

Different approaches to strategy view sources of wealth creation and the essence of the strategic problem faced by firms differently. The competitive forces framework sees the strategic problem in terms of market entry, entry deterrence, and positioning; game-theoretic models view the strategic problem as one of interaction between rivals with certain expectations about how each other will behave;[13] resource-based perspectives have focused on the exploitation of firm-specific assets. Each approach asks different, often complementary questions. A key step in building a conceptual framework related to dynamic capabilities is to identify the foundations upon which distinctive and difficult to replicate advantages can be built.

A useful way to vector in on the strategic elements of the business enterprise is to first identify what isn't strategic. To be strategic, a capability must be honed to a user need[14] (so that there is a source of revenues), unique (so that the products/services produced can be priced without too much regard to competition), and difficult to replicate (so profits won't be competed away). Accordingly, any assets or entity which

---

[12] Thus Eastman Kodak's core competence might be considered imaging, IBM's might be considered integrated data-processing and service, and Motorola's untethered communications.

[13] In sequential move games, each player looks ahead and anticipates his rivals' future responses in order to reason back and decide action, i.e. look forward, reason backward.

[14] Needless to say, users need not be the current customers of the enterprise. Thus a capability can be the basis for diversification into new product markets.

is homogeneous and can be bought and sold at an established price cannot be all that strategic (Barney 1986). What is it, then, about firms which undergirds competitive advantage?

To answer this, one must first make some fundamental distinctions between markets and internal organization (firms). The essence of the firm, as Coase (1937) pointed out, is that it displaces market organization. It does so in the main because inside the firms one can organize certain types of economic activity in ways one cannot using markets. This is not only because of transaction costs, as Williamson (1975, 1985) has emphasized, but also because there are many types of arrangements where injecting high-powered (market like) incentives might well be quite destructive of the cooperative activity and learning.[15] Inside an organization, exchange cannot take place in the same manner that it can outside an organization, not just because it might be destructive to provide high-powered individual incentives, but because it is difficult if not impossible to tightly calibrate individual contribution to a joint effort. Hence, contrary to Arrow's (1969) view of firms as quasi-markets, and the task of management to inject markets into firms, we recognize the inherent limits and possible counterproductive results of attempting to fashion firms into simply clusters of internal markets. In particular, learning and internal technology transfer may well be jeopardized.

Indeed, what is distinctive about firms is that they are domains for organizing activity in a non-market-like fashion. Accordingly, as we discuss what is distinctive about firms, we stress competences/capabilities which are ways of organizing and getting things done which cannot be accomplished by using the price system to coordinate activity.[16] The very essence of capabilities/competences is that they cannot be readily assembled through markets (Teece 1982, 1986a; Kogut and Zander 1992). If the ability to assemble competences using markets is what is meant by the firm as a nexus of contracts (Fama 1980), then we unequivocally state that the firm about which we theorize cannot be usefully modelled as a nexus of contracts. By contract we are referring to a transaction undergirded by a legal agreement, or some other arrangement which clearly spells out rights, rewards, and responsibilities. Moreover, the firm as a nexus of contracts suggests a series of bilateral contracts orchestrated by a coordinator, where our view of the firm is that the organization takes place in a more multilateral fashion, with patterns of behaviour and learning being orchestrated in a much more decentralized fashion, but with a viable head-quarters operation.

The key point, however, is that the properties of internal organization cannot be replicated by a portfolio of business units amalgamated through formal contracts as

---

[15] Indeed, the essence of internal organization is that it is a domain of unleveraged or low-powered incentives. By unleveraged we mean that rewards are determined at the group or organization level, not primarily at the individual level, in an effort to encourage team behaviour, not individual behaviour, in order to accomplish certain tasks well.

[16] We see the problem of market contracting as a matter of coordination as much as we see it as a problem of opportunism in the face of contractual hazards. In this sense, we are consonant with both Richardson (1960) and Williamson (1975, 1985).

many distinctive elements of internal organization simply cannot be replicated in the market.[17] That is, entrepreneurial activity cannot lead to the immediate replication of unique organizational skills through simply entering a market and piecing the parts together overnight. Replication takes time, and the replication of best practice may be illusive. Indeed, firm capabilities need to be understood not in terms of balance sheet items, but mainly in terms of the organizational structures and managerial processes which support productive activity. By construction, the firm's balance sheet contains items that can be valued, at least at original market prices (cost). It is necessarily the case, therefore, that the balance sheet is a poor shadow of a firm's distinctive competence.[18] That which is distinctive cannot be bought and sold short of buying the firm itself, or one or more of its subunits.

There are many dimensions of competitors and the business firm that must be understood if one is to grasp firm-level distinctive competences and capabilities. In this chapter we merely identify several classes of factors that will help determine a firm's distinctive competence and dynamic capabilities. We organize these in three categories: processes, positions, and paths.

3.3. Processes, positions, and paths

We advance the argument that the competitive advantage of firms lies with its managerial and organizational processes, its present position, and the paths available to it.[19] By managerial and organizational processes, we refer to the way things are done in the firm, or what might be referred to as its routines, or patterns of current practice and learning. By position we refer to its current endowment of technology and intellectual property, its complementary assets, its customer base, and its external relations with suppliers and complementors. By paths we refer to the strategic alternatives available to the firm, and the presence or absence of increasing returns and attendant path dependencies. Our focus throughout is on asset structures for which no ready market exits, as these are the only assets of strategic interest. A final section focuses on replication and imitation, as it is these phenomena which determine how readily a competence or capability can be cloned by competitors, and therefore distinctiveness of its competences and the durability of its advantage.

The firms' processes and positions collectively encompass its competences and capabilities. A hierarchy of competences and capabilities ought be recognized, as some competences may be on the factory floor, some in the R&D labs, some in the

---

[17] As we note in Teece *et al.* (1994), the conglomerate offers few if any efficiencies because there is little provided by the conglomerate form that shareholders cannot obtain for themselves simply by holding a diversified portfolio of stocks.

[18] Owners' equity may reflect, in part, certain historic capabilities. Recently, some scholars have begun to attempt to measure organizational capability using financial statement data. See Baldwin and Clark (1991) and Lev and Sougiannis (1992).

[19] We are implicitly saying that fixed assets, like plant and equipment which can be purchased off-the-shelf by all industry participants, cannot be the source of a firm's competitive advantage. Inasmuch as financial balance sheets typically reflect such assets, we point out that the assets that matter for competitive advantage are rarely reflected in the balance sheet, while those that don't are.

executive suites, and some in the way everything is integrated. A difficult to replicate or difficult to imitate competence/capability was defined earlier as a distinctive competence. As indicated, the key feature of a distinctive competence is that there is not a market for it, except possibly through the market for business units. Hence competences and capabilities are intriguing assets as they typically must be built because they cannot be bought.

Organizational and managerial processes   Organizational processes have three roles: coordination/integration (a static concept); learning (a dynamic concept); and reconfiguration (a transformational concept). We discuss each in turn.

Coordination/integration. While the price system supposedly coordinates the economy, managers coordinate or integrate activity inside the firm. How efficiently and effectively internal coordination or integration is achieved is very important (Aoki 1990).[20] Likewise for external coordination.[21] Increasingly, strategic advantage requires the integration of external activities and technologies. The growing literature on strategic alliances, the virtual corporation, and buyer–supplier relations and technology collaboration evidences the importance of external integration and sourcing.

There is some field-based empirical research that provides support for the notion that the way production is organized by management inside the firm is the source of differences in firms' competence in various domains. For example, Garvin's (1988) study of eighteen room air-conditioning plants reveals that quality performance was not related to either capital investment or the degree of automation of the facilities. Instead, quality performance was driven by special organizational routines. These included routines for gathering and processing information, for linking customer experiences with engineering design choices, and for coordinating factories and component suppliers.[22] The work of Clark and Fujimoto (1991) on project development in the automobile industry also illustrates the role played by coordinative routines. Their study reveals a significant degree of variation in how different firms coordinate the various activities required to bring a new model from concept to market. These differences in coordinative routines and capabilities seem to have a significant impact on such performance variables as development cost, development lead times, and quality. Furthermore, they tended to find significant firm-level differences in coordination routines and these differences seemed to have persisted for a long time. This suggests that routines related to coordination are firm-specific in nature.

---

[20] Indeed, Ronald Coase, author of the pathbreaking 1937 article 'The Nature of the Firm', which focused on the costs of organizational coordination inside the firm as compared to across the market, half a century later has identified as critical the understanding of 'why the costs of organizing particular activities differs among firms' (Coase 1988: 47). We argue that a firm's distinctive ability needs to be understood as a reflection of distinctive organizational or coordinative capabilities. This form of integration (i.e. inside business units) is different from the integration between business units; they could be viable on a stand-alone basis (external integration). For a useful taxonomy, see Iansiti and Clark (1994).

[21] Shuen (1994) examines the gains and hazards of the technology make vs. buy decision and supplier co-development.

[22] Garvin (1994) provides a typology of organizational processes.

Also, the notion that competence/capability is embedded in distinct ways of coordinating and combining helps to explain how and why seemingly minor technological changes can have devastating impacts on incumbent firms' abilities to compete in a market. Henderson and Clark (1990), for example, have shown that incumbents in the photolithographic equipment industry were sequentially devastated by seemingly minor innovations that, nevertheless, had major impacts on how systems had to be configured. They attribute these difficulties to the fact that systems level or 'architectural' innovations often require new routines to integrate and coordinate engineering tasks. These findings and others suggest that productive systems display high interdependency, and that it may not be possible to change one level without changing others. This appears to be true with respect to the 'lean production' model (Womack *et al.*) which has now transformed the Taylor or Ford model of manufacturing organization in the automobile industry.[23] Lean production requires distinctive shopfloor practices and processes as well as distinctive higher-order managerial processes. Put differently, organizational processes often display high levels of coherence, and when they do, replication may be difficult because it requires systemic changes throughout the organization and also among inter-organizational linkages, which might be very hard to effectuate. Put differently, partial imitation or replication of a successful model may yield zero benefits.[24]

---

[23] Fujimoto (1994: 18–20) describes key elements as they existed in the Japanese auto industry as follows: 'The typical volume production system of effective Japanese makers of the 1980s (e.g. Toyota) consists of various intertwined elements that might lead to competitive advantages. Just-in-time (JIT), *jidoka* (automatic defect detecton and machine stop), total quality control (TQC), and continuous improvement (*kaizen*) are often pointed out as its core subsystems. The elements of such a system include inventory reduction mechanisms by *kanban* system; levelization of production volume and product mix (*heijunka*); reduction of '*muda*' (non-value adding activities), '*mura*' (uneven pace of production), and *muri* (excessive workload); production plans based on dealers' order volume (*genyo seisan*); reduction of die set-up time and lot size in stamping operation; mixed model assembly; piece-by-piece transfer of parts between machines (*ikko-nagashi*); flexible task assignment for volume changes and productivity improvement (*shojinka*); multi-task job assignment along the process flow (*takotei-mochi*); U-shape machine layout that facilitates flexible and mutliple task assignment, on-the-spot inspection by direct workers (*tsukurikomi*); fool-proof prevention of defects (*poka-yoke*); real-time feedback of production troubles (*andon*); assembly line stop cord; emphasis on cleanliness, order, and discipline on the shopfloor (5-S); frequent revision of standard operating procedures by supervisors; quality-control circles; standardized tools for quality improvement (e.g. 7 tools for QC, QC story); worker involvement in preventive maintenance (total productive maintenance); low-cost automation or semi-automation with just-enough functions; reduction of process steps for saving tools and dies, and so on. The human-resource management factors that back up the above elements include stable employment of core workers (with temporary workers in the periphery); long-term training of multiskilled (multitask) workers; wage system based in part on skill accumulation; internal promotion to shopfloor supervisors; cooperative relationships with labour unions; inclusion of production supervisors in union members; generally egalitarian policies for corporate welfare, communication, and worker motivation. Parts procurement policies are also pointed out often as a source of the competitive advantage; relatively high ratio of parts out-sourcing; multilayer heirarchy of suppliers; long-term relations with suppliers; relatively small number of technologically capable suppliers at the first tier; sub-assembly functions of the first-tier parts makers; detail-engineering capability of the first-tier makers (design-in, black box parts); competition based on long-term capability of design and improvements rather than bidding; pressures for continuous reduction of parts price; elimination of incoming parts inspection; plant inspection and technical assistance by auto makers, and so on.'

[24] For a theoretical argument along these lines, see Milgrom and Roberts (1990).

The notion that there is a certain rationality or coherence to processes and systems is not quite the same concept as corporate culture, as we understand the latter. Corporate culture refers to the values and beliefs that employees hold; culture can be a *de facto* governance system as it mediates the behaviour of individuals and economizes on more formal administrative methods. Rationality or coherence notions are more akin to the Nelson and Winter (1982) notion of organizational routines. However, the routines concept is a little too amorphous to properly capture the congruence amongst processes and between processes and incentives that we have in mind. Consider a professional service organization like an accounting firm. If it is to have relatively high-powered incentives that reward individual performance, then it must build organizational processes that channel individual behaviour; if it has weak or low-powered incentives, it must find symbolic ways to recognize the high performers, and it must use alternative methods to build effort and enthusiasm. What one may think of as styles of organization in fact contain necessary, not discretionary, elements to achieve performance. Recognizing the congruences and complementarities among processes, and between processes and incentives, is critical to the understanding of organizational capabilities. In particular, they can help us explain why architectural and radical innovations are so often introduced into an industry by new entrants. The incumbents develop distinctive organizational processes that cannot support the new technology, despite certain overt similarities between the old and the new. The frequent failure of incumbents to introduce new technologies can thus be seen as a consequence of the mismatch that so often exists between the set of organizational processes needed to support the conventional product/ service and the requirements of the new. Radical organizational re-engineering will usually be required to support the new product, which may well do better embedded in a separate subsidiary where a new set of coherent organizational processes can be fashioned.[25]

Learning. Perhaps even more important than integration is learning. Learning is a process by which repetition and experimentation enable tasks to be performed better and quicker and new production opportunities to be identified.[26] In the context of the firm, if not more generally, learning has several key characteristics. First, learning involves organizational as well as individual skills.[27] While individual skills are of relevance, their value depends upon their employment, in particular organizational settings. Learning processes are intrinsically social and collective and occur not only through the imitation and emulation of individuals, as with teacher-student or master-apprentice, but also because of joint contributions to the understanding of complex problems.[28] Learning requires common codes of communication and coordinated search procedures. Second, the organizational knowledge generated by

---

[25] See Abernathy and Clark (1985).

[26] For a useful review and contribution, see Levitt and March (1988).

[27] See Mahoney (1994).

[28] There is a large literature on learning, although only a small fraction of it deals with organizational learning. Relevant contributors include Argyres and Schon (1978), Levitt and March (1988), Levinthal and March (1981), Nelson and Winter (1982), and Leonard-Barton (1995).

such activity resides in new patterns of activity, in 'routines', or a new logic of organization. As indicated earlier, routines are patterns of interactions that represent successful solutions to particular problems. These patterns of interaction are resident in group behaviour, though certain subroutines may be resident in individual behaviour. The concept of dynamic capabilities as a coordinative management process opens the door to the potential for inter-organizational learning. Researchers (Doz and Shuen 1989; Mody 1990) have pointed out that collaborations and partnerships can be a vehicle for new organizational learning, helping firms to recognize dysfunctional routines, and preventing strategic blindspots.

Reconfiguration and transformation. In rapidly changing environments, there is obviously value in the ability to sense the need to reconfigure the firm's asset structure, and to accomplish the necessary internal and external transformation (Amit and Schoemaker 1992; Langlois 1994). This requires constant surveillance of markets and technologies and the willingness to adopt best practice. In this regard, benchmarking is of considerable value as an organized process for accomplishing such ends (Camp 1989). In dynamic environments, narcissistic organizations are likely to be impaired. The capacity to reconfigure and transform is itself a learned organizational skill. The more frequently practised, the easier accomplished.

Change is costly and so firms must develop processes to minimize low pay-off change. The ability to calibrate the requirements for change and to effectuate the necessary adjustments would appear to depend on the ability to scan the environment, to evaluate markets and competitors, and to quickly accomplish reconfiguration and transformation ahead of competition. Decentralization and local autonomy assist these processes. Firms that have honed these capabilities are sometimes referred to as 'high flex'.

Positions The strategic posture of a firm is determined not only by its learning processes and by the coherence of its internal and external processes and incentives, but also by its location at any point in time with respect to its business assets. By business assets we do not mean its plant and equipment unless they are specialized; rather we mean its difficult-to-trade knowledge assets and assets complementary to them, as well as its reputational and relational assets. These will determine its market share and profitability at any point in time.

Technological assets. While there is an emerging market for know-how (Teece 1981), much technology does not enter it. This is either because the firm is unwilling to sell it[29] or because of difficulties in transacting in the market for know-how (Teece 1980). A firm's technological assets may or may not be protected by the standard instruments of intellectual property law. Either way, the ownership protection and utilization of technological assets are clearly key differentiators among firms. Likewise for complementary assets.

Complementary assets. Technological innovations require the use of certain related assets to produce and deliver new products and services. Prior commercialization

---

[29] Managers often evoke the 'crown jewels' metaphor. That is, if the technology is released, the kingdom will be lost.

activities require and enable firms to build such complementarities (Teece 1986*b*). Such capabilities and assets, while necessary for the firm's established activities, may have other uses as well. Such assets typically lie downstream. New products and processes either can enhance or destroy the value of such assets (Tushman *et al.* 1986). Thus the development of computers enhanced the value of IBM's direct sales force in office products, while disc brakes rendered useless much of the auto industries' investment in drum brakes.

Financial assets. In the short run, a firm's cash position and degree of leverage may have strategic implications. While there is nothing more fungible than cash, it cannot always be raised from external markets without the dissemination of considerable information to potential investors. Accordingly, what a firm can do in short order is often a function of its balance sheet. In the longer run, that ought not be so, as cash flow ought be more determinative.

Locational assets. Geography matters too. Uniqueness in certain businesses can stem from locational assets which are non-tradeable (e.g. positioning of a refinery in a certain geographic market). While real estate markets are well developed, land use and environmental restrictions often make locational assets non-tradeable, and hence may be the source of difficult-to-replicate advantages which manifest themselves in lower transport costs, superior convenience, and the like.

Paths   *Path dependencies.* Where a firm can go is a function of its current position and the paths ahead. Its current position is often shaped by the path it has travelled. In standard economics textbooks, firms have an infinite range of technologies from which they can choose and markets they can occupy. Changes in product or factor prices will be responded to instantaneously, with technologies moving in and out according to value maximization criteria. Only in the short run are irreversibilities recognized. Fixed costs—such as equipment and over-head—cause firms to price below fully amortized costs but never constrain future investment choices. 'Bygones are bygones'. Path dependencies are simply not recognized.

The notion of path dependencies recognizes that 'history matters'. Bygones are rarely bygones, despite the predictions of rational actor theory. Thus a firm's previous investments and its repertoire of routines (its 'history') constrains its future behaviour.[30] This follows because learning tends to be local. That is, opportunities for learning will be 'close in' to previous activities and thus will be transaction- and production-specific (Teece 1988). This is because learning is often a process of trial, feedback, and evaluation. If too many parameters are changed simultaneously, the ability of firms to conduct meaningful natural quasi-experiments is attenuated. If many aspects of a firm's learning environment change simultaneously, the ability to ascertain cause–effect relationships is confounded because cognitive structures will not be formed and rates of learning diminish as a result. One implication is that many investments are much longer term than is commonly thought.

---

[30] For further development, see Bercovitz *et al.* (1996).

The importance of path dependencies is amplified where conditions of increasing returns to adoption exist. This is a demand-side phenomenon, and it tends to make technologies and products embodying those technologies more attractive the more they are adopted. Attractiveness flows from the greater adoption of the product amongst users, which in turn enables them to become more developed and hence more useful. Increasing returns to adoption has many sources including network externalities (Katz and Shapiro 1985), the presence of complementary assets (Teece 1986) and supporting infrastructure (Nelson 1996), learning by using (Rosenberg 1982), and scale economies in production and distribution. Competition between and amongst technologies is shaped by increasing returns. Early leads won by good luck or special circumstances (Arthur 1983) can become amplified by increasing returns. This is not to suggest that first movers necessarily win. Because increasing returns have multiple sources, the prior positioning of firms can affect their capacity to exploit increasing returns. Thus, in Mitchell's (1989) study of medical diagnostic imaging, firms already controlling the relevant complementary assets could in theory start last and finish first.

In the presence of increasing returns, firms can compete passively, or they may compete strategically through technology-sponsoring activities.[31] The first type of competition is not unlike biological competition amongst species, although it can be sharpened by managerial activities that enhance the performance of products and processes. The reality is that companies with the best products will not always win, as chance events may cause 'lock in' on inferior technologies (Arthur 1983) and may generate switching costs for consumers. However, while switching costs may favour the incumbent, in regimes of rapid technological change switching costs can become quickly swamped by switching benefits. Put differently, new products employing different standards will appear with alacrity in market environments experiencing rapid technological change, and incumbents can be readily challenged by superior products and services that yield switching benefits. Thus the degree to which switching costs cause 'lock-in' is a function of the rapidity of technological change and the amount of ferment in the competitive environment.

Technological opportunities. The concept of path dependencies is forward meaning through the consideration of an industry's technological opportunities. It is well recognized that how far and how fast a particular area of industrial activity can proceed is in part due to the technological opportunities that lie before it. Such opportunities are usually a lagged function of foment and diversity in basic science, and the rapidity with which new scientific breakthroughs are being made.

However, technological opportunities may not be completely exogenous to industry, not only because some firms have the capacity to engage in or at least support

---

[31] Because of huge uncertainties, it may be extremely difficult to determine viable strategies early on. Since the rules of the game and the identity of the players will be revealed only after the market has begun to evolve, the pay-off is likely to lie with building and maintaining organizational capabilities that support flexibility. For example, Microsoft's recent about-face and vigorous pursuit of Internet business once the NetScape phenomenon became apparent is impressive, not so much because it perceived the need to change strategy, but because of its organizational capacity to effectuate a strategic shift.

basic research, but also because technological opportunities are often fed by innovative activity itself. Moreover, the recognition of such opportunities is affected by the organizational structures that link the institutions engaging in basic research (primarily the university) to the business enterprise. Hence, the existence of technological opportunities can be quite firm-specific.

Important for our purposes is the rate and direction in which relevant scientific frontiers are being rolled back. Firms engaging in R&D may find the path dead ahead closed off, though breakthroughs in related areas may be sufficiently close to be attractive. Likewise, if the path dead ahead is extremely attractive, there may be no incentive for firms to shift the allocation of resources away from traditional pursuits. The depth and width of technological opportunities in the neighbourhood of a firm's prior research activities thus are likely to impact a firm's options with respect to both the amount and level of R&D activity that it can justify. In addition, a firm's past experience conditions the alternatives management is able to perceive. Thus, not only do firms in the same industry face 'menus' with different costs associated with particular technological choices, they also are looking at menus containing different choices.[32]

Assessment   The assessment of a firm's competitive advantage and strategic capability is presented here as a function of the firm's processes, positions, and paths.[33] What it can do and where it can go is thus heavily constrained by the typography of its processes, positions, and paths. Each component of this capability framework needs to be analysed in a strategic audit.

We submit that if one can identify each of these components and understand their interrelationships, one can at least predict the performance of the firm under various assumptions about changes in the external environment. One can also evaluate the richness of the menu of new opportunities from which the firm may select, and its likely performance in a changing environment.

The parameters we have identified for determining performance are quite different from those in the standard textbook theory of the firm, and in the competitive forces and strategic conflict approaches to the firm and to strategy.[34] Moreover, the agency-theoretic view of the firm as a nexus of contracts would put no weight on processes, positions, and paths. While agency approaches to the firm may recognize that opportunism and shirking may limit what a firm can do, they do not recognize the opportunities and constraints imposed by processes, positions, and paths. Moreover, the firm in our conceptualization is much more than the sum of its parts—or a team tied together by contracts.[35] Indeed, to some extent individuals can be moved in and out of organizations and, so long as the internal processes and structures remain in place, performance will not necessarily be impaired. A shift in the environment is a

---

[32] This is a critical element in Nelson and Winter's (1982) view of firms and technical change.

[33] We also recognize that the processes, positions, and paths of customers also matter. See our discussion above on increasing returns, including customer learning and network externalities.

[34] In both, the firm is still largely a black box. Certainly, little or no attention is given to processes, positions, and paths.

[35] See Alchian and Demsetz (1972).

far more serious threat to the firm than is the loss of key individuals, as individuals can be replaced more readily than organizations can be transformed. Furthermore, the dynamic capabilities view of the firm would suggest that the behaviour and performance of particular firms may be quite hard to replicate, even if its coherence and rationality are observable. This matter and related issues involving replication and imitation are taken up in the section that follows.

3.4. *Replicability and imitatability of organizational processes and positions*

Thus far, we have argued that the competences and capabilities (and hence competitive advantage) of a firm rests fundamentally on processes, positions, and paths. However, competences can provide competitive advantage and generate rents only if they are based on a collection of routines, skills, and complementary assets that are difficult to imitate.[36] A particular set of routines can lose their value if they support a competence which no longer matters in the market place, or if they can be readily replicated or emulated by competitors. Imitation occurs when firms discover and simply copy a firm's organizational routines and procedures. Emulation occurs when firms discover alternative ways of achieving the same functionality. There is ample evidence that a given type of competence (e.g. quality) can be supported by different routines and combinations of skills. For example, the Garvin (1988) and Clark and Fujimoto (1990) studies both indicate that there was no one 'formula' for achieving either high quality or high product development performance.

Replication. Replication involves transferring or redeploying competences from one concrete economic setting to another. Since productive knowledge is embodied, this cannot be accomplished by simply transmitting information. Only in those instances where all relevant knowledge is fully codified and understood can replication be collapsed into a simple problem of information transfer. Too often, the contextual dependence of original performance is poorly appreciated, so unless firms have replicated their systems of productive knowledge on many prior occasions, the act of replication is likely to be difficult (Teece 1976). Indeed, replication and transfer are often impossible absent the transfer of people, though this can be minimized if investments are made to convert tacit knowledge to codified knowledge. Often, however, this is simply not possible.

In short, organizational capabilities, and the routines upon which they rest, are normally rather difficult to replicate.[37] Even understanding what all the relevant routines are that support a particular competence may not be transparent. Indeed, Lippman and Rumelt (1992) have argued that some sources of competitive advantage are so complex that the firm itself, let alone its competitors, does not understand them.[38] As Nelson and Winter (1982) and Teece (1982) have explained, many

---

[36] We call such competences distinctive (see Section 3.1). See also Dierickx and Cool (1989) for a discussion of the characteristics of assets which make them a source of rents.

[37] See Szulanski's (1993) discussion of the intra-firm transfer of best practice. He quotes a senior vice-president of Xerox as saying 'you can see a high performance factory or office, but it just doesn't spread. I don't know why.' Szulanski also discusses the role of benchmarking in facilitating the transfer of best practice.

[38] If so, it is our belief that the firm's advantage is likely to fade, as luck does run out.

organizational routines are quite tacit in nature. Imitation can also be hindered by the fact few routines are 'stand-alone'; coherence may require that a change in one set of routines in one part of the firm (e.g. production) requires changes in some other part (e.g. R&D).

Some routines and competences seem to be attributable to local or regional forces that shape firms' capabilities at early stages in their lives. Porter (1990), for example, shows that differences in local product markets, local factor markets, and institutions play an important role in shaping competitive capabilities. Differences also exist within populations of firms from the same country. Various studies of the automobile industry, for example, show that not all Japanese automobile companies are top performers in terms of quality, productivity, or product development (see e.g. Clark and Fujimoto, 1990). The role of firm-specific history has been highlighted as a critical factor explaining such firm-level (as opposed to regional or national level) differences (Nelson and Winter 1982). Replication in a different context may thus be rather difficult.

At least two types of strategic value flow from replication. One is the ability to support geographic and product line expansion. To the extent that the capabilities in question are relevant to customer needs elsewhere, replication can confer value.[39] Another is that the ability to replicate also indicates that the firm has the foundations in place for learning and improvement. Considerable empirical evidence supports the notion that the understanding of processes, both in production and in management, is the key to process improvement. In short, an organization cannot improve that which it does not understand. Deep process understanding is often required to accomplish codification. Indeed, if knowledge is highly tacit, it indicates that underlying structures are not well understood, which limits learning because scientific and engineering principles cannot be as systematically applied.[40] Instead, learning is confined to proceeding through trial and error, and the leverage that might otherwise come from the application of scientific theory is denied.

Imitation. Imitation is simply replication performed by a competitor. If self-replication is difficult, imitation is likely to be even harder. In competitive markets, it is the ease of imitation that determines the sustainability of competitive advantage. Easy imitation implies the rapid dissipation of rents.

Factors that make replication difficult also make imitation difficult. Thus, the more tacit the firm's productive knowledge, the harder it is to replicate by the firm itself or its competitors. When the tacit component is high, imitation may well be impossible, absent the hiring away of key individuals and the transfer of key organizational processes.

---

[39] Needless to say, there are many examples of firms replicating their capabilities inappropriately by applying extant routines to circumstances where they may not be applicable, e.g. Nestlés transfer of developed-country marketing methods for infant formula to the Third World (Hartley 1989). A key strategic need is for firms to screen capabilities for their applicability to new environments.

[40] Different approaches to learning are required depending on the depth of knowledge. Where knowledge is less articulated and structured, trial and error and learning-by-doing are necessary, whereas in mature environments where the underlying engineering science is better understood, organizations can undertake more deductive approaches or what Pisano (1994) refers to as 'learning-before-doing'.

However, another set of barriers impede imitation of certain capabilities in advanced industrial countries. This is the system of intellectual property rights, such as patents, trade secrets, and trademarks, and even trade dress.[41] Intellectual property protection is of increasing importance in the USA, as since 1982 the legal system has adopted a more pro-patent posture. Similar trends are evident outside the USA. Besides the patent system, several other factors cause there to be a difference between replication costs and imitation costs. The observability of the technology or the organization is one such important factor. Whereas vistas into product technology can be obtained through strategies such as reverse engineering, this is not the case for process technology, as a firm need not expose its process technology to the outside in order to benefit from it.[42] Firms with product technology, on the other hand, confront the unfortunate circumstances that they must expose what they have got in order to profit from the technology. Secrets are thus more protectable if there is no need to expose them in contexts where competitors can learn about them.

One should not, however, overestimate the overall importance of intellectual property protection; yet it presents a formidable imitation barrier in certain particular contexts. Intellectual property protection is not uniform across products, processes, and technologies, and is best thought of as islands in a sea of open competition. If one is not able to place the fruits of one's investment, ingenuity, or creativity on one or more islands, then one indeed is at sea.

We use the term appropriability regimes to describe the ease of imitation. Appropriability is a function both of the ease of replication and the efficacy of intellectual property rights as a barrier to imitation. Appropriability is strong when a technology is both inherently difficult to replicate and the intellectual property system provides legal barriers to imitation. When it is inherently easy to replicate and intellectual property protection is either unavailable or ineffectual, then appropriability is weak. Intermediate conditions also exist.

4. Conclusion

The dynamic capabilities orientation to strategy we have put forth clearly is different from the 'competitive market force' and 'strategic play' views that were dominant earlier. But are these paradigms complementary or competitive? Our view is that complex problems are likely to benefit from insights obtained from all of the paradigms we have identified plus more. The trick is to work out which frameworks are appropriate for the problem at hand. Slavish adherence to one class to the neglect of all others is likely to generate strategic blindspots. The tools themselves then

---

[41] Trade dress refers to the 'look and feel' of a retail establishment, e.g. the distinctive marketing and presentation style of The Nature Company.

[42] An interesting but important exception to this can be found in second sourcing. In the microprocessor business, until the introduction of the 386 chip, Intel and most other merchant semi-producers were encouraged by large customers like IBM to provide second sources, i.e. to license and share their proprietary process technology with competitors like AMD and NEC. The microprocessor developers did so to assure customers that they had sufficient manufacturing capability to meet demand at all times.

generate strategic vulnerability. We now explore these issues further. Table 12.1 summarizes some similarities and differences.

4.1. Efficiency versus market power

The competitive forces and strategic conflict approaches generally see profits as stemming from strategizing—that is, from limitations on competition which firms achieve through raising rivals' costs and exclusionary behaviour (Teece 1984). The competitive forces approach in particular leads one to see concentrated industries as being attractive—market positions can be shielded behind entry barriers, and rivals' costs can be raised. It also suggests that the sources of competitive advantage lie at the level of the industry, or possibly groups within an industry. There is almost no attention at all devoted to discovering, creating, and commercializing new sources of value.

The dynamic capabilities and resources approaches have a different orientation. They see competitive advantage stemming from high-performance routines operating 'inside the firm', reflected in processes and positions. Path dependencies (including increasing returns) and technological opportunities shape the road ahead. Because of imperfect factor markets, or more precisely the non-tradeability of 'soft' assets like values, culture, and organizational experience, distinctive competences and capabilities generally cannot be acquired; they must be built. This sometimes takes years—possibly decades. In some cases, as when the competence is protected by patents, replication by a competitor is ineffectual as a means to access the technology. The capabilities approach accordingly sees definite limits on strategic options, at least in the short run. Competitive success occurs in part because of policies pursued and experience and efficiency obtained in earlier periods.

Competitive success can undoubtedly flow from both strategizing and economizing,[43] but along with Williamson (1992) we believe that 'economizing is more fundamental than strategizing ... or put differently, that economy is the best strategy'.[44] Indeed, we suggest that, except in special circumstances, too much 'strategizing' can lead to firms to underinvest in core competences and thus harm long-term competitiveness.

4.2. Normative implications

The field of strategic management is avowedly normative. It seeks to guide those aspects of general management that have material effects on the survival and success of the business enterprise. Unless these various approaches differ in terms of the framework and heuristics they offer management, then the discourse we have gone

---

[43] Phillips (1971) and Demsetz (1974) also made the case that market concentration resulted from the competitive success of more efficient firms, and not from entry barriers and restrictive practices.

[44] We concur with Williamson that economizing and strategizing are not mutually exclusive. Strategic ploys can be used to disguise inefficiencies and to promote economizing outcomes, as with pricing with reference to learning-curve costs. Our view of economizing is perhaps more expansive than Williamson's as it embraces more than efficient contract design and the minimization of transactions costs. We also address production and organizational economies, and the distinctive ways that things are accomplished inside the business enterprise.

TABLE 12.1 Paradigms of strategy: salient characteristics

Paradigm no.	Intellectual roots	Representative authors addressing strategic management questions	Nature of rents	Rationality assumptions of managers	Fundamental units of analysis	Short-run capacity for strategic reorientation	Role of industrial structure	Focal concern
(1) Attenuating competitive forces	Mason Bain	Porter (1980)	Chamberlinean	rational	industries firms products	high	exogenous	structural conditions and competitor positioning
(2) Strategic conflict	Machiavelli Schelling Cournot Nash Harsanyi Shapiro	Ghemawat (1986) Shapiro (1989) Brandenburger and Nalebuff (1995)	Chamberlinean	hyper-rational	firms products	often infinite	endogenous	strategic interactions
(3) Resource-based perspectives	Penrose Selznick Christensen Andrews	Rumelt (1984) Chandler (1966) Wernerfelt (1984) Teece (1980, 1982)	Ricardian	rational	resources	low	endogenous	asset fungibility
(4) Dynamic capabilities perspective	Schumpeter Nelson Winter Teece	Dosi, Teece, and Winter (1989) Prahalad and Hamel (1990) Hayes and Wheelwright (1984) Dierickx and Cool (1989) Porter (1990) Ghemawat (1991)	Schumpeterian	rational	processes positions paths	low	endogenous	asset accumulation, replicability, and inimitability

through is of limited immediate value. In this chapter, we have already alluded to the fact that the capabilities approach tends to steer managers toward creating distinctive and difficult-to-imitate advantages and avoiding games with customers and competitors. We now survey possible differences, recognizing that the paradigms are still in their infancy and cannot confidently support strong normative conclusions.

Unit of analysis and analytic focus. Because in the capabilities and the resources framework business opportunities flow from a firm's unique capabilities, strategy analysis must be situational.[45] This is also true with the strategic conflict approach. There is no algorithm for creating wealth for the entire industry. Prescriptions that apply to industries or groups of firms at best suggest overall direction, and may indicate errors to be avoided. In contrast, the competitive forces approach is not particularly firm-specific; it is industry and group-specific.

Strategic change. The competitive forces and the strategic-conflict approach, since they pay little attention to skills, know-how, and path dependency, tend to see strategic choice occurring with relative facility. The capabilities approach sees value augmenting strategic change as being difficult and costly. Moreover, it can generally only occur incrementally. Capabilities cannot easily be bought; they must be built. From the capabilities perspective, strategy involves choosing among and committing to long-term paths or trajectories of competence development.

In this regard, we speculate that the dominance of competitive forces and the strategic conflict approaches in the USA may have something to do with observed differences in strategic approaches adopted by some US and some foreign firms. Robert Hayes (1985) has noted that American companies tend to favour 'strategic leaps' while, in contrast, Japanese and German companies tend to favour incremental, but rapid, improvements.

Entry strategies. Here the resources and the capabilities approaches suggest that entry decisions must be made with respect to the capabilities which new entrants have, relative to the competition. Whereas the other approaches tell you little about where to look to find likely entrants, the capabilities approach identifies likely entrants. Relatedly, whereas the entry deterrence approach suggests an unconstrained search for new business opportunities, the capabilities approach suggests that such opportunities lie close in to one's existing business. As Richard Rumelt explains it, 'the capabilities approach suggests that if a firm looks inside itself, and at its market environment, sooner or later it will find a business opportunity'.

Entry timing. Whereas the strategic conflict approach tells little about where to look to find likely entrants, the resources and the capabilities approach identifies likely entrants and their timing of entry. Brittain and Freeman (1980) using population ecology methodologies argued that an organization is quick to expand when there is a significant overlap between its core capabilities and those needed to survive in a new market. Recent research (Mitchell 1989) showed that the more industry-specialized assets or capabilities a firm possesses, the more likely it is to enter an emerging

---

[45] On this point, the strategic conflict and the resources and capabilities are congruent. However, the aspects of 'situation' that matter are dramatically different, as described in Section 3.2.

technical subfield in its industry, following a technological discontinuity. Additionally, the interaction between specialized assets such as firm-specific capabilities and rivalry had the greatest influence on entry timing.

Diversification. Related diversification—that is diversification that builds upon or extends existing capabilities—is about the only form of diversification that a capabilities framework is likely to view as meritorious (Rumelt 1974; Teece 1980, 1982; Teece *et al.* 1994). Such diversification will be justifiable when the firms' traditional markets decline.[46] The strategic-conflict approach is likely to be a little more permissive; acquisitions that raise rivals' costs or enable firms to effectuate exclusive arrangements are likely to be seen as efficacious in certain circumstances.

Focus and specialization. Focus needs to be defined in terms of distinctive competence capability, not products. Products are the manifestation of competences, as competences can be moulded into a variety of products. Product market specialization and decentralization that configure around product markets may cause firms to neglect the development of core competences and dynamic capabilities, to the extent to which competences require accessing assets across divisions.

The capabilities approach places emphasis on the internal processes that a firm utilizes, as well as how they are deployed and how they will evolve. The approach has the benefit of indicating that competitive advantage is not just a function of how one plays the game; it is also a function of the 'assets' one has to play with, and how these assets can be deployed and redeployed in a changing market.

4.3. Future directions

We have merely sketched an outline for a dynamic capabilities approach. Further theoretical work is needed to tighten the framework, and empirical research is critical to helping us understand how firms get to be good, how they sometimes stay that way, why and how they improve, and why they sometimes decline.[47] Researchers in the field of strategy need to join forces with researchers in the fields of innovation, manufacturing, organizational behaviour, and business history if they are to unlock the riddles that lie behind corporate as well as national competitive advantage. There could hardly be a more ambitious research agenda in the social sciences today.

---

[46] Cantwell shows that the technological competence of firms persists over time, gradually evolving through firm-specific learning. He shows that technological diversification has been greater for chemicals and pharmaceuticals than for electrical and electronic-related fields, and he offers as an explanation the greater straight-ahead opportunities in electrical and electronic fields compared with chemicals and pharmaceuticals. See Cantwell (1993).

[47] For a gallant start, see Miyazaki (1995) and McGrath *et al.* (1996). Chandler's (1990) work on scale and scope, summarized in Teece (1993), provides some historical support for the capabilities approach.

References

Abernathy, W. J., and K. Clark (1985). 'Innovation: Mapping the Winds of Creative Destruction', *Research Policy*, 14: 3–22.

—— and J. M. Utterback (1978). 'Patterns of Industrial Innovation', *Technology Review*, 80 (7): 40–7.

Alchian, A. A., and H. Demsetz (1972). 'Production, Information Costs, and Economic Organization', *American Economic Review*, 62: 777–95.

Amit, R. and P. Schoemaker (1990). 'Key Success Factors: Their Foundation and Application', unpublished working paper, University of British Columbia and University of Chicago.

—— —— (1992). 'Strategic Assets and Organizational Rent', Working Paper, University of British Columbia, Canada.

Andrews, K. (1987). *The Concept of Corporate Strategy*, 3rd edn. Homewood, Ill: Dow Jones-Irwin.

Aoki, M. (1990). 'The Participatory Generation of Information Rents and the Theory of the Firm', in M. Aoki *et al.* (eds.), *The Firm as a Nexus of Treaties*. London: Sage.

Argyris, C., and D. Schon (1978). *Organizational Learning*. Reading, Mass: Addison-Wesley.

Arrow, K. (1969). 'The Organization of Economic Activity: Issues Pertinent to the Choice of Market vs. Nonmarket Allocation', in *The Analysis and Evaluation of Public Expenditures: The PPB System*, 1, US Joint Economic Committee, 91st Session. Washington, DC: US Government Printing Office: 59–73.

—— (1996). 'Technical Information and Industrial Structure', *Industrial and Corporate Change*, 5(2).

Arthur, W. B. (1983). 'Competing Technologies and Lock-in by Historical Events: The Dynamics of Allocation under Increasing Returns', Working Paper WP-83-90. International Institute for Applied Systems Analysis, Laxenburg, Austria.

—— (1988). 'Competing Technologies: An Overview', in G. Dosi *et al.* (eds.), *Technical Change and Economic Theory*. London: Pinter Publishers: 115–135.

Bain, J. S. (1959). *Industrial Organization*. New York: Wiley.

Baldwin, C., and K. Clark (1991). 'Capabilities and Capital Investment: New Perspectives on Capital Budgeting', Harvard Business School, Working Paper 92-004.

Barney, J. B. (1986). 'Strategic Factor Markets: Expectations, Luck, and Business Strategy', *Management Science*, 32(10): 1231–41.

Baumol, W., J. Panzar, and R. Willig (1982). *Contestable Markets and the Theory of Industry Structure*. New York: Harcourt Brace Jovanovich.

Bercovitz, J. E. L., J. M. de Figueredo, and D. J. Teece (1996). 'Firm Capabilities and Managerial Decision-Making: A Theory of Innovation Biases', in Z. Shapira (ed.), *Technological Oversight and Foresight*. Cambridge: Cambridge University Press.

Brandenburger, A. M., and B. J. Nalebuff (1966). *Co-operation*. New York: Doubleday & Co.

—— —— (1995). 'The Right Game: Use Game Theory to Shape Strategy', *Harvard Business Review*, July–Aug.

Brittain, J., and J. Freeman (1980). 'Organizational Proliferation and Density-Dependent Selection', in J. R. Kimberly and R. Miles (eds.), *The Organizational Life Cycle*. San Francisco: Jossey-Bass: 291–338.

Camp, R. (1989). *Benchmarking: The Search for Industry Best Practice that Leads to Superior Performance*. White Plains, NY: Quality Resources.

Cantwell, J. (1993). 'Corporate Technological Specialization in International Industries', in M. Casson and J. Creedy (eds.), *Industrial Concentration and Economic Inequality*. Aldershot: Edward Elgar.

Chandler, A. D., Jr. (1966). *Strategy and Structure*. New York: Doubleday & Co., Anchor Books edn.

—— (1990). *Scale and Scope: The Dynamics of Industrial Competition*. Cambridge, Mass.: Harvard University Press.

Clark, K., and T. Fujimoto (1991). *Product Development Performance: Strategy, Organization and Management in the World Auto Industries*. Cambridge, Mass.: Harvard Business School Press.

Coase, R. (1937). 'The Nature of the Firm', *Economica*, 4: 386–405.

—— (1988). 'Lecture on the Nature of the Firm, III', *Journal of Law, Economics and Organization*, 4: 33–47.

Cool, K., and D. Schendel (1988). 'Performance Differences among Strategic Group Members', *Strategic Management Journal*, 9: 207–24.

David, P. A., and J. A. Bunn (1988). 'The Economics of Gateway Technologies and Network Evolution: Lessons from Electricity Supply History', *Information Economics and Policy*, 3: 165–202.

De Figueiredo, J. M., and D. J. Teece (1996). 'Mitigating Procurement Hazards in the Context of Innovation', *Industrial and Corporate Change*, 5(2): 537–59.

Demsetz, H. (1974). 'Two Systems of Belief About Monopoly', in H. Goldschmid *et al.* (eds.), *Industrial Concentration: The New Learning*. Boston: Little, Brown & Co.

Dierickx, I., and K. Cool (1989). 'Asset Stock Accumulation and Sustainability of Competitive Advantage', *Management Science*, 35(12): 1504–11.

Dixit, A. (1980). 'The Role of Investment in Entry Deterrence', *Economic Journal*, 90: 95–106.

Dosi, G., D. J. Teece, and S. Winter (1989). 'Toward a Theory of Corporate Coherence: Preliminary Remarks', unpublished paper, Center for Research in Management, University of California at Berkeley.

Doz, Y., and A. Shuen (1990). 'From Intent to Outcome: A Process Framework for Partnerships', INSEAD Working Paper.

Eaton, C., and R. G. Lipsey (1981). 'Capital, Commitment, and Entry Equilibrium', *Bell Journal of Economics*, 12 (Autumn): 593–604.

Fama, E. F. (1980). 'Agency Problems and the Theory of the Firm', *Journal of Political Economy*, 88 (Apr.): 288–307.

Freeman, J., and W. Boeker (1984). 'The Ecological Analysis of Business Strategy', in G. Carroll and D. Vogel (eds.), *Strategy and Organization*. Boston: Pitman.

Fujimoto, T. (1994). 'Reinterpreting the Resource-Capability View of the Firm: A Case of the Development-Production Systems of the Japanese Automakers', draft working paper, Faculty of Economics, University of Tokyo.

Garvin, D. (1988). *Managing Quality*. New York: Free Press.

—— (1994). 'The Processes of Organization and Management', Harvard Business School Working Paper, 94-084.

Geroski, P. A. (1988). 'Book Review of James Friedman, *Game Theory with Applications to Economics*', *International Journal of Industrial Organization*, 6(2): 155–281.

Ghemawat, P. (1984). 'Capacity Expansion in the Titanium Dioxide Industry', *Journal of Industrial Economics*, 33 (Dec.): 145–63.

—— (1986). 'Sustainable Advantage', *Harvard Business Review* (Sept.–Oct.).

—— (1991). *Commitment: The Dynamics of Strategy*. New York: Free Press.

Ghemawat, P., and R. E. Caves (1986). 'Capital Commitment and Profitability: An Empirical Investigation', *Oxford Economic Papers*, 38 (Nov.): 94–110.

Gilbert, R. J., and D. M. G. Newberry (1982). 'Preemptive Patenting and the Persistence of Monopoly', *American Economic Review*, 72 (June): 514–26.

Gittell, J. H. (1995). 'Cross Functional Coordination, Control and Human Resource Systems: Evidence from the Airline Industry', Ph.D. thesis, MIT.

Hansen, G. S., and B. Wernerfelt (1989). 'Determinants of Firm Performance: The Relative Importance of Economic and Organizational Factors', *Strategic Management Journal*, 10: 399–411.

Hartley, R. F. (1989). *Marketing Mistakes*. New York: Wiley.

Hartman, R., and D. J. Teece (1990). 'Product Emulation Strategies in the Presence of Reputation Effects and Network Externalities: Some Evidence from the Micro-computer Industry', *Economics of Innovation and New Technology*, 1: 157–82.

Hayes, R. (1985). 'Strategic Planning: Forward in Reverse', *Harvard Business Review* (Nov.–Dec.): 111–19.

——and K. Clark (1985). 'Exploring the Sources of Productivity Differences at the Factory Level', in K. Clark *et al.* (eds.), *The Uneasy Alliance: Managing the Productivity-Technology Dilemma*. Boston, Mass.: HBs Press.

——and S. Wheelwright (1984). *Restoring Our Competitive Edge: Competing Through Manufacturing*. New York: Wiley.

————and K. Clark (1988). *Dynamic Manufacturing: Creating the Learning Organization*. New York: Free Press.

Henderson, R. M. (1994). 'The Evolution of Integrative Capability: Innovation in Cardio-vascular Drug Discovery', *Industrial and Corporate Change*, 3(3): 607–30.

——and K. B. Clark (1990). 'Architectural Innovation: The Reconfiguration of Existing Product Technologies and the Failure of Established Firms', *Administrative Science Quarterly*, 35 (Mar.): 9–30.

——and I. Cockburn (1994). 'Measuring Core Competence', MIT Working Paper.

Iansiti, M., and K. B. Clark (1994). 'Integration and Dynamic Capability: Evidence from Product Development in Automobiles and Mainframe Computers', *Industrial and Corporate Change*, 3(3): 557–605.

Itami, H., and T. W. Roehl (1987). *Mobilizing Invisible Assets*. Cambridge, Mass.: Harvard University Press.

Jacobson, R. (1988). 'The Persistence of Abnormal Returns', *Strategic Management Journal*, 9: 41–58.

Jensen, M. C., and W. H. Meckling (1976). 'Theory of Firm: Managerial Behavior, Agency Costs and Ownership Structure', *Journal of Financial Economics*, 3(4): 305–60.

Johnson, R. N., and A. Parkman (1983). 'Spatial Monopoly, Non-Zero Profits and Entry Deterrence: The Case of Cement', *Review of Economics and Statistics*, 65: 431–9.

Jorde, T. M., and D. J. Teece (eds.) (1992). *Antitrust, Innovation, and Competitiveness*. New York: Oxford University Press.

Katz, M. L. (1986). 'An Analysis of Cooperative Research and Development', *RAND Journal of Economics*, 17: 527–43.

——and C. Shapiro (1985). 'Network Externalities, Competition and Compatibility', *American Economic Review*, 75: 424–40.

Kogut, I., and U. Zander (1992). 'Knowledge of the Firm, Combinative Capabilities, and the Replication of Technology', *Organizational Science*, 3: 383–97.

Kreps, D. M., and R. Wilson (1982*a*). 'Sequential Equilibria', *Econometrica*, 50 (July): 863–94.

——(1982*b*). 'Reputation and Imperfect Information', *Journal of Economic Theory*, 27 (Aug.): 253–79.

Langlois, R. (1994). 'Cognition and Capabilities: Opportunities Seized and Missed in the History of the Computer Industry', Working Paper, University of Connecticut. Presented at the conference on Technological Oversights and Foresights, Stern School of Business, New York University, 11–12 March.

——and P. L. Robertson (1995). *Firms, Markets and Economic Change: A Dynamic Theory of Business Institutions*. London: Routledge.

Learned, E., C. Christensen, K. Andrews, and W. Guth (1969). *Business Policy: Text and Cases*. Homewood, Ill.: R. Irwin.

Leonard-Barton, D. (1995). *Wellsprings of Knowledge*. Boston, Mass.: Harvard Business School Press.

Lev, B., and T. Sougiannis (1992). 'The Capitalization, Amortization and Value-Relevance of R&D', unpublished MS, University of California at Berkeley, and University of Illinois, Urbana-Champaign.

Levin, R. (1982). 'The Semiconductor Industry', in Richard Nelson (ed.), *Government and Technical Progress*. New York: Pergamon Press.

Levinthal, D. (1990). 'A Microeconomic Model of Population Ecology', unpublished MS, University of Pennsylvania.

——and J. March (1981). 'A Model of Adaptive Organizational Search', *Journal of Economic Behavior and Organization*, 2: 307–33.

Levitt, B., and J. March (1988). 'Organizational Learning', *Annual Review of Sociology*, 14: 319–40.

Lieberman, M. (1987). 'Excess Capacity as a Barrier to Entry', *Journal of Industrial Economics* (June).

Link, A. N., D. J. Teece, and W. F. Finan (1996). 'Estimating the Benefits from Collaboration: The Case of SEMATECH', *Review of Industrial Organization* (Oct.).

Lippman, S. A., and R. P. Rumelt (1992). 'Demand Uncertainty and Investment in Industry-Specific Capital', *Industry and Corporate Change*, 1(1): 235–62.

Mahoney, J. (1992). 'The Management of Resources and the Resources of Management', *Journal of Business Research*.

Mason, E. (1949). 'The Current State of the Monopoly Problem in the U.S.', *Harvard Law Review* (June).

Milgrom, P., and J. Roberts (1982*a*). 'Limit Pricing and Entry Under Incomplete Information: An Equilibrium Analysis', *Econometrica*, 50 (Mar.): 443–59.

————(1982*b*). 'Predation, Reputation and Entry Deterrence', *Journal of Economic Theory*, 27 (Aug.): 280–312.

————(1990). 'The Economics of Modern Manufacturing: Technology, Strategy, and Organization', *The American Economic Review*, 80(3): 511–28.

Mitchell, W. (1989). 'Whether and When? Probability and Timing of Incumbents' Entry into Emerging Industrial Subfields', *Administrative Science Quarterly*, 34: 208–30.

Miyazaki, K. (1995). *Building Competences in the Firm: Lessons from Japanese and European Optoelectronics*. New York: St Martins Press.

Mody, A. (1990). 'Learning through Alliances', Working Paper, World Bank, Washington, DC.

Nelson, R. (1996). 'The Evolution of Competitive or Comparative Advantage: A Preliminary Report on a Study', WP-96-21, International Institute for Applied Systems Analysis, Laxenburg, Austria.

——and S. Winter (1982). *An Evolutionary Theory of Economic Change*. Cambridge, Mass.: Harvard University Press.

Penrose, E. (1959). *The Theory of the Growth of the Firm*. London: Blackwell.

Peteraf, M. (1990). 'The Resource Based Model: An Emerging Paradigm for Strategic Management', Discussion Paper 90-29, Kellogg School of Management, Northwestern University.

Peters, T. J., and R. H. Waterman (1982). *In Search of Excellence*. New York: Harper & Row.

Phillips, A. C. (1971). *Technology and Market Structure*. Toronto: Lexington Books.

Pisano, G. (1990). 'The R&D Boundaries of the Firm', *Administrative Science Quarterly*, 34(1): 153–76.

Porter, M. E. (1980). *Competitive Strategy*. New York: Free Press.

——(1981*a*). 'Strategic Interaction: Some Lessons from Industry Histories for Theory and Antitrust Policy', in S. Salop (ed.), *Strategy, Predation and Antitrust Analysis*. Washington, DC: Bureau of Economics, Federal Trade Commission.

——(1981*b*). 'The Contributions of Industrial Organizations to Strategic Management', *Academy of Management Review*, 6(4): 612.

——(1990). *The Competitive Advantage of Nations*. New York: Free Press.

——and M. O. Lawrence (1978). 'Note on the Corn Wet Milling Industry 1973–1977', *Intercollegiate Case Clearinghouse*, no. 9-378-206.

——and A. M. Spence (1982). 'The Capacity Expansion Process in a Growing Oligopoly: The Case of Corn Wet Milling', in J. J. McCall (ed.), *The Economics of Information and Uncertainty*. Chicago: University of Chicago Press.

Prahalad, C. K., and G. Hamel (1990). 'The Core Competence of the Corporation', *Harvard Business Review* (May–June), 79–91.

Putterman, L. (ed.) (1986). *The Economic Nature of the Firm: A Reader*. Cambridge, Mass.: Cambridge University Press.

Richardson, G. B. H. (1960). *Information and Investment*. Oxford: Oxford University Press.

Rosenberg, N. (1982). *Inside the Black Box: Technology and Economics*. Cambridge, Mass.: Cambridge University Press.

Rumelt, R. P. (1974). *Strategy, Structure, and Economic Performance*. Cambridge, Mass.: Harvard University Press.

——(1984). 'Towards a Strategic Theory of the Firm', in R. B. Lamb (ed.), *Competitive Strategic Management*. Englewood Cliffs, NJ: Prentice-Hall.

——(1987). 'Theory, Strategy, and Entrepreneurship', in D. Teece (ed.), *The Competitive Challenge*. Cambridge, Mass.: Ballinger.

——(1991). 'How Much Does Industry Matter?' *Strategic Management Journal*, 12: 167–85.

——D. Schendel, and D. Teece (1994). *Fundamental Issues in Strategy*. Cambridge, Mass.: Harvard Business School Press.

Schelling, T. C. (1960). *Strategy of Conflict*. Cambridge, Mass.: Harvard University Press.

Schmalensee, R. (1983). 'Advertising and Entry Deterrence: An Exploratory Model', *Journal of Political Economy*, 91(4): 636–53.

Schumpeter, J. A. (1934). *Theory of Economic Development*. Cambridge, Mass.: Harvard University Press.

——(1942). *Capitalism, Socialism, and Democracy*. New York: Harper & Row.

Shapiro, C. (1985). 'Patent Licensing and R&D Rivalry', *American Economic Review Papers and Proceedings* (May).

—— (1989). 'The Theory of Business Strategy', *RAND Journal of Economics* (Spring).

Shuen, A. (1994). 'Technology Sourcing and Learning Strategies in the Semiconductor Industry', unpublished Ph.D. dissertation, University of California at Berkeley.

Spence, A. M. (1979). 'Investment Strategy and Growth in a New Market', *Bell Journal of Economics*, 10: 1–19.

Sutton, J. (1992). 'Implementing Game Theoretical Models in Industrial Economies', in A. Del Monte (ed.), *Recent Developments in the Theory of Industrial Organization*. Ann Arbor, Mich.: University of Michigan Press.

Szulanski, G. (1993). 'Intrafirm Transfer of Best Practice, Appropriate Capabilities, Organizational Barriers to Appropriation', Working Paper, INSEAD.

Teece, D. J. (1976.) *The Multinational Corporation and the Resource Cost of International Technology Transfer*. Cambridge, Mass.: Ballinger.

—— (1980). 'Economics of Scope and the Scope of an Enterprise', *Journal of Economic Behavior and Organization*, 1: 223–47.

—— (1981). 'The Market for Know-how and the Efficient International Transfer of Technology', *The Annals of the Academy of Political and Social Science* (Nov.): 81–96.

—— (1982). 'Towards an Economic Theory of the Multiproduct Firm', *Journal of Economic Behavior and Organization*, 3: 39–63.

—— (1984). 'Economic Analysis and Strategic Management', *California Management Review*, 23(3): 87–110.

—— (1986*a*). 'Transactions Cost Economics and the Multinational Enterprise', *Journal of Economic Behavior and Organization*, 7: 21–45.

—— (1986*b*). 'Profiting from Technological Innovation', *Research Policy*, 15(6).

—— (1988). 'Technological Change and the Nature of the Firm', in G. Dosi *et al.* (eds.), *Technical Change and Economic Theory*. London: Pinter Publishers.

—— (1992). 'Competition, Cooperation, and Innovation: Organizational Arrangements for Regimes of Rapid Technological Progress', *Journal of Economic Behavior and Organization*, 18(1): 1–25.

—— (1993). 'The Dynamics of Industrial Capitalism: Perspectives on Alfred Chandler's Scale and Scope (1990)', *Journal of Economic Literature*, 31 (Mar.).

—— and G. Pisano (1994). 'The Dynamic Capabilities of Firms: An Introduction', *Industrial and Corporate Change*, 3(3): 537–56.

—— R. Rumelt, G. Dosi, and S. Winter (1994). 'Understanding Corporate Coherence: Theory and Evidence', *Journal of Economic Behavior and Organization*, 23: 1–30.

Tirole, J. (1988). *The Theory of Industrial Organization*. Cambridge, Mass.: MIT Press.

Tushman, M. L., W. H. Newman, and E. Romanelli (1986). 'Convergence and Upheaval: Managing the Unsteady Pace of Organizational Evolution', *California Management Review*, 29(1): 29–44.

Vasconcellos, J. A., and D. C. Hambrick (1989). 'Key Success Factors: Test of a General Framework in the Mature Industrial-Product Sector', *Strategic Management Journal*, 10(4): 367–82.

Wernerfelt, B. (1984). 'A Resource-Based View of the Firm', *Strategic Management Journal*, 5: 171–80.

—— and C. Montgomery (1988). 'Tobin's Q and the Importance of Focus in Firm Performance', *American Economic Review*, 78(1): 246–50.

Williamson, O. E. (1975). *Markets and Hierarchies*. New York: Free Press.

—— (1985). *The Economic Institutions of Capitalism*. New York: Free Press.

—— (1992). 'Strategizing, Economizing, and Economic Organization', *Strategic Management Journal*, 12: 75–94.

Womack, J., D. Jones, and D. Roos (1991). *The Machine That Changed the World*. New York: Harper-Perennial.

13

Organizational Capabilities in Complex Worlds

Daniel A. Levinthal

The title of this chapter both serves to identify its content as well as raise questions—the questions being what is meant by the terms organizational capability and complex worlds. While these phrases have reasonably clear connotations, as we develop more formal representations of these ideas, we need to be much clearer and more explicit about their meaning. This chapter is a partial response to that need. Some basic concepts are introduced that seem central in thinking about issues related to the notion of organizational capabilities. The aspiration, however, is not to be exhaustive but rather to identify some critical underlying features and indicate the associated possibilities for formal modelling.

Let us first turn our attention to the second of the two questions raised by the title—what is meant by the term 'complex worlds'. The discussion here builds closely on the work of Simon (1972) and the issue of interrelatedness of elements of a system. This interrelatedness, or complexity, may take the form of spatial or temporal interrelatedness. Spatial interrelatedness implies that one facet of a system affects other facets of the system. The effect may be in terms of eliciting a given behaviour or in terms of the pay-off associated with a given behaviour. Interrelatedness may also be temporal. Chess is a complex game primarily due to temporal interrelatedness. The value of moves is, in large measure, associated with their 'stage setting' properties; how does a move position the player for subsequent moves and ultimately for the capture of the opponent's king.

The notion of organizational capabilities, as distinct from individual capabilities, is intimately related to this issue of complementarities. As Nelson and Winter (1982) suggest, for a capacity to be viewed as an organizational capability, as opposed to an individual skill, it must involve collective action. More precisely, their concept of organizational routine reflects a series of patterned stimulus response actions on the part of a set of actors within the organization.

In the absence of complementarities, the notion of organizational capabilities would be meaningless. If the pay-off to the actions, skills, and competencies are independent of one another, then there would be no reason to observe patterned sets of interactions among individuals. Routines, or other forms of linked behaviour, are

This chapter is based on research which was supported by Sol Snider Center for Entrepreneurship at the Wharton School, University of Pennsylvania and the International Institute for Applied Systems Analysis, Vienna, Austria. The chapter has benefited from the comments of Giovanni Dosi, Luigi Marengo, Dick Nelson, Jan Rivkin, and Sid Winter.

powerful devices to enhance capabilities in a setting in which there are important complementarities in the behaviour of the various actors. Alternatively, in the language put forth earlier, they are important in complex worlds.

The presence of complementarities raises important questions regarding the appropriate unit of analysis. While organizational routines reflect the presence of complementarities among individual actors, we see broader assemblages of behaviour emerge that result from complementarities among routines themselves. Furthermore, selection pressures are brought to bear on the phenotype, the overall organization, and not at the level of underlying organizational routines, or genotypes. Such a perspective offers important insights for efforts at imitating the behaviour of high-performing organizations as well as for efforts at benchmarking particular organizational practices.

What are the implications of complementarities for the emergence of intelligent, collective action? First, the presence of significant complementarities makes the problem of intelligent action one which is highly combinatorial. The appropriateness, or put more tersely, the pay-off of a given behaviour depends on a wide set of other actions within the organization and, indeed, actions external to the organization as well. These interdependencies are reciprocal as well. Given the vast combinatorial nature of intelligent, interdependent collective action, the behaviour of individual actors cannot be characterized as being optimal. It is not, in general, possible to determine what optimal behaviour is in such a setting (Lewis, 1985*a*, 1985*b*; Casti 1992). By necessity, behaviour that is not the outcome of fully calculative decision processes must be examined and alternative bases of behaviour considered.

There are obviously a wide variety of alternatives that one might specify, ranging from divine inspiration to individual disposition. The focus here is on processes of search. Search processes themselves may take a variety of forms, from algorithms of gradient search to the employment of sophisticated heuristics in the form of 'theories of the world'. The importance of search behaviour is not simply a behavioural postulate about individual cognition, as is often presumed, but an inherent outcome of choice in complex task environments.

If collective, organizational capabilities are to emerge via a search process, what are some of the basic properties that underlie the effectiveness, or ineffectiveness, of search? Drawing heavily on the work of Simon (1972), Holland (1975), and Holland *et al.* (1989), the focus here is on a few basic features. First, is the notion of parallelism (Holland 1975). Given a highly combinatorial problem, such as the development of organizational capabilities, it is critical for an effective adaptive mechanism to engage in highly parallel search efforts. Parallelism not only greatly enhances the speed at which adaptation may occur, it is also critical to the preservation of variety of initiatives and perspectives within an organization. Indeed, a critical question is the degree to which variety can be sustained within a single organization versus a population of organizations. Marengo (1992) points out that the degree of parallelism, or variety, sustainable by an organization is constrained by the need for effective coordination and communication within the organization.

Another central property is that of hierarchy. Learning and adaptation take place at multiple levels. As Levinthal and March (1993) suggest, adaptation at one level may substitute for adaptation at another. However, beliefs and actions at one level may also constrain behaviours at lower levels of the organization. This is reflected in Simon's (1969) notion of decision premises, the structural context influenced by executives in Bower's (1970) discussion of resource allocation processes, and, in a more abstract manner, the nested levels of selection in Warglien's (1995) model of organizational adaptation.

An effective adaptive system, in the face of complementarities, must be able to link individual behaviours into larger assemblies of action. This is the critical role of routines in the Nelson and Winter (1982) structure. The idea of routine is generally treated as a kind of horizontal form of linkage. Hierarchy of action and authority are critical in creating sub-assemblies of action and behaviour that are vertical in nature.

The problem of the design of an organization is usefully informed by considering these basic properties, but it is not fully solved with the knowledge of them. Organizational structures are the outcome of a variety of influences. They reflect the intended design efforts of organizational architects, the past structures and behaviours with which these architects have to work, and various social forces that influence beliefs about appropriate forms. The problem of design is never fully solved. Not only is the problem space extraordinarily complex, but the problem space itself changes, in part in response to exogenous events and in part in response to the organization's own actions.

The *NK* model of Kauffman (1993) is introduced as a simple, canonical representation of spatial interrelatedness. In particular, the model allows one to specify a fitness landscape that, in Kauffman's words, can be 'tuned' according to the degree of complementarity, or spatial interrelatedness. The presence of complementarities results in multiple local peaks in a fitness landscape. Adaptive search in such a rugged landscape has important implications for the organization of economic activity. In particular, both the emergence of heterogeneity across organizations and inertia in the face of changing environmental conditions result as properties of adaptive search in rugged fitness landscapes (Levinthal 1997).

1. Units of Analysis: Routines and Broader Assemblages

How then should we proceed in studying the emergence of organizational capabilities in such complex worlds? A critical element of this choice, and indeed in any social science research programme, is the choice of unit of analysis (Freeman 1978). For much of its modern history, microeconomics has focused on the behaviour of markets as its units of analysis. In analysing such questions, the field was largely satisfied with relatively trivial characterizations of firms. A central element of the contribution of Nelson and Winter has been the introduction of a new, more microlevel, unit of analysis—that of organizational routines. The introduction of this concept has provoked a substantial rethinking not only of firm behaviour itself, but also of more macrolevel behaviour, such as the level of industry concentration

(Nelson and Winter 1978) and rates and pattern of innovative activity (Nelson and Winter 1982; Dosi 1988). Recently, the idea that knowledge is largely tacit and embedded in organizational routines has been applied to gain insights into the relative competitiveness of national economies (Kogut 1991, Nelson 1993, and 1994).

Complementarities are central to the existence and formation of routines, but routines themselves are critical building blocks for broader assemblages of capabilities. In some cases, these broader assemblages become a sufficiently distinct and coherent of practices that they are given a label, such as the Fordist or Toyota production system. A central element of such systems of behaviour is the degree to which they are coherent; the degree to which one element reinforces or complements other elements. One set of policies, whether it be the management of supply relations or the design of a production process, influences the emergence and desirability of other policies and sets of routines. For instance, the automated assembly line provided the motivation for a new set of human resource practices involving new compensation structures and policies of recruitment and retention (Raff 1991).

It is these systems of practices to which we typically use the label organizational capabilities. The fact that these various elements may have an important degree of coherence (Dosi *et al.* 1994) should not mask the other reality that these systems are composed of a number of 'sub-assemblies'. The particular constellation that emerges is influenced by the presence of existing sets of practices, but it is not preordained.

The popular concept of core competence (Prahalad and Hamel 1990) is, seen in this light, unclear. One conception is that a core concept is a central assemblage of routines and practices which should form the basis of all other assemblages within the organization. Put in the terminology developed here, an organization will achieve competitive advantage if there are important complementarities between this 'core competence' and other assemblages of routines.

Henderson and Clark's (1990) work suggests a quite different possible interpretation of the concept of core competence. The notion of 'architectural' capability that they develop refers to the capacity to effectively reconfigure component knowledge; it is the organization's capacity to redesign the linkages among the sub-assemblies of routines and practices. Presumably this capability to reconfigure assemblages is itself, however, restricted to some domain of activity. A financial 'engineer' may be able to reconfigure the elements of a conglomerate organization. Henderson and Clark, however, are clearly referring to instances, unlike a conglomerate organization, in which the sub-elements have significant complementarities among themselves. The prior discussion in this chapter on the unsolvability of highly combinatorial problems suggests both the rareness and, in turn, distinctive value of such recombinative capabilities, as well as the inherent limits of such capabilities.

One may also usefully think of assemblages of capabilities that span the bounds of the organization. Organizations engage in formal and informal alliances with other organizations for which they have complementary capabilities. This sort of logic underlies the importance of Marshallian regional externalities which have received much recent attention (Porter 1990; Krugman 1991). Nelson (1993, 1994) has pursued such ideas at the level of national systems and considered the co-evolution of university systems, technology, and industry.

1.1. *Units of analysis: phenotypes and genotypes*

The presence of complementarities raises important issues for the nature of selection processes. Selection operates at the level of the organization or, in the terminology of biology, at the level of the phenotype. An organization earns a profit or loss. The environment does not directly reward a particular business practice. The profitability of Wal-Mart Stores cannot be directly attributable to its particular organizational capabilities (Stalk *et al.* 1992) or its market position (Ghemawat 1991). While it is possible to make intelligent inferences, there is inevitably some degree of ambiguity.

These issues of the appropriation of rewards to particular actions and initiatives are manifestations of the more general issue of 'credit assignment' (Holland 1975). For a system to effectively adapt, whether it be an individual organization or the economy as a whole, actions that are associated with favourable outcomes need to be reinforced relative to those actions associated with less favourable outcomes. At the level of the economy, this is reflected in the flow of financial capital to organizations that succeed, or demonstrate the prospect of succeeding, in product markets. Within an organization, problems of credit assignment occur in the evaluation of the contribution of a particular function within the organization or a particular individual within the firm to the overall organization's success. As suggested above, credit assignment is made difficult by the degree of interrelationships among parts of a system.

This problem of inference is not only a challenge to academics attempting to unravel the sources of firm profitability, but to practitioners as well. Consider the implications of credit assignment problems for issues of imitation and replication of capabilities. Imagine the challenge of an automobile manufacturer wishing to replicate the 'Toyota system' of manufacturing. The problem is at least threefold.

First, there is the challenge of imitating the underlying practices. However, these practices themselves are likely to be composed of many sub-assemblies of routines and more microlevel practices. Thus, there is a recursive element to the problem.

Second, there is the challenge of making inferences as to what elements in the set of practices and behaviours are in fact underlying the desired performance and which are simply spuriously related. For instance, prior to the initial Japanese transplant automobile assembly plants in the USA, some observers speculated that the success of the Toyota system, or lean manufacturing, was contingent upon elements of the Japanese culture. As it has turned out, whatever complementarities exist between Japanese culture and these business practices, they are not sufficiently powerful to impede the success of the 'transplant' operations (MacDuffie 1988).

Finally, issues of unit of analysis and complementarities raise important questions about the desirability of the identification and transfer of 'best practices'. Implicit in such efforts is the assumption that 'best practice' is independent of the firm's context. Such a perspective not only ignores external contingencies (Lawrence and Lorsch

1967), but also ignores issues of internal coherence and consistency (Miller and Friesen 1984). Are 'best practices' in fact decomposable from the broader set of organizational processes of which they are a part?

By the same token, the identification and measurement of performance of isolated business processes represent a profound change in the unit of selection. Rather than market forces operating on the overall organization, the phenotype, selection-like pressures are brought to bear on a particular practice, the genotype. This fundamental shift in unit of analysis has, in many instances, led to dramatic discoveries on the part of firms regarding the effectiveness or ineffectiveness of particular practices. Business practices whose gross inefficiencies had previously been masked by strong, or at least adequate, overall corporate profitability are brought to light.

One can interpret the effect of this shift in unit of analysis using the notions of organizational slack (March and Simon 1958; Cyert and March 1963). When the overall organization is the unit of selection and adequate or satisficing performance is achieved, there is little impetus to search for new ways to refine the 'technology' of the current operations. In contrast, performance failure triggers efforts at local problem-solving.

Benchmarking, the comparison of a given business process with some standard, where the standard is typically not a behavioural norm but an ideal type, has a number of powerful implications when seen in this light. Slack is reduced, or in some respects eliminated, by two effects. First, the buffering provided by 'success', or effective business practices and performance elsewhere in the organization, is eliminated. Second, the aspiration level is set to correspond to some ideal type. This ideal type is sometimes best practice within the organization and in other cases it is defined with respect to an external population, where that external population may be a class of firms or the 'world'. These two effects make a performance failure almost inevitable and, in turn, lead to an inducement to engage in local problem-solving. In some instances, these discoveries of performance failure motivate a decision to outsource the activity, while in other instances it provokes efforts to enhance the performance of the processes themselves.

2. Search, Design, and other Mechanisms of Movement on Rugged Landscapes

Higher-order capabilities, by definition, involve multiple actors. Through their collective behaviour, they generate outcomes of which the participating actors are not individually capable. But how is this collective intelligence to emerge? Broadly speaking, one could imagine two sorts of processes. One would be a process of design. To take the overworked example of Adam Smith's pin factory, a social planner or entrepreneur (for the present purposes there is no clear distinction between the two roles) could assign individuals to various stages of the production process. This act of design would not in and of itself result in the development of distinctive, collective capabilities. These capabilities would emerge over time as the individuals acquired greater skill in their particular roles. Thus, the capability development that occurs with time is one of individual skill development. The achievement of collective capabilities is not an emergent property of the system.

This story of collective design and individual skill development, while interesting, seems rather distant from Nelson and Winter's (1982) discussion of organizational routines. The division of tasks does not seem to be preordained in the Nelson and Winter characterization of organizational capabilities. Rather, the spirit of the discussion seems to be more that individuals engage in actions that have joint consequences and that, over time, patterns of behaviour emerge that exhibit collective intelligence. Thus, in contrast to the characterization of the pin factory, not only do individual skills evolve as agents repeatedly engage in similar tasks, but patterns of interaction emerge as well.

When the contrast is made between the ability of markets and social planners to achieve effective solutions to the problem of the design of collective action, there now seems to be a global consensus as to greater efficacy of markets. By the same token, one should be equally sceptical of administrative solutions to complex design problems of a micro, organizational variety. This is not to say that there is not a role for intentional design, but the scope of such efforts is inherently limited.

2.1. Necessity of search: computational arguments

Complexity results in the necessity of a search process. Simon (1955) has made this point by contrasting the computational demands posed by decision problems and the cognitive capacity of human beings. However, theoretical work in computer science suggests that problem complexity may exceed the capacity of any computation device based on the principle of a Turing machine (Casti 1992). Computational problems are termed NP-complete if the difficulty in finding a solution increases at a rate faster than a polynomial expression of the number of variables being considered. Furthermore, complexity, the degree of interaction within a system, generally underlies the intractability of NP-complete problems. Simon's arguments for bounded rationality rested on a comparison of human cognitive capacity relative to the complexity of decision problems. However, consider the calculative limits of modern computers relative to the complexity of well-posed, but NP-complete, computational problems. Radical increases in calculative power result in only a modest expansion of the frontiers of solvable problems in the face of such complexity.

The particular 'engineering' solutions to NP-complete problems vary, ranging from 'branch and bound' techniques (Garfinkel and Nemhauser 1972) to algorithms of gradient search, but they all reflect methods to search over the space of possible solutions. Such processes appear to be analogous to Simon's notion of satisficing (1955) and Cyert and March's (1963) discussion of decision rules.[1] Simon's human decision-makers cannot find optimal solutions to the problems posed to them. Nor, it turns out, can any machine based on the logic of a general Turing machine.

---

[1] Indeed, the connection is not coincidental given the involvement of some of the same individuals in the early stages of both research programmes.

The connection to behavioural theories of firm decision-making (Cyert and March 1963; Nelson and Winter 1982) becomes even more striking when one considers the actual mechanisms by which heuristic search algorithms operate: 'the most widely applied technique is that of "neighbourhood search", in which a preselected set of local operations is used to repeatedly improve an initial solution, continuing until no further local improvements can be made and a "locally optimum" solution has been obtained' (Garey and Johnson 1979: 122). The development of heuristic algorithms seems to mirror the emergence of heuristics or routines within organizations. A priori, it is difficult to judge the effectiveness of a particular algorithm. However, through trial and analysis, algorithms are refined and often prove quite effective in practice, at least in relation to the competitive challenges of a particular time and place.[2]

Heuristics can themselves be quite complex. Indeed, Winter (1994*b*) argues that the techniques of calculative rationality are themselves properly viewed as particular sorts of heuristic devices. Such theories on the part of actors may provide more or less useful representations of the true pay-off structure.[3] When applying more formal optimization techniques, it is important to bear in mind that while an 'optimum' solution is identified, this is an optimum only with respect to the representation of the problem space. In general, the connection between this identified solution and the actual problem space is ambiguous.

While the analogy between the challenge of designing computational algorithms to address NP-complete problems and the challenge of an organization moving in a rugged landscape offers some insight, it is also misleading in important respects. Both involve searches through vast combinatorial spaces; however, the speed of feedback and the cost of the search effort itself are vastly different in the context of organizations and a symbolic representation of a problem space. In the case of computational search, the feedback is essentially instantaneous; for organizations, feedback from 'experimentation' must be measured in fractions of years not seconds.[4] In addition, computation search processes are typically treated as 'off-line' search processes. In contrast, organizations must simultaneously survive in the present while discovering new bases of advantage for the future.

3. Fitness Landscapes and Complementarities

How might we think analytically about the performance implications of alternative organizational policies in the face of complementarities? In his work on the foundations of population genetics, Kauffman has considered this question in the context of biological organisms, examining the relationship between interaction effects in the

---

[2] Survival in an evolutionary context is a function of relative, or competitive performance (Winter 1964). Thus, an evolutionary perspective makes the satisficing 'hurdle' an external referent, rather than an internal one; nonetheless, one is left with a 'competitive' notion of satisficing, not optimizing behaviour.

[3] I thank Dick Nelson for making clearer to me the idea that the topography need not be fixed but is in an important respect a function of the actor's understanding of the world.

[4] I thank Sid Winter for making this observation.

fitness contribution of elements of an organism and the topography of the fitness landscape (Kauffman 1993). The fitness landscape refers to the change in fitness, or performance, with changes in elements of the organism. In the organizational context, we can specify a landscape to reflect performance differences as facets of the organization vary, where those facets, for example, could be elements of human resource policies, manufacturing policies, and distribution logistics.

What, in turn, determines the structure of the fitness landscape? For instance, does the landscape consist of a single, global peak, or are there a variety of local peaks? Furthermore, how smooth is the landscape? That is, is the fitness value of neighbouring points likely to be similar or do fitness values change in an abrupt manner with a change in location? What might determine the smoothness of the fitness space?

An important contribution of Kauffman's work is the finding that the topography of the fitness landscape is determined by the degree of interdependence of the fitness contribution of the various attributes (genes) of an organism. In the literature on population genetics, such interaction effects are termed epistatic effects (Smith 1989). If organizational fitness is highly interactive, that is the value of a particular feature of the organization depends on a variety of other features of the organization, then the fitness landscape will tend to be quite rugged. In such a setting, even if only one element is changed, the fitness contribution of those attributes that did not change might still be affected. Perhaps the most prominent example of such interdependence in the organizations' literature is Chandler's work (1962) on the relationship of a firm's strategy and organizational structure. Recent work in the economics literature by Milgrom and Roberts (1990) also points to the need to examine the complementarity among a firm's choices of product lines, production strategies, and technology. In the context of human resource management, the presence of complementarities has been explored empirically, where 'bundles' of human resource practices, such as screening and selection, team-based work systems, flexible job assignments, and skills training, are shown to be more effective when used in conjunction than when used separately (Ichniowski *et al.* 1995; MacDuffie, 1995).

Despite the importance of such interactive effects on fitness, much of the population genetics literature, as well as the organizations' literature, has tended to treat facets of the organism (organization) as if their fitness contribution is independent of other attributes of the organism (organization). Kauffman (1993) has developed a simple but powerful analytic structure to represent epistatic interactions, which he terms the NK model. An entity, an organization for our purposes here, is characterized as consisting of N attributes where each attribute can take on A possible values. Thus, the fitness space consists of A^N possible types of organizations. The degree to which the fitness of the organization depends on interaction effects among the attributes is specified by the variable K.

In particular, the contribution of a given attribute of the organization to the organization's overall fitness is assumed to be influenced by K other attributes. Therefore, if K equals zero, then the contribution of each element of the organization (such as strategy, personal system, structure, etc.) is independent of all other attributes. At the other extreme, if K equals $N - 1$, then the fitness contribution of any one attribute depends on the value of all other attributes of the organization. As a result, adjacent locations in the fitness space need not have similar fitness values. In this sense, the value K determines the intensity of interaction effects and, in turn, how rugged or correlated is the fitness space.[5]

4. Emergence of Heterogeneity: Search and Basins of Attraction

Consider the problem of identifying a coherent set of policies, that is a set of behaviours for which there are positive complementarities. This is a problem of finding an attractive peak in a rugged fitness landscape. If organizational capabilities are an outcome of such a search process, what general statements can we make about such a process?

Intelligent, non-exhaustive, search processes are sensitive to the topography of the problem space being explored. This may be the actual topography or, as in many efforts at calculative rationality, a representation of the actual topography. At one level, this sensitivity to the topography is a statement of minimal intelligence of the search process. Clearly, if a search process is to reflect any intelligence, it should be sensitive to the fitness value of alternative locations in the space of possible solutions. In particular, the engineering challenge is to design an algorithm that is effective at finding extreme points in such a space.

However, search processes tend to be sensitive to the topography of the solution space in a stronger sense as well. The particular extreme value that is identified by a given algorithm is typically sensitive to the initial proposed solution at which search started. Furthermore, the extreme value that is identified will be (or quite close to) a local peak in the solution space.

Consider the outcome of a process of local search on a rugged landscape. In particular, suppose that search takes the form of examining alternatives in the immediate neighbourhood of the current proposed solution and that search ceases when a local optimum is obtained. Finally, imagine carrying out a large number of such search efforts at randomly chosen starting locations in the space of possible solutions. Except by chance, the initial 'solutions' for each of the search efforts will differ. However, after a few iterations of local search, the number of distinct solutions will decline radically (Kauffman 1993; Levinthal 1997). This reduction in the number of identified 'solutions' reflects the fact that while the solutions were initially distributed randomly in the landscape, many initial starting points share the same local optimum. Kauffman (1993) terms the set of locations in the landscape for which

---

[5] A random number, typically assumed to be distributed by a uniform distribution over the unit interval, is assigned to each of the N attributes, where a distinct number is assigned contingent on the value of the K other attributes with which it interacts. As a result, each attribute can take on A^{K+1} different values, depending on the attribute itself (which can take on A possible values) and the value of the K other attributes with which it interacts. This assignment is repeated for each of the N attributes, with the overall fitness treated as the average over the N attributes.

local search results in a common local optimum as belonging to a common 'basin of attraction'.[6]

The number of local optima that are reached increases as the landscape becomes more 'rugged'. In particular, consider the landscape that results when $K = 0$. As noted earlier, when $K = 0$ there is a single maximum in the space of alternative solutions. If a policy array is located at any point other than the optimum, there is a location in the immediate neighbourhood, involving a change in a single attribute that enhances performance. Since $K = 0$, changing this attribute improves the performance independent of the other $N-1$ attributes. Therefore, a process of local search results in a 'walk' to the optimum from all starting positions.

For $K > 0$, the landscape has multiple local optima. More generally, as K increases the landscape becomes less correlated and the number of local optima increases. As a result, search efforts may become 'trapped' at a suboptimal local peak. This property is clearly an implication of the limited nature of local search. The 'ruggedness' of the landscape has an impact on organizational form to the extent that there are peaks and valleys beyond the 'vision' of the search algorithm. Thus, greater vision attenuates the effect of a given level of K. However, as long as the search effort is not exhaustive, the qualitative properties of search leading to, possibly inferior, local peaks remains. Furthermore, the number of such peaks increases with K for a given range, or vision, of neighbourhood search.

This analysis of local search in complex landscapes has important implications for contingency theory arguments regarding variation in organizational forms in a population. Contingency theory is typically expressed as an argument for a correspondence between facets of organizations and features of the environment in which organizations function (Lawrence and Lorsch 1967). In this discussion of movement on rugged fitness landscapes, all organizations face the same environment. What differs is their initial composition. As a result of these different starting points, organizations are led to adopt distinct organizational forms. Local search in a multi-peak landscape results in organizational adaptation being path- or history-dependent. As a result, the observed distribution of organizational forms in a population may reflect heterogeneity in the population of organizations at earlier points in time rather than variation in niches in the environment, as suggested by ecological analyses (Hannan and Freeman 1977), or a set of distinct external conditions, as generally suggested by contingency theories (Lawrence and Lorsch 1967).

For example, both United Parcel Service and Federal Express are very successful companies operating in the same business of delivering mail and packages. Their organizational solutions to this common mission, however, are quite distinct (Cappelli and Crocker-Hefher 1993). These differences reflect the imprinting at founding (Stinchcombe 1965) of distinct systems of control. United Parcel Services was founded at a time when Taylorism and the principles of scientific management

---

[6] The term 'basin of attraction', while conventional in the literature, is a bit confusing in the imagery that it evokes. The points share a common local peak (i.e. point of 'attraction') and through local search are drawn *uphill* to this common local peak.

were dominant. Federal Express was developed in more recent years and the organization reflects the emphasis in recent years on information technology and employee empowerment. Despite the apparent differences in their organizational form, they both appear viable despite sharing the same niche.[7]

Organizations are complex social systems and, as a result, are likely to be subject to a large number of epistatic interactions. This suggests that the mapping from organizational form to effectiveness measures, whether these measures are survival rates as in ecological analysis or financial performance as in the case of many applications of contingency theory, may be exceedingly complex. In particular, there is unlikely to be a unique mapping from an effectiveness measure to organizational forms and the observed distribution of forms is likely to reflect both the demands of the environment and the organization's unique history that has led it to a particular peak in the landscape.

To the extent that variation in organizational form results from a process of local search and adaptation, then the observed variation in forms may have more to do with an organization's structure at founding than current environmental contingencies. The impact of initial imprinting persists even though organizations engage in considerable adaptation. This persistence is the result of two properties. First, the terrain over which organizations search has many local peaks when organization effectiveness is influenced by interaction effects among organizational attributes. However, as long as the fitness space of alternative organizational forms is somewhat correlated (i.e. similar organizational forms tend to have similar fitness values), local search provides a powerful mode of organizational adaptation. The combination of local search in conjunction with a rugged landscape results in the persistent impact of imprinting effects, despite the absence of organizational inertia. Thus, Stinchcombe's (1965) arguments regarding imprinting effects do not depend on organizational inertia in the narrow sense of an absence of organizational change. Local search in a rugged landscape is sufficient to generate a persistent effect of founding on organizational form.

4.1 Inertia and adaptation in changing landscapes

Questions of organizational-level adaptation are posed typically with respect to organizational changes in response to changing external environments (Tushman and Romanelli 1985). A particular variant of this question which has received considerable recent interest is the challenge posed for established firms by Schumpeterian environments (Abernathy and Clark 1985; Tushman and Anderson 1986). Therefore, it is interesting to consider how shifts in the topography of a fitness landscape affects processes of organizational-level adaptation and population-level selection.

Despite the fact that the immediate impact of the change in the environment on organizational fitness is independent of K, the likelihood of an organization surviving

[7] Of course, asymptotically, the principle of competitive exclusion still applies. If there are differences in relative fitness, in the limit only the more fit form will persist in a given niche.

such a change is quite sensitive to the intensity of epistatic interactions within the organization. This contrast results from the fact that the ability of the organization to adapt effectively to the new landscape is influenced by the level of epistatic interactions within the organization.

With a low K value, an organization can change a particular attribute without significantly impacting the fitness contribution of other organizational attributes. Put more abstractly, with a low K value, the organization faces a highly correlated fitness landscape and is therefore able to engage in effective local adaptation. This consideration of the impact of epistatic interactions on the ability of organizations to adapt to changes in their environment corresponds to Henderson and Clark's (1990) discussion of the challenges posed by architectural innovations. Architectural innovations, as characterized by Henderson and Clark, do not involve substantial changes in the underlying components of a firm's products or production process, but change the linkages among the components. They observed the drastic impact on the competitive viability of firms in the photolithographic alignment equipment industry of modest changes in the underlying technology. Architectural changes are changes in a tightly coupled system (i.e. a system with a high degree of epistatic interactions) and, as a result, organizations have great difficulty adapting despite the modest degree of technical change.

With higher levels of K, local adaptation is not an effective response to a change in the fitness landscape. A change in a single organizational attribute is likely to have repercussions for the fitness contribution of a variety of other organizational attributes. As a result, with a higher level of K, survival subsequent to a change in the fitness landscape is much more dependent on a successful long-jump or reorientation than local adaptation (Levinthal 1997). Thus, as suggested by the work of Tushman and Romanelli (1985), there may be a correlation between survival and reorientations, but the analysis implies that this correlation should be present only for organizations that have a relatively high intensity of epistatic interactions. When organizations are tightly coupled, and as a result the fitness space is only weakly correlated, local adaptation is not very effective. Under such conditions, survival in the face of a changing environment becomes more linked to a successful (lucky or visionary) long-jump or reorientation.

5. Conclusion: 'Packaging' Problems in Complex Worlds

Current observers of business enterprises suggest that the present environment poses extraordinary challenges on business organizations in the form of rapid changes in technologies and global markets. The challenge that such changes imply for business organizations seems to revolve around the need to re-evaluate and often repackage a firm's set of capabilities. Changes in the competitive environment may render some capabilities less valuable than they were previously and, at the same time, may make other capabilities of greater value. More subtly, changes may influence the complementarity among sets of capabilities. New manufacturing techniques may place a premium on a different set of human-resource practices. Innovations in information technology may facilitate the emergence of a new set of retailers with strategies premissed on high volume and rapid turnover of merchandise.

Why are these issues so challenging for architects of business strategy? This question raises the broader issue of what one might mean by the term complexity. Following Simon (1969), complexity has been interpreted here to be a function of the degree of interrelationships among parts of a system. Thus, an economy is complex to the extent that it is tightly coupled. To what extent does activity in one market (product or geographic) affect behaviour and performance in another? To what extent do advances in one technological domain influence the opportunity structure associated with other domains? This characterization of complexity provides some structure to address the question of the relative complexity of one time period or another. For the purposes of this chapter, the application of these ideas revolves around the development of organizational capabilities.

Organizational capabilities are an interesting phenomenon because of their central role in contributing to this 'packaging' problem—contributing both as a source of the problem as well as a partial solution. The existence of organizational capabilities, as distinct from a collection of individual skills, reflects the need to coordinate patterns of behaviour that have an enormous set of interactions, many of which are opaque to the actors themselves. These interactions range from microlevel behaviours of individual co-workers to broader assemblages of routines that may constitute a production system.

Which particular routines will emerge cannot be well specified in advance, only that stable collective patterns of behaviour are likely to emerge (Cohen and Bacdayan 1994; Egidi 1994). Similarly, how particular sets of routines may link up to broader assemblages is, in general, uncertain. Furthermore, a given organization is unlikely to have a fully coherent assemblage of routines. 'Islands' of complementarities are likely to emerge within an organization with few, or possibly negative, interaction effects with other facets of the organization.

What is clear is that complementarities generate a rugged fitness landscape and, assuming that actors are guided by limited 'vision' when moving on this landscape, the particular set of behaviours that emerges is importantly conditioned by the current set of actions. The factors that cause organizational capabilities to be a central factor in considering the profitability of firms and, indeed, the performance of the broader economy, also result in the need for humility in articulating appropriate organizational designs for their incubation. We are making progress, however, in articulating the logical foundations underlying organizational capabilities and this emerging logic holds some promise for these challenges of design.

References

Abernethy, W., and K. Clark (1985). 'Mapping the winds of creative destriction', *Research Policy*, 14: 3–22.

Bower, J. L. (1970). *Managing the Resource Allocation Process: A Study of Corporate Planning and Investment.* Cambridge, Mass.: Harvard Business School Press.

Cappelli, P., and A. Crocker-Hefher (1996). 'Distinctive human resources are a firm's core competencies.' *Organizational Dynamics*, 24: 7–22.

Casti, J. L. (1992). *Reality Rules: II.* New York: Wiley.

Chandler, A. (1962). *Strategy and Structure: Chapters in the History of the American Industrial Enterprise.* Cambridge, Mass.: MIT Press.

Cohen, M., and P. Bacdayan (1994). 'Organizational routines are stored as procedural memory: Evidence from a laboratory study', *Organizational Science*, 5: 554–68.

Cyert, R., and J. March (1963). *A Behavioral Theory of the Firm.* Englewood Cliffs, NJ: Prentice-Hall.

Dosi, G. (1988). 'Sources, procedures, and micro economic effects of innovation', *Journal of Economic Literature*, 26: 1120–71.

—— D. Teece, R. Rumelt, and S. Winter (1994) 'Understanding corporate coherence: theory and evidence', *Journal of Economic Behavior*, 23: 1–30.

Egidi, M. (1994). 'Routines, hierarchies of problems, procedural behavior: Some evidence from experiments', Working Paper 94-58. Laxenburg, Austria: International Institute for Applied Systems Analysis.

Freeman, J. (1978). 'The unit of analysis in organizational research', in M. Meyer (ed.), *Environments and Organizations.* San Francisco: Jossey Bass.

Garey, M., and D. Johnson (1979). *Computers and Intractability.* San Francisco: W. H. Freeman & Co.

Garfinkel, R., and G. Nemhauer (1972). *Integer Programming.* New York: Wiley.

Ghemawat, P. (1991). *Commitment.* New York: Free Press.

Hannan, M., and J. Freeman (1977). 'The population ecology of organizations', *American Journal of Sociology*, 82: 929–64.

Henderson, R., and K. Clark (1990). 'Architectural innovations: The reconfiguration of existing product technologies and the failure of established firms', *Administrative Science Quarterly*, 35: 9–30.

Holland, J. H. (1975). *Adaptation in Natural and Artificial Systems.* Ann Arbor: University of Michigan Press.

—— K. Holyoak, R. Nisbett, and P. Thagard (1989). *Induction: Processes of Inference, Learning, and Discovery.* Cambridge, Mass.: MIT Press.

Ichniowski, C., K. Shaw, and G. Prennushi (1995). 'The effects of human resource management practices on productivity', *American Economic Review*, 87: 291–313.

Kauffman, S. (1993). *The Origins of Order.* New York: Oxford University Press.

Kogut, B. (1991). 'Country capabilities and the permeability of borders', *Strategic Management Journal*, 12: 33–47.

Krugman, P. (1991). *Geography and Trade.* Cambridge, Mass.: MIT Press.

Lawrence, P., and J. Lorsch (1967). *Organization and Environment: Managing Differentiation and Integration.* Boston, Mass.: Harvard University.

Levinthal, D. (1996). 'Organizations and capabilities: The role of decompositions and units of selection', Working Paper, University of Pennsylvania.

—— (1997). 'Adaptation on rugged landscapes', *Management Science*, 43(7): 934–50.

—— and J. G. March (1993). 'The myopia of learning', *Strategic Management Journal*, 14: 95–112.

Lewis, A. (1985*a*). 'On effectively computable realizations of choice functions', *Mathematical Social Sciences*, 10: 43–80.

—— (1985*b*). 'The minimum degree of recursively representable choice functions', *Mathematical Social Sciences*, 10: 179–88.

MacDuffie, J. P. (1988). 'The Japanese auto transplants: Challenges to conventional wisdom', *Industrial Labor Relations*, 28: 12–18.

—— (1995). 'Human resource bundles and manufacturing performance: Organizational logic and flexible production systems in the world auto industry', *Industrial and Labor Relations Review*, 48: 197–221.

March, J., and H. Simon (1958). *Organizations*. New York: Wiley.

Marengo, L. (1992). 'Coordination and organizational learning in the firm', *Journal of Evolutionary Economics*, 2: 313–26.

Milgrom, P., and J. Roberts (1990). 'The economics of modern manufacturing', *American Economic Review*, 80: 511–28.

Miller, D., and P. Friesen (1984). *Organizations: A Quantum View*. Englewood Cliffs, NJ: Prentice-Hall.

Nelson, R. (1993). *National Innovation Systems: A Comparative Study*. New York: Oxford University Press.

—— (1994). 'The co-evolution of technology, industrial structure, and supporting institutions', *Industrial and Corporate Change*, 3: 47–63.

—— and S. Winter (1978). 'Forces generating and limiting competition under Schumpeterian competition', *Bell Journal of Economics*, 9: 524–48.

—— —— (1982). *An Evolutionary Theory of the Firm*. Cambridge, Mass.: Harvard University Press.

Newell, A., and H. Simon (1972). *Human Problem Solving*. Engelwood Cliffs, NJ: Prentice-Hall.

Porter, M. E. (1990). *The Competitive Advantage of Nations*. New York: Free Press.

Prahalad, C. K., and G. Hamel (1990). 'The core competence of the corporation', *Harvard Business Review*, May–June: 79–91.

Raff, D. (1991). *Buying the Peace: Wage Determination Theory, Mass Production, and the Five Dollar Day at Ford*. Princeton, NJ: Princeton University Press.

Stalk, G., P. Evans, and L. Shulman (1992). 'Competing on capabilities: The new rules of the game', *Harvard Business Review*, 70: 57–69.

Simon, H. A. (1955). 'A behavioral model of rational choice', *Quarterly Journal of Economics*, 69: 99–118.

—— (1969). *The Sciences of the Artificial*. Cambridge, Mass.: MIT Press.

—— (1976). *Administrative Behavior*. New York: Free Press.

Smith, A. (1776). *An Inquiry into the Nature and Causes of the Wealth of Nations*, Glasgow edn. Oxford: Clarendon Press.

Smith, J. M. (1989). *Evolutionary Genetics*. New York: Oxford University Press.

Stinchcombe, A. (1965). 'Social structure and organizations', in J. March (ed.), *Handbook of Organizations*. Chicago: Rand McNally.

Tushman, M., and P. Anderson (1986). 'Technological discontinuities and organizational environments', *Administrative Science Quarterly*, 31: 587–611.

—— and E. Romanelli (1985). 'Organizational evolution: A metamorphosis model of convergence and reorientation', in L. Cummings and B. Staw (eds.), *Research in Organizational Behavior*, 7: 171–222.

Warglien, M. (1995). 'Hierarchical selection and organizational adaptation', *Industrial and Corporate Change*, 4: 161–86.

Winter, S. (1964). 'Economic "natural selection" and the theory of the firm', *Yale Economic Essays*, 4: 225–72.

—— (1987). 'Knowledge and competence as strategic assets', in David J. Teece (ed.), *The Competitive Challenge*. Cambridge, Mass.: Ballinger.

—— (1994). 'Organizing for continuous improvement: Evolutionary theory meets the quality revolution', in Joel Baum and Jitendra Singh (eds.), *Evolutionary Dynamics of Organizations*. New York: Oxford University Press.

Index